HISTORY DERAILED

HISTORY DERAILED

CENTRAL AND EASTERN EUROPE
IN THE LONG NINETEENTH CENTURY

IVAN T. BEREND

UNIVERSITY OF CALIFORNIA PRESS

Berkeley / Los Angeles / London

University of California Press
Berkeley and Los Angeles, California

University of California Press, Ltd.
London, England

Library of Congress Cataloging-in-Publication Data

Berend, T. Ivan (Tibor Ivan), 1930–
    History derailed : Central and Eastern Europe in the long nineteenth
century / Ivan T. Berend.
        p.   cm.
    Includes bibliographical references and index.
    ISBN 0–520–23299–2 (alk. paper)
    1. Europe—History—1789–1900.   2. Industrialization—Europe,
Western—History—19th century.   3. Industrialization—Austria—
History—19th century.   4. Europe—Economic conditions—19th
century.   5. Industrialization—Europe, Eastern—History—19th
century.   6. Europe—Ethnic relations.   7. Europe—Intellectual life—
19th century.   I. Title.
D359 .D55 2003
943'.0009'034—dc21   2002003303

Manufactured in the United States of America

12   11   10   09   08   07   06   05   04   03
10   9   8   7   6   5   4   3   2   1

CONTENTS

ILLUSTRATIONS

FIGURES

(following p. 46)

(following p. 258)

MAPS

TABLES

PREFACE

As so many times in their modern history, the peoples of Central and Eastern Europe find themselves in an era of dramatic transformation. The caravan of nations in the region is in rapid movement once again. Their ideal and the pattern they follow is the West, just as it was in the nineteenth century. The historical parallel is plain to see. The nineteenth century was a crucial period in modern Central and Eastern European history and offers a key to a better understanding of the area's stormy twentieth-century history and the major turmoil of the present. As Joyce Appleby, Lynn Hunt, and Margaret Jacob observe: "[W]hat historians do best is to make connections with the past in order to illuminate the problems of the present and the potential of the future" (Appleby et al. 1995, 9).

Although this volume stands as an entirely independent work, it can also be regarded as the first part of an informal trilogy on modern Central and Eastern Europe. During the 1990s, I published two volumes about the history of the region in the first and the second halves of the twentieth century (Berend 1996, 1998). To find and analyze the origins of the twentieth-century tragedy of the region, I turn in this volume to the "long" nineteenth century.[1] This book, like the previous two, discusses the entire area between Germany and Russia and follows a topical organization, in contrast to the more conventional country-by-country type of examination. The analysis is highly comparative and seeks to capture the historical complexity of events—that is, the important interrelations of social, political, economic, and cultural facts and perceptions in a single and

---

1. My late friend György Ránki and I introduced this term in our *The European Periphery and Industrialization, 1780–1914* (Cambridge: Cambridge University Press, 1982).

ultimately indivisible process, called history. To present a broad synthesis is the object of my work.

This volume is therefore rather different from most of the works on nineteenth-century Central and Eastern Europe. Most of the books in this vast literature discuss only a single country. In a small number of works, one can also find brief, mostly descriptive, political histories or presentations, in a "one-country-one-chapter" format, of the foundation of independent states in the Balkans and the emergence of small-nation nationalism. Other books present histories of the economic development of the area. Too often, however, the relationships and mutual influences of cultural, economic, social, and political trends, which constitute the complexity of the nineteenth-century transformation in Central and Eastern Europe, are not addressed in scholarly literature. My main effort, then, has been to analyze these interrelationships: the impact of "enlightened" romanticism upon political reforms and economic performance; the consequences of partial economic modernization on societal transformation; and the influence of cultural and socioeconomic development on the rise of nationalism and authoritarian political regimes.

Of course, regional history requires generalization, highlighting the basic similarities of the historical path of an entire region. Several historians, however, question this regional generalization. That is, historians sometimes question whether Central and Eastern Europe can be regarded as a unit. They remind us of major national differences within the region. "The core-periphery model is not consistent with the huge diversity within Central and Eastern Europe . . . the Polish and Hungarian cases were, for example, vastly different from the Bulgarian and the Romanian," David Good asserts (Good 1997). Certain "considerations call into doubt the appositeness of the category 'Central and Eastern Europe' as a unit of historical analysis," John Connelly says. "Instead of 'two parts,' it is perhaps more helpful to conceive of several zones of historical development extending gradually eastward in Europe" (Connelly 1999). It is true that major differences and several "zones" exist within Central and Eastern Europe. The further east a country lies from the river Elbe, the further removed it tends to be from the Western European pattern: Hungary, more than the Czech lands, Romania more than Hungary, and Bulgaria more than Romania.

This book, of course, discusses such differences and dissimilarities among various countries and subregions within Central and Eastern Europe, especially between Central Europe and the Balkans.

Generalization, however, is a useful as well as unavoidable aspect of writing history. Someone who discusses the history of a particular period in a single country also generalizes implicitly about various and often strikingly different regions. Bucharest and Budapest, for example, were entirely different worlds from the Romanian and Hungarian countrysides. Northern Italy had more in common with Belgium in the late nineteenth century than it did with southern Italy. Certainly, Mecklenburg constituted more of an "Eastern world" within Germany than did the Western-style Ruhrgebiet. Sidney Pollard has warned us as well about the importance of regional rather than country-based units, carved out by (often artificial) political borders. Central and Eastern Europe as a region between Germany and Russia is, of course, an abstraction, similar to notions of "Europe," the "Nordic countries," "Mediterranean Europe," and the "Near East." One can always argue against these abstractions by pointing to important national differences. However, as I try to show in this volume, regional comparisons and generalizations have real meaning and can help us to understand individual national cases.

Western Europe was the point of reference for the Central and Eastern European elites from the turn of the eighteenth throughout the nineteenth century. It is through comparison with Western Europe that the region's basic characteristics are defined: the lack of the nation-state, a lack of industrialization, and the absence of modern, urbanized society. Traditional agricultural economies and rural-peasant societies were preserved. The unfinished processes of nation-building and socioeconomic modernization had dramatic consequences on society and politics. Above all, they blocked the road to parliamentary democracy.

Polish, Hungarian, Slovak, and Slovene national elites have tried desperately to prove that their countries do not belong to the "East"; that they are, indeed, Central Europeans. Ongoing debate continues to define and redefine the western border of the Balkans: Is it the eastern side of the Ringstrasse in Vienna, or the eastern border of Hungary? Do Croatia and Romania belong to Central Europe or to the Balkans?

Cultural traits exhibit basic regional similarities. All of these countries are multiethnic and multicultural, because the area between the Baltic Sea and the Adriatic Sea was, as C. A. Macartney observes, a "belt of mixed population" (Macartney 1968). Most of the peoples in the area, however, spoke Slavic languages. Those who did not, such as the Romanians and Hungarians, borrowed a great number of Slavic words. Even the cuisine is mixed. Folk music and songs of this region are closely related. Béla Bartók, who was among other things a scholar and collector of folk music, spoke of an "East European international musical jargon" (Bartók 1952, 3–28).

Although markedly different from Western Europe, all of these countries began to follow the Western European pattern of establishing a modern economy, society, and nation-state. They all created modern literary languages and national theaters. They all struggled to be independent nation-states. They all adopted the achievements of the Western European agricultural revolution and built up extensive trade with Western Europe by exporting agricultural products and raw materials. They all initiated railroad construction, founded banks and industrial firms, and tried to develop industries. The results of all these policies, however, were mixed: they were more successful along the western rim of the region, less so in the middle, and only to a very limited degree on the eastern edge of the area. Still, some basic characteristics are common throughout Central and Eastern Europe.

In spite of tragic hostility and violent confrontations, a Central and Eastern European identity and consciousness also emerged and put down deep roots among intellectuals: the mid-nineteenth-century Romanian historian Nicolae Bălcescu believed in the brotherhood of the neighboring nations, the turn-of-the-century Czech politician Karel Kramář propagated *novoslovaství,* a new pan-Slav concept of the connectedness of the Slavic people. The mid-twentieth-century Hungarian populist writer László Németh spoke about the "milk-brotherhood" of the Eastern European peoples. Thus, in spite of important national and even subregional differences, Central and Eastern Europe developed a special self-identification and exhibited basic similarities compared to Western Europe and other parts of the world.

Besides such comparisons and contrasts to Western Europe, this book also emphasizes the interrelations of East and West: chapter 2 discusses romanticism, which came from Western Europe via Germany and brought the Western European zeitgeist of freedom and nationalism. These concepts were spread throughout the area by the representatives and disciples of exalted romanticism, an artistic-spiritual trend that became the driving force in the region's history. Cultural-linguistic nationalism inspired a folklorizing movement and triggered the creation of literary languages, national poetry and drama, and national theater and opera. Romanticism in Central and Eastern Europe, however, unlike in the West, combined romanticist ideals with the ideas of the Enlightenment and rationality. Enlightened romanticism unleashed a tremendous creative force: the strong belief in progress and in the possibility of changing history through passionate action, reform, and education. This became the prime mover of political struggles and economic modernization. Furthermore, the agitated cultural and political elite played a central role in the creation of romantic nationalism, an ideology that generated heroic struggles for independence all over the region (described in chapter 3).

In addition to the impact of Western European culture, Western Europe's markets inspired the modernization of the traditional economy and the creation of new export sectors in the East. This was considered an important form of nation-building. Enlightened national elites emphasized the need for "organic work" in the form of railroad construction, industrialization, agricultural modernization, and urbanization.

Indeed, modernity became a leading slogan, penetrating and transforming society, politics, and economy alike. However, the transformation was incomplete. The ancient economic regime was still in place. It was reformed, but not radically destroyed (discussed in chapter 4). Some parts of Central and Eastern Europe profited from these interconnections and followed, albeit at a certain distance, the transformation of Western Europe. Other countries of the region were unable to do so. The story of the region is that of a partially successful modernization, along with the social consequences and ambiguity arising from the coexistence of the old with slowly emerging new societies: the "dual society" in Central Europe and the "incomplete societies" in the Balkans. As a result, the social conflicts of the nineteenth century were mostly considered racial and minority problems: the conflicts between Polish and Hungarian landlords and Ukrainian and Romanian peasants, respectively; between German and Jewish entrepreneurs and Polish and Hungarian workers. The need for scapegoats generated the so-called Jewish question, which later became one of the most tragic elements of social conflict in the area (chapter 5). Political frustration and fundamentalist nationalism blocked the road toward political democracy. Arising out of the region's legacy of autocratic regimes, authoritarian systems became the rule in Central and Eastern Europe (chapter 6).

The long nineteenth century—a century and a third—is a lengthy period in itself. Yet I take a *longue durée* approach that embraces an even longer period by comparing the different historical paths of Western and Central and Eastern Europe from the sixteenth to the early nineteenth centuries (chapter 1).

The long nineteenth century started with the eruption of the "twin volcanoes" of the French sociopolitical revolution and the British Industrial Revolution (see Hobsbawm 1962) and ended with World War I. This period became the stage of a historical drama in Central and Eastern Europe: attempts at political, social, and economic modernization, their partial success and partial failure. The seeds of later revolts, bitter hatreds, extremism, and aggressive nationalism were sown during these years, when the history of the area was, so to speak, derailed.

In this critical age of transition in the region, the existing establishment became intolerable, but a new system had not yet fully emerged. I present a rich selection of facts and information in an attempt to reconstruct the relevant historical trends. Some historians do not believe in this possibility any longer. While I recognize the usefulness of their epistemological criticism, I do not share their conclusion. "At best," to quote Appleby, Hunt, and Jacob again, "the past only dimly corresponds to what the historians say about it, but practical realists accept the tentativeness and imperfections of the historians' accounts"; we still "can uncover evidence, touch lives long passed, and 'see' patterns in events that otherwise might remain inexplicable"; we also know that "knowledge seeking involves a lively, contentious struggle among diverse groups of truth-seekers" and "telling the truth takes a collective effort" (Appleby et al. 1995, 248, 251, 309). "Facts are facts," Robert Darnton says cleverly but unphilosophically, "despite the fact that they cannot be separated clearly from interpretation" (Darnton 1997, 11).

Writers, composers, conservative and enlightened aristocrats, and political thinkers interpreted the struggles, successes, and frequent failures of their nations. I also therefore delve into their reflections, their ways, and the consequences of their thinking. Their narratives constitute an integral part of the historical reality I seek to present here. Although primary sources, some archive materials, statistics, memoirs, travelers' reports, correspondence, poetry, and literature of the period have been used broadly to reconstruct the past, as well as contemporary perceptions of it, I have relied chiefly on secondary sources in writing this book. The historian cannot open the files of innumerable archives in twelve countries and thus must rely on the findings of the hundreds of historians who have dug deeply into those various national archives and histories.

MAP 1. Central and Eastern Europe in 1815

MAP 2. Central and Eastern Europe in 1910

ACKNOWLEDGMENTS

This book was born at the University of California in Los Angeles, where I began teaching the history of nineteenth-century Central and Eastern Europe more than a decade ago. While teaching the topic, I gradually built up the main concept and worked out several important parts of the book. Various historical questions and parts of the manuscript were discussed with my colleagues in the History Department and at the Center for European and Russian Studies, and I benefited from the assistance of graduate students, most of all Joan Hackeling and Carla Thorson. I am also indebted to the Young Research Library for its exceptional collection of most of the secondary sources. Grants from the Academic Senate and the International Studies and Overseas Programs at UCLA provided financial assistance.

The ideas of colleagues and friends have played a great role in developing the overall concept and interpretation. The works of Zsigmond Pál Pach, Eric Hobsbawm, Isaiah Berlin, Arno Mayer, Peter Sugar, Miroslaw Hroch, and Norman Davies, to name only a few, have provided important inspiration. Daniel Chirot's comments also offered valuable help in completing the manuscript, and I have profited immensely from the interest and questions of my students.

My wife, Kati, who originally suggested this book and encouraged me to write it, as well as providing invaluable assistance in library research and critical readings of and commentary on various versions of the manuscript, was the single most important contributor to the writing.

Last, but not least, I am very grateful to David C. Summers and Peter Dreyer for their thorough copyediting and polishing of the manuscript.

I collected illustrations from eight countries and twenty-three museums, libraries, publishers, and institutions in Central and Eastern Europe. Mária

Sárosi worked efficiently to help me in this work. For their assistance and generosity in giving me, and on occasion even waiving, copyright permissions, I would like to thank the Muzeul National de Artă al României, Bucharest; Meridiane Publishing House, Bucharest; Slovenske Narodne Muzeum, Etnograficke Muzeum, Martin, Slovakia; SPN Pedagogicke Nakladelstvi, Prague; Muzeum Narodowe w Warszawie, Warsaw; Muzeum Historyczne Miasta, Warsaw; Muzeum Narodowe w Krakowie, Kraków; Muzej Grada Beograda, Belgrade; Bulgarian Academy of Sciences, Center for Architectural Studies, Sofia; the Research Center for Islamic History Art and Culture of the Organization of the Islamic Conference, Istanbul; Magyar Nemzeti Múzeum, Budapest; Magyar Nemzeti Múzeum Történeti Fényképtára, Budapest; Magyar Nemzeti Galéria, Budapest; Néprajzi Múzeum, Budapest; Budapesti Történeti Múzeum Kiscelli Múzeuma, Budapest; Fotográfiai Múzeum, Kecskemét; Fővárosi Szabó Ervin Könyvtár, Budapest; Hadtörténeti Múzeum, Budapest; Magyar Mezőgazdasági Múzeum, Budapest; Országos Széchenyi Könyvtár, Budapest; Magyar Tudományos Akadémia, Budapest; Magyar Tudományos Akadémia Történettudományi Intézete, Budapest; and Petőfi Irodalmi Múzeum, Budapest.

THE EMERGING WEST AS AN IDEAL AND MODEL FOR THE EAST

IN THE LATE EIGHTEENTH and early nineteenth centuries, the Central and Eastern European elite, national prophet-poets, intellectuals, and enlightened aristocrats, looked to the West with the greatest admiration. They expressed their dissatisfaction with the state of their own "backward," "underdeveloped," "sleeping" countries, societies in their "childhood," which lacked modern institutions, such as industry, railways, and educational systems, and lagged behind Western Europe by a century. Reformers warned of the danger posed by the inability of their countries to "sustain an independent state" and of the threat of being pushed back "to Asia." They saw that their countries remained outside the main thrust of the modern Western European metamorphosis and were thus defenseless against their more powerful neighbors, subordinate to the more advanced world, and relegated to the periphery of the continent.

These reformers were convinced, however, that they could turn their countries around. Like all those influenced by the zeitgeist of the century, the Enlightenment and the idea of progress, they viewed history as a ladder for climbing from lower to higher stages.

Freedom and progress, progress and economic growth, went together in their minds. These ideas were also borrowed from the West, where the "idea of progress reached its zenith" during the period 1750–1900. Progress, "from being one of the important ideas . . . became the dominant idea" (Nisbet 1980, 171). As Franz (or Ferenc) Liszt, the romantic virtuoso pianist-composer par excellence, said: "We believe in one unending progress, in one untrammeled social future" (Einstein 1947, 347). Karl Marx expressed this way of thinking in the preface to *Das Kapital* when he compared Britain to continental Europe. The latter suffered from "the incompleteness of [capitalist] development," he wrote. "Alongside of modern evils, a whole series of inherited evils oppress us, arising from the passive survival of antiquated modes of production." Expressing the nineteenth-century belief in progress, he added, "the country that is more developed industrially only shows, to the less developed, the image of its own future" (Marx [1867] 1932, 13).

Stanisław Konarski, who had spent a decade in the West and had been an observer of the early years of the British Industrial Revolution, became the editor of the first modern Polish periodical, *Monitor,* and made an urgent plea: "Let us govern ourselves like sensible people. . . . For the God of nature did not search for different clay when he made Poles from what he used for Englishmen" (Brock 1972, 12). At about the same time, in 1791, István Batsányi, a twenty-eight-year-old Hungarian member of Maria Theresa's famous Regiment of Guards in Vienna, wrote "A franciaországi változásokra" (On the Changes in France), a poem celebrating the French Revolution. He passionately warned both the common people and their oppressors to turn their eyes to Paris:

> Who have not shaken off the collar of the slave
> The yoke that drags you down into your grave
> And you, too, sacred kings, who, consecrated, kill—
> Since Earth cries out for blood—the subject of your will
> To Paris turn your eyes!!! Let France elucidate
> For king and shackled slave your future and your fate.
>
> (Makkai 1996, 142)

Nearly a century later, the Albanian poet Naim Frashëri drew attention to the great ideas of France:

> Europe's was a sorry plight,
> Dark confusion was her share,
> To shake her and put things right,
> She needed Rousseau and Voltaire.
>
> (Bihiku 1980, 38)

In 1911, Constantin Dobrogeanu-Gherea, a Romanian socialist, published his *Asupra socialismului în ţările înapoiate* (On Socialism in Backward Countries), in which he maintained that "bourgeois capitalism would eventually revolutionize social and economic relations and the mental climate in Eastern Europe" (Hitchins 1994, 76).

From the late eighteenth century to the early twentieth, a series of Central and Eastern European political thinkers, poets, statesmen, and reformers closely watched the ideas and transformation of Western Europe. The leading Hungarian reformer, József Eötvös, a member of the revolutionary government of 1848 and one of the main architects of liberal legislation establishing the modern educational system after the Austro-Hungarian Compromise in 1867, noted after the revolution: "Since the time of the French Revolution, the development of most of the European countries demonstrates that the model for new institutions was taken from England; ideas and concepts were copied from France" (Eötvös 1902a, 39). Victor Hugo, Walter Scott, Byron, Schiller, Hobbes, Locke, Rousseau, Voltaire, Montesquieu, and Hegel all inspired him; their books were among the two thousand in his library (Bénye 1972). Eastern European reformers, comparing the situation of their own countries to that of the sparkling ideas and spectacular transformation of the West, noticed the growing gap between the two and looked to the latter as a model to follow. István Széchenyi, an enlightened young Hungarian aristocrat, traveled to Britain in 1822. "England has reached a level higher than ever before achieved by any people, but it is still climbing," he commented in his diary in January of that year. Some months later, he compared what he saw to the Hungarian reality: "I feel profound pain and downheartedness at the situation . . . of our country. . . . *Our country is sleeping*" (Széchenyi and Wesselényi 1985, 110, 212; emphasis added). In his milestone book *Hitel* (Credit), published in 1830, Széchenyi complained about the *"pitiful situation* of our country . . . *following other nations a century-long distance behind."* He expressed his admiration for Britain, which he claimed was "practically the core of the world," and argued that "copying others presents no danger, we can adopt their century-long experiences" (Széchenyi 1830, 139–40, 155–56, 258; emphasis added).

In 1830s Turkey, where one-quarter of the top military-administrative leaders had personal experience of the West (Todorova 1977), reformers also urged their compatriots to follow the Western model. "Only through reforms that will bring Turkey closer to *the norms of European life* can we get over the enduring political and economic crisis," wrote Mustafa Reshid Pasha. Halil Pasha, the Turkish commander-in-chief and son-in-law of the Sultan, considered the relative weakness of the Ottoman army when he warned, "If we do not adopt European ways, we shall have *no choice left but to return to Asia*" (quoted by Petrosjan 1977, 63–65; emphasis added).

"France has become our ideal," stated Ion Brătianu, a prominent revolutionary leader of mid-nineteenth-century Romania, and "has the mission to preside over the regeneration of Europe." The French consul in

Bucharest reported during the revolutionary days of 1848: "France has there, on the banks of the Danube, an inevitable *clientele* . . . which tries every day to assimilate her language, her legislation, her literature and even her most futile fashions" (Seton-Watson [1934] 1963, 139–40). In Iaşi, in 1863, five young Romanians who had returned from the West founded the Junimea (Youth) movement. The movement's chroniclers described the feelings and beliefs of the young reformers, who considered Romanian society to be in its *"childhood"* but "accepted the need for Rumania to evolve toward a *modern civilization on the Western model."* Titu Maiorescu and his friends "also discovered in Henry Buckle's 'History of Civilization in England' scientific confirmation of the theories about social change and the course of development which their own country should follow" (Hitchins 1994, 61–64). The Bulgarian national bard and hero Hristo Botev wrote in an article in *Zname:* "Our *unfortunate Bulgarian people have no Parliament,* no tribune from which to express their will, their needs and their sufferings" (Botev 1976, 7). The "Warsaw Positivists," a group of Polish reformers, bitterly criticized the situation in their country during the 1860s and 1870s after the failure of a series of national uprisings: "The cultural and economic resources of the Polish nation were as yet *underdeveloped* to sustain an independent state. In order to take their place among the modern nations of Europe, the Poles must first improve trade and industry . . . build towns and railways, and raise the rate of literacy" (Davies 1986, 170).

Most of the reform-oriented Central and Eastern European elite were convinced that the rise, the "century-long experience," of Northwestern Europe offered a model to follow. They would have to educate themselves, set goals, implement the needed reforms, build the required institutions, and "adopt the norms of European life." Only then could they elevate their nations. As the Albanian Frashëri expressed it:

May the dawn
That will bestow upon us
A great light,
Giving birth to:
Civilization,
Prosperity . . .
Knowledge
And progress,
Goodness
And Humanity
. . . arise,
Never to stray.
      (Elsie 1995, 234–35)

CHAPTER 1

THE CHALLENGE OF THE RISING WEST AND THE LACK OF RESPONSE IN THE "SLEEPING" EAST

THE RISE OF NORTHWESTERN EUROPE

THE EMERGENCE OF THE Western European model has a history at least three centuries long. On October 12, 1492, the Genoese Christopher Columbus reached America, initiating a period of European dominance. The Florentine Amerigo Vespucci explored the New World further with his voyages between 1497 and 1504. The Portuguese colonized Brazil in 1500. The Spaniard Hernando Cortés conquered Mexico in 1519–20. Jacques Cartier founded Montréal in 1536. Jamestown was founded in Virginia in 1607. These milestones in the European colonization of the New World signaled a new age. The rise of Western Europe, indeed, began with these risky adventures of courageous sailors and ruthless conquistadors.

By the end of the eighteenth century, most of the major overseas centers had been established and the "white colonies" had been settled. Only the interior of Africa and the Australian desert remained unexplored by Europeans. "In little more than a century," Carlo Cipolla observes, "first the Portuguese and the Spaniards, then the Dutch and the English, laid the basis of worldwide European predominance. It was the gun-carrying ocean-going sailing ship developed by Atlantic Europe during the fifteenth, sixteenth, and seventeenth centuries that made the European saga possible" (Cipolla 1994, 212). The triumph of Europe was based on the multitude of ships and more ships, ports, and shipyards (Braudel 1979).

When the saga began, at the end of the fifteenth century, Mediterranean Europe was the powerhouse of the old continent and the prime force behind the expansion. Northern Italy, Flanders, and above all Spain, the main beneficiary of the astonishing sixteenth- and seventeenth-century inflow of more than 36 million pounds of silver and nearly 400,000 pounds of gold, were among the richest and most advanced areas of Europe. By the end of the seventeenth century, however, the center of power in Europe had shifted to Holland, Britain, and, to a lesser degree, France. The New World discoveries and the rise of the new Atlantic trade played an important role in this change, but they are not sufficient to explain the new dominance of Northwestern Europe.

What other factors brought about the change? Geography, for one thing. Both Holland and Britain enjoyed easy access to the Atlantic trade route, and no part of either country was very far from the sea. Both countries capitalized on this advantage in the seventeenth and eighteenth centuries by building networks of canals into the most extensive water transportation system in the world. By the beginning of the nineteenth century, the cost of water transportation in these countries had dropped to one-quarter the cost of ground transportation. Compared to large landlocked countries, they held a unique advantage in cheap mass transportation.

They also had other, greater advantages. They experienced the earliest "bourgeois revolutions" in Europe, which cleared the road for social and institutional transformation and eliminated feudal obstacles. The new societies put major political turmoil behind them. During the last third of the sixteenth century, a bloody revolt began in the Netherlands that lasted a full eight decades, but during that time, the United Provinces of the Netherlands evolved into the most democratic and tolerant country, founded on a constitution. The flourishing scholarly and artistic life of the time reflected the rising prosperity. Both Holland and Britain created unparalleled religious freedom and a new attitude toward life and business based on the Protestant ethic. In tandem with a few Swiss cantons and German free cities, they developed a new social pattern that gave prestige and autonomy to merchants and financiers and free rein for economic and technical innovation (McNeill 1963, 40). Holland and Britain instituted genuine market economies and developed into merchant and maritime great powers. They dominated the emerging "modern trade" that replaced the old "medieval trade" in oriental spices and luxury articles, which met the demands of the upper classes and did not imply an exchange of goods. Instead, both countries, based initially on a modern division of labor and then on an increased commodity production for a permanently widened buyer's market, became traders in vast quantities of goods for mass consumption

(Pach, 1994, 218). A triangular Atlantic trade emerged: textiles and other manufactured products were shipped from Europe to Africa, slaves were bought and transported to the overseas colonies, and sugar, rum, coffee, cotton, indigo, and other items were sent back to Europe as cargo.

A flexible merchant class emerged in Holland by the end of the seventeenth century. The Dutch, thanks to an advanced shipbuilding industry, became merchants on a world scale. They built a thousand ships a year and created the world's strongest navy and a merchant marine of twenty thousand units. This was four times larger than the fleet of the nearest competitor, Britain, and thirty times larger than that of France. The Dutch middlemen bought to sell and became the masters of the Baltic, the Russian, and distant overseas trades. They also began to process and resell imported goods: they used imported copper to cast bronze cannon, wove imported raw silk, produced cigars from imported tobacco, and refined imported sugar. Holland harnessed its unlimited natural resource, wind, as its main energy source, and had built more than three thousand windmills by the mid seventeenth century. Amsterdam, the real center of Europe's first modern state, emerged as the center of world trade and dictated market prices.

Britain advanced still further. The elimination of serfdom and the flourishing wool production of the fourteenth century led to gradually increasing sales of manufactured goods. The amount of woolen fabric exported surpassed that of raw wool as early as the mid fifteenth century. However, Britain's real breakthrough occurred in the mid sixteenth century with the development of iron, lead, and other manufacturing sectors. England also pioneered a new energy source: coal. The amount mined jumped from 210,000 tons to 11 million tons between 1550 and 1800.

Trade expansion and rising sea power represented the real strength of a modernizing Britain by the mid sixteenth century. The defeat of the legendary Spanish Armada in 1588 and three Anglo-Dutch wars, ending in the mid 1670s, eroded Holland's control of the waters and established Britain as the most powerful world power. Protectionist measures included curbs on foreign ships in English harbors and use of foreign-built ships. Britain soon boasted the world's most powerful navy and merchant fleet, serving the world's largest colonial empire. London became the world's capital, with half a million inhabitants by the end of the seventeenth century.

The absolute state paved the road toward a unified nation-state. In 1543, the House of Tudor began the unification of the British Isles through ruthless homogenization of languages and peoples to forge a British identity. Starting in the mid seventeenth century, as a consequence of the

British Civil War and the so-called Glorious Revolution of 1688–89, a unique parliamentary system emerged that transformed the absolute monarchy into a constitutional one. Finally, in 1707, the United Kingdom of England, Wales, Scotland, and Ireland was created.

France emerged as the third most powerful country of Europe, a model absolutist state, in the seventeenth and eighteenth centuries. Under the seventy-two-year rule of the *Roi Soleil,* Louis XIV, France became the most powerful country on the Continent and also one of the largest colonial powers. Its strength rested on colonial trade. Together with Britain, France was a pioneer of modern colonialism and dynamic expansion. In the course of the first half of the eighteenth century, French colonial trade quadrupled.

Unlike Holland and Britain, absolutist France established its economy by state interventionism and became the model mercantilist state. Louis XIV's powerful minister Jean-Baptiste Colbert introduced strict state regulations. Besides various foreign trade companies and port and road constructions, major state-owned manufacturing firms were established. In the eighteenth century, the coal mines of Anzin, with four thousand workers, became the country's largest venture. Coal production increased eightfold during the eighteenth century. The textile firm of Mulhouse, the forges of Creusot, and the wallpaper factory of Réveillon typified the industrial progress of the country. With lavish royal sponsorship, science and culture flourished. The Académie Française (1635), the Académie des Sciences (1666), and the Comédie-Française (1680) were founded. The works of Molière and Racine elevated France to become a cultural leader in Europe.

Louis XIV's four major wars also established France as the most important military power on the Continent. Europe's first modern army was created, replacing the feudal nobles' army with strong artillery and infantry, a well-trained officer corps, and a chain of fortresses, barracks, and arsenals. In contrast to the great French army, however, the French navy was gradually dwarfed on the seas by the British. The Bourbon state, despite all its power, remained far behind both Holland and Britain. The absolute state remained frozen in its ancien régime.

DEMOGRAPHIC CHANGES, AGRICULTURAL REVOLUTION, AND PROTO-INDUSTRIALIZATION IN THE WEST

The most drastic changes in Northwestern Europe were demographic. For centuries, high birthrates had been offset by high death rates. Famine and disease—smallpox, plague, and cholera—regularly decimated the population, so that the growth rate stayed low, about 0.5 percent annually. The population of Europe in the second half of the seventeenth century was only slightly greater than in the thirteenth century (Armengaud and Reinhard 1961).

From the sixteenth century on, however, population growth accelerated. According to Roger Mols's evaluation, the number of Europe's inhabitants increased from roughly 82 million in 1500 to roughly 105 million by 1600 and more than 120 million by 1700. And while the total population of the Continent increased by nearly 50 percent during these two centuries, the population of Britain and the Netherlands combined grew twice as fast: from 6.3 million in 1500 to 12.7 million in 1700. In contrast, the Mediterranean countries, Spain, Portugal, and Italy, increased in population by less than 60 percent (Mols 1974).

The population of the Continent grew impressively (64 percent) in the eighteenth century, but Britain and the Netherlands, again, nearly doubled their population (to 21.1 million), while the Mediterranean countries grew by only 40 percent.

Sparsely populated Europe became a densely populated continent, "probably the most highly populated part of the whole world, with a density of about 18.7 inhabitants per square kilometer" in 1800, compared with 14 inhabitants per square kilometer in Asia and only 5 in Africa and America (Armengaud 1973, 28). The European average, however, does not reflect the high population density in the Northwestern countries, which increased from 30–40 inhabitants per square kilometer in the early seventeenth century to 60–80 people per square kilometer at the end of the eighteenth century. This meant many more hands available in the fields and workshops, many more mouths to feed, and many more feet in need of shoes.

Closely connected to the new demographic trends, an agricultural revolution took place in eighteenth-century Europe. Like the question of the chicken or the egg, whether the new agriculture was a cause or a consequence of demographic change is endlessly discussed. Europe was, however, able to avoid the trap posited by the pessimistic eighteenth-century scholar Thomas Malthus by which the food supply grew only arithmetically, while population growth increased geometrically. Malthus realized that agricultural producers for centuries had not been able to produce more than 20 to 25 percent of marketable (or taxable) surplus—exactly the amount that was taken by the landlord, the Church, and the state (the so-called feudal fifth, ninth, or tenth). The only way to increase output, the extension of cultivation, led to use of marginal, less fertile land, which decreased productivity. This old practice, however, became obsolete. As E. L. Jones, a historian of British agriculture in the seventeenth and eighteenth centuries, observes, a miraculous change occurred between 1700 and 1800: England became able not only to feed twice as many people but also to produce enough fodder to feed three times as many horses (Jones 1967).

However miraculous the change appeared, it was not sudden, for it was based on a gradual development of capitalistic agriculture, first in its genuine "laboratory," Holland, but then mostly in Britain. The long process of eliminating feudal landownership, serfdom, and communal farming and developing capitalist landownership, tenant farming, and yeomanry was the main achievement of British development between the fourteenth and seventeenth centuries. From the fourteenth to the nineteenth centuries, sanctioned by the General Enclosure Act of 1801, peasants' strip fields were incorporated into big landowners' estates and the enclosed peasants became wage workers. This created a wage-earning class and, with the emergence of a market system that led to a more advanced form of division of labor, laid the foundations for a major breakthrough.

Dynamic technological innovations followed. Among them, the modern crop-rotation system deserves special attention. The old method of preventing soil depletion through two- or three-field crop rotation meant that half or a third of the arable land remained fallow at any given time. Modern scientific crop rotation—the so-called Townshend four-crop rotation (wheat, turnips, barley, and clover) decreased fallow land dramatically. The more sophisticated Norfolk system used seventeen kinds of rotating crops, which successfully preserved and even enriched the soil, thanks to the nitrogen-fixing mechanism of the legumes. This single innovation increased the area of cultivated land by at least one-third. Land amelioration also advanced tremendously. Manure, previously used for heating, was discovered to improve the soil. Drainage, canalization, and other methods of soil reclamation all contributed to higher yields. Improved farming equipment also increased productivity. Heavier, steel-tipped plows drawn by horses rather than oxen yielded 50 percent faster and deeper plowing and better soil preparation. Other horse-drawn machinery also appeared.

The new methods spread, partly as a result of enthusiasts publishing books. Among the pioneers of agricultural literature were John Dorne, a Dutch bookseller who established his headquarters in Oxford as early as 1520, and John Fitzherbert, whose *Boke of Husbondrye* came out in 1523.

During the seventeenth century, Hugh Platt and Walter Blith publicized the potential of manuring land and drainage, which had a large impact on modern farming, and various landowner-writers, the best known being Viscount Charles "Turnip" Townshend and the gentleman farmer and propagandist Jethro Tull, later shared their experiences with modern rotation and new crops (Ernle 1925).

According to some estimates, the yield of wheat per acre increased only from 8 to 11 bushels during the half-millennium before 1650. By 1800, however, the yield had increased to 20 bushels per acre, and the marketable surplus product more than doubled, increasing output by roughly 50 percent. Scientific farming resulted in another revolutionary innovation in animal husbandry: livestock, traditionally grazed in pastures, began to be kept in stables and fed new forage crops such as clover and turnips in the crop-rotation system. This way, farmers could avoid slaughtering a great part of their stock in wintertime, a necessity that had for centuries prevented an increase in animal stock. Consequently, herds sharply increased: during the seventeenth century, the average size of sheep flocks on farms in the upland region of Oxfordshire increased more than four times (Jones 1967). The milk production of Dutch cows increased by three to four times during the second half of the eighteenth century.

As a unique consequence of these efficiencies, much of the agricultural labor force was released from farming and hence was ready to work in other branches of the economy. In the late seventeenth century, fully 60 percent of the active population was engaged in agriculture in Britain. By the early 1810s, this share had dropped to 33 percent. The advancing enclosure system and the increasing population spurred this trend.

The Dutch and British economies had become capitalistic market systems by the eighteenth century. The huge income from transatlantic trade contributed to the capital accumulation that led to the rise of a rich merchant stratum. Analyzing the market's influence, Michael Flinn concludes that "the expansion of the overseas markets remains a development of the utmost significance for the industrial advance of Britain . . . [however], home demand predominated," and domestic markets and trade were far more important (Flinn 1966, 57, 62). At the end of the eighteenth century, England had a very strong domestic market: its per capita iron and cotton consumption reached a level matched by the continental countries only a century later. According to Paul Bairoch, foreign trade accounted for about 10–12 percent of capital accumulation during the eighteenth century (Bairoch 1976b). The emerging new merchant class, making use of its enormous wealth and the exceptionally free market conditions, turned to the countryside, employing cheap rural labor in cottage industries to produce industrial products for marketing. The merchant-led putting out, or *Verlag*, system triggered a boom in industrial activity. During the eighteenth century, proto-industrialization facilitated the rise of the factory system. The merchant entrepreneurs founded huge factories, employing hundreds and sometimes thousands of workers in six- to eight-story modern buildings to perform a single element of a well-organized industrial operation. The industrial division of labor—as Adam Smith enthusiastically described it in his famous example of a pin factory—increased productivity. A new type of entrepreneur emerged who became the organizer and planner of output and trade, a "captain of industry" commanding thousands of workers and employees. Something new appeared on the horizon—the era of industrialization.

THE NEW SCIENTIFIC THINKING AND WESTERN VALUES

The rise of Northwestern Europe during the seventeenth and eighteenth centuries was also driven by a highly revolutionized science and philosophy, which evolved into a new zeitgeist. A widespread new concept of human society and the universe, a new value system and a new way of thinking, emerged in the West. The people of the age developed an unquestionable belief that reason and experience can uncover the laws of nature and society and facilitate the reorganization of societies.

The initiators of this scientific and ideological transformation from the mid seventeenth to the late eighteenth centuries were concentrated in Northwestern Europe, especially in the Netherlands, which attracted émigré philosophers; in Britain; and, later in the eighteenth century, in France.

Forerunners of the new trend included Joost Lips in Leiden, whose translations of the classics introduced a major change in the European worldview, and René Descartes, who presented the first modern concept of a universe operating under mathematical laws in his *Discours de la méthode* published in 1637, eight years after he moved to Holland. First Descartes and then his disciple Benedict (Baruch) Spinoza became philosophers of rationalism and natural law. The latter, an exponent of the causal explanation of nature and society, developed the concepts of a social contract, rule by the majority, and individual freedom. Spinoza rejected religion as the product of human fear of the unknown forces of nature and of ignorance preserved by poverty.

The Enlightenment philosophy developed in Holland paved the road toward the revolution of thought in Britain. The son of an illiterate English farmer, Isaac Newton, who spent most of his time in the study of alchemy, theology, and ancient philosophy, published his *Philosophiae naturalis principia mathematica* in London in 1687, the "capstone of the Scientific Revolution of the sixteenth and seventeenth centuries and . . . often said to be the greatest work of science ever published" (Dobbs and Jacob 1995, 10). In this and his next three works in the early eighteenth century, based on his rigorous experimentation and scholarly methodology, Newton explained the laws of the physical world, the "laws of motion, the laws of optics, the calculus, the concept of universal gravitation. . . . In addition to its grand unified vision of the universe, [Newton's work] provided a rational mechanics for the operations of machines on earth" (ibid., 38, 44). The Newtonian concept of the universe depicted a secure, harmonious system and presented science as a prime mover of human progress. Lectures and publications, including Voltaire's, popularized the Newtonian views and generated practical works on applied mechanics and machine building. The Newtonian scientific weltanschauung changed people's ways of thinking about nature and society. It became a pillar, not only of Enlightenment scholarship, but of civil engineering.

The scientific revolution most of all diverted people's interest from metaphysical to physical problems and to the utilitarian opportunities of applied science. Important links developed between the philosopher-scientists and the humble instrument makers. As A. E. Musson and Eric Robinson have shown, mathematics became a practical tool for artisans in the early seventeenth century. Traders, merchants, seamen, and carpenters developed it more than academics did. Various cheap textbooks became available. Gresham's College in London encouraged collaboration between scholars and craftsmen. The newly founded Royal Society "was actively concerned with the practical applications of natural philosophy," and its members aimed at improving "mechanic arts" such as building, metalsmithing, shipbuilding, and agriculture. Around the end of the eighteenth century, many craftsmen bought Francis Walkingame's best-selling textbook *The Tutor's Assistant,* which appeared in numerous editions of 5,000–10,000 copies each (Musson and Robinson 1969, 12–25). The new weltanschauung became the worldview and guiding compass of thousands of entrepreneurs.

Besides Newton, Thomas Hobbes occupies a special place among the seventeenth-century pioneers of thought as the first plebeian English philosopher and the founder of modern political philosophy. In his mature work *Leviathan,* Hobbes challenged basic feudal concepts such as the ancient bonds of loyalty to sovereigns and established in their place the concept of individualism. "The condition of man . . . is a . . . condition of war everyone against everyone . . . everyone is governed by his own reason and every man has a right . . . of doing anything he likes," Hobbes wrote ([1651] 1956, 122–23). The recognition of self-interest as the key incentive in life led Hobbes to the logical conclusion of the need for an absolute state. Since in the society of selfish individuals, everybody is "in the condition of war," people must mutually transfer their rights, that is, make a *contract* and, via an absolute monarch, create laws (ibid., 125). Hobbes recommended an omnipotent rational state that guaranteed individual rights and personal security and kept society in "peace."

John Locke, the most popular philosopher of the late seventeenth century, the age of the "Glorious Revolution" in Britain, went even further. In his *Two Treatises on Government,* he posited the central role of laws, the most important "guarantor of freedom," and the need for a social contract between king and people that limited power and made it constitutional. "All men by nature are equal," he stated, "being born . . . with a title to perfect freedom and an uncontrolled enjoyment of all the rights and privileges of the law of Nature. . . . It is evident," he continued, "that absolute monarchy . . . is indeed inconsistent with civil society, and can be no form of civil government" (Locke [1690] 1947, 801). Locke also propagated the separation and mutual limitation of legislative and executive powers. He became one of the most influential apostles of the modern *Rechtsstaat* and the parliamentary system.

If one begins the list of influential and pioneering British thinkers and scholars of the seventeenth and eighteenth centuries with Isaac Newton, one must conclude it with Adam Smith, the founder of "economics as physics," describing and explaining the laws of the economic universe. Smith, a pupil and later the successor of Francis Hutcheson in the chair of moral philosophy at Glasgow University, began his career as one of the British moral philosophers by publishing his *Theory of Moral Sentiment* (1759). Seventeen years later, however, he published his *Wealth of Nations* (1776), a thousand-page book that became "the crowning peak of the early development of economic theory" (Heimann 1964, 63–64). Just as preordained harmony rules Newton's universe, the preordained harmony of the self-regulated market rules Smith's economic world. Smith introduced the concepts of the laissez-faire economy governed by an "invisible hand," supply and demand, and the "infallible panacea" of the price mechanism under competitive conditions. Smith deemed intervention harmful, including protective tariffs.

The innovative British philosophy strongly influenced the French Enlightenment. François-Marie Arouet (who, in 1722, adopted the name Voltaire), a recognized poet who had already been imprisoned in the Bastille, traveled to England and stayed for three years. He was impressed by the intellectual freedom there and impassioned by the teaching of Newton and Locke. In his *English Letters* (1734), he expresses admiration for Britain and alludes to the rather different French intellectual environment. Through his poems, novels, essays, and pamphlets, he became one of the most powerful proponents of natural law, "the instinct which makes us feel justice," and tolerance, since "intolerance is absurd and barbaric, it is the right of the tiger" (Voltaire 1946, 833, 841). Voltaire advocated an intellectual revolt against an antiquated Church and state, and his slogan "Écrasez l'infâme" ("Crush the infamy," i.e, superstition) took on political significance in the late 1770s when he returned to France.

The French Enlightenment showcased a number of writers' and philosophers' wit, sarcasm, and lucidity. Charles-Louis de Secondat, baron de Montesquieu, idealized the British parliamentary system and attacked absolute power. Political liberty cannot exist, he argued, "when the legislative and executive powers are united in the same person, or in the same body . . . there is no liberty, if the judiciary power be not separated from the legislative and executive." Moreover, "the legislative power should reside in the whole body of the people" that can be represented by their delegates (Montesquieu [1748] 1946, 936, 938).

The ideas of a revolutionary social and political system were in the making. The Geneva-born Jean-Jacques Rousseau, who moved to Paris in the mid eighteenth century, expressed the aura of revolution most eloquently. The very first sentence of his *Social Contract* sounded like a declaration of war on the establishment: "Man is born free and everywhere he is in chains." Whereas all the previous thinkers had appealed to elites, Rousseau addressed the masses. He defined liberty as obedience to the general will and offered society "a form of association which will defend and protect with the whole common force the person and goods of each associate, and in which each, while uniting himself with all, may still obey himself alone, and remain as free as before." Rousseau established an entirely new concept of legitimate power, stating that only the "state that [is] governed by laws . . . [and in] the public interest . . . [has a] legitimate government" (Rousseau [1762] 1946, 954, 957, 965). Rousseau went even further by denouncing private property and wealth that makes even the law itself unjust, since "laws are always useful to those who have possessions and harmful to those who have nothing." The just society requires a "social state . . . [in which] all have something and none of them has too much." Rousseau emotionally condemned private ownership as the cause of wars, crimes, murders, and other misfortunes of the human race, passionately declaring "that the fruits of the earth belong to all and the earth to no one!" (Rousseau [1755] 1983, 29, 140).

THE STAGNATION AND RELATIVE DECLINE
OF THE EUROPEAN "PERIPHERIES"

The other areas of the European continent could not follow in the footsteps of the Northwestern countries. This was true even of previous leaders of Europe, such as Italy, Portugal, and Spain, although they could also profit from the discovery of America and, potentially, from the Atlantic trade. "Although our kingdoms could be the richest in the world for the abundance of gold and silver that have come into them," stated the 1588–93 Cortes, "they end up as the poorest because they serve as a bridge across which gold and silver pass to other kingdoms" (Cipolla 1994, 239). The rigid medieval social-institutional system and the associated noble-hidalgo attitude led to conspicuous consumption and a parasitic lifestyle. Spain did not make any attempt to increase productivity and output, but it opened its border to duty-free French products (in 1659) and English goods (in 1667). As Adam Smith clearly recognized, "It is not [through] the importation of gold and silver that the discovery of America has enriched Europe. . . . [It] made a most essential [change] . . . by opening a new and inexhaustible market to all the commodities of Europe, it gave occasion to a new division of labour [which] . . . in the narrow circle of the ancient commerce, could never have taken place" (Smith [1776] 1976, 1: 469–70). Spain, Portugal, and Italy, unable to exploit this situation, exhausted their gold and silver income. When the inflow of precious metals drastically decreased during the seventeenth century, Spain's debt exceeded income by from three to four times. Decline was inevitable.

Italy's decline began earlier. The export of woolen and silk cloth declined sharply during the seventeenth century. The exports of Genoa, Venice, and Milan dropped by 75, 90, and 96 percent, respectively, between the end of the sixteenth century and that of the seventeenth. With its rigid social structure, dominant guilds, and outdated institutions, Italy could not compete with the emerging Northwestern countries. The Italian market was flooded by imports from England, Holland, and France, while Italy began to export unprocessed silk and agricultural products.

If the Mediterranean countries began lagging behind Northwestern Europe, Central and Eastern Europe lagged even further. This region lay far from modern Atlantic trade routes and had no contact with overseas colonies. Instead, it lost its previous role in the so-called Levantine trade of the medieval period, whose main routes crossed the area. Mostly land-locked, these countries were excluded from the advantages of the emerging modern age. The geopolitical situation was only one of the causes of stagnation and decline. Here, too, the reasons were deeply rooted in history and in domestic social, political, and institutional factors. It is outside the scope of this study to evoke the century-long discourse on the origins of the different historical performance of Central and Eastern Europe from that of the West. Following the publication in 1824 of Leopold von Ranke's *Geschichte der romanischen und germanischen Völker*, many historians took the view that Europe had from the seventh century onward always been divided into a "Latino-Germanic West . . . having been united" by Charlemagne, and, "East of the Saale and Elbe" line, a mostly Slavic and Byzantine-Islamic East, which did not belong among the Western nations. From "that time they never exercised any independent influence, they only appear either subservient or antagonistic; they receive . . . only the ebb of the tide of the general movements" (Ranke [1824] 1909, 5–6). When Europe as a whole joined the Christian community in the tenth century and the forms of feudalism were established, its substance was not integrated into the social fabric of Eastern Europe, and "genuine Eastern characteristics" distinguished the area from the West (Makkai 1976). Additionally, the two-hundred-year Mongol occupation of Russia from the thirteenth century on and the five-hundred-year Ottoman occupation of large parts of the Balkans from the late fourteenth century on drove a wedge into the body of Europe as far as Hungary, impeding the Western type of feudal development in much of the region. Central and Eastern Europe thus cannot be regarded as structurally part of the West:

Social structural elements that developed organically in the west . . . over almost 500 years [ninth–thirteenth centuries], through the dismantling of parts of previous achievements and the rearranging of the main elements . . . appeared in the eastern zone, including Hungary, in a concentrated form . . . in little more than one and a half centuries. It is hardly surprising that the forms they took were in some places inorganically truncated or raw, in others still unarticulated, rough, or mixed, and in yet others demonstrating here and there various archaic features. (Szűcs 1983, 153)

Several historians, on the other hand, underline the basic similarity of Western and Eastern European feudalism. Zsigmond Pál Pach, one of the most knowledgeable scholars of the topic, concluded that "European economic development tended . . . to equalize the difference in the development levels of Western and Eastern Europe [up to the second half of the fifteenth century by advancing] the East European societies that had started later on the road to feudal development" (Pach 1994, 287). Some of the countries of the region, such as Hungary and Poland, became medieval great powers. Jerzy Topolski also maintains that Polish, Bohemian, Hungarian, Baltic, and Russian "feudalism was developing in a similar way . . . [to that in the West]. Nor do these areas reveal any essential differences in chronological terms" (Topolski 1994, 375–77). In his interpretation, the similar paths of socioeconomic development taken in Western and Eastern Europe diverged at the end of the fifteenth century.

This latter turning point is not debated: between the sixteenth and eighteenth centuries, the Continent became divided into two halves. The vast area of Central and Eastern Europe, however, was by no means uniform. Each country had its peculiarities, and subregions are clearly distinguishable. Central and Eastern Europe somehow broke into at least two zones: the Central European and Russian and Balkan areas (Berend 1986). The split between Greek Orthodoxy and Roman Catholicism strengthened and stabilized that divergence. The western zone—encompassing Poland, the Baltic countries, Bohemia, Hungary, and Croatia—was strongly influenced by the West, while the eastern zone, Russia and the Balkans, remained isolated from the West, lacked private property, and preserved the communal system until early modern times or even longer (Gunst 1996). It is for this reason that Jenő Szűcs speaks of three, rather than two, regions of Europe.

The history of Central and Eastern Europe from the sixteenth century to the eighteenth consequently followed an opposite trend from that of Western Europe. Instead of eliminating feudal institutions and adopting a market system and merchant capitalism, the Baltic, Polish, Bohemian, Hungarian, and Croatian area regressed to an earlier stage of feudalism, a manorial-serf economy—a "second serfdom." Self-managing latifundia based on socage reappeared. Serfs were again bound to the land, and feudal dues were paid in crops and then in labor. Juhan Kahk speaks of Estonian peasants who, from "the middle of the sixteenth century were required to work on the demesne all through the summer," and in the eighteenth century, "in addition to the regular corvée . . . the peasant was required to send [a second, and] a third person to work on the demesne during . . . reaping season." The average corvée was fixed at two days a week, but throughout August, it rose to three and even four days (Kahk 1989, 170, 173).

After having suppressing the country's most dramatic peasant uprising, led by György Dózsa, the Hungarian Diet assembled in Buda in October 1514 and enacted "bloody laws" that abolished the free movement
of the peasants and tied them to the soil. Labor service, the *robot,* was also
reintroduced (52 days a year, performed with two yokes of oxen, or 104
days without the use of draft animals). This legal framework of the "second serfdom" became a reality largely in the mid seventeenth century,
when the latifundia became dominant in the country, replacing the peasant tenure of previous centuries.

The Polish Sejm of 1520 also introduced labor service and restricted it
to 52 days a year. In the seventeenth century, however, when manorial land
already occupied roughly one-quarter of the arable land, the mandatory
labor service was increased to three days a week. The free migration of
the peasantry that had become common during the fifteenth century was
curbed, and the serfs were tied to the soil (Topolski 1982). In Bohemia,
after the Battle of the White Mountain (1620), the *Verneurte Landesord-
nung* (Renewed Land Ordinance) of 1627 was introduced. The bulk of
the rural population was tied to the soil and was not permitted to move
without the agreement of the landlord. Additionally, the Labor Service
Decree *(Robot-patent)* of 1680 declared that the serfs were obliged to perform labor service on the demesne of the lord, who even had the right to
increase the *robot* "at will" (Klíma 1991). When Maria Theresa restricted
excesses of the *robot* system, and the new Patent of 1775 limited labor service to three days a week, "the Empress . . . found it difficult to enforce
even the three days' outer limit" (Kann 1974, 197).

While the West experienced an emerging modern capitalism, the East
thus reinstituted earlier feudal structures. The fifteenth to the eighteenth
centuries were disastrous for the area in many respects. Historical cata-
clysms and national tragedies followed one after the other, and independent statehood collapsed. The Serb defeat at Kosovo Polje (1389), "an ir-
retrievable disaster for the South Slavs," led to the Ottoman occupation
of the Balkans. The battles of Mohács (1526) and Buda (1541) ended Hungarian independence and led to the partition of Hungary and a hundred
and fifty years of Ottoman rule in the middle of the country. Following
the Battle of the White Mountain (1620), the Thirty Years' War resulted
in the death of 40 percent of the population of Bohemia and virtually de-
capitated the Czech elite, changing the social situation of the country—now
a province of the Habsburg empire. In the North, the Swedish-Russian
rivalry ended with the Treaty of Nystad (1721), and Swedish hegemony in
the Baltic area was replaced by Russian dominance. During internal Polish warfare (1715–16), the Russian tsar subordinated the Polish-Lithuanian

kingdom to Russian rule, effectively making it a "Russian protectorate." The war of the Confederation of Bar had an even more tragic consequence: the partition of Poland (1772).

During the early modern centuries, when strong absolutist states emerged in Western Europe, foreshadowing nation-states and modern capitalist transformation, all the Central and Eastern European countries lost their independent statehood and were absorbed by huge, mostly despotic empires. At the end of the eighteenth century, the entire area belonged to the Ottoman, Russian, and Habsburg empires.

The dramatic deviation from the Western model of transformation was, however, more a consequence than a cause of genuine internal weaknesses, which mostly predated foreign occupation. While Western Europe responded to demographic catastrophe and the scarcity of peasant labor by lowering rents and decreasing labor services and by increasing peasant mobility, which led to the fall of serfdom, "in Eastern Europe . . . decline in population . . . was accompanied by an ultimately successful movement towards imposing extra-economic controls, that is, serfdom" (Brenner 1985, 23). In the same way, the West responded to the rise of modern trade and markets with the advent of capitalism. The East reacted to the favorable opportunities for grain export by enforcing serfdom and preserving feudal institutions for centuries longer. "The emergence of a specific set of class- or social-property relations in the countryside—that is, capitalist class relations" led to a breakthrough from a traditional economy to a self-sustaining modern system in the West (ibid., 30), while, in contrast, the preservation of the traditional class and social-property relations, the "strong position of the nobility in the state and society" (Rutkowski 1928), preserved the feudal system in the East.

The dominant position of the nobility in state and society gradually led to an idealized noble, or gentlemanlike, mentality, soon considered a "national characteristic," that was completely different from either the Protestant ethic and Puritan morality—the "spirit of capitalism," as Max Weber put it ([1904–5] 2001)—or the ideas of Judaism, with its traditional business sense, in which Werner Sombart (1911) saw the origins of capitalism. Zsigmond Pál Pach describes the antibusiness mentality of the Hungarian nobility: "A type of *'absentee'* landlord came into being, living far from his domain, spending money excessively, keeping up a luxurious residence in Vienna." He adds, "The Hungarian country gentleman who lived mainly on the serf's services . . . on his medium-sized or small estate . . . engaged at most in local county affairs . . . besides going to weddings and hunting and offering hospitality to neighbours and county notables" (Pach 1994, 148, 150). The mid-nineteenth-century Hungarian historian Mihály Horváth noted that "common opinion, based on the biases and prejudices . . . of the noble classes, cherished the most absurd ideas concerning commerce," and the mid-twentieth-century Hungarian historian Gyula Szekfű concluded that the "Hungarian race . . . [has an] anti-commercial and anti-capitalist talent" (Pach 1994, 151, 155). The hidalgo attitude in Spain and the "anti-capitalist national character" in Hungary and in other "noble societies" of Central and Eastern Europe, consequences of a special class and property structure in these areas, became strong and eventually insuperable obstacles on the road to modern transformation.

This is not to say that Central and Eastern Europe did not join the emerging modern world system. Zsigmond Pál Pach has suggested that the generalization that the region "failed to join in this great process of transformation" may not explain the negative trend in the development of Central and Eastern Europe. On the contrary: "In the first period of the development of [a] modern world economy, it was not yet the overseas colonies, but rather the countries of East-Central Europe that were joined [to] the economy of Western Europe in the sense of a modern market . . . by exports of mass-consumption foodstuffs and imports of mass-consumption manufactures" (Pach 1994, 288, 306). The reestablished manorial-serf system of the East, paradoxically, had a "capitalist origin." The region did become a part of an emerging capitalistic world system (Wallerstein 1974, 91–92). In the emerging modern world, however, it acquired a subordinate and peripheral role.

The area east of the Elbe River was distinguished by the preservation of its agrarian character and retarded urban development. Urban centers of a Western type did not emerge in Central and Eastern Europe in the early modern period. By 1800, quite a few modern cities existed in the West. First and foremost was London, with its 1.1 million inhabitants, and next Paris, with more than half a million. Amsterdam, Milan, Marseille, Berlin, and Hamburg, among several other cities, had populations of between 100,000 and 200,000. Central and Eastern Europe, however, remained rural. Its largest cities in 1800 were Warsaw, with 100,000 inhabitants; Prague, with 75,000; and Pest and Buda (later Budapest), which together had 54,000. The Hungarian census of 1785–87 recorded 400,000 urban citizens—only 5 percent of the total. The Balkan capital cities remained dusty, sleepy little settlements. Around the end of the eighteenth century, Bucharest had 30,000 inhabitants. Belgrade had 25,000. Serbia's urban dwellers accounted for hardly more than 4 percent of the population in the early nineteenth century. Central and Eastern European urbanization was one-tenth of that of the West around the beginning of the nineteenth century. Even the Central and Eastern European villages were "extremely tiny, often no more than a dozen houses" (Braudel 1979, 56–57).

The Balkan subregion's deviation from the West was even more dramatic. From the nineteenth century on, national historiography has traditionally blamed the Ottoman conquest for Balkan backwardness. The conquerors destroyed grain-growing villages in the lowlands and decimated the population, the argument goes; the survivors escaped to wooded, mountainous areas, where they supported themselves by raising animals. The consequence of Ottoman occupation was thus the depopulation of the Balkans and a reversion to seminomadic pastoral life (Lampe and Jackson 1982). Maria Todorova sums up the "dominant discourse" in Balkan historiography thus: "On the eve of the Ottoman conquest, the medieval societies of the Balkans had reached a high degree of sophistication that made them commensurate with, if not ahead of, development in Western Europe. . . . The arrival of the Ottomans was a calamity of unparalleled consequences because it disrupted the natural development . . . isolated the peninsula from European development and left it untouched by the great ideas and transformations . . . [bringing] a deep cultural regression and even barbarization" (Todorova 1997, 182). Even Hungarian historiography has accounted for the unfortunate non-Western development pattern of the country from the sixteenth century on in terms of the catastrophe of the Ottoman occupation of the middle part of the country for over a century and a half. "The Ottomans destroyed the normal development of the Hungarian state and nation by their three hundred years of wars," stated Gyula Szekfű, the leading interwar historian. "The Ottoman rule is the most severe, moreover, probably the only major catastrophe of Hungarian history. . . . That was the cause of all later misfortunes of Hungary" (Szekfű 1935, 498–99, 584).

More recent research, however, has challenged this traditional view. Zsigmond Pál Pach has convincingly proved that a divergent trend in socioeconomic development had begun in Hungary at the end of the fifteenth century, before the Ottoman conquest of 1526 and 1541. Moreover, the *elkanyarodás,* diversion from Western trends, was caused by the rise of modern Atlantic trade and the marginalization of Central and Eastern Europe in the world system (Pach 1963). Fikret Adanir also offers a critical revision regarding the Balkans. "The Balkan Peninsula had experienced demographic and economic decline long before the foundation of the Ottoman state," he argues. Desertion of land became typical during earlier centuries, and Thessaly, the lowlands of Macedonia, and Danubian Bulgaria were grazing grounds for the herds of the Wallachians (Adanir 1989, 133–34). The leading Romanian agrarian historian Henri Stahl argues that Romanian society was essentially nomadic and pastoral, based on a marginal "itinerant agriculture" that did not employ crop-rotation systems before 1864. Grain-growing villages, in this interpretation, did not exist. The pastoral population cultivated virgin land for three years and then moved to other places with their herds and cultivated virgin land again. Private ownership did not exist, and the warrior elite engaged in fiscal exploitation of the communal villages. The Romanian Domnie was thus a sui generis type of social formation, "at any rate, not that of feudalism" (Stahl 1980, 53, 214–16). The leading nineteenth-century Romanian historian Nicolae Iorga called the Romanian state a *stat de pradă,* a predatory state. This characterization was certainly appropriate to most of the Balkans, which were referred to by late medieval sources as Magna Valachia.

Regarding the Balkans, but also the rest of Central and Eastern Europe, it is thus fair to ask, Why did this area become dependent, occupied by neighboring great powers, and peripheral to Europe? Why did other countries become colonial powers or dominant in the area? "Why did it not turn out the other way around?" — as György Ránki and I have asked in our work on the nineteenth-century European periphery. "Most of the authors dealing with backwardness do not go back to prior to the sixteenth century, and few go back even that far," we wrote twenty years ago. "The 'optical illusion' that this gives rise to will be obvious." The answer to the previous question is that "the seeds of this 'departure' from the Western model were already well embedded in the preceding centuries." The lack of feudal structures, "barbarian feudalism," "state serfdom," and the peculiar tenacity of communal landholding had a major impact on the later history of the region (Berend and Ránki 1982, 10–12).

Besides, a historical debate about the consequences of the Ottoman occupation of the Balkans attempts to revise the traditional view of the Ottoman empire, maintaining that the Ottoman system was no more backward than any other non-Western regime in the world. The Ottoman empire was, in fact, a rather typical successful large agrarian empire. Some writers entirely reject the concept of Ottoman "backwardness" and regard Ottoman civilization simply as an alternative to the Western European model. Maria Todorova discusses the rise of Western stereotypes of the Balkans, which, from the eighteenth century on, became a "frozen image" of industrial backwardness, primitive social relations and institutions, irrational and superstitious cultures, and tribal barbarity—a "repository of negative characteristics against which a positive and self-congratulatory image of the 'European' and the 'West' has been constructed" (Todorova 1997, 7, 11, 188). Opposing this biased perception, she cites Ágnes Heller's view: "The myth of Occident and Orient is not a juxtaposition of civilization with barbarism but rather of one civilization with another" (Heller 1992, 14).

The various perceptions and interpretations cannot cover existing differences and require noting some basic facts. In the classical Ottoman system, created by Mehmed II in the mid fifteenth century and characteristic of the entire sixteenth century, the peasants had a "quite tolerable condition of life," and the "tax load . . . was not unduly heavy." The state eventually acquired nearly 90 percent of the territory, but it was given to the spahi cavalry officers, a military elite of about 20,000 soldiers in the Balkans in the mid fifteenth century, for an indefinite period of time to collect taxes (the *timar* system). Power, however, was strictly centralized, and the spahis could be removed at any time (Lampe and Jackson 1982). Ottoman occupation of the Balkans actually helped to replace the nomadic transhumance way of life with permanent settlements and agricultural activity. Turkish immigration and settlements in northeast Bulgaria, Thrace, the flatland of Macedonia, and Thessaly repopulated deserted areas. The state encouraged the cultivation of unused land by granting private ownership, which led to rice cultivation in the river valleys. The Ottoman military-administrative districts (sanjaks) at last became a corn surplus area (Adanir 1989, 134–39). It is also true and important that the empire was open to ethnic differences and tolerant of religious minorities.

The Ottoman regime, however, started to change at the end of the sixteenth century. The classical *timar* system, which was rather similar to other feudal tax systems, was replaced by tax farming. Later, tax farms were leased on a hereditary basis *(malikâne)*. In the Ottoman "command economy," to use John Lampe's term, the peasants had to sell their products to the Sultan at a low official mandatory price, which amounted to an extra form of taxation. Head tax became personal tax, instead of household tax, all kinds of tax exemptions were abolished, and so-called extraordinary taxes were collected annually to cover the vast expenses of permanent warfare, in 1593–1606, in 1645–69, and in 1683–99. The tax burden, Fikret Adanir concludes, became three times higher in constant prices than it had been in the sixteenth century.

The dissolution of the *timar* system undermined the well-being of the rural population. Provincial governors recruited private armies and became absolute rulers of the land they governed. "Overtaxation, brigandage . . . famines, and epidemics" led to a steep decline in the population. "Social banditry" became the main characteristic of the Balkans. People escaped from the lowlands to the hills and woods. An Austrian envoy noted of his travels across the Balkans in the early seventeenth century that he did not see developed agriculture except on the Thracian plain around Plovdiv, and that "wild stretches between Belgrade and Niš were wilderness." "The Ottoman system . . . in the long run . . . proved to be an obstacle to substantial increases in agricultural productivity and rendered more difficult the transition to the capitalistic mode of production" (Adanir 1989, 142–56). Kemal Atatürk—who was, of course, strongly motivated to legitimize his revolutionary regime by sharply rejecting the Ottoman era—encouraged his people "to regard the old empire as a backward despotism whose guiding ideology, Islam, had prevented its Turkish elite from keeping up with western technology and economic progress" (De Bellaigue 2001). The Ottoman empire was thus not just another type of economic regime, and it was definitely not a successful agricultural empire in terms of modern agricultural and capitalistic transformation in the early modern centuries. In fact, it was a serious burden and an obstacle to the kind of modernization that Atatürk's revolution aimed to achieve after World War I.

The worst long-term consequence of being incorporated into the Ottoman empire was virtual exclusion from the emerging world system, isolated in a rigid Ottoman bureaucratic-military regime that eschewed private ownership. The agricultural surplus was used to sustain the huge military establishment of a vast empire that was preoccupied with warfare, either to enlarge the empire or to preserve it.

Balkan societies were mutilated during the half-millennium of Ottoman rule. The elite became a bureaucratic-military Ottoman class. They were joined by a group of partly Islamized Balkan mediators who served as spokesmen for the local peasantry and assisted the Ottoman elite with tax collection. Each Serbian village elected a local leader, or *knaz,* and larger provinces elected a grand knaz. "Balkan Christian locals," Maria Todorova observes, "were integrated in the bureaucracy only at the lowest level, if at all," so that there was a "lack of political elites in the Balkans" (Todorova 1997, 171). Balkan societies thus became "incomplete societies," scarcely more than huge peasant communities. Blood relations remained the main organizational principle, and the peasants lived in extended family or communal units, working together and dividing the fruits of their labor equally. Since their surplus products were in effect confiscated, the peasant communities relied on a subsistence economy with practically no market connections. Neither the peasants nor the spahis who were responsible for tax collection engaged in improving agricultural methods or increasing output.

The Balkans remained almost entirely rural, but small towns with limited merchant-artisan populations emerged. In the centralized Ottoman empire, the *esnafi* system, a strict, guild-type organization, controlled what was produced and in what quantity, blocking any kind of unauthorized change. Prices were fixed, and profit was limited to 10 percent.

When the centralized Ottoman system began to decline, the situation worsened. As the regime lost control over security, local warlords and plundering janissary troops preyed on the Balkan peasantry. Anarchy and terrorism prevailed. The Western powers, together with Russia, defeated the Ottomans several times during the seventeenth and eighteenth centuries, and the empire became a free hunting ground for Dutch, French, and English merchants, who acquired special privileges. Export and import duties were fixed at the extremely low rate of 3 to 5 percent ad valorem, which, in the age of protectionism, left the empire's markets vulnerable. "The Ottoman Empire did not experience the so-called Commercial Revolution which basically transformed Western economic institutions and practices between the fifteenth and eighteenth centuries. . . . The Ottoman economy was remaining static during this period. . . . The curtain separating the Ottoman Empire from the West did not lift appreciably until the mid-nineteenth century" (Stavrianos [1958] 1963, 125, 134). The Balkans, dominated by a subsistence-communal economy, could not join the world system.

TRADITIONAL DEMOGRAPHIC TRENDS; ABSENCE OF
AGRICULTURAL REVOLUTION AND PROTO-INDUSTRIALIZATION

Lifestyle, nutrition, marriage customs, health conditions, and the entire communal-rural environment of the medieval type of village life changed little in Central and Eastern Europe during the early modern centuries. While the mortality level declined in the West—to about 26–27 deaths per 1,000 inhabitants in England in 1800—it remained essentially unchanged in Central and Eastern Europe. In the early 1800s, there were 39.5 deaths per 1,000 inhabitants in Bohemia, and the mortality rate rarely dropped below 35–36 deaths, which was, as in previous centuries, nearly counterbalanced by an equally high birthrate (between 35–45 births per

1,000 inhabitants). The calculations of Roger Mols (1974) and B. R. Mitchell (1975) indicate that the population of Central and Eastern Europe, unlike that of Western Europe, grew very slowly, from 16 million in 1500 to 20 million in 1600, 22.8 million in 1700, and somewhat more than 30 million in 1800. In contrast to the rapid growth in the West during the sixteenth century, only a 25 percent increase occurred here, followed by an 11 percent increase during the seventeenth century, and roughly 35 percent in the eighteenth. Most experts speak of "continuous population decline" in the Balkans between the mid seventeenth and early nineteenth centuries (see, e.g., Palairet 1997). Although the exact figures are disputable — Mols estimates that the seventeenth- and eighteenth-century Balkans had a "minimum" of 8 million inhabitants, whereas Michael Palairet registers only 3.7 million in 1700 and 5.5 million in the early nineteenth century — they certainly demonstrate the demographic trends and the marked difference between the Balkans and the West. Using much more reliable data, the demographers of nineteenth-century Europe registered a continued slow population growth in Central and Eastern Europe during the first decades of the century (Glass and Eversley 1965, 62). Around 1800, there were some 18–28 people per square kilometer in Central Europe, and the Balkans hardly surpassed 8–12, compared to 60–80 in Western Europe. The contrast was distinct.

B. H. Slicher van Bath and many students of the agricultural revolution in Western Europe have maintained that the major technological innovations and the increase of productivity were generated by necessity, namely, the population explosions of the sixteenth and eighteenth centuries; but there was no such pressure in sparsely populated Central and Eastern Europe. Moreover, socioeconomic institutions created insurmountable barriers to agricultural modernization. Until the end of the eighteenth century, the peasant economy thus preserved "its traditional level of production technique, unchanged, unmodernized . . . the land [was cultivated] in the same manner as the West European peasantry had been doing in the fifteenth and sixteenth centuries" (Gunst 1996, 76–77). When, in the mid to late eighteenth century, Western European yields significantly increased (for wheat: 7–8 times the sown seed in Holstein, 6–8 times in France, and 10–12 times in Great Britain), grain productivity remained unchanged in Central Europe, three to five times the amount of the sown seed in Poland, Hungary, and Bohemia, as in the sixteenth century (Magdalena 1974). The first signs of improvement appeared only in the second half of the eighteenth century (Kann and David 1984). In the mid and late seventeenth century, the ancient two-field rotation system still existed in the mountainous northern parts of Hungary and in Transylvania (on the Rákóczi estates), meaning half of the land remained fallow for grazing, while in the other areas, the three-field rotation system persisted (Várkonyi 1985). It did not change until the late eighteenth century. Crop rotation and new crops, including corn, potatoes, and feed crops, appeared on the most advanced large estates in the 1780s.

The Balkans did not feel any population pressure. Moreover, as Palairet observes, "The density of Balkan settlement . . . was too low to permit an efficient division of labor . . . peasants engaged in subsistence farming" (Palairet 1997, 22). Agricultural practice in the area during the early modern centuries declined into seminomadic animal husbandry, because settled farming became almost impossible. Peasants were ruthlessly exploited by warlords and robbed and murdered by savage janissaries. In various parts of the Balkans, "banditry was an essential branch of economic life" (ibid., 149). A Russian traveler in the early nineteenth century warned that the "Bulgars of the uplands were 'ferocious brigands . . . who rob and mutilate their victims.'" Late seventeenth- and even early nineteenth-century Western travelers describe the deserted Balkan countryside: "I am confident, above two-thirds of the land lyes unoccupied. . . . In many, many miles riding, we saw neither corn-field, nor pasture, nor flocks, nor herds," Reverend John Covel observed in 1675. "I should have mentioned . . . a great part of European Turkey . . . as almost destitute of inhabitants," reported an early nineteenth-century British traveler (Stavrianos [1958] 1963, 141–42). An "anti-capitalist character" emerged during these centuries in Hungary and Poland, and according to Palairet, armed violence became a kind of "national characteristic" in the Balkans. "[A]rmed struggle against an external enemy" was considered virtuous. Outlaws embodied freedom and courage, so that "the value system of this pastoral society could not only tolerate banditry but glory in it" (Palairet 1997, 149). "Our people think and sing in their songs that men become *hajduks* in Serbia as the result of Turkish terror and misrule," Vuk Karadžić noted in his Serbian Dictionary of 1818. The outlaws in the Balkans, organized in bands, received their food and shelter from the peasants who protected them, especially in wintertime. They were, in most cases, legendary heroes of the Robin Hood type (Holton and Mihailovich 1988, 120).

The peasants who fled to the uplands turned to transhumant stockraising in place of agriculture and used the mountain grasslands for grazing sheep and cattle. Only one-fifth to one-quarter of the arable land was plowed in both the Bulgarian Vidin province and Serbia. The agricultural revolution was not yet on the horizon.

In the eighteenth century, local warlords in the Turkish empire introduced private landownership, which became a factor in the disintegration of the centralized Ottoman state after being legalized by the Porte.[1] The resulting *chiflik* system was a kind of manorial economy operated either by serfs or by wage workers. *Chiflik* estates of 15–30 acres, cultivated by ten to twenty families, partly by sharecropping, appeared along the Danube in northern Bulgaria, in southern Bulgaria, in Macedonia, and in northern Greece, "almost always clustered around, or on the same rivers as, a Balkan commercial center" (Lampe and Jackson 1982, 34). This sort of manorial commercial farming remained limited even in Bulgaria, where it was practiced on roughly 20–23 percent of the arable land in some regions, but on no more than 5 percent of the total area of the country. Market-oriented *chiflik* farming nonetheless produced the bulk of the empire's agricultural exports.

Most of the peasant households in Central and Eastern Europe remained self-sufficient during the seventeenth and eighteenth centuries. Women produced a large amount of textiles and clothing and processed food; men manufactured most of their own tools, crafted woodwork, and did construction. A medieval guild system served the small urban population. There was scant room for Western-style proto-industrial development.

The only exception was Bohemia and Moravia, which experienced a flourishing proto-industrialization during the eighteenth and early nineteenth centuries. Merchants, burghers, well-to-do peasants, and landed aristocrats became industrial entrepreneurs in eighteenth-century Bohemia and employed a surprising number of peasants, mostly as home workers. In 1798, nearly 700,000 people were employed in the textile industries and roughly 200,000 people in the glass, iron, and paper industries in the Czech lands.

In other areas of Central and Eastern Europe, instead of proto-industrialization, a kind of feudal revival took place. In Hungary and Croatia, there was a late rekindling of guilds in the seventeenth and early eighteenth centuries. In places freshly liberated from Ottoman rule in the early seventeenth century, guilds were reorganized. Some guilds were small, formed by a handful of master craftsmen, and some, as in Varaždin and Zagreb in the second half of the century, represented more than one craft.

---

1. The Ottoman government was called the Porte, or the Sublime Porte, a name deriving from the Bab-i-Hümayün, or Imperial Gate (translated into French as "la Sublime Porte," "the High Gate"), of the Topkapi Palace in Istanbul, from which the Sultan's edicts went out.

They were highly conservative and opposed any artisan work outside the guild. Industrial activity stagnated in both Croatia and Hungary during the sixteenth and seventeenth centuries, with only 1 percent of the population working in industry and trade. Even in the cities, this figure only rose to between 10 and 20 percent. Later, by the second half of the eighteenth century, a quarter of the urban population belonged to 50 to 60 artisan guilds, but most of the craftsmen also cultivated land—mostly vineyards—to make a living.

The techniques and organization of artisan production did not change much between the fifteenth and early nineteenth centuries in Hungary and Croatia. Poland exhibited somewhat greater progress in this respect, and cottage industries advanced there during the eighteenth century, with from 8 to 10 percent of families earning the largest part of their incomes from textile piecework at home, while a similar proportion of peasants were occupied mainly with food processing. In Hungary, emerging proto-industries faced strong competition, but this was not the case in the Polish-Lithuanian kingdom, even after the partition of the country, because unlike the Habsburg empire, occupying Russia was economically weaker than the lands it dominated politically and militarily. However, industrial advances were very slow in a generally declining and crisis-ridden Poland, where even in 1830, only 2–3 percent of the population worked in industry.

The first putting-out industries and organized factories were established in Hungary in the late eighteenth and early nineteenth centuries. Proto-industrialization was, nevertheless, very limited, since little merchant capital was available and it was not drawn to industrial investment (Mérei 1951). Trade was much more lucrative, especially selling Hungarian agricultural products in the Austrian-Bohemian market and buying textiles and other manufactured goods there for Hungarian consumers. "The influx of cheaper industrial goods not only depressed the inefficient Hungarian crafts, it undermined a number of capitalist enterprises of the manufactory type, established in the preceding era of prosperity" (Kann and David 1984, 242). At the end of the eighteenth century, only 66 relatively large industrial, capitalist-type firms existed in Hungary. In Croatia, 28 textile, potash, glass, paper, and leather factories were established between the 1750s and 1790s, but only 11 survived after the turn of the century.

Elek Fényes, the father of modern Hungarian statistics, counted 530 nonmechanized "factories" in mid-nineteenth-century Hungary; only five steam engines were in use, with a capacity of about 50 horsepower. "The darkest side of our country," Fényes concluded, "is the lack of industry" (Fényes 1865–66).

Hillside animal husbandry was typical in the barely urbanized Balkans. Manufacturing was not separated from agriculture and took place in peasant households. Subsistence farming did not serve as a basis for any kind of early industrial development. During the late eighteenth and early nineteenth centuries, however, in certain areas, especially in northern Bulgaria, necessity generated proto-industrial advances. In relatively densely populated mountainous and hillside areas—the regions that escaped janissary atrocities—where arable farmland was inadequate, cottage industry became the main source of family income. Marketability was, however, the sine qua non for development, and Balkan peasant society was not a suitable market for the products of cottage industry. The physical proximity of an urban market or easy access to a transportation route (i.e., a major river) by way of which products could be exported offered exceptional opportunities. Istanbul and Salonika possessed these advantages and also supplied woolen cloth and clothing to the Ottoman army. Mills "were established exclusively for state contract work, to supply uniform cloth for cutting and sewing by the Bulgarian tailors at the Hambarya" (Palairet 1997, 9). Cotton processing for Austrian merchants also flourished in the Ambelakia and Tirnavos areas during the continental blockade of the Napoleonic wars. Around the turn of the nineteenth century, industrial villages appeared, and an increasing number of peasant households embarked on manufacturing. In most of the other parts of the Balkans, however, this was not the case. Serbian peasants were not engaged in industry. In a paradoxical way, proto-industrialization gained momentum in the later decades not as a path toward mechanized, modern big industry but rather as a substitute for it.

THE WESTERN WORLDVIEW AND LOCAL VALUES

In a virtually static socioeconomic environment, traditional value systems survived a long time. Count József Teleki, a leading Hungarian aristocrat who spent two years in Holland, France, and Switzerland, returned to Hungary to publish an anti-Enlightenment pamphlet (1760) attacking Voltaire even before he became known in the country. Pál Bertalanffy, the Jesuit who in 1757 wrote one of the first Hungarian geography books, a work of more than a thousand pages, sarcastically attacked Copernicus, saying his "brain [was] turned upside down." Mihály Szatmári Paksi's

Physica contracta (1719) attempted to refute Newton. A "populist" cult of ancient Hungarianness was confronted by "alien" Western ideas. The Tripartitum, an early sixteenth-century summary of noble privileges by the Counter-Reformation leader István Werbőczy, remained the Bible of the Hungarian nobility. In Bohemia and Poland, education was the province of the Church, and schooling concentrated, even at the secondary level, on theology and Latin. Culture and science remained subordinate to religion and the feudal worldview. The Jesuits controlled most of the schools and censored publications. In the anachronistic social environment of Poland, Stanisław Konarski established the Collegium Nobilium, a special school for nobles, and Adam Czartoryski opened a school of knights (1765). The feudal worldview and practices continued to gain momentum in these countries. Witchcraft trials and witch burning—thirteen defendants were burned in one single case in Szeged, Hungary—continued for another century in Hungary and Poland after the last case in France in 1670. Maria Theresa, after a few unsuccessful attempts, banned witchcraft trials in 1768. The last case in Poland occurred in 1776 (Kosáry 1980). The Polish nobility, in percentage terms the most numerous in Europe, jealously guarded its "golden freedom" and did not want to change the social hierarchy. The concept of the nobility reinforced notions of superiority over other nations, inasmuch as Poland was considered the "bulwark of Christianity" and also a protectorate of the Virgin Mary. A similar idea flourished in Hungary. Accordingly, the Polish nobility nurtured the idea of its "Sarmatian" origin, and the Hungarians, based on medieval tales, cherished their legendary Hun ancestry, which they believed differentiated them ethnically from their Slavic neighbors and serfs. Provincial hostility to foreign influences and a stressed "Polishness" (including special Polish noble dress, the *kontusz*) blocked the road to Western ideas (Topolski 1982; Cynarski 1974). Like the hidalgo mentality in Spain, Polish Sarmatianism and its Hungarian counterpart led the noble elite to reject trade and industry as alien and look down on the social strata representative of them. Instead of a Northwestern European Protestant ethic, wasteful consumption and a parasitic lifestyle became characteristic of the elite in Central and Eastern Europe. The Enlightenment did not prevail in these noble societies. Moreover, the nobility represented itself as the embodiment of dignity and grandeur, an ideal that would influence both the better-off peasant and urban populations.

The old value system remained predominant. Seventeenth- and eighteenth-century Hungary, Bohemia, and Poland experienced the overwhelming victory of the Catholic Counter-Reformation and a late blossoming of a provincial version of the religious-feudal baroque. These values, first embraced by the higher and lower nobility and even the urban craftsmen, had by the first half of the eighteenth century penetrated peasant society. The Reformation engulfed Bohemia during the sixteenth century: two-thirds of the population joined one of the Protestant faiths. After the Battle of the White Mountain in the late 1620s, however, a ruthless and highly successful Counter-Reformation, led by the Habsburgs and implemented by the Jesuits, forced all of the Protestants who had the right to migrate to leave the country. In that decade, roughly one-fifth of the population departed. The serfs, on the other hand, were forced to convert to Catholicism in special ceremonies. By 1787, only 2 percent of the population was Protestant (Kadlec 1987). Catholicism became the state religion after 1628. The Counter-Reformation was not so successful in Hungary, where the noble resistance of the seventeenth century safeguarded large areas of the country. The Protestant majority (once 70 percent of the inhabitants) shrank, however, and by 1804, 60 percent of the population had returned to the Catholic Church. In Croatia, 60 to 65 percent of the population were Catholic, and the remainder were not Protestant but Greek Orthodox. The conservative Jesuit worldview prevailed.

In the early modern era, however, the revolutionary ideas of the West began to infiltrate the "sleeping" countries of the European periphery, albeit only among the relatively small group of enlightened nobility. The road to an acceptance of the Newtonian worldview began to open only in the last third of the eighteenth century. A total acceptance of Newtonian physics is evident in the works of Pál Makó, Antal Radics, and János K. Horváth in Hungary in the late 1760s and 1770s. The first physics textbook in Hungarian expressed this in its title, *A fisikának eleji: A természetiekről Newton tanitványainak nyomdoka szerént* (Elementary Physics: On Nature, Based on the Pupils of Newton) (1777). During those decades, the reforms of Hungary's Hapsburg queen Maria Theresa (r. 1740–80) introduced a unified secular educational system. State control and the introduction of mathematics and science as a regular part of the curriculum opened the way to a modern educational system in the 1770s, although compulsory universal education had not yet been introduced. A National Educational Committee was similarly established in Poland in 1773 to secularize and modernize the educational system.

In addition to the enlightened monarch's moderate reforms, the ideas of the Enlightenment made their way both to Hungary and to the other countries of the region. As in the West, freemasonry was one of the vehicles. The first Masonic lodges were founded in Prague in 1726, in Warsaw in 1755, and in Hungary by the mid eighteenth century. During the last decade of the century, there were twenty-eight to thirty Masonic lodges distributed throughout Hungary, with 600 to 2,000 members. The ideas of tolerance, fraternity, and equal membership for nobles and non-nobles paved the way to the Enlightenment. However, even freemasonry remained an institution of noble society, representing the more enlight-ened groups of the county's nobility. Leading Freemasons represented the most prominent aristocratic families: in Poland, Stanisław-August, the last king, and the wealthy noble Poniatowski family; in Hungary, the Rádays, Vays, Orczys, and Podmaniczkys. Very few burghers participated, although intellectuals, medical doctors, and other professionals joined. In the mid 1780s, Hungarian freemasonry expressed the anti-Habsburg, anticentralization ideas of the enlightened nobility and urged noble re-sistance against the emperor Joseph II. In 1789, in the "First Innocence Lodge" of Buda, a lecture stressed the role of "sense and freedom against despotism and stupidity." The author even quoted Montesquieu (Balázs 1967). Paradoxically, Enlightenment ideas in Hungary and Poland were closely connected both with moderate reform and with safeguarding no-ble privileges, although the majority of the Polish nobility, or *szlachta*, re-jected all liberal political and social notions.

Although books, theaters—among them the National Theater in War-saw (1765)—and publications such as the *Merkuriusz Polski Ordynaryjny* (1661) and the *Kurier Polski* (1730), the first Polish periodical and daily newspaper, respectively, transmitted modern Western ideas, their impact always remained limited. The elite, partly by traveling to the West, as in the case of the Hungarian count Ferenc Széchenyi in 1787, who went to the Netherlands and Britain to study modern agriculture and the ideas of Adam Smith, and partly as a result of reading Western literature, became acquainted with modern British and French thinkers. The noble En-lightenment developed more firmly and more quickly in Poland than in Hungary. Hugo Kołłątaj's influential political club, the Kuznica, discussed the ideas of the Enlightenment, but envisioned only limited reforms as the foundation of an enlightened, democratic noble state. The works of Locke, Voltaire, Rousseau, and Smith became popular in these circles, but their ideas circulated exclusively among a noble elite, whose focus did not take in the Third Estate. Whereas in the West, 60 to 90 percent of the population was literate by 1800, literacy in Central Europe had spread mostly among the upper nobility, and only partially among the lower no-bility and urban population. In Poland, roughly 70 percent of the higher nobility and 60 percent of the small urban patrician layer were literate as early as the beginning of the eighteenth century, but 90–95 percent of the lower nobility and peasantry remained illiterate. The peasantry in Poland, Hungary, and Bohemia remained outside the educated classes. According to detailed research, in spite of eighteenth-century progress, fewer than 10 percent of the younger generation were enrolled in school in Hungary at the end of the century. Nearly a century later, in 1869, 68 percent of the population were still illiterate. Pride and arrogance among the nobility, and backwardness, superstition, and ignorance among the bulk of the population, were typical of the societies of Central and Eastern Europe.

Ottoman rule in the Balkans isolated society from European influences. "Henceforth people will be looking at the universe with the eyes of oxen," said Kâtib Çelebi, a famous Turkish encyclopedist and historian who in the mid seventeenth century criticized contemporary Ottoman scholarship for ignoring philosophy and science. The Ottoman empire, including its European part, the Balkans, "remained unaffected and unchanged . . . [by] the discoveries, the commercial revolution, the scientific advances, and the rise of the absolutist monarchies . . . [the] developments [that] transformed and strengthened immensely the Western world. . . . The failure of the Ottoman Empire was . . . a failure of adjustment, a failure to respond to the challenge of the new dynamic West," L. S. Stavrianos, one of the best authorities on the area, observes (Stavrianos [1958] 1963, 132–33, 136). Even the Ottoman upper class lacked anyone to transmit the new innovations and ideas of the advanced world to them. Not only were the peasants illiterate, but the local elite were too. "[A]n intellectual iron curtain separated the Ottoman Empire from the West," Stavrianos writes. The subjects of the Sublime Porte "knew nothing of the epoch-making achievements of Paracelsus in medicine, Vesalius in anatomy, and Copernicus, Kepler, and Galileo in astronomy."

Norman Davies elaborates on the often-mentioned impact of Ottoman control combined with anti-Western Greek Orthodoxy: "None of the great civilizing movements . . . Reformation, Science, Enlightenment . . . could effectively penetrate the Balkan countries. Political traditions owed little to rationalism, absolutism, or constitutionalism; kinship politics dominated at all levels, nepotism lubricated by bribery was a way of life" (Davies 1996, 646).

REVOLUTION IN THE WEST AND HIBERNATION IN THE EAST

On July 14, 1789, the Bastille, a symbol of oppression and the establishment, was attacked by a Paris mob and quickly taken. Three days later, the French Third Estate constituted itself into a National Assembly, which on August 27 proclaimed the Rights of Man, paraphrasing the first sentence of Rousseau's Social Contract: "Men are born free and remain free and equal in rights." The French Revolution began to realize the ideas of the Enlightenment.

A revolutionary crescendo between the 1770s and the 1810s signaled the conclusive accomplishment of the gradual transformation and rise of the West. The French Revolution of 1789 itself lasted a quarter of a century, if one takes into account its several phases. During these years, however, France and the entire Western European world—mostly reformed and remodeled by Napoleon—opened a new chapter of human history. Antiquated feudal institutions, serfdom, the guild system, and noble privileges were eliminated. The modern state, political system, and legal order were founded. Serfs and Jews were emancipated. Human rights were guaranteed for all: "no person should be troubled for his opinion," "every citizen can write, speak, and publish freely," and "every man is presumed innocent till found guilty," proclaimed the Declaration of the Rights of Man, which also termed property "a sacred and inviolable right." Church estates were nationalized, and Church and state were separated (1801). The codification of the revolutionary legislation in the French Civil Code, or Code Napoléon (1804), influenced the modernization of countries throughout Western Europe. The revolutionary and Napoleonic wars led to the birth of the modern army and the modern nation. National citizenship was established in keeping with the abbé Sieyès's concept of an "unmediated, undifferentiated, individual membership of the state" (Brubaker 1992, 39). The French Revolution became a "landmark in all countries," Eric Hobsbawm observes, and was thus not only a French event but *"the* revolution of its time" (Hobsbawm 1962, 54–55).

Although the French Revolution became the "mother of all revolutions" of the nineteenth and twentieth centuries and was rich in valiant gestures, violent terror, attractive ideas, theatrical statements, and historic actions, it was only one part of a dual revolution. Parallel to the dramatic events taking place in France, a much less dramatic and less heroic revolution was emerging in Britain—the Industrial Revolution—whose impact, though delayed, has probably been greater in the long run, causing sensational repercussions around the world. "It is not unreasonable to regard this dual revolution—the rather more political French and the industrial (British) revolution—not so much as something which belongs to the history of the two countries which were its chief carriers . . . but as the twin crater of a rather larger regional volcano. That the simultaneous eruptions should occur in France and Britain . . . is [not] accidental . . . [and it could not have happened] at this time in any other part of the world" (Hobsbawm 1962, 2).

As the French Revolution "translated" the ideas of the Enlightenment into actions and a social system, the Industrial Revolution was born from a Newtonian worldview and from applied mechanics. It was, in a way, "in the air." "It was possible to learn more about applied mechanics at a London coffeehouse lecture series than it was in any French college prior to the 1740s" (Dobbs and Jacob 1995, 115). After James Hargreaves, a Lancashire weaver, invented his spinning "jenny" (1767), Richard Arkwright, a hairdresser, created a spinning water frame (1768), and Samuel Crompton combined the two into his spinning "mule" (1779), the textile industry was revolutionized. The first spinning jennies were over twenty times more productive than hand spinning, but Crompton's mule was several hundred times more productive than the jenny. Once Edmund Cartwright had perfected his power loom in 1787, a child working on two machines could produce fifteen times more cloth than a traditional master weaver. The technical innovations of the Industrial Revolution, as Hobsbawm noted, "practically made themselves." One invention precipitated the need for another, and a virtually monopolized world market offered an unlimited market for the products. In 1769, James Watt patented his modern steam engine with a separate condenser. "This was the decisive breakthrough to an 'age of steam' . . . [it] brought the steam engine within reach of all branches of the economy and made of it a universal prime mover" (Landes 1969, 102). Watt's improved rotary steam engine (1784) and continuous improvements decreased the coal consumption of the machine to one-tenth. In a few decades, the capacity of steam engines in Britain reached 4 million horsepower and could do the work of 40 million people.

A mechanized factory industry emerged, increasing production by 20–50 percent a decade until the mid nineteenth century. Britain became the world's first industrialized nation. Annual British cotton consumption had already reached two kilograms per capita by 1790. The Continent matched that level only in 1885. Within half a century, British cotton consumption increased by fifteen times. Per capita iron production in Britain was 15 kilograms in 1790. Continental Europe reached this level only in 1870. More than 40 percent of the gainfully occupied population of Britain worked in industry in 1841. In the mid nineteenth century, Britain produced roughly two-thirds of the world's coal and more than half of its iron and cotton cloth (Landes 1969).

A new stage of the technological-industrial revolution emerged with the opening of the world's first railroad, the Stockton–Darlington line in

September 1825: the Railway Age had begun. J. M. W. Turner, the painter of the ocean and light, painted the Great Western Railroad. Édouard Manet and Claude Monet painted a series of paintings of the Gare Saint-Lazare, fascinated by the steam, strength, and beauty of the locomotive. "The iron road, pushing its huge smoke-plumed snakes at the speed of wind . . . [with its] bridges and stations, formed a body of public building beside which the pyramids and the Roman aqueducts and even the Great Wall of China paled into provincialism. . . . [It] was the very symbol of man's triumph through technology" (Hobsbawm 1962, 44). By 1850, 23,000 miles of railroad were operating in the world, reducing the cost of transportation dramatically, along with the cost of mass consumption goods. The railroad had, however, a much greater importance. It also opened a huge market for coal, iron, steel, and engineering products, greatly boosting industry: between 1830 and 1850, British iron and coal production tripled. The railway became the symbol of modernity, speed, and progress.

Like the French Revolution in the sociopolitical arena, the advances of the British Industrial Revolution also penetrated the western half of the European continent. This process, however, was somewhat delayed. In 1800, in the middle of her takeoff, according to Paul Bairoch's calculations, Great Britain had a per capita gross national product two-thirds higher than that of the continent of Europe as a whole (Bairoch 1976a). In the mid nineteenth century, continental Europe was still about a generation behind Britain in industrial development. However, "the continental countries were part of the same larger civilization as Britain; and they were certainly her equals, in some respects her superior, in science and education for the elite" (Landes 1969, 125). In the first half of the century Belgium, Holland, France, Switzerland, and Denmark more than doubled their per capita GNP and came close to (roughly 80 percent of) the British level. Since the 1850s, all of Western Europe has been industrialized (Bairoch 1976a, 279).

The "regional volcano" with its twin crater erupted and destroyed the ancién regime with its antiquated institutions and traditional economy. A modern Western Europe emerged and became the world's first highly industrialized zone. Soon industry and related services accounted for 50 to 60 percent of the countries' GNP. The structure of the workforce radically changed, together with the settlement pattern: the bulk of the gainfully employed people of Western Europe, for the first time in history, worked in industry and services, leaving the rural countryside for urban settlements. The Industrial Revolution replaced the old civilization with a new one.

TABLE 1. *Per capita GNP in 1800 and in 1860 (in 1960 U.S.$)*

	1800	Britain = 100	1860	1860 as % of 1880	Britain = 100
Great Britain	345	100	558	162	100
Continental Western Europe	211	61	454	215	81
Austria-Hungary	190	55	288	152	51
Eastern Europe	170	49	180	105	32

SOURCE: Paul Bairoch, "Europe's Gross National Product, 1800–1975," *Journal of European Economic History* 5, no. 2 (1976).

As another result of the dual revolution, the industrialized West built up strong nation-states with homogenized populations that spoke the same language, read the same newspapers, served in the same army, learned the same history, and proudly shared a new national identity. The new modern nation-states that adopted the British parliamentary system and the French *état de droit* all accepted democratic constitutions and demanded equal citizenship and human rights. Western Europe emerged as the rich, industrialized, urbanized core of the world with its strong nation-states and democratic parliamentary system.

István Széchenyi and his friend Baron Miklós Wesselényi, two young Hungarian aristocrats, sought the miracle with their own eyes, traveling to the West in 1822. The comparison was disheartening. "What is preposterous in our country?" Széchenyi asks rhetorically in his diary, and answers: "That the representatives of the peasants are noblemen: wolves protect the sheep." In a detailed note from April 12, 1822, Wesselényi describes the crop-rotation system he had seen in France. Another note in his diary, written in England in June, describes the British Industrial Revolution with consternation. "One glass factory, coal mine, and ironworks next to the other. The entire area is covered by fire and smoke like the scenery of the last judgment. . . . Everything, stone and men alike, is black. . . . The steam-engines are used everywhere, and they are exquisite." In July, the impressive, hectic scene at the West and East India Company docks, with hundreds of ships, warehouses, and paved roads to the city, stunned him. "I feel like a small-town tradesman in his Sunday suit, ludicrously stiff and afraid to move," he wrote (Széchenyi and Wesselényi 1985, 166, 192, 198). The depressing feeling of inferiority is evident.

Serfdom and noble privileges, the manorial system and *robot* work in the fields, lack of modern credit and mechanized industry in Central and Eastern Europe, and a seminomadic system of hillside grazing and subsistence farming in the Balkans remained almost unchanged until the mid nineteenth century. In 1841, only five steam engines served Hungarian industry, with a capacity of roughly 50 horsepower. The first mechanized factory in Bulgaria was established in Sliven in 1834. Central and Eastern Europe, including the vast Russian empire, contained hardly more than three thousand kilometers of railroad in 1860, whereas Western Europe was covered with a network of thirty-eight thousand kilometers. In the same year, 75 to 89 percent of the active population of Hungary, Poland, Romania, Bulgaria, and Serbia still worked in agriculture. The gap between the rapidly advancing West and the hibernating Central and Eastern Europe dramatically widened.

According to Angus Maddison's newest calculations, the Central and Eastern European countries together reached 58 percent of Western per capita GDP in 1820, but this had declined to 49 percent by 1870 (Maddison 1995). While the exact figures are uncertain, the faster growth in the West and the slow advance in the East make the relative decline of the latter irrefutable.

However, it was during these decades that Central and Eastern Europe at last saw attempts to respond to the Western challenge. Some of the people in the western zone of the region embarked on modernization. Bohemia's industrial growth was impressive, and Hungary began its agricultural revolution. Even the formerly rigid Ottoman empire introduced major reforms. Reform and modernization became the leitmotivs of the region's history in the nineteenth century.

CHAPTER 2

ROMANTICISM AND NATIONALISM IN CENTRAL AND EASTERN EUROPE

ROMANTICISM AS VEHICLE OF NATION-BUILDING

THE POOR CENTRAL and Eastern European soil was neither fertile nor cultivated enough to nourish the fruits of the Enlightenment and the "dual revolution." The modern science- and philosophy-based worldview was unable to penetrate the noble elite or take root among the illiterate masses. The Newtonian scientific revolution and the revolutionary ideas of the age had only a limited impact in the eighteenth century. The existing institutions, customs, biases, and superstitions were more or less frozen in place until the early to mid nineteenth century.

Romanticism was primarily responsible for introducing the Western values of freedom, liberty, and nation. Romanticism also mobilized enthusiastic emissaries in Central and Eastern Europe. Although the western and eastern parts of Europe followed different paths of social, economic, and political development, they were components of the same European system and shared the same cultural heritage. Nothing could halt the spread of inspiring and rejuvenating ideas. And travelers from both West and East—Napoleon's *Grande Armée,* Western European entrepreneurs, artisans, and experts, Eastern European writers, political thinkers, aristocrats, and adventurers—often crossed the borders and spread information and knowledge on the spectacular transformation of the West.

Romanticism, nevertheless, did break through with the fortissimo of Berlioz's exalted *Symphonie fantastique,* with the seduction of Schubert's songs, the soul-stirring chorus of Verdi's *Nabucco,* the heroic stance of Byron, and the revolutionary effect of Victor Hugo. The new weltanschauung began to take hold not only among the old social elite but also among a small new group of intellectuals, and even among the masses in the early nineteenth century. The elite of the Central and Eastern European countries, or at least a part of it, looked to the West with great admiration (see introduction), and sought to adjust to the transforming world. People heard about a new world without noble privileges and serfdom and about a new national community that included all citizens, not just strictly insulated estates. Reforms from above and revolutionary attempts from below began to undermine the establishment. The apparently unchangeable regimes gradually lost their stability and strength. Beneath the calm surface, dangerous fault lines became active again. Romanticism, like an irresistible undercurrent, cut away at the rock of an old and rigid society.

Western and Eastern European romanticism were not exactly the same. In the West, romanticism was "an intellectual reaction against the eighteenth-century ideals of order, discipline, and reason" (Eugen Weber 1960, 13) and an effort to liberate *sentiment,* emotion, instinct, and even the subconscious. It underwent various stages during its brief but dominant presence between the late eighteenth and early nineteenth centuries, including the early (rococo) and the late (Biedermeier) periods. It remained a cultural-intellectual movement, although it profoundly transformed the value system of the West. While French romanticism was rather sensitive to social problems, German romantics revolted most against reason and the ideas of the French Revolution (Reiss 1995, 3). In Central and Eastern Europe, these various stages overlapped and intermingled. Moreover, a great deal of Enlightenment thinking arrived with romanticism, which turned out to be less a revolt against reason and the Enlightenment than a breakthrough combining messages of reason *and* emotion (Krejci 1958; Sziklay 1962).

Romanticism was a revolutionary movement. Sir Isaiah Berlin equated its importance with the two major revolutions of the age, maintaining that its importance and lasting consequences were "no less far-reaching" than the impact of the British Industrial Revolution and the French Revolution (Berlin 1999, xiii). "If the essence of Romanticism is 'freedom'—its central themes are entwined around the new concept[s] of 'people' and 'brotherhood'—now envisioned not as phantasms, but as realities" (Ewen 1984, 40). The key words for understanding romanticism are, indeed, "freedom" and "people." Others stress the passionate desire for change. As Friedrich von Schlegel, one of the "fathers" of romanticism, wrote in his milestone novel *Lucinde* (1799): "only in longing do we find our rest . . . no higher goal may be attained than longing itself" (quoted in Thorlby 1966, 149). Romanticism, indeed, was an "intoxicated dreaming," an artistic "Protestantism, Liberalism, the rule of laissez-faire" (Lucas 1948, 46). As the most authentic romanticist, Victor Hugo, expressed it in his famous preface to *Hernani:* "Romanticism, so often ill-defined, is only . . . if we look at it from its combative side—liberalism in literature . . . liberty in art, liberty in society, behold the double end towards which consistent and logical minds should tend" (Eugen Weber 1960, 59). Romanticism, thus, was a war against the rules of convention and existing reality.

Romantic "longing" and "dreaming" took on a very specific meaning in Central and Eastern Europe: longing for the achievements of the West, freedom, and liberty; and dreaming of a just society and a new community that included the entire nation—in short, becoming an equal part of Europe. Central and Eastern European romantics followed in the footsteps of the philosophers of the age from Voltaire to Spencer, and regarded liberty, commerce, and progress as inseparable. They believed that the realization of freedom would open the door to progress, and that progress would in turn lead to an ever-ascending realization of freedom (Nisbet 1980, 236).

Central and Eastern European romanticism was strongly influenced by the German trend (Roguski 1996). The German romantic understanding of the "difference between German and Western thought," the perception of a distinct, non-Western German "national individuality," became extremely influential in Central and Eastern Europe. Romanticism arrived as a militant national idea, expanding the notions of freedom and individualism beyond the realm of the person. It was transformed into a matter that required the mobilization of the nation. The romantic cult of genius shifted from the sphere of art to that of politics, with the credo that "man is capable of fashioning the whole of society." German romantic historians preached the view that if the "West was declining because of its skepticism, its rationalism, its materialism . . . the Germans . . . should be viewed as a fresh and youthful nation . . . barbarous indeed, but full of violent energy" (Berlin 1978, 120). German romanticism became the vanguard of romantic nationalist thought (Reiss 1995, 6, 7, 41). Romanticism "found it truest home [in Germany]. But it traveled beyond the confines of Germany to every country where there was some kind of social discontent and dissatisfaction, particularly to countries oppressed . . . especially in Eastern Europe" (Berlin 1999, 131). These concepts spread like wildfire in Central and Eastern Europe, where independent nation-states did not yet exist. Central European nationalists "took . . . [German romantic] reasoning one step further . . . [and claimed that] they had an even more powerful hope" of a "glorious future" (Berlin 1978, 120).

Romantic writers and artists of the region "were not primarily interested in the programme and artistic aspiration of romanticism . . . but far more in the development of their own national characteristics"(Sőtér 1973, 140). Glorified individualism and exalted egotism—important characteristics of the trend in the West—were transformed into, or at least combined with, an exhilarating cult of the nation. Romantic individual *Weltschmerz* and passion were connected here with national cataclysm and national oppression. Romantic longing conjured up a glorious past and a victorious future, stirring desire to rejuvenate the ailing nation.

Romanticism became a paramount nation-building movement in the East: a newly created literary language fueled romantic arts, poetry, and drama, which joined forces with music, architecture, and history writing in the struggle for nationhood. This idea also grew from German soil. The lack of national unity, manifest in the political environment of the fragmented German states, led to the concept of the *Kulturnation,* as the historian Friedrich Meinecke later phrased it. In the admired and envied West, the "melting pot" of the nation was the state, which created an integrated national market and homogenized various ethnic, linguistic, and religious groups into Frenchmen and Britons. The various institutions of the state, especially a modern army and a unified educational system, promoted a common self-identification and camaraderie among these disparate groups. It also established a "historicized national memory." This development was crowned by the revolutionary transformation that replaced the traditional "political nations" of the nobility with modern nations based on the so-called Third Estate. This brought the entire people, including the peasantry, into the body of nation. The "smooth functioning of the state . . . in its slow, long-term evolution . . . [the] unifying force of a common political history," Meinecke concluded, created the nation and nation-state in the West (Meinecke 1908). During this "long-term evolution," all the previously dominant feudal and religious myths were eliminated and a new myth of a united national community and a common national consciousness emerged. Although, as Benedict Anderson maintains, the nation was an "imagined community"(Anderson 1983), an abstraction, a virtual reality, it became an absolute reality because people believed in its existence. The nation became a sacrosanct notion, to die and kill for.

In Central and Eastern Europe, this "smooth functioning of the state," the major historical "driving force" in the West, was absent. The process of nation-building therefore had to go the other way around, from nation to state. In the fragmented German states and among subordinated peoples of the multinational empires of Central and Eastern Europe, the first task was to create a homogeneous national culture, and then a nation-state. In this region, nations had to be built first from "cultural property . . . commonly acquired and experienced. . . . Nations that for centuries had had only a cultural existence" could be reborn as nations and then could establish themselves as nation-states. What was needed was a strong sense of self-determination, or *Selbsbestimmung:* "a nation is a community that *wishes* to be a nation" (Meinecke 1908, 7, 9).

Most students of the history of nation-building, including Hans Kohn, a pioneer of modern studies of nationalism, agree with Meinecke that the most important prerequisite for the emergence of a nation is the *will* to be a nation. "Although some . . . objective factors . . . [such as a common territory, statehood, and even the memory of past statehood] are of great importance for the formation of nationalities, the most essential element is a living and active corporate will" (Kohn 1944, 15). Culture, language, and history thus constitute a highly politicized sphere necessary for the creation of this corporate will.

The romantic concept of nation-building was closely connected with the romantic belief in progress. Peoples developed the self-confidence that they were able to shape history and realize desired changes. What the admired West achieved was realized within the newly created nation-state. The advanced West had broken the chains of serfdom and accomplished spectacular socioeconomic and political progress. Nation-state and progress seemed inseparable. Progress and advancement appeared to be an automatic consequence of the creation of a nation-state. Romanticism thus paved the way for revolt against ossified establishments and for modernization of life.

The real significance of romanticism in the region extended far beyond art itself. Romanticism was "not only an artistic movement but perhaps the first movement . . . when arts dominated other aspects of life, when there was a kind of tyranny of art over life" (Berlin 1999, xi). Romanticism emerged as a comprehensive worldview, which influenced an entire generation of the educated elite of these nations. It is interesting to recognize that many influential reformers who actively contributed to the modernization of their countries were first inspired by romantic art. Baron József Eötvös, one of the central personalities in the modernization of Hungary, was introduced to literature by reading Schiller, Byron, and

Scott. "Schiller was my only ideal," noted Eötvös in his notebook at the age of twenty. In 1836–37, he traveled to the West and spent nine months there, mostly in Paris and London. He met, among others, Victor Hugo and was impressed for a lifetime: "His goal is not to please us, but to be of use," he noted in one of his essays on Hugo (Eötvös 1902a, 226). Romanticism mobilized the emotions and minds of the best part of Central and Eastern European elite. It permeated the public spirit and all spheres of life, including public opinion, individual attitudes toward life and society, politics, philosophy, and the arts.

Romanticism also offered mystical explanations and unassailable solutions to burning questions about history, which impinged on the final rationalization of life and society. It elevated historiography to new heights. Benedetto Croce called the nineteenth century *il secolo della storia,* the century of history (Peckham 1970; 1995, 33). Historicism and the rediscovery of the past, so characteristic of romanticism, gained central importance in Central and Eastern Europe and laid the foundation for building the future of the nation itself.

The memory of the past became the essence of the nation in the entire region. Romanticism became the essence of "Polishness" after the final defeat of the Polish uprisings (Jedlicki 1999, 210). The past, and even more often an imagined glorious past, offered a refuge for all of the rising nations of the area and was equally essential for "Hungarianness," "Czechness," and "Romanianness."

Messianic romanticism, accordingly, became a complex leading trend in political and intellectual life. What was a short-lived art trend in the West became a century-long movement in the East. In fact, romanticism persisted into the closing decades of the nineteenth century (Sőtér 1973, 193). Historiography, literature, theater, music, musical theater, opera, fine arts, and architecture all entered the age of romanticism and exemplified its main characteristics. Heroic advocacy of freedom and social justice, rebellion against an obsolete and unjust society, revolt against all kinds of oppression—this became the mission of literature and art, expressed with passionate subjectivism.

All of these elements put the visionary poet in the foreground. He became the messenger of truth and embodied his ideas in his personal life. Schiller, Byron, Petőfi, and Botev were romantic heroes who died young, mostly fighting for freedom and against oppression. Romantic attitudes and gestures gained momentum in Central and Eastern Europe: poets and artists, self-appointed romantic revolutionaries, became national heroes and the leading critics of the oppressive outmoded world. "Poetry,"

FIGURE 1. Art in the service of nation-building in Romania: Constantin Lecca, *The Murder of Mihai the Brave*. Courtesy Muzeul National de Artă al României, Bucharest.

FIGURE 2. . . . and in Poland: Wojciech Gerson, *The Death of Przemysł* (1881). Courtesy Muzeum Narodowe w Warszawie, Warsaw.

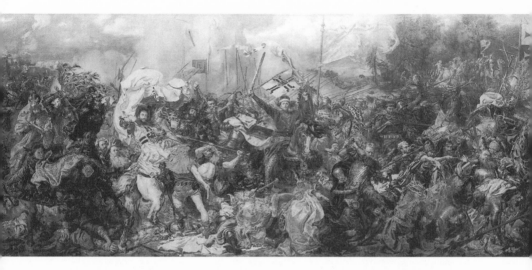

FIGURE 3. . . . and in Poland: Jan Matejko, *The Battle of Grünewald*. Courtesy Muzeum Narodowe w Warszawie, Warsaw.

FIGURE 4. . . . and in Hungary: Mihály Munkácsy, *The Arrival of the Hungarians in the Danube Valley*. Courtesy Magyar Nemzeti Galéria, Budapest.

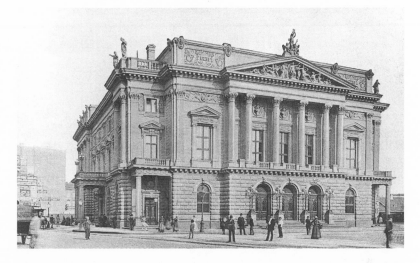

FIGURE 5. The National Theater in Budapest. Courtesy Hungarian National Museum, Budapest.

FIGURE 6. The National Theater in Bucharest. Reproduced from Florea, *Romanian Art,* 24. Courtesy Meridiane Publishing House, Bucharest.

FIGURE 7. Brno Opera House, 1882. Courtesy SPN Pedagogicke Nakladelstvi, Prague.

FIGURE 8. A Polish romantic visionary. Walenty Wankowicz, *Adam Mickiewicz* (1828). Courtesy Muzeum Narodowe w Warszawie, Warsaw.

FIGURE 9. A Polish romantic historian and revolutionary. Seweryn Oleszczynski, *Joachim Lelevel* (1830). Courtesy Muzeum Narodowe w Warszawie, Warsaw.

FIGURE 10. Viktor Madarász, *The Death of Sándor Petőfi* (1875). Courtesy Petőfi Literary Museum, Budapest.

FIGURE 11. Miklós Barabás, *Franz Liszt* (1842). Courtesy Magyar Nemzeti Galéria, Budapest.

FIGURE 12. A Romanian romantic poet. Niccolo Livaditti, *Vasile Alecsandri and His Family*. Courtesy Muzeul National de Artă al României, Bucharest.

FIGURE 13. Jósef Peszka, *Hugo Kołłątaj* (1791). Courtesy Muzeum
Narodowe w Warszawie, Warsaw.

FIGURE 14. Friedrich von Amerling, *István Széchenyi*. Courtesy Magyar Tudományos Akadémia, Budapest.

FIGURE 15. The first Polish uprising. Franciszek Smuglewicz, *Kościuszko Takes the Oath*. Courtesy Muzeum Narodowe w Warszawie, Warsaw.

FIGURE 16. J. N. Lewicki, *The Second Polish Uprising in 1831.* Courtesy Muzeum Narodowe w Krakowie, Kraków.

FIGURE 17. Jaroslav Dąbrowski, leader of the third Polish uprising in 1863. Courtesy Muzeum Historyczne m. st. Warsawy, Warsaw.

FIGURE 18. The 1848 Hungarian revolution. Mihály Than, *The Battle of Tápióbicske.* Courtesy Hungarian National Museum, Budapest.

FIGURE 19. Ignác Tyroler, *Lajos Kossuth.* Courtesy Hungarian National Museum, Budapest.

FIGURE 20. A Romanian peasant revolutionary. Barbu Iscovescu,
Avram Jancu. Courtesy Muzeul National de Artă al României,
Bucharest.

FIGURE 21. A Romanian revolutionary in 1848. Gheorge Tattarescu,
Nicolae Bălcescu. Courtesy Muzeul National de Artă al României,
Bucharest.

FIGURE 22. Costache Petrescu, *Demonstration for the 1848 Constitution in Romania*. Reproduced from Florea, *Romanian Art*, 59. Courtesy Meridiane Publishing House, Bucharest.

FIGURE 23. George Karajordje, the leader of the Serbian
uprising in 1804. Courtesy Hadtörténeti Múzeum, Budapest.

said Shelley, "is indeed . . . the centre and circumference of knowledge; it is that which comprehends all science, and that to which all science must be referred." "Poetry is the genuine absolute Reality," declared Novalis (Friedrich von Hardenberg), one of the leading German initiators of the trend. The artist thus "stands above the human being," because, Novalis said in his *Blütenstaub,* "we are engaged in a mission: we are called to give shape to the earth . . . [and] poetry shapes the beautiful social order—the world family—the beautiful establishment of the universe" (Furst 1980, 57–59, 63, 69).

Shelley called the poet a "lawgiver for humanity." Few people in England and in the West, Czesław Miłosz notes, took that claim seriously. However, when the German romantic F. W. J. Schelling (following Herder) explained the romantic notion "that poets or painters may understand the spirit of their age more profoundly and express it in a more vivid and lasting manner than academic historians" (Berlin 1978, 140), his view was taken at face value in Russia, Poland, and throughout the region. Was it a kind of psychological idiosyncrasy of the nations of the area? Probably yes, and it grew out of their special historical circumstances.

Poets and writers had become the most important messengers of Western ideas in the East. Writers and artists, indeed, filled a social and intellectual vacuum in these countries, where a modern citizenry and middle class had been unable to emerge from the rigid framework of noble society. Nor was there a strong native elite in the "incomplete societies" of the Balkans under Ottoman rule. The small intelligentsia therefore played a central political role in the region. Moreover, Isaiah Berlin observes:

The concept of intelligentsia must not be confused with the notion of intellectuals. Its members thought of themselves as united by something more than mere interests in ideas; they conceived themselves as being a dedicated order, almost a secular priesthood. . . . The notion of the artist as a sacred vessel . . . was exceedingly widespread. . . . He is a wholly dedicated being . . . his fate is peculiarly sublime and tragic . . . [to] sacrifice himself totally to his idea. (Berlin 1978, 117, 128–29)

A dedicated order of self-sacrificing writers and artists became the fonts of change. Borrowing from Herzen, Berlin recalls that Russian literature is "one vast bill of indictment against Russian life." Romantic literature and art, thus, acquired unique importance in the entire area: "A modified . . . romanticism," Virgil Nemoianu asserts, "is more evident and more significant in Eastern and Central European literature than anywhere else" (Nemoianu 1984, 120).

It was not easy to follow the Western transformation and get access to its ideas, but the French Revolution and the Napoleonic wars broke through the barriers in a fundamental way. "Only the French Revolution and the revolutionary wars, the rise and fall of Napoleon, made history a Europe-wide mass experience," György Lukács writes. "The people of Europe experienced more changes between the decades of 1789 and 1815 than they had for centuries. . . . People realized . . . that history influences everyday life and they are part of it" (Lukács 1977, 22, 25). However, the ideas of the Enlightenment and the French Revolution were censored in most places. The intellectual isolation of the Central and Eastern European countryside was pervasive, but capital cities soon emerged as intellectual centers with access to Paris and "French ideas." People met with travelers, and got access to foreign books and papers. Vienna became an important center of information for the peoples of the Habsburg empire. The Slovene Bartolomeus Kopitar, the Czech Josef Dobrovský, the Hungarian "guardsmen writers," such as György Bessenyei and István Batsányi, and the Serb Vuk Karadžić all learned the new Western zeitgeist in Vienna. Most of the Polish and some of the Romanian thinkers and writers made a pilgrimage to Paris. Others went to St. Petersburg. The great Polish romantic trio of Adam Mickiewicz, Juliusz Słowacki, and Zygmunt Krasiński spent long years in the French capital. Pest-Buda (later Budapest) also played an important role for Slovak, Croat, and Serb writers. It was the first center of Serb and Bulgarian book publication, and home to the first Serb newspapers. The Slovak Ján Kollar and the Croat Ljudevit Gaj studied and worked there. They became the pioneers of the romantic cultural movement of language reforms and the discovery of the past.

LINGUISTIC NATIONALISM: FOLKLORE
AND LANGUAGE REFORMS

The German Johann Gottfried Herder, who was strongly influenced by Rousseau, was the first and most influential advocate of the importance of genuine folk poetry, folk song, and vernacular language. Herder strongly influenced his contemporaries in Central and Eastern Europe. In his twenty-volume *Ideen zur Philosophie der Geschichte der Menschheit*, he developed the idea that the history of the world or mankind is the history of independent peoples, *Völker,* who have their unique individuality and communal pattern of feeling based on inherited traditions, rituals, folk songs, and poetry, knit together by language. Individuals can think freely only in one language, their native tongue, which determines their personality. Language and tradition carry the national soul, that is, the "original national character." Mankind is made up of a series of "wonderfully separated nations, not only by woods and mountains . . . rivers and climates, but more particularly by languages, inclinations, and characters." Cultural identity is based on a vernacular language. The advancement of the nation is tied to the promotion of the vernacular language: "The cultivation of the mother-tongue alone can lift a nation out of the state of barbarism: and this very reason [the lack of cultivation of the mother tongue] kept Europe so long barbarous; a foreign language fetters . . . robbing them even of the . . . native code of laws . . . and a national history" (Herder [1784–91] 1968, 78, 328).

Herder was an advocate for and a pioneer of the collection of folk poetry and folk songs; he published his *Volkslieder* in 1778 and his *Stimmen der Völker* in 1807. Turning against the artificial imitation of classicism, he launched the romantic renewal of language and the drive toward the creation of national poetry. Herder's lifelong devotion to folk poetry combined the national concept with the democratic idea. By making a fetish out of folk poetry and the folk, Herder culturally incorporated the peasantry into the nation. His work led to the concept of "cultural-linguistic nationalism," a vital element of Central and Eastern European nation-building. Herder influenced the entire region. Slavic peoples echoed his ideas because Herder had a high view of them. His works also inspired Hungarians, despite his dark prophecy about the disappearance of the endangered island of the Hungarian language beneath a Slavic and Germanic ocean.

The national movement of Central and Eastern Europe began with romantic folklorizing by a handful of intellectuals. "In the midst of the illiterate masses, there appeared one or two hundred striking figures, who, with their own hands, began to construct new edifices on the old foundation" (Kadić 1983, 88). Miroslaw Hroch characterizes the beginnings of the rising national movement as nonpolitical. It was cultivated by a small number of enthusiasts who followed in Herder's footsteps by collecting folk poetry and songs (Hroch 1985). Polish, Czech, Slovak, Serb, Slovene, Bulgarian, and Hungarian collections were published. The Polish Zorian Dołęga Chodakowski (born Adam Czarnocki) began collecting folk tales and poetry in the 1810s: "Happiness . . . to wander among the folk," he noted in 1816, "to live the poetical life of the villagers! When they tell me their tales. . . . Virtue has its abode among the people, and poetry too." Chodakowski developed a scholarly program: "Let us undertake a search for information among our own people . . . in the haunts of our forefathers. . . . One must go to various remote localities and stoop beneath the peasant's thatched roof. One must be present at his feasts, at his play, and at the various events of his life." The wandering scholar became a myth and model for the romantic generation in Poland (Brock 1992, 4, 5, 8, 11–12).

Vuk Karadžić, Chodakowski's contemporary, published his influential collection of Serbian and other Slavic folk poems, *Mala prostonarodna slavenosrpska pjesmarica,* which was admired even by Goethe (Halpern and Halpern 1972). János Arany discovered ancient Hungarian, while Pál Gyulai unearthed old Transylvanian folk ballads. Ivan Bogorov published a collection of Bulgarian folk poetry and songs, *Blgarski narodni pesni i poslovici.* The Albanian literary renaissance also began with the publication of folk poems and songs by Zef Jubani (1871). Folk poetry was collected, and sometimes even falsified and presented as a sensational discovery. The Czech romantic poet Josef Linda reported the finding of a thirteenth-century Czech ballad, "Píseň Vyšehradská," in 1816 . The following year, Václav Hanka, the librarian of the National Museum, "discovered" medieval Czech poems in the cellars of the Dvůr Králové cathedral. The "discovery" of the "Judgment of Libuša" brought to light early written legislation. The falsification of medieval manuscripts sought to "demonstrate that the Czechs were both different from and superior to their German-speaking neighbors," Hillel Kieval observes (Kieval 2000, 122–23). The Hungarian Kálmán Thaly falsified "early eighteenth century *kuruc* poems." Young lyric poets, such as the Czechs František Čelakovský and Karel Mácha, the Hungarian Sándor Petőfi, and the Bulgarian Hristo Botev, copied the rhythm and atmosphere of folk songs, and based their poetry entirely on folk motifs (Sőtér 1973, 141–43).

The birth of national literature required the creation of a standard literary language. Language renewal and reform took on a tremendous momentum. Multifunctional standardized languages already had a long history of spontaneous and gradual development. In the West, from the Renaissance and Reformation to the nineteenth century, hundreds of spoken dialects were replaced by standard national languages. Both the reformed Church and the modern, centralized state, with its educational and legal institutions and emerging media, needed a standardized language. These all led to the rise of modern literary languages with standardized grammar, spelling, and orthographic rules. That did not happen in Central and Eastern Europe. A successful Counter-Reformation eliminated Protestantism there, and Greek Orthodoxy was not even challenged. The nations within the multiethnic empires of Central and Eastern Europe had separate official and popular languages. Noble and peasant speech was also quite often different. Moreover, various ethnic groups used several distinct native languages. In most cases, cities were German-speaking and legislation written in Latin. Nonvernacular languages served education, culture, scholarship, public life, and legislation.

The written language of much of the Balkans was Old Church Slavonic, a petrified historic language, impenetrable to the people and far removed from all spoken Slavic dialects. The gap was even greater in Romania, where the Church used Church Slavonic while the peasants spoke various dialects of Wallachian. In Hungary, peasants spoke the Hungarian language, while the noble elite used Latin (even in the parliament) and German in everyday communication. The vernacular, spoken in a number of dialects, was not developed enough to be anything but an informal peasant language. The official language of the Czech lands was German. Many language reformers and advocates of national language and history, such as the Slovene Bartolomeus Kopitar, the Czech František Palacký, and the Slovak Antony Bernolák, published their first works in German.

A language-reform movement emerged with the mission to create a modern literary language in the service of nation-building. "One may see a nation in its language, as in a mirror," the Bulgarian romantic nationalist Ljuben Karavelov wrote. "Every nation should take pride in its language . . . [and] purify it of foreign garbage—namely, Turkish, Greek, Russian and Church Slavonic words." To boost Bulgarian pride, Georgi Rakovski created the myth in his *Pokazalec* (1859) that the Bulgarian language was older than Sanskrit, and thus superior to Greek (*Monumenta Bulgarica* 1996, 445–47, 476–77).

A standardized language was necessary to meet the demands of modern life. Writers and political thinkers, who had turned toward the ideas of the Enlightenment and romantic nationalism, elevated the importance of their unique national languages and sought to create the linguistic vehicle, the modern national language, that could spread their ideas. Enlightened romanticism thus became the initiator of a vigorous movement of language reform. "I am happy to see that Hungarians begin understanding the importance of cultivation of their language. This is the only way for the most miserable peoples to emerge and hope in the coming more fortunate times," the Hungarian poet Dániel Berzsenyi (1776–1836) wrote to his friend Mihály Helmeczi on January 25, 1814 (Berzsenyi 1938, 36). This intention, and not a spontaneous gradual development, created the Polish, Czech, Slovak, Serbo-Croat, Hungarian, Bulgarian, and Romanian languages as we know them today. A strong, "linguistically mostly false assumption . . . [emerged that] nations are constituted by the multifunctional standardized literary languages they use and the culture they represent. . . . People belonging to a specific language and culture constitute a nation. . . . Foreign elements . . . of language and culture threaten the genuine character of a nation" (Radics 1997, 18).

Language reformers thus sought to purify the vernacular, purging foreign words and expressions and replacing them with ones they considered genuine. Dialectal and archaic elements were renewed, German and other foreign words were "nationalized" by part-by-part translations, and loan words from "brotherly" languages and "nationalized" Latin, French, and other words were introduced. Turning to the peasant dialect—a Herderian approach—became the basis of most of the language-reform movements in the region. Several language reforms changed the alphabet from the previously used Cyrillic (in Romania) and Gothic (in Bohemia and the Baltic area) to the Latin, or at least modernized and simplified the old Cyrillic script (in Serbia).

The noble resistance to Josephinist reforms and forced Germanization gave special impetus to the cultivation of the Hungarian language. The 1790–91 parliament enacted a law on compulsory Hungarian language education in all high schools and in higher education. To create a literary language, however, along with standardized grammar and spelling, required the introduction of new words to refer to elements absent from simple everyday life. The scholarly works of János Sajnovics and Sámuel Gyarmathi cleared the way to understanding the history of the language. Various grammars and dictionaries were published between the 1770s and 1810s. Dozens of writers and scholars participated in this movement between 1772 and 1849. Ferenc Kazinczy, Ferenc Kölcsey, Mihály Vörösmarty, Ferenc Verseghy, and Miklós Révai played central roles in this effort. Tens of thousands of new words were created, partly by renewing old, unused words and partly by elevating words from local dialects into the standardized language. Various foreign words were also magyarized and translated, most via German, which represented the Western world. A small dictionary could be compiled of the borrowed Latin words as well. Derivation, word composition, and word splitting also created new words. Although some vocabulary proved to be alien and artificial and never took hold, most of these new words were gradually accepted. The publication of *Zalán futása* (1825) by Mihály Vörösmarty—poet laureate of the romantic age—became a milestone in the breakthrough of language reform. Sándor Petőfi, the most popular poet of the 1840s, used between one and two thousand new words in his poems. After 1825, various professional fields expanded their vocabularies, and legal, philosophical, scientific, mathematical, military, and economic dictionaries were published (Bárczi 1975).

A modernized, standardized Hungarian language was created and the results were sanctioned by the Magyar Tudós Társaság (Hungarian Scholarly Society), later renamed the Magyar Tudományos Akadémia (Hungarian Academy of Sciences) (1825). The Academy produced standard publications on spelling and orthographic rules (*A magyar helyesírás,* 1832), and grammar (*A magyar nyelv rendszere,* 1845). A standardized everyday spoken language gradually supplanted local dialects. By the mid nineteenth century, a modern Hungarian literary language had been elaborated and was broadly used.

The Romanian way to standardized language was somewhat different. Western ideas arrived on Romanian soil via Greece and Transylvania. Locke, Voltaire, and Rousseau were translated into Greek almost immediately, due to Greece's geographic situation, its shipping and trading traditions, and Greek trading colonies abroad. Phanariot officials—Greeks in the service of the Sublime Porte—and Greek merchants and teachers all played important roles in the Romanian principalities under Ottoman rule. "Bucharest society," according to L. S. Stavrianos, "was essentially Greco-Romanian in character, and it was directly and fully influenced by intellectual currents in the Greek world" (Stavrianos [1958] 1963, 147). The other determining influence came from the Transylvanian Romanian community. The Şcoala Ardeleana, or Transylvanian School, as it was called later, initiated a discourse, a romantic theorizing on national identity and culture. It was made up of a group of philologists, writers, and historians, some of them theological students in Uniate seminaries in Rome and Vienna.

The hypothesis that they were the descendants of the Roman colonizers of ancient Dacia supplied Romanians with a vision of past greatness and generated a radical language reform. George Sincay, Petru Maior, and Samuil Klein-Micu became the apostles of this movement. *Elementae linguae Daco-Romanae sive Valachicae* (Elements of the Daco-Roman or Wallach Language), the first modern Romanian grammar, was published in 1780, followed by the first *History of the Origins of the Romanians in Dacia* (1812). The Latin alphabet replaced the Cyrillic, and Slavic words were purged from the vocabulary, while tens of thousands of newly created words based on Latin, Italian, and French were added. The *Lexicon Bu-*

dense (1825), started by Klein-Micu and completed by Maior, was the first Romanian etymological dictionary with a consistent Latinist concept. Jenachita Văcărescu and Eliade Rădulescu, in 1787 and 1828, respectively, turned against latinization and used the Italian language to modernize Romanian orthography, grammar, and vocabulary. Rădulescu maintained that Romanian and Italian were merely different dialects of the same language. Italian and Spanish had developed as literary languages, he argued, but Romanian could not reach that level of sophistication because of barbarian (Slavic) influences. Thousands of Italian and French words were adopted to replace Slavic ones. Consequently, only the Romanian language reform did not turn to a peasant language among the various efforts to codify literary languages in Central and Eastern Europe. Only in Romania did language reformers not base the standardized language on one of the original dialects. Instead, a new, initially artificial, literary language was created (Serban 1983–94). Romanian, which had been a mixed Slavic-Romance language written with a Cyrillic Old Church Slavonic alphabet, became a purified Romance language written with the Latin alphabet and replaced Greek as the language of education and higher culture.

Literature using and propagating the renewed literary Romanian language flourished between the 1830s and 1870s. Grigore Alexandrescu, Dimitrie Bolintineanu, Vasile Alecsandri, the greatest poet of the period, and, later in that century, Mihai Eminescu took leading roles in this effort (Dogaru 1982; Schifernet 1996). The modern Romanian language thus became established. The language-reform and cultural movement, influenced by an emerging historical myth and national ideology, sought to prove that Romanian culture was an outpost of Latin or Romance language and culture.

Outside influences also generated a Serbian, or rather a Serbo-Croatian, language-reform movement. The first Serbian reformers came mostly from Serbian communities outside Serbia, especially from Hungary. Greek influence was important here as well. Dositej Obradović, born in Hungary (at Temesvár), became the founder of modern Serbian literature. He had been a student of the Greek school in Smyrna in 1765 and then studied in Vienna and Halle in the 1770s. Obradović advocated "rational piety" and "enlightened virtue." The ideas of the Enlightenment, as in so many other cases, were mixed with passionate nationalism and a strong conviction that he had to create a Serbian literary language and literature that did not exist at that time. "Let us cast a brief glance at the enlightened nations of all Europe. At the present time every one of those nations is striving to perfect its own dialect. . . . [W]hen learned men write their thought in the general language of the whole nation, then the enlightenment of the intellect and the light of learning are not confined to persons who understand the old literary language, but are spread abroad and reach even the villagers, being taught to the humblest peasant" (quoted in Stavrianos [1958] 1963, 242).

The Serbo-Croatian language-reform movement gained a decisive impetus from the work of the romantic-nationalist Vuk Karadžić, who spent years in Vienna and was inspired to collect Serbian folk poetry by Bartolomeus Kopitar, a Slovene scholar who created the first Slovene grammar and codified a Slovene literary language. Karadžić published a volume of collected folk poems in 1814 and then an enlarged, four-volume work in 1824. As an accomplished linguist, Karadžić introduced phonetic reform to the Cyrillic alphabet, enriched and elevated the vernacular to the level of a literary language, and selected a Herzegovinian dialect nearest to both Serbian and Croatian as a common basis for a standardized Serbo-Croat language. His first Serbian dictionary and grammar were crucial to Serbo-Croat's success.

Karadžić's work, although initially criticized by the Orthodox Church, succeeded, partly because of its association with the rising romantic-national, so-called Illyric movement of the 1830s and 1840s. Its program was based on the idea of South Slavic unity traced back to the ancient Illyrioi of the Balkan Roman province of Illyricum. The Illyric concept gained a tremendous stimulus when Napoleon restored its old Roman name to the occupied Balkan province in 1809. This idea won great support in Croatia from Ljudevit Gaj, an enthusiastic journalist and writer who broadly popularized the South Slavic idea and the common "Illyrian literary language" in his periodicals *Novine Hrvatska* and *Ilirske Narodne Novine*. In late-eighteenth-century Croatia, there were three main dialects, the so-called *štokavian, cakavian,* and *kaykavian* dialects, based upon the three distinctive pronunciations of the word *what*. Gaj advocated the southern Dalmatian *štokavština* idiom, although it was not the dialect spoken in Croatia. Gaj believed it would help to create a common Serbo-Croat language. Toma Mikloušić's *Encyclopedia* (1821) and various grammars and orthographic works of the 1820s and 1830s assisted in the creation of a unified Croat language. By the mid nineteenth century, with the publication of Petar Petrović-Njegoš's novel *Gorski vijenac* and of Branko Radičević's collection of poems *Pjesme*, modern Serbo-Croat became accepted as a written language, replacing the Old Church Slavo-Serb.

The Czech and Slovak language-reform movements were also influenced by romantic historical concepts. Josef Dobrowský, a Czech Jesuit priest, became a pioneer in language reform when he published his Old Slavic grammar, a dictionary, and a history of the Bohemian language and literature. Josef Jungmann, an enthusiastic pan-Slavic nationalist, maintained that "language and nation live in symbiosis; when the first is destroyed, the second dies." He advocated Slavic language unification through the creation of a common literary language. The movement was sustained by his five-volume Czech-German dictionary (1834–39), which introduced Polish, Russian, Serb, and Croat expressions "in order to prepare the ground for the expected emergence of a pan-Slavic language" (Kieval 2000, 120). He also translated Milton's *Paradise Lost,* Goethe, and Chateaubriand into Czech. His struggle for Czech language education in the schools and the foundation of an association for the scholarly cultivation of the Czech language (1830) strongly contributed to the success of the language movement. As a model, Jungmann turned back to the Králická Bible, a sixteenth-century translation. Jungmann also borrowed words and expressions from other Slavic languages, however, mostly from Russian and Polish. A third leading figure, Pavel Josef Šafařík, argued for the existence of a common Slavic mother language, subdivided among the various Slavic tribes. As an "enlightened pan-Slav" of Slovak origin and professor of Slavic philology in Prague, Šafařík built a bridge between the Czech and Slovak language movements.

Language standardization began in Slovakia, part of Hungary at that time, with the pioneering work of Father Antony Bernolák, who published the first Slovak dictionary, *Slowar slowenski česko-latinsko-nemecko-uherski,* in six volumes in 1787, and a grammar in 1790. The dictionary was later enlarged by another priest, Juraj Palkovič. A Slavic mission in Europe was proclaimed by pan-Slavs in Slovakia, such as the poet and collector of Slavic folk songs Ján Kollár, who became one of the initiators of language reforms that would bring the Slovak and Czech languages nearer to one another. His idea was to create a common, uniform Slavic language. Juraj Palkovič, a professor of Czecho-Slovak languages and literature in Pozsony (Bratislava), published a rhyming geography, *Vlastivěda,* used the Czech Bible as a source and basis for the modern Czech or Czechoslovak language, and collected Slovak folklore. He also advocated a unified Czecho-Slovak language. The west Slovak dialect, Palkovič argued, would be the best foundation for it.

On the other hand, Ludevít Štúr, a central figure of the Slovak language movement and also a collector of folk songs and fairy tales, advocated an independent Slovak language based on a mid-Slovak dialect, one more distant from the Czech (Matuška 1948). Štúr started to use an independent Slovak vernacular in the Pozsony *lycée* in 1843 and argued that the Slovaks constituted a nation entirely separate from the Czechs, *narod slovansky*, a separate tribe (nation) within Slavdom. Kollár wrote of four Slavic tribes. Štúr claimed that there were eleven, including the Slovaks. "We have our own language, which is quite separate from the Czech," he said. The Tatrin society, founded in 1844, initiated Slovak cultural activities "on the basis of the new literary language." Opposing both Czechoslovakism and the concept that the Slovaks were part, albeit an equal part, of a greater Hungarian political nation, Štúr and his followers argued for an independent Slovak nation. Slovaks, they maintained, had settled their homeland before the Hungarians reached the Danube valley, and thus had both the right to use the Slovak language and to political autonomy. This claim was put forward publicly in 1848 (Brock 1984, 43, 48–50, 53).

From the 1770s to the 1840s, with few exceptions, all the Central and Eastern European languages were modernized and standardized literary languages were created. In several cases, these movements were closely connected to historical concepts, often myths, and ambitious national goals. Their practical importance, however, was overwhelming. They provided a vehicle for the creation of national literatures and scholarship, education, journalism, and legislation. The same vehicle transmitted modern Western ideas and scholarship, conveyed burning national problems and dreams, and united the nation's elite with the masses. Above all, it prepared the soil for a national cultural revival. From the 1820s and 1830s on, the major language obstacles had been eliminated and the road was open for a literary and poetic revolution. Its essence in Central and Eastern Europe was the creation of a national literature. All the trends in art, whether directly or indirectly, were at the service of the national agenda. They attacked ossified medieval institutions and attitudes and played an important role in the diffusion of national ideas and self-confidence.

LITERATURE, MUSIC, ART, AND HISTORIOGRAPHY
IN THE SERVICE OF THE NATIONAL IDEA

The main road to nation-building was paved by a cultural renewal in the oppressive framework of multinational empires. In contrast to the role of the state in the West, the popular German concept of the *Kulturnation,* which stressed the importance of culture in nation-building, elevated the national-cultural movements to a higher stage. The early apolitical, romantic folklorizing on the part of a rather small group of intellectuals was followed—mostly up through the middle of the nineteenth century—by a second phase of the national movement, an aggressive cultural-national propaganda aimed at influencing the great masses of the population and building a new national consciousness. Poets, composers, painters, and architects followed their romantic feelings and expressed their personal beliefs, often deliberately hoping to mobilize the people. This second phase of the national movement exhibited a strong drive for national and modernizing propaganda (Hroch 1985). Some of the romantic writers, artists, and freedom fighters clearly expressed this deliberate goal: "Science, as well as literature, poetry and journalism . . . should have the character of political propaganda," the Bulgarian poet-prophet Hristo Botev proclaimed (Botev 1976, 83). Poetry, in this interpretation, was a part of political struggle. As the Hungarian Sándor Petőfi wrote in a letter to his friend and fellow poet János Arany in 1847: "Let's make . . . [the poetry of the people] predominant in the realm of literature. When the people are prominent in poetry, they are very near to power in politics" (Czigány 1984, 191). Writing in the July and August 1847 issues of the Hungarian periodical *Életképek,* József Irinyi passionately confessed: "I love our century because it attacks class walls with elemental strength and is leading the entire human race toward equality. Because of the introduction of machines, matter is ruled by the human spirit; guided by rational politics, philosophy penetrates the mud huts [of the peasantry]" (*Az Életképek* 1970, 121).

This purposeful sense of mission, combined with a strong belief in reason and the unlimited potential of human action, generated a turning point. Central and Eastern Europe gave birth to new national literatures, music, and art, whose cultural-political impact was almost independent of their international standing. A great many national cultural heroes who had a tremendous impact on the development of their countries did not represent the highest standards of contemporary art and literature. Regardless of their European importance, however, romantic literature and art in Central and Eastern Europe successfully propagandized the main idea of enlightened romanticism: freedom, both in social and national terms. They advocated self-sacrificing struggle against the oppressors and raised the national consciousness and self-esteem of the region's peoples. Culture became the prime mover of nationalism and nation-building in Central and Eastern Europe and gradually transformed the entire political environment of the region. At its best, moreover, Central and Eastern European literature, scholarship, and art enriched the entire romantic movement and became part of the international high culture of the age.

The Czech scholar František Palacký, one of the leading historians of the age, studied original documents and carried out research in more than seventy European archives. The first volume of his monumental six-volume *History of the Czech Nation* appeared in 1836, but he needed thirty years to complete it. Palacký became well known in Germany and Europe and chaired the first pan-Slav Congress. His international standing made him all the more credible and influential at home. He presented an alternative interpretation to the famous German nationalist historian Leopold von Ranke's analysis of the contrast between the Western, Germanic, and Eastern, Slavic, nations. In Palacký's work, the peaceful, constructive character of the Slavs was opposed by aggressive-expansionist Germanic-Roman qualities. It strengthened the feeling that "we are not worse, but actually even better than the so-called advanced nations." The author clearly expressed his ideological goal: "I had no higher wish for my earthly life than to serve my beloved nation by giving a faithful account of its past, in which it would recognize itself as in a mirror and regain consciousness of what it needs." Palacký's history ends in 1526, when the Habsburgs gained the Czech throne. One of his maxims sums up what he sought to prove: "We were here before Austria, and we will also be here after it!" (quoted in Sayer 1998, 128–29). Palacký reinterpreted Czech history from a national point of view and ascribed a national component to religious struggles. The Hussite movement, in his interpretation, was a part of the Slav-German conflict. Jan Hus was cast as a national hero who stood up "against all." The Czechs appeared as the very first crusaders fighting against authority and hierarchy and for equality and freedom of conscience. "This interpretation of Czech history made the Czechs the eastern outpost of the liberal West, instead of the western outpost of the Slav East" (Kohn 1944, 560).

Exceptional achievement and international fame also characterized the Serb Vuk Stefanović Karadžić, who was born into a peasant family in a western Serbian village in 1787 but became a Renaissance-type scholar-artist on the European scale. Karadžić produced the first grammar and dictionary of the vernacular Serbian language, created a new, simplified alphabet, translated the New Testament, and assembled a monumental collection of Serbian and South Slav oral poems and folk songs, published in his *Srpske narodne pjesme* in six volumes between 1824 and 1833. His work was comparable to Herder's. All these achievements led to early world fame: much of his collection of folk poetry and songs became part of the European romantic culture. The first German translations appeared in 1818, then a huge collection during the 1820s, which was admired by

Goethe. In 1826, an English translation appeared. The next year, John Browning translated more than a hundred songs and ballads from Karadžić's anthology (Holton and Mihailovich 1988, 79–82).

Karadžić accomplished two related goals: he elevated the status of the peasant language to a literary level and focused on the national question. The central themes of the folk poems he collected were the fate of the two Serbian insurrections, the heroic struggle for freedom, and the fighting spirit of the nation. Karadžić "consciously laid stress on this nationalism and its political implications" (Barac 1955, 89). With publication of folklore-epic poems on "The Fall of the Serbian Empire," "The Maid of Kosovo," and the "Death of the Mother of the Jugovići," Karadžić's *Hajduk* and the *Uskok* cycles became instrumental in establishing the Kosovo legend as the pillar of Serb national self-consciousness (*Antologija srpske* 1974; Novaković 1995). Karadžić's famous *Srbi svi i svuda* (All Serbs and Serbs Everywhere) became a milestone in the development of a South Slav, or Yugoslav, national ideology.

Two charismatic musicians, outstanding international representatives of romantic music, Liszt and Chopin, deserve special notice. Ferenc Liszt, best known by the German form of his first name, Franz, was born in Sopron, Hungary, to a German family. His father, Adam, was an official serving Prince Esterházy, and the family lived in Hungary until Franz turned twelve years old. The young Liszt spent a great part of his formative years in the country, though he never learned the Hungarian language. For most of his life, Liszt lived in Paris, Weimar, and later Rome. He was, however, considered Hungarian. Mihály Vörösmarty, a leading Hungarian romantic poet, addressed a poem "To Ferenc Liszt," the first lines of which read:

> Renowned musician, freeman of the world,
> and yet our kinsman everywhere you go,
> have you a cadence for the ailing land
> to set to strings that play in the marrow?
> (translated in Makkai 1996, 224–26)

Liszt expressed his Hungarian patriotic feelings in a letter in 1843 to a prominent Hungarian reformer, Miklós Wesselényi, in which he promised to learn Hungarian: "I shall be happy and proud when I understand and speak my mother tongue . . . that expresses the noble ideas of Hungary. . . . If Hungary accepts me as her own son . . . I do not need heaven—the goal of my life has been realized" (Liszt 1989, 83–84). Liszt was a larger-than-life revolutionary composer and a virtuoso pianist, probably the greatest ever. Along with the somewhat older virtuoso violinist

Niccolò Paganini, he was welcomed in royal courts and the most elegant salons and concert halls of Europe. Liszt was also a writer, an exquisite correspondent (with ten thousand published letters), an essayist whose works were published in six volumes, one of the leading advocates of program music, and inventor of a classic romantic genre, the symphonic poem. He and Richard Wagner, his son-in-law, became the leading representatives of romantic music. Because of his Hungarian pieces, the symphonic poem *Hungaria,* the *Hungarian Coronation Mass, Hungarian Rhapsodies,* and "Ungarische Sturmmarsch," Liszt became an envoy of romantic Hungarian music (based, in reality, mostly on Gypsy music).

Fryderyk Chopin, who was born into a Polish-French family, left Poland in his early twenties after the defeat of the Polish uprising of 1830–31 and joined the great Polish emigration to Paris. He spent the second half of his short life abroad or, more accurately, in his second home. Yet his études, preludes, nocturnes, and other pianoforte compositions made their Polish melodies world renowned. His music expressed "alternating moods of rousing protest and melancholic languor. For some, he translated Polish history into notes on the keyboard"; Robert Schumann said of what was perhaps Chopin's most famous piece, the "Revolutionary Étude," op. 10, no. 12, that it spoke of "guns buried in flowers" (Davies 1996, 820).

Polish romantic drama, which was central to Polish nation-building and became an integral part of romantic European culture, was one of the greatest achievements of Central and Eastern European romanticism (Gutowski 1991). The legendary charismatic "national bards" Mickiewicz, Słowacki, and Krasiński played key roles in its birth, but after the defeat of the 1830 uprising, all three emigrated to Paris (Piasecka 1992).

Mickiewicz was born in the Byelorussian-speaking region of the Grand Duchy of Lithuania into a Polish petit gentry family. Voltaire, Schiller, Goethe, and Byron were all influences on him. His first book of poems, *Ballady i romanse,* published in 1822, opened the romantic era in Poland. His life was archetypically that of a romantic hero, including imprisonment by the oppressive Russian authorities and forced emigration after the defeat of the Polish uprising. He lived in Paris, fought in Italy against Austrian oppression, and died in Istanbul in 1855 at the age of fifty-seven while organizing a Polish legion of liberation.

Mickiewicz's world fame was established by his drama in verse, *Dziady,* or "Forefather's Eve," a forceful indictment of Russian oppression. The pagan rite of *dziady* preserved in Lithuanian folklore—calling on the dead and offering them food—offered a framework for the poet to "invite" ghosts and, by means of their earthly and ethereal experiences, con-

vey his "anti-Sarmatian," antifeudal Enlightenment credo, combined with
an exalted romantic nationalism (Kowalczykowa 1991). He developed the
messianic idea that Poland would reclaim the world and liberate it
through her suffering and spiritual superiority. In part three of *Dziady,*
completed later, Konrad the poet, captive in a tsarist prison, is no longer
preoccupied with his personal and social problems, but dedicated to the
national cause. He feels equal to God and challenges him: if God allows
suffering and injustice, he is "not the father of the world but a . . . ," and
a choir of good spirits finishes the sentence, "tsar." Mickiewicz was convinced of his mission and believed that the strength of words can build
and destroy the real world. (He was actually right: his "sacred national
play" was able to generate an uprising against oppression in Poland even
a century and a half later.)

Juliusz Słowacki and Zygmunt Krasiński, the two other members of
the "Holy Trinity" of Polish romanticism, were both rivals of and com-
plements to Mickiewicz. During his short life (he died at forty), Słowacki
produced an impressive oeuvre of passionate national dramas, such as
his *Kordian* (1834), which is comparable to Mickiewicz's *Dziady.* Unlike
Mickiewicz, Słowacki was critical of the failure and shortcomings of the
Polish noble uprising and the tragic neglect of the peasantry: his hero
Kordian symbolically realizes only at the end of his life, while awaiting
execution, that his peasant servant Grzegorz is actually his father.

Krasiński, an aristocrat and son of one of the tsar's generals, who betrayed the Polish cause, had by the age of twenty-one written his "Undi-
vine Comedy," *Nieboska komedia* (1833), and *Iridion,* which express their
author's disappointment and fears. Krasiński took up social issues: in his
works, democrats fight aristocrats, the poor fight the rich, and, above all,
Christians fight non-Christians. Foreigners in the typical Central and Eastern European drama embody immorality and sin (Ratajczak 1992). Polish romantic drama created a special concept of "Polishness," an "ethereal entity requiring loyalty and existing even without embodiment in a
state" (Miłosz 1983, 200).

Poets, writers, and artists became sacrosanct national heroes, legends
who influenced their nation even after their early deaths. Central and Eastern European intellectuals became extremely influential in part because
they themselves believed in their mission and in the myths they created.
They believed in the victory of their nation and the possibility of transforming it overnight: they lived in the world of dreams and confused their
daydreams with reality. They were dedicated to their mission, and the best
of them were thus very convincing. On the other hand, desperate peoples

wanted to believe in a glorious past, in the great potential of their nation, and that it was an innocent victim of other countries. They shared in self-pity and hatred of the numerous foreign enemies of the nation, which were held responsible for all of their troubles. In this atmosphere, intellectuals often became sacrosanct idols, burning torches to follow.

Two strikingly similar cases illustrate this. Both the Hungarian Sándor Petőfi and the Bulgarian Hristo Botev became quintessential national poets. Their poems, writings, and political activities placed them in the vanguard of the revolutionary national struggles of their countries. Each died on the battlefield (at the ages of twenty-six and twenty-seven, respectively). Their corpses were never found, and both became legends in the national pantheons of their homelands. Petőfi had a special role in the history of Hungary, not only because of his plebeian revolutionary poetry and his commitment to the romantic unity of love and freedom, but also because the 1848 revolution began when he declaimed his "Nemzeti Dal" (National Song) to a crowd on March 15, 1848. The poet fought the invading Russian army and died for the revolution. Botev's role in Bulgarian history is equally central. As poet, writer, founder of journals, and freedom fighter, he mobilized his nation. When the April uprising began in 1876, he raised money abroad, organized an armed group of volunteers, crossed the river Danube at Kozlodui, and attacked Turkish troops in the Milinkamak area.

Both Botev and Petőfi sought out and prophesied their early deaths on the battlefield. Botev wrote:

Perhaps I shall die in my youth
But enough for me is this guerdon
That people may say of me one day
"He died, poor fellow, for Justice,
For the cause of Justice and Freedom."
(quoted in Topencharov 1982, 28)

Petőfi expressed his worry and wish in a similar way:

One thought torments me: that I lie
Upon a featherbed to die!
Slowly wither, slowly waste away,
Flowerlike, the furtive earthworm's prey;
Like a candle, slowly to be spent
In an empty, lonely tenement.
No death like this, my Lord Divine,
No death like this, be ever mine!

Let me be a tree through which the lightning flashes,
Or the tempest plucks up by the roots and smashes;
Let me be a rock from mountain rent asunder,
Hurtled to the gorge by skyearthshaking thunder . . .
When once they rise, all fettered folk
Who've had enough of chain and yoke,
With faces red and banners red, in line
Emblazoned there this sacred countersign:
"World Liberty!"

                                        (Petőfi [1948] 1976, 30–31)

Romantic Byronic gestures became building blocks of the nation. Romantic self-sacrificing heroism excluded pragmatic considerations and rational compromises. Central and Eastern European romantic nationalism embodied the basic romantic attitude: "the motive is more important than the consequences, the intention is more important than the effect" (Berlin 1999, 10).

EMANCIPATING THE PEASANTRY—THROUGH ART

Romantic literature and art were in the vanguard of the struggle for sociopolitical modernization. Following in Herder's footsteps, collectors of oral folk tales, proverbs, and poetry recognized the foundation for modern poetry based on peasant dialect and the rhythms of folk poetry. Poetry and music emancipated the peasantry before revolutionary politics was able to do so. The new national poetry built a new national identity. Huge collections of folk poetry were published throughout the region: Kradžić's six-volume anthology of Serbian folk poetry; two volumes of Bulgarian proverbs and sayings collected by Petko Slavejkov; Hadzi Hajden Jovanovic's publication of Bulgarian folk songs; and Ljuben Karavelov's anthology of three thousand Bulgarian sayings and proverbs (*Monumenta Bulgarica* 1996, xxxviii–ix). The Czech romantic Karel Jaromír Erben published five volumes of collected folk songs with piano accompaniment in the 1840s, a typical romantic ideal of unifying poetry and music.

Folk poetry became a model of modern national poetry. One of the earliest pioneers of this new trend was the Czech Karel Hynek Mácha, who published his first nineteen variations on the folk song "The Dear Little Moon" during the 1830s. The breakthrough of a *népies* (peasant) style occurred in Hungary during the 1840s and 1850s. Sándor Petőfi's early poems were written in folk style, using the typical folk-song device of an introductory line describing nature entirely unrelated to the subject. His effortless rhymes produced a natural effect, and the poems dealt with everyday life (Czigány 1984, 182). Petőfi's *János Vitéz* (1844) established the love story of two village orphans, Jancsi and Iluska, as national poetry and made them poetic heroes with a democratic message of poetic justice. Petőfi's contemporary János Arany based his ballads on old folk ballad traditions:

> Yea, swords do clash and armors crash
>   And blood-red is the sun,
> And birds of prey descend to stay;
>   Edward! this thou hast done.
>
> A thousand of our race are slain
>   In gory battle lost
> Who lives today may sadly say:
>   "This is thy holocaust."

sings a courageous old bard instead of toasting and praising the oppressor king in his "The Bards of Wales" (Arany 1914, 162).

Using reworded folk motifs and even the rhythm of folk songs, Mickiewicz expressed a classical romantic credo:

> Faith and love are more discerning
> Than lenses or learning.
> You know the dead truth, not the living,
> The world of things, not the world of loving.
> Where does any miracle start?
> Cold eye, look in your heart!
>
>   (Miłosz 1983, 211)

The Bulgarians Petko Slavejkov and Hristo Botev also drew on original folk songs. Botev's poetry recalls the simplicity and rhythm of folk songs. In his "Hadzhi Dimitar," wild animals take care of the fallen hero:

> By day a mother eagle lends him shade
> And a wolf meekly licks his wound,
> While on high a falcon—heroic bird—
> Keep[s] watch over her brother hero!

Then the wood nymphs take over:

> One binds his wound with herbs
> Another splashes him with water
> A third hastens to kiss his mouth
> As he gazes at her—lovely, smiling
>   (*Monumenta Bulgarica* 1996, 463)

A similar pattern may be found in Serbia, where from the 1860s on, Jovan Jovanović-Zmaj adopted the rhythm and language of folk poetry in his late romantic patriotic poems.

As with poetry, romantic music drew inspiration from folk songs. In 1835, Liszt wrote in his manifesto "Zur Stellung der Künstler" about the "mission" of music and musicians. One of the expressions of this mission was the cult of the folk song, born, as he phrased it, "from the very womb of the 'nation.'" Folk elements had appeared in music before: Bach, Telemann, and Mozart had used the polonaise. Beethoven and Haydn had used Hungarian tunes. Folk-song motifs, however, served only for the enrichment of melodies. In the romantic age, a methodical collection and publication of folk songs began: the first volumes of Scottish and German folk songs appeared in the late eighteenth century. Brahms published about fifty folk songs with German texts. One of his own songs, "In stiller Nacht," was published as an anonymous folk melody.

Liszt and Chopin, although entirely international, elevated Hungarian and Polish folk songs to the highest level of European music. Via Chopin's work, Polish national dances, such as the polonaise, mazurka, and krakoviak, became part of the international musical repertoire. Liszt, especially, with his *Hungarian Rhapsodies* and Piano Sonata in B Minor, made the Hungarian *verbunkos* and Gypsy music world renowned. Romanticism, observed Alfred Einstein, thus "began to separate the nationalities in music."

Like other forms of folk literature, "folk songs" took on sacrosanct national importance, notwithstanding that most—perhaps 80 percent of them—had actually been written during the eighteenth and nineteenth centuries, as demonstrated by Béla Bartók, who collected Hungarian, Romanian, Slovak, and other folk songs in the early twentieth century. Some 10 to 20 percent were *népies müdal*—urban, folk-like art songs, often called "Gypsy music," which, as Bartók notes, was the "song of the noble elite" in nineteenth-century Hungary. Half of these "folk songs" were, moreover, of foreign origin—in the case of Hungary, often adaptations of German and Slavic songs. Slovene "folk music" was of German origin, and many Czech folk songs also came from Germany. Folk songs of neighboring countries often closely resembled each other, and Bartók speaks of an "East European international musical jargon" (Bartók [1934] 1986, 310). In the Hungarian case, the most important songs were *verbunkos* (from the German *Werbung*, recruiting) dances originally used to persuade young men to join the army. During the first half of the nineteenth century, these songs became "the national Hungarian instrumental music idiom, including its transformation into the *csárdás* dance forms" (Suchoff 1995, 20).

The national profile of music was a new phenomenon in the romantic age. In earlier centuries, music had been entirely international, and, as Alfred Einstein has noted, "before 1800 a strongly national coloring was shown only by those composers whose stature did not reach the lofty heights of greatness" (Einstein 1947, 18). Berlioz, however, was strongly French, and Wagner was explicitly Teutonic. A total romantic "nationalization" of music characterized the most important art genre of the age in the Czech lands (ibid., 296). The pioneer of Czech national music was Bedřich Smetana. Just as romantic drama was a leading literary trend in Poland, Czech romantic music and opera were among the greatest achievements of Central and Eastern European romanticism and European romanticism at large.

Smetana established Czech national music with his pieces for piano, such as *Czech Dances* and *Memories of Bohemia,* and with his string quartets, among them *From My Life.* Smetana's work was carried on by Antonín Dvořák, who drew extensively on folk song and dances in his symphonies, string quartets, Slavic rhapsodies, and, most of all, songs and choruses.

This national phase of music ended with the end of the romantic age. In the Czech lands, it ended with Leoš Janáček (d. 1928). "*Janůfa* is not a Czech national opera, it has nothing to do with national historical dreams," Max Brod argued in one of his letters. "The music, which throughout has been of sharply national character . . . suddenly becomes really universal, purely musical music" (quoted in Spector 2000, 216). This was also true in the case of Hungary, where, despite Bartók's scholarly work and collection of folk music, he himself heralded a turn toward international modern music. In an editorial in its first issue in 1890, the Hungarian literary journal *A Hét* (The Week) expressed a similar turn: it would be a forum only for "literature, and not the great force to form and create state and nation" (Frigyesi 1998, 95).

It should be recalled that music escaped in the romantic era from the churches and the exclusive salons of the aristocracy. Handel's "*Messiah* was the first work that was given mass-performances. . . . [N]ew festive auditoriums had to come into existence, the secular, clear, free counterparts to the dark and solemn halls of the church" (Einstein 1947, 13–14). Before the romantic era, musicians had served the Church, the king, and the aristocrats (as court conductor at Kismarton and Esterháza, Alfred Einstein reminds us, Haydn wore the prince's livery), and composed their works when they were ordered to do so. Now they were free musicians. Beethoven was probably the very first among them (ibid., 12). Romantic music thus reached a broad audience and became a decisive vehicle for romantic feelings and ideas.

As in music, romantic folklorization also generated national styles in architecture. In Romania, the so-called neo-Romanian style used historicized folk decorative elements. Ion Mincu's veranda, with arcades and round arches, the Lahovay Mansion (1886) and Girls' Central School (1890) in Bucharest, and the Administrative Palaces of Galaţi and Craiova all represented this romantic national style (Sasarman 1983). The Hungarian Ödön Lechner's "Hungarian" style, using tiled roofs and national decorative elements, richly decorated Budapest and Kecskemét around the turn of the century and expressed a similar trend.

THE CREATION OF NATIONAL MYTHS

The rivers and mountains, woods and plains, the landscape, the beauty of the fatherland inspired poets and painters alike. This feeling was passionately expressed by the Albanian Naim Frashëri (1846–1900):

> Oh mountains of Albania and you, oh lofty trees!
> Broad blossoming plains, you are in my thoughts day and night!
> You fair highlands and you sparkling streams!
> Peaks, hills, slopes, cliffs and verdant forests!
> I shall sing of the herds you hold and feed,
> Oh blessed places! How you nourish and delight me!
> You, Albania, bestow upon me honor and the name Albanian.
> You have filled my heart with flame and desire.
>
> (translated in Elsie 1995, 232)

Vojislav Ilić similarly links the scenery of the fatherland with patriotic Serbianness in his poem "On the River Vardar":

> Oh waves, oh Serbian river! Centuries vanish so,
> And sink like waves into the sea of somber eternity.
> But your drops like pearls forever kiss the foothills
> On which stand memorials of the glorious national past.
> Some day, like the heavenly phoenix, freedom will dawn . . .
>
> (translated in Dordevic 1984, 3)

Karel H. Mácha, the main representative of Czech romanticism, who was influenced by Byron and Scott, visited 129 old castles in search of the glorious Czech past. The ruins of Bezděz inspired his *The Evening at Bezděz,* a "poem in prose" (Součkova 1958, 49–50). Ruins also attracted romantic painters: the Czech Julius Mařak painted the "sacred places" of his country. Ruins were likewise the main themes of the Romanians Theodore Aman, Nicolae Grigorescu, and Ion Andrescu. The Serbians Djura Jaksić, Novak Rakonić, Stefan Todorović, and the Croat Vjekoslav Karas painted the landscapes of their native lands, village life, historical events, and national heroes. The Polish romantic painters Aleksander Orlowski, Piotr Michalowski, Jan Matejko, and Artur Grottger followed the same pattern.

Epic poetry was one of the most important genres for constructing national historical myths, which raised people's self-confidence, gave them a sense of belonging to a national community, and formed traditions (Bahlcke 2000). The most hallowed task of such romantic national poetry was the "discovery," or rather the construction, of a glorious national past. The model was Virgil's *Aeneid,* and the compulsory rhythm the heroic hexameter. At the age of twenty-five, in 1825, for example, Mihály Vörösmarty published his epic poem *Zalán futása* (The Flight of Zalán), which describes the conquest of Hungary by the Hungarians under "brave Arpád, the noble commander, wearing the skin of a leopard and strong enough to lead the nation." With the help of Hadúr, the god of hosts, Arpád defeats the Bulgarian ruler Zalán. The story of the winning of the fatherland carried Hungarians back to the ancient glory of their ailing nation. The poet, according to a typical romantic pattern, seeks to mobilize the nation: "Where are you, glory of old? Lost deep in the night of the shadows?" "Where are you, Arpád . . . in this impotent age?" (Makkai 1996, 214–15). Distinctive romantic-national features figure powerfully in Vörösmarty's poems. In *Szózat* (Appeal, 1836), the characteristic Central and Eastern European romantic vision of *nemzethalál,* the extinction of the nation, is tragically exhibited:

> Or there shall come, if come there must,
> a death of fortitude;
> and round about our graves shall stand
> a nation washed in blood.
> Around the graves where we shall die
> a weeping world will come . . .

For Magyars, however, there is no place but the fatherland,

> for it has borne you and at death
> will consecrate your dust!
> No other spot in all the world

can touch your heart as home;
let fortune bless or fortune curse,
from hence you shall not roam!
(Makkai 1996, 228)

In *Zrinyi* (1828), Vörösmarty expresses the tragic and heroic loneliness of the nation: "The Hungarian looks West, and then looks back to the East with dismal eyes; he is an isolated, brotherless branch of his race" (Czigány 1984, 128).

Romantic national poetry spread messages of freedom, liberty, and the rebirth of the nation throughout the region (Topolski et al. 1991). Rather than speaking of the Enlightenment or romanticism, Czech literary historians call the period between 1780 and 1830 the *národni obrozeni*, or "national renaissance." In 1802, in the fourth volume of an anthology edited by Jaroslav Puchmajer, the twenty-nine-year-old Josef Jungmann published his *Těžké vybrání*, the country's first romantic poem. The mission of national literature was "to arouse the national consciousness and to bring Czech culture to the level of other European nations" (Součkova 1958, 39). Jungmann, an admirer of Voltaire and Goethe, was an emotional nationalist, who "rhapsodized about a fantastically modified past of the Slavs." Ján Kollar, a leading representative of the "Czech renaissance" became an ardent pan-Slav nationalist and, glorifying the Slavs, identified the Slavic zodiac with the Indian-Egyptian one and developed a "patriotic-national vision of Slavic grandeur and mythical potential" (Nemoianu 1984, 129).

Sima Milutinović-Sarajlija (1791–1847) published lyric and national epic poems glorifying the sufferings, struggle, and glory of the Serbs. In *Srbijanka* (1826), he glamorized the first Serbian insurrection. The central topic of Milovan Vidaković's writings—epic poems and novels, such as *Karija carica* (1827)—was Serbian history. Jovan Sterija Popović's national epic poems—*Svetislav i Mileva, Miloš Obilić,* and *Nahod Simeon*—eulogized the Serbian past, the horror of the Turks, and the Kosovo legend. The patriotic feeling of Serbdom, the glory of the medieval Serbian state, and fanatical hatred of Serbia's enemies, especially the Turks, motivated all of these writings.

In his *Sonetni venec,* the Slovene Francè Prešeren combines the classic romantic unity of love and patriotism. His *Krst pri Savici,* the Slovene "Flight of Zalán," describes the last struggle of the pagans with victorious Christianity and the christening of the nation. The Croat Ivan Mažuranić, a believer in the messianic role of the Slavs and the Illyrian theory of Slav unity, who later became *banus* (governor, sometimes called viceroy) of Croatia, expressed the need to confront the common enemy (especially Hungarians) in poems such as *Smrt smailage čengića* (1846) (Barac 1955, 97, 103, 111). The Văcărescu brothers and the Şcoala Ardeleană in Romania pioneered a poetic revolution focused on the national cause using heroic, nationalistic themes.

The central topic of Albanian poetry, drama, and novels was the fifteenth-century national hero George Kastrioti, known as Skanderbeg (a corruption of the Turkish Iskander Bey). Poems by Jeronim De Rada, Anton Santori, and Gabriel Dara all harked back to Albania's "ancient glory." In *Paradise* (1894), a poetic narrative of the glorious history of the Albanians in battle with various enemies, the most important late romantic national poet of Albania, Naim Frashëri, proudly proclaimed that in the past, Albanians had "stood up to Turkey, honored Albania, took up arms and fought and saved all of Europe" (Bihiku 1980, 38). In his extremely popular *The History of Skanderbeg* (1898), Frashëri erected a monument to Albanian resistance to the Ottomans and the struggle for freedom.

Albanians, Serbs, Hungarians, and Poles equally shared the belief that their country, and their country *alone,* was the bastion of Christendom and Western civilization. This "rampart" myth, based on a fourteenth-century papal letter on the occasion of the coronation of Ladislaus I, the Short, became the backbone of Polish historical myths in the nineteenth century. In 1807, both Jan Paweł Woronicz and Andrzej Horodyski described Poland as the strong *przedmurze,* or rampart, of Europe, which "repelled the Eastern storms from the rest of the world" and made it possible that "in the womb of Europe human rights, religion, arts and knowledge of various kinds useful in social life could be preserved." Stanisław Staszic and Adam Mickiewicz maintained that all of Slavdom was "the unshakable rampart of Europe's rising civilization" (Tazbir 1983, 7, 10, 109, 111).

The rampart myth included a sense that the rising nations of Eastern Europe had borne the brunt of defending the Continent, and, consequently, that they deserved the gratitude of the West, which, however, had "repaid the debt with ingratitude," although it ought to do so by restoring the victims' independence.

National drama and theater also played an exceptional role in propagating the national cause. The nationalist drama and nationalist tragedy were responsible for creating a history with a glorious past, which is to be recaptured in a lackluster present. The topic and mission are found throughout the entire region: an idealized national past with exceptional national kings and heroes representing truth and justice, often solitary romantic champions battling external enemies, with the nation's very existence always at stake. Anyone who attacks the nation is evil and treacherous. Politics becomes a moral struggle between good and evil. The characters are not complex. Their morality is their goal, good or bad, according to whether they are defenders or enemies of the nation. They are moved by passion, patriotism, love, and hatred. They do their heroic or evil deeds for a cause. Most of these historical tragedies are ahistorical: every historical period and event seems analogous to the problems of the present (Spiró 1986).

The literary standard of these genres was rather uneven. Good plays and trash—both produced in great numbers—had the same mission and played similar political roles. Aesthetic value, in this context, was only of secondary importance. The national drama attracted thousands of people, a performance became a festive, almost religious event, and the mobilizing effect was extraordinary.

Hungarian national drama was born during the 1810s with József Katona's *Bánk bán,* which followed the stereotypical pattern: wicked foreigners, in this case, the queen and her brother (from "Meran") are punished by rebellion and the assassination of the queen, and an old peasant, Tiborc, has a long, passionate monologue about peasant misery and Hungary's decline. In Bohemia, the story of Jan Hus inspired a play by the actor-director Josef Kajetan Tyl, as well as Václav Brožik's monumental painting *The Sentencing of Master Jan Hus.* (The Czech poet Mácha planned to write four dramas about Bohemia's kings but failed to do so.) Meanwhile, typical Central and East European national tragedies also flourished in mid-nineteenth-century Romania, including, besides those of Michai Eminescu (see Massoff 1964), Vasile Alecsandri's *Despot Voda* and Bogdan Haşdeu's *Domnita* and *Rosanda;* and the Slovak Jonás Záborsky, the Croats Matija Ban and Mirko Bogović, and the Bulgarians Dobri Vojnikov and Ivan Vazov all produced—mostly second-rate—national tragedies.

Some of the best national tragedies, however, were Serbian. Popović's *Smrt Stefan Dečanskog* exemplifies Central and East European romantic-national drama, and Djura Jakšić's *Jelizaveta, kneginja crnogorska* (1864), although quite similar to *Bánk bán,* is a much more mature work and rises above the stereotypical conflict between the bad foreign and good national forces. Jakšić clearly realized that the real tragedy of the small nations of the region was that they were the pawns of foreign powers. Within each nation, indigenous forces played humiliating, suicidal satellite roles, accusing one another (with reason) of treason and slaughtering one another, leading finally to total collapse.

The message of the national drama was forcefully repeated by the romantic genre of so-called program music, which successfully merged literature with music to express not only emotions but ideas as well. The main advocates of program music, among them Brahms and Liszt, argued that "more and more, the masterpieces of music will absorb the masterpieces of literature." Liszt spoke about the "fusion of the two." In this sense, Schubert's *Liedern* created a new trend in art by merging the romantic poem with romantic music. In *Má Vlast* (My Native Land), a program-music cycle of six symphonic poems (a Lisztian genre), Smetana employed a musical dialect that was unmistakably Czech. Smetana's eight operas, especially *The Brandenburgers in Bohemia* (1862), *The Bartered Bride* (1864), *Dalibor* (1867), and *Libuše* (1872), became the foundation of Czech opera. In Hungary, Ferenc Erkel's *Hunyadi László* (1844) and *Bánk bán* (1861), an opera based on Katona's play, were highly patriotic too, and Polish patriotism is expressed in Stanisław Moniuszko's *Halka* (1847) and *The Haunted Castle* (1865).

Romantic painters often chose the same topics that engaged writers and musicians: for example, the new Hungarian drama, opera, and painting all retold the story of László Hunyadi, the older son of János Hunyadi, who defended Hungary in the late fourteenth century and defeated an Ottoman army. The atmosphere of tragic history is presented by Viktor Madarász's *The Mourning of László Hunyadi*, a large canvas depicting the victim of a conspiracy that almost ended the continuous reign of the great national dynasty of the Hunyadis. The same heroic treatment was accorded to Skanderbeg in Albania, and to the role of Kosovo in Serbian art. Romania's glorious national history was embodied in Mihai the Brave, who briefly united Transylvania with Wallachia and is depicted on horseback by Mihai Lipaty and in the painting *Mihai the Brave Entering Alba Iulia* by Constantin Lecca, who also produced two huge paintings of Mihai's death in 1601 (Oprescu 1984).

Historical myths were developed by national poet-prophets, missionary artists, and, not least, pseudo-scholars. It was during these decades, from the late eighteenth century onward, that modern historiography was born. Jacob Talmon speaks about a "religion of history" that actually was a "structure of ideas . . . an entity moving towards a pre-ordained goal" (Talmon 1960, 24–25). The publication of medieval sources, codices, and various documents, as well as multivolume histories of the nations of the area, established modern scholarship in most of these countries. However, even the most serious and scholarly works could not avoid bolstering historical myths. Many others focused explicitly on the latter goal of mythmaking, glorifying the national past, but also inspiring a vigorous new movement of nation-building. Paradoxically, the most irrational national myths served the most rational modernization goals.

The myth of an ancient, united "Illyrian" nation of southern Slavs mobilized Serbs, Croats, Slovenes, and Bosnians to join forces to regain their independence and build a modern nation. Histories that hypothesized the Illyrian basis of South Slav unity appeared, one of the earliest being the *History of Various Slavic Peoples, Namely, Bulgarians, Croats, and Serbs* (1794–95) by Jovan Rajić, an Orthodox monk.

An exuberant nationalist movement also sprang up to create a Great Romania by uniting all the Romanians living under Ottoman, Hungarian, and Russian authority. Mihai the Brave and other Romanian heroes had waged a "splendid struggle for freedom and national unity," Nicolae Bălcescu wrote in an unfinished work; "the memory of the heroic past has to generate the desire of generations to come to enrich this brilliant legacy" (quoted in Arató 1971, 195). Romanians believed that their nation had been born from the intermixing of Romans and Dacians after Trajan's conquest of Dacia (Transylvania), the last province of the Roman empire to be established; but "foreign authors . . . cast aspersions on the Romanians, the grandsons of the ancient Romans," Petru Maior said in his 1812 *History of the Origins of the Romanians in Dacia* (quoted in ibid., 194). In fact, Henri Stahl notes, "the first document confirming the existence of state-like forms set up by Romanians dates from 1247," and it is likely that a unified Romanian state was formed only in the following centuries when the *voivode* (originally, chief of the warriors) "declared himself autonomous and absolute master of his territory" (Stahl 1980, 211–12).

The concept of the Hun origins of the Hungarians, and the Poles' belief in their descent from the ancient Sarmatae, a nomadic people related to the Scythians, equally stressed (or made up) heroic military traditions and strengthened and prepared these nations to fight against oppressors of overwhelming power.

The feeling of lagging behind a rising West that haunted the reformist elites of these countries was countered by a sense of national moral superiority. Slavophiles idealized the Slav peoples and ascribed a higher value system to them. In this vein, Adam Mickiewicz condemned Western materialism and the "diabolic forces of money" in his Paris lectures, saying: "The general idea of political economy is the enemy of the Slav people, for this idea is *par excellence* material." The Slavs, he declared, had not "given over their spirit to the work of reason and industry," so they still retained "pure and profound religious feelings." Like many other Polish and Russian political thinkers, Mickiewicz saw the Slav community of property, embodied in the village commune, as the realization of the ideal property relations hypothesized by the French utopian philosopher Charles Fourier (Walicki 1991, 117–28).

The concept of the "difference between German and Western thought" (Reiss 1995, 3), a central idea of German romantics, also attracted various Slavic romantics, such as the influential Russian Slavophiles. "My thought is far from Western Europe," Joachim Lelewel, the leading Polish romantic historian, proclaimed. "My entire attention is turned toward the east, toward Slavdom." He differentiated between Western and Slavic heritages and emphasized that "ancient Slavic communalism" was distinct from Western traditions. Bishop Jan Pavel Woronicz talked about a separate Slav civilization, superior to that of the West. The Polish populists in their manifesto of 1834 reformulated the German romantic concept of "national individuality" and declared Slavdom to be the national individual, the "new Christ of the new faith" (Walicki 1991, 7, 12–13, 16).

"It is time to realize that we shall not purchase the favor of the West," wrote Ivan Aksakov, a Russian Slavophile, "[their] hatred . . . towards the East and towards Orthodoxy is a traditional, instinctive . . . feeling. . . . Everything that is happening in Europe is nothing but a plot against us. . . . The future Europe will be divided into two camps: on the one side Russia, with all Orthodox Slavic tribes, on the other—the entire . . . Europe together" (quoted in Riasanovsky [1952] 1965, 32, 83–85).

A modern national identity remained to be created. It was very weak in the Balkans, where Greek Orthodoxy was the basis of self-identification for non-Turkish peoples. This "age of theocracy," however, was gradually replaced by an age of nationalism. While Christianity—with a solid base of supreme loyalty for centuries under Muslim Ottoman rule—still remained an important factor in the Balkan self-image, a secular national concept also emerged and began playing an important role. A half-religious, half-ethnic "confessional-nationality" became characteristic in the Balkans (Turczynski 1976).

A new national identity gradually emerged among the various peoples of the Habsburg empire. Derek Sayer cites a report of the Prague Statistical Commission from 1871 whose authors said that attempts to investigate nationality in 1851 had been "premature" because "a clear consciousness of national identity among the majority of Austro-Hungarian nations was, so to speak, still in diapers" (Sayer 1998, 29). The Polish, Hungarian, Serbian, Bulgarian, and even Albanian historical concepts of being (each, of course, alone) the "Christian fortress and defender of Europe against the Asian horde" simultaneously served to strengthen national self-confidence and consciousness.

Early historiography had great importance in this process. In 1762, a Bulgarian monk, Father Paisii Hilendarski, wrote one of the earliest "national histories" of the region, although it remained in manuscript for eighty years. He sought to strengthen national self-esteem: "Why are you ashamed to be called a Bulgarian?" he asked. "It is necessary and useful . . . to know . . . about the deeds of your fathers. . . . Of the whole Slavic race the most glorified were the Bulgarians: they were the first to appoint tsars, the first to have patriarchs, the first to be Christianized, and they conquered the most land . . . [they defeated the Greeks] many times and had taken tribute from them" (*Monumenta Bulgarica* 1996, 340–41).

As an expression of emerging Slovak national consciousness, Ján Baltazár Magin's *Apologia* reinterpreted Slovak history: instead of a Hungarian conqueror who defeated and subordinated the Slavs of the Danube basin, he posited an "alliance" of two coexisting and equal nations. Juraj Papánek went even further in his Slovak history (1780) and presented a glorious past of the great Moravian empire.

Polish historiography, beginning with Adam Naruszewicz's six-volume *History of Poland* (Naruszewicz 1780–86), was one of the most developed in the area. The historical studies of K. B. Hoffman, Maurycy Mochňacki, and especially Joachim Lelewel became part of the mobilization for continuous struggle.

The historical myths were mixed with romantic heroicism. "We are alone, an Eastern people in the West, without relatives," István Széchenyi declared in his *A kelet népe* (People of the East) (Széchenyi 1925). Romanians like Samuil Klein-Micu, Petru Maior, and other Daco-Roman theorists felt likewise: we are alone, the last outpost of Latin culture, surrounded by Slavic and Hungarian barbarism. We are subordinated at the moment, although we arrived in the area much earlier than all the others.

The Polish credo after the partition of the country could be summarized as: "We defended the West and are the Crucified, the Jesus Christ of nations, who will rise again or be resurrected and redeem the human race." The whole nation shared the view that Poland's national poet Adam Mickiewicz expressed in his essay "Books of the Polish Nation and Pilgrimage" in 1832: "a satanic Trinity . . . [Frederick II of Prussia, Catherine II of Russia, and Austria's Maria Theresa] fashioned a new idol . . .

political interest. . . . But the Polish nation alone did not bow down . . . the Kings crucified the Polish nation, and laid it in its grave. . . . [But] the Polish nation did not die. Its body lieth in the grave; but its spirit has descended into the abyss . . . the Soul shall return again to the Body; and the nation shall arise, and free all the peoples of Europe from slavery" (Mickiewicz 1986, 202).

In sum, the popular ethos went something like this: "We western and southern Slavs have to accomplish the Herculean task of uniting the great Slavic nation, which lives in various countries and mostly under a foreign yoke." Romantic missions, romantic struggles, romantic rebellions were put on the agenda.

The enemies, the despotic multinational empires and the unchangeable establishment, however, were too numerous and strong, and the hope of victory too small and distant. That was probably the reason for an expanded, century-long, romantic age in Central and Eastern Europe. Moreover, the romantic attitude, gesture, and pose have inseparably mingled with the national cause and become an organic and permanent element of it. The romantic attitude not only became part of the national character but penetrated personal lives and mentalities as well. Emotional overreaction, self-destructive lifestyles, and an extremely high rate of suicide, these "Wertherian gestures," became the pattern. Theatrical emotion, heroic poses, and bombastic rhetoric became a requirement for discussing the national issue. Poets and writers continued to be self-appointed national prophets. Leadership required charisma, not modern rational political institutions and procedures. Temporarily declining birthrates or other sociopolitical crises immediately revived the fear of the extinction of the nation. Confrontations with other countries and political and economic losses in a difficult period, imagined or real, immediately generated a sense of betrayal. A critical remark about the backwardness of the nation or major policy mistakes made by a fellow citizen were often considered high treason. Self-pity, a kind of romantic-national *Weltschmerz,* became a national characteristic. The nation was often considered a victim surrounded by enemies. National feeling was mixed with xenophobia. Czesław Miłosz comments on the "abnormal" nature, not only of Polish history during the period, but also of thought and literature: "[An] enormous talent for self-pity was displayed, and Poland was presented as an innocent victim suffering for the sins of humanity" (Miłosz 1983, 200). Otherness generated suspicion and hostility. If the nation was at stake, reason was often suppressed by emotion. Because of its "tribal" ethnocultural character, a romantic, deformed, and pathetic national consciousness in Central and Eastern Europe carried within it the seeds of xenophobic, exclusive, aggressive nationalism, an ideology the German Eugen Diderichs called "new romanticism" in the late nineteenth century (Mosse 1966, 52).

Central and Eastern Europe became a hotbed of various kinds of extremism, wrong political decisions, and internal and international conflicts.

CULTURAL INSTITUTIONS AND PUBLIC BUILDINGS

The spread of enlightened-romantic messages was assisted by important new "national" cultural institutions. One of the most important of these was the school system, discussed in a later chapter. By its establishment and gradually increasing enrollment, the school system became a strong pillar of national education, despite a rather limited curriculum. The new generations studied a common vernacular language and the same history of the nation. The teachers, in most cases, played a central role in the education of even the adult population in small towns.

Various other national institutions were also established around this time, including national theaters, libraries, and museums. Theater in the West developed over centuries and was an integral part of urban life and an institution of entertainment. In Central and Eastern Europe, without that tradition, theater was not a consequence but rather a planned means of creating urban development. The work of cultural nation-building, however, made the need for "national" theaters a central political issue. The principle of the public, nonprofit *Nationaltheater* for serious drama and responsible programming emerged in Germany, appearing first in Hamburg (Senelick 1991, 231). The theater, the home of the national drama, was essentially a church of the national language and the national ideal, a cradle for the cultivation of new historical myths, and a voice against oppression and for independent nationhood. Although an entertaining, cosmopolitan German theater, traveling French and Italian companies, and amateur theatrical companies were well established, Hungarian, Romanian, Czech, Serbian, and Bulgarian theater did not exist before the romantic age. The need to create national theater as an institution emerged from German romantic national ideology. The building of large national theaters became an obsession of religious proportions that mobilized the best patriots of the age. In the Czech lands, instead of "national theater," they often spoke of *vlastenské divadlo*, "patriotic theater."

Some independent nations of the area established national theaters in

the late eighteenth century—Russia in 1756, Poland in 1765, and Austria
in 1776 (that is, nearly a century before the others). These national theaters used native languages. The national theater was Poland's most important cultural institution up until the 1820s. German theater and culture had no role in Poland. All of the other nations put a national theater
on their list of national requirements. Noblemen, such as Count František Antonín Nostit-Rieneck, maintained private and then public German theaters in Bohemia, and in November 1821, a group of patriots sent
a petition to the emperor urging the foundation of a Czech theater as a
"fundamental means for the revival of the Czech language . . . [and] fertile soil for Czech literature . . . which would also deal with our patriotic
past." However, as late as April 1849, Havlíček Borovský had to state in
the *Narodní Novini,* "for a long while we have worked so that our nation
would have what every cultured nation has—its own theater." During the
1850s, nationwide fund-raising began, and in 1856, the site of the theater
was acquired. Meanwhile, a provisional theater was opened in 1862. The
construction of the permanent building on the bank of the Vltava River
began in 1867. The foundation stone was brought from Řip Mountain, a
symbolic gesture, since, according to historic legend, the ancestor of the
Czech nation, Čech, had claimed the surrounding country for his people
at that place.

By decision of the Transylvanian Diet, the Kolozsvár Theater was
opened in 1821. Two years later, another Hungarian theater opened its
doors in Miskolc. The movement for a national theater in the capital, however, was more protracted. The first draft of a plan was ready in 1819. Eight
years later, the national poet and politician Ferenc Kölcsey argued that
"every refined European nation" had theaters, and, if Hungary did "not
wish to be expelled from among the respected nations," and because "national life without national language is unthinkable," it must create a national theater with "the participation of the nation." In 1836, motivated
by the goal of "advancement of the nation, the refinement of the language . . . and morality," the Hungarian reform parliament enacted a law
on the foundation of "a national theater to be erected in Pest." In August
1837, the Hungarian Theater of Pest, renamed the National Theater in
1840, was opened. As a symbolic message, the opening performance presented *Árpád's Awakening,* a play by Mihály Vörösmarty about the conqueror and founder of Hungary, Árpád (Senelick 1991, 285–86, 293, 296).
The Belgrade Theater similarly opened its doors with the historical play
Smrt Stefana Dečanskog (The Death of Stefan Dečanskog) in 1841. In 1834,
the Romanian Heliade-Rădulescu published an article in *Curierul Romá-*

nesc urging the "establishment of a national theater that will serve as a model to other peoples as well." In 1840, the Wallachian general assembly discussed a petition on a state-subsidized theater, but the Great Theater, with its thousand seats, was opened only in 1852 and renamed the National Theater in 1877 (ibid., 305–8).

During the same decades, similar movements advocated the foundation of national libraries and museums. In most cases, they were called "national": *országos* or *nemzeti* in Hungary; *narodna* in Serbia. As in the case of the national theaters, these libraries and museums were also established by the "nation," that is, through donations, including entire collections donated by enlightened aristocrats, such as the library and other collections of the Hungarian Ferenc Széchenyi. In many cases, nationwide fund-raising even financed the erection of the buildings.

Besides the institutions, the buildings themselves served the same mission and gained symbolic importance in strengthening national consciousness and confidence. Public buildings played an important role in mass education. This is equally true of the exalted, religiously symbolic gothic, the pompous baroque, and the nationalist romantic-eclectic. Architecture was one of the most influential art forms: accessible to all and visible every day in the centers of emerging capital cities. In nations unable to keep step with the rise of the West, the era of industrialization generated a special effort to imitate modernization. John Kenneth Galbraith has called this phenomenon, so typical of the nineteenth century, "symbolic modernization" (Galbraith 1964, 5). Public buildings best fulfilled the desire for symbolic modernization.

Monumental public buildings were constructed in the typical romantic neostyles: neoclassical and neorenaissance museum buildings housed treasures of the national past or collections of international art. The neorenaissance National Museum in Prague by Josef Schulz, the neoclassical Hungarian National Museum by Mihály Polláck (built in 1837–46), and the Museum of Fine Arts in Bucharest are excellent examples. The Atheneul Român (Romanian Atheneum) in Bucharest, designed by the French architect Albert Galleron and completed in 1888, is a typical romantic combination of a neoclassical façade, with six huge ionic columns, and a neorenaissance interior. Neorenaissance or eclectic opera houses such as the Paris Opéra, theaters, and public libraries (e.g., the Budapest Opera by Miklós Ybl and the Czech National Theater in Prague by Joseph Zitek, both in neorenaissance style, and the eclectic Biblioteca Centrala in Bucharest) attempted to elevate the stature of national culture. These public buildings became secular cathedrals of the nation.

Special mention should also be made of the completion of Saint Vitus's Cathedral in Prague. The cathedral, a genuine gothic work from the fourteenth and fifteenth centuries, had remained unfinished because of the Hussite wars. In 1859, a society was established for the completion of the building and work began in the 1870s. The concept was for a "re-gothicization" of the church, "a quite breathtaking piece of cultural hubris"—as Derek Sayer calls the neogothic plan. But the symbolic meaning of the enterprise was historical: "What testimony to the continuity of Czech identity could be more compelling than this realization of Charles IV's project after a five-hundred year hiatus? It triumphantly confirmed . . . that 'We were here before Austria, and look, here we are after it!'" (Sayer 1998, 180). The same can be said about the impressive, eclectic neogothic Hungarian parliament building (by Imre Steindl). Its dimensions alone were meant to communicate a clear message. It was the second-largest parliament building in Europe, next to the Houses of Parliament in London, at the end of the nineteenth century. Every passerby could decode the meaning: we are powerful, inferior to none.

Impressive new public buildings played a central role in rebuilding and modernizing capital cities that had evolved from small, traditional communities. The rebuilding of Bucharest, for example, carried a strong message, "We belong to Europe!" In the 1830s, the churches, dwellings, and public buildings along the main streets were those of an oriental Balkan town, as captured in Charles Doussault's lithographs. In the Romanian Principalities—as in the Balkans in general—gothic and Renaissance architecture did not exist. The dominant style was Ottoman-Byzantine. By the end of the century, however, Bucharest had become a European city. Romanians "started adopting the Western way of living, to assimilate aspects of civilization and cultural assets characteristic of . . . modern man," Vasile Florea observes. "Giving up the patriarchal forms of life of the Eastern type, people began to change even their houses" (Florea 1984, 12–13).

Monumental city halls and aristocratic palaces copying Versailles and Schönbrun were erected all over Central and Eastern Europe to express national grandeur. A series of neoclassical palaces—the Mycielski palace in Pepow, the Raczyński palace in Rogalin, the Lipski palace in Czerniejewo, and the Széchenyi, Esterházy, and Festetics palaces in Hungary— symbolized Polish and Hungarian noble power and tradition. The romantic arts and a passionate secular romantic national religion emerged and inspired the generations of early- and mid-nineteenth-century Central and Eastern Europe.

"Enlightened romanticism" fulfilled its mission and transferred the modern worldview of the West to the eastern half of Europe. A kind of romantic national religion was born, a strong, devout belief in self-sacrificing struggle for freedom and independence and for the rejuvenation and elevation of the ailing fatherland to Western standards by revolutions and radical reforms. The peoples of Central and Eastern Europe, as equal members of the family of European nations, wanted to join Europe. The national poet-musician-missionaries were no longer isolated, unknown eccentrics. They became celebrated, highly esteemed national prophets, often haloed with legendary fame. They began to influence a larger group of people, and their ideas gradually penetrated the intellectual-political elite, urban plebeian strata, and the youth.

SPREADING THE NATIONAL GOSPEL:
THE MEDIA AND THE COFFEEHOUSES

The propagandizing phase of the national movement increased the importance of the media. How could national prophets, a few dozen poets, artists, composers, and political thinkers, reach the public? Public buildings, published poems, books (usually several hundred copies), and drama performances displayed and disseminated their ideas, but definitely were not enough to mobilize a reform-oriented elite, much less the masses. Modern media were needed—dailies, magazines, calendars, and extensive correspondence—to reach thousands of households and tens of thousands of people. Meetings and gatherings in churches, clubs, saloons, and coffeehouses had an equally important role in facilitating public discourse. All these institutions were created around the turn of the nineteenth century.

Modern journals appeared in Central and Eastern Europe as early as the late eighteenth century. The very first Polish paper, Bishop Ignacy Krasicki's Warsaw weekly the *Monitor,* was first published in 1765, followed by *Zabawy* (1770–77), and *Pamietnik* (1782–92). Journalism gained major importance during the 1830s and 1840s (Kawyn 1953). Polish dailies, weeklies, and monthlies multiplied from 20 in the 1860s to 140 by the early twentieth century, diversified according to readers' interests. Illustrated magazines such as the *Biesiada Literacka, Bluszcz,* and *Tygodnik Ilustrowany* were highly popular. The latter, established in 1859, had a circulation of seven thousand, but reached twenty thousand by the early twentieth century. The daily *Kurier Warszawski* had a readership of 25,000 in 1896, while *Goniec* attracted 60,000 subscribers (Porter 2000, 77). "Despite their loss of independence," Alina Słomowsak observes, "Poles could read and think in national terms, not submitting to germanification or russification or other attempts at deracination" (Słomowska 1974, 12; see also Holmgren 1998, 151–52).

One of the first Hungarian biweeklies, published by Sámuel Szacsvay in Vienna, was the *Magyar Kurír* (1786). The first weekly, *Hazai Tudósítá-sok* (1806), which was published in Pest by István Kultsár, was followed by numerous journals and magazines. In 1801, only eight journals existed in the country. By 1830, there already were twenty-three, and in 1848, fifty-nine. Among them, modern political newspapers such as the liberal *Pesti Hírlap*, the conservative *Világ*, and the religious *Nemzeti Ujság* represented various political trends.

In the early nineteenth century, various Serb and Croat journals were published as well. Dimitrij Davidović's *Srbske Novine* was published in Vienna between 1814 and 1822. Nine hundred copies in all of this journal and *Šumadinka*, a women's magazine, were published in 1856. In that year, 138 foreign newspapers from various countries were sent to Serbia, as well as 600 newspapers in the Serbian language from Hungary and more than 200 papers in German. Altogether more foreign newspapers were sent to Serbia than were printed at home (Karanovich 1995, 181). A scholarly-literary journal, the *Srbske Letopis*, was founded in 1824, and the *Srbski Narodni List* in 1835. In 1834, Ljudevit Gaj published his *Novine Hrvatske* and *Danica*.

Journals also played an important role in informing the intellectual and political elite in the Romanian Principalities and Transylvania. Eliade Rădulescu's *Curierul Românesc*, Gheorghe Baritiu's *Gazeta de Transilvania* (1836), Zahari-Karkaleki's almanac and journal *Biblioteca Romaneasca*, Ion Barac's *Foaie de Dumineaca* and its rival the *Gazeta de Transylvania* (1838) all had a few hundred subscribers: the *Foaie*, for example, had 150, and the *Gazeta*, 800.

The first Bulgarian journal, *Ljuboslovie*, was founded in 1844 by Konstantin Fotinov in Smyrna, followed by Ivan Bogorov's *Balgarski Orel* in Leipzig in 1846. The *Balgarska dnevnica* (1857) appeared in Ujvidék (Novi Sad), Hungary. Some papers expressed the orientation and mission of the journal in their title, such as *Svoboda* (Freedom) and *Nezavisimost* (Independence). Altogether, sixty-six Bulgarian journals were founded before the liberation of the country, more than half of them in neighboring Romania.

Several hundred journals, with a circulation of a few thousand each, reached only the most involved and interested of the urban elite. The influence of these periodicals was, however, much broader than the mere number of their copies. A journal of which 800–900 copies were printed often reached tens of thousands of people. The information and message were in part orally transmitted and in part institutionally distributed. In various Balkan countries, *citaliste* (reading rooms) offered free access to the papers. A public reading place, *kasina,* was opened in Belgrade in 1843 in the most beautiful new building in the city, the Zdanije kod Jelena. In three years, the Srbsko čitalište u Beogradu (Serbian Reading Club in Belgrade) opened its doors. "Thanks and honor to those patriots who made possible the establishment of this very important institution," Maksim Simonović said in his opening speech. "We have made one step more toward European education." The reading club had, in the first year of its existence, 358 members, that is, 2.5 percent of the population of Belgrade in that year. The importance of these kinds of institutions is clearly expressed by the fact that the club had its own library, the first circulating library in Serbia, which, according to an order by the Ministry of Education, received a free copy of every book printed by the state Printing Office of the Principality. In 1847, the club published its own newspaper, the *Novine Čitališta Beogradskog* (Karanovich 1995, 179–83). In small Balkan villages, priests and teachers of the illiterate read newspapers aloud and discussed the important news.

Calendars probably played an even more important role in spreading information and communicating a specific worldview. Calendars surfaced in average households, even in remote villages, and for many families, they represented the only source of national literature and history. Short novels, patriotic historical studies, poems, and popular scholarly writings became very common and reached peasant families in this way. The Serb Vuk Karadžić published his views in his *Danica* pocketbook with a popular calendar (1826), and the Croat Antun Nagy's calendar appeared in 1818. The most important messengers of the Daco-Roman historical concept were the calendars that published parts of Petru Maior's work and spread the national gospel among Romanians. The patriotic poems of the Bulgarian Hristo Botev were published by *The Wall Calendar:* "Hadzhi Dimitar" in 1875, and "The Hanging of Vasil Levski" in 1876. The following lines from the latter poem were to be found in every home:

Oh my Mother, dear Motherland
Why weep you so mournfully, so plaintively?
Ah, I know—I know you're weeping, Mother
Because you are a dismal slave,
Because your holy voice, Mother

Is a helpless voice—a voice in the wilderness.
Weep! There, near the edge of Sofia town
Stretches—I saw it—a dismal gallows
And one of your sons, Bulgaria
Hangs from it with a terrible power.
                    (*Monumenta Bulgarica* 1996, 469)

Personal correspondence was also of major importance in this era. The Slovene Bartolomeus Kopitar, a pioneer linguist, and Josef Dobrovský, the "father" of the Czech language movement, corresponded for twenty years between 1808 and 1828. Liszt conducted a widespread correspondence with hundreds of people, as his ten thousand published letters prove, and Ferenc Kazinczy, the spiritual leader of Hungarian language reform and national literature, had an extensive correspondence with dozens of intellectuals from his home in remote Széphalom, which thus became a cultural center. In the early stages of the Albanian national movement, Naum Veqilharxhi reportedly circulated a letter in which "he pointed to the backwardness and misery of the Albanians as a result of long centuries of Turkish rule," and in 1844, he printed an eight-page Albanian spelling book, using a new thirty-three-letter Albanian alphabet he had invented (Elsie 1995, 213–14).

Besides printed journals and calendars, oral forms of preaching the national and enlightened gospel and a new scientific view on the universe also played an exceptional role. Various associations were founded and held regular meetings. The Czech Scholarly Association (1770), for example, cultivated the Czech language. Cultural associations also arose around newly established museums (in Brno in 1817, and in Prague in 1822), and knowledge of the Czech language was a prerequisite for membership. The Association of Friends of Science, which met twice a month for discussions, was established in Warsaw in 1800 and had 185 members by 1828. Bernolák established a Slovak scientific society in 1792, with various branch organizations and a correspondence service, and a Slovak literary association was launched in 1801. In Romania, a scientific society and a literary association were established in Iaşi in 1833 and 1843, respectively. A Bulgarian scientific society was founded in Istanbul in 1856. A Serb cultural association, Matica srpska, was established in 1826. The Croat *citaonica,* a reading association with a huge network of branches in Varasdin, Zagreb, and other places, was formed by Metel Osegović. The Slovak Jednota, under the enthusiastic leadership of Ludevit Štúr, held meetings twice a week to discuss literary, linguistic, and historical questions, began a collection of folk songs, and organized youth programs. Its "correspondence department" built up a huge information network. Similar organizations were founded in Lőcse (1832) and Késmárk (1838). Mlada Hrvatska was a Croat organization of the same kind. Freemasonry also offered an organizational network. Its importance was exhibited by the strength of the Polish organization, which had thirty-two local chapters and four thousand members.

Secret organizations were founded in Poland, Hungary, and Transylvania as well. The Association of Free Brothers, a Polish society in Vilna, with 200 members, was active in the second half of the 1840s. The Warsaw-based "Slav Unity," the Wrocław-based Polonia (1817–24) (Mościcki 1924), and V. M. Stefański's "Plebeian Association" (1842–43) also created a huge network throughout Poland. S. Goszczyński established a Polish folk association in 1835. The Hungarian Ignác Martinovics established the secret Association of Reformers and the Society of Freedom and Égalité in 1794 and recruited about 200–300 members. The number was not very great, but the cream of Hungarian intellectuals belonged to these secret societies. Adolf Dawid founded a secret organization in Transylvania to mobilize the Romanians for the creation of a united Romanian republic, sending emissaries to priests and teachers in the 1830s.

The coffeehouses of Warsaw, Prague, and, most of all, Budapest were among the most important public sources of information and a forum for the exchange of ideas, discussions, and even lecture series. The coffeehouse emerged as the new urban agora, a meeting place for intellectuals, young people, and the urban middle class. The 1848 Hungarian revolution started from the Pilvax Coffee House in Pest, where poets met and read their poems. Later in the century, Oktogon Square, with its various coffeehouses, some of them open twenty-four hours a day, and the New York Coffeehouse, a famous gathering place of writers and intellectuals, played a central role in intellectual-political life. The same was true of the Skadarlija neighborhood, around Ulica Skadarska in Belgrade, which resembled "a small Montmartre teeming with creative ferment" in the mid nineteenth century (Holton and Mihailovich 1988, 156–57). The *kahvehane,* the Balkan coffeehouses, traditional centers of male social life since the sixteenth century, played a similar role. Meeting and discussing the news of the world belonged to the mandatory everyday program of adult males.

Various urban clubs and aristocratic and bourgeois private salons also served as important institutions for cultural and political discourse. It is impossible to estimate the number of people who read papers, joined legal or secret societies, and gathered and discussed issues in coffeehouses and other public or private places. Most of the newspapers, however, had only a few hundred, or at best a few thousand, readers, and political associations and cultural organizations also generally attracted members in similar numbers. The number of culturally and politically active people certainly reached a few thousand in each country of the region, however, thus constituting a great and influential part of the cultural, political, and intellectual elite, especially among the urban youth.

The list of subscribers to the *Časopis Českého Musea,* the Bohemian Museum's influential national-oriented publication, and the list of donors to the Czech scholarly and scientific publication fund Matice česká offer unique information about the emerging patriotic vanguard in the Czech lands. According to Miroslaw Hroch's findings, roughly 2,800 patriots contributed to the above-mentioned national institutions between 1827 and 1848. Their number was 175 in 1830 and 1,135 in 1848. In the beginning, nearly 45 percent of the contributors were clergymen and nearly 9 percent noblemen, while another 27 percent belonged to other groups of educated people, such as teachers, students, and various kinds of officials. Less than 10 percent belonged to burgher and artisan groups. By the mid nineteenth century, the number not only increased significantly, but the social composition of the vanguard of patriots had also changed. The contingent of noblemen virtually disappeared, and the percentage of clergymen declined to 29 percent. The most significant change was the dramatic increase in the number of students (from 5 to 30 percent) and commoners—burghers, artisans, peasants, and workers (from less than 10 to more than 15 percent). The intelligentsia played the determinant role in the movement in the middle of the century, although 44 percent of the activists originated from merchant, artisan, and burgher families and 20 percent from peasant and worker families. The masses, including the peasantry, joined during and after the 1848 revolution and played an important role at a new stage of the national movement (Hroch 1985, 47, 53).

The institutional vehicles for spreading Western ideas and the concept of romantic nationalism helped mobilize the most influential sectors of society. The new ideas propelled a vanguard of revolutionaries and reformers into action and transformed the originally apolitical folkloristic and cultural movement into an actively political and often militant organization. An influential younger generation, intellectuals, and an important part of the cultural and political elite developed the will to form their people into a nation. Successful emotional indoctrination established a new loyalty: devotion to the nation. The modern, enlightened concept of nation, incorporating the entire population, including the peasantry, and the idea of equal citizenship emerged hand in hand with a new basis for self-identification. Peoples of the region began to feel that they were members of a mystic national community—a nation that demanded absolute and unquestioned loyalty. Nationalism, furthered by a strong emotional-romantic movement, thus arrived in the region before the nation actually was born. Although certainly "imagined," as Benedict Anderson suggests, it became very real once the notion took root. Nation-building became the central issue on the area's political agenda. During the second half of the nineteenth century, the national movement of Central and Eastern Europe entered into its third and most advanced stage—it became an organized and vigorous political movement capable of mobilizing the masses. East of the river Elbe, nationalism became the paramount driving force of modern history.

CHAPTER 3

UPRISINGS AND REFORMS

The Struggle for Independence and Modernization

THE WESTERN CHALLENGE AND EASTERN WESTERNIZERS

THE MODERN WESTERN ideals of freedom, liberty, and the independent nation-state gradually penetrated Central and Eastern Europe and sharpened the contrast between ideals and realities. Most of the countries of Europe experienced the frustration of remaining far behind the West in the early decades of the nineteenth century. Between 1800 and 1860, the Northwest European countries more than doubled their per capita gross national product—the most comprehensive parameter of the level of economic development. The Scandinavian and Mediterranean countries, as well as the Habsburg empire, however, increased their income level only by 40 percent. Russia and the Balkans experienced stagnation, achieving only a 10 percent increase, and many of the Balkan countries saw a drop in GNP. During the 1860s, all these countries, from Sweden and Spain to Poland and Bulgaria, remained almost unchanged in their traditional agrarian structure: between 70 to 85 percent of the labor force continued to work in agriculture.

While this caused continued landlessness, *robot* work on the big estates, illiteracy, suffering for the majority of the population, and humiliation for the minority intellectual elite and enlightened nobility, it also produced a strong mobilizing effect. The broadening gap in economic development challenged the slow-moving countries, causing a frightening feeling of stagnation, "backwardness," and even military danger, a fear of the final "extinction" of the nation, as romantic poets and desperate reformers often expressed it (see introduction and chapter 1).

These countries nevertheless had a path to follow. They could adopt Western ideas and copy the legal systems, laws, and institutions of the West. They could invite experts, court investors, import skilled workers, and buy modern technology.

The challenge of the West, meanwhile, offered tremendous opportunities as well. The nonindustrializing countries could enjoy the advantage of an ever-growing Western marketplace and export potential. The rapidly industrializing West was hungry for food and raw materials. Agrarian and raw material–producing countries could sell everything they produced; indeed, they were unable to deliver enough to the Western markets. Around 1830, 86 percent of British wheat and 92 percent of French wool imports came from agricultural Europe, which, in the 1870s delivered more than 20 percent of the world's food and raw material exports. During the nineteenth century, Britain increased its imports by nearly thirty-twofold. The imports of France and Germany increased by seven- and fourfold, respectively, between 1830 and 1914. In the late 1870s, nearly two-thirds of world trade consisted of food and raw materials (Kuznetz 1967). Meanwhile, more than two-thirds of world trade remained intra-European trade. In 1831, 86 percent of the wheat imported by Britain was from the European agricultural countries, and 78 percent of Holland's imports in 1880 came from Europe. World trade increased fiftyfold between 1750 and 1913, and ninefold during the sixty years between 1820 and 1880. The traditional division of labor was intensified and an unlimited market was opened for the agricultural countries. "The 'pull' of industrialized Western Europe . . . opened the way. . . to joining in world trade. . . . The old socio-economic conditions, however . . . presented some fundamental impediments to progress. . . . For . . . [answering the Western challenge], the *ancien régime* had to be destroyed. . . . The temptation to do so was extraordinary" (Berend and Ránki 1982, 25).

The enlightened Hungarian reformer István Széchenyi clearly expressed this recognition in his landmark book *Hitel* (Credit), published in 1830: "The annual wheat, rye, barley, and oat consumption of Britain is much more than 200 million Pozsony measures! Only 1.2 million is transported to the West between Buda and Pest on the Danube. . . . A bit more or less rain and starvation follows, such as in 1816 and 1817." "Hungary," Széchenyi wrote bitterly, "has no commerce, and the landowners are poorer than they should be. . . . Did we do enough to increase our output, improve its quality, and promote its marketing? Did we do our best to build connections with other nations? . . . We love harvesting but not plowing and sowing. . . . Many look down on commerce" (Széchenyi

1830, 131–32, 139–40, 155–56). Széchenyi became an initiator of social reforms attacking serfdom and advocated the introduction of modern
banking and credit systems, railroads, and food-processing factories.

The Western markets and the English model similarly attracted enlightened Polish aristocratic landowners. Dezydery Chłapowski, who, like
Széchenyi, traveled in England between 1811 and 1819, established his estate as a model modern farm. Andrzej Zamoyski, the founder of the Polish Agricultural Society in Warsaw in 1858, organized regular meetings at
his Klemenson estate in the mid 1840s, demonstrated modern plowing,
and held cattle shows (Trzecinkowski 1995, 147–49).

Count Camillo di Cavour, the leading Italian enlightened reformer,
clearly realized what the impact of the opening of Western markets would
be on the noble elite of the nonindustrialized countries when he wrote
in 1845: "The commercial revolution which is now taking place in England . . . will have a mighty impact on the Continent. By opening up
the richest market in the world to foodstuffs, it will encourage their production, the principal aim, that is, of all agricultural industries. . . . Trade
will then become an essential element in the prosperity of the agrarian
classes, who will then naturally tend to join the supporters of the liberal
system" (quoted by Mori 1975, 91–92).

Aristocratic conservative-reformer landowners, indeed, often became
supporters of the liberal system of the West, while enlightened priests,
radical intellectuals, and romantic poets and artists sought to follow the
French and English pattern of social, economic, and political modernization. They all were students of enlightened romanticism, shared in the
zeitgeist, and believed in progress and the possibility of changing history
by reforms from above and mobilizing the nation. The oppressive, antiquated Habsburg, Russian, and Ottoman empires, however, blocked the
road to change. In the Russian empire, the expression of progressive views
and "conspiracy" to realize them were sufficient "crimes" to warrant de-
portation to Siberia. Nearly 100,000 Poles had suffered that fate in occupied "Russian Poland" during the nineteenth century.

The peoples under Ottoman rule had no opportunity for realizing their
dreams through independent actions, and they remained shackled to the
most outmoded regime in Europe. Any attempt at revolt generated ruthless repercussions. Turkish garrisons kept Ottoman subjects in line. Two
British ladies who traveled throughout the Balkans during the 1860s
recorded: "Having noted down all we heard from the lips of the speak-
ers, and compared all accounts together, we must give it as our testimony . . . [that] Christians represented the native Mussulmans as op-

pressing, robbing, and insulting the rayah [non-Muslim subjects of the Ottoman empire]—for a rayah to be prosperous is to mark him out for destruction—thus industry is deterred and the country ruined" (Mackenzie and Irby 1867, 391).

Even the relatively more liberal Habsburg empire did not tolerate reforms that weakened the centralized regime. Although the Hungarians had limited autonomy and their noble Diet initiated halfhearted reforms during the 1830s and 1840s, most of these were rejected by the Habsburg king, who long resisted introducing Hungarian as an official language in the Hungarian kingdom and flatly refused to institute protective tariffs accepted by the Hungarian parliament in 1844 to promote industrial development in the country. The leading reformers were persecuted: intellectuals who sympathized with the French Revolution, such as the outstanding language reformer Ferenc Kazinczy and the "guardsman-poet" István Batsányi, were arrested and sentenced to long prison terms in the 1790s. Those who openly argued for freedom of speech, such as Baron Miklós Wesselényi and the radical reformers Lajos Kossuth and Mihály Táncsics, were all arrested and spent years in prison during the 1830s and 1840s.

Reforms and national independence thus became inseparable. Romantic national poetry, drama, music, and art successfully propagated the powerful message of freedom and equality. The oppressed peoples became ever more convinced that they had to gain back independence in order to realize their dreams, implement the ideas of the Enlightenment, introduce modern Western institutions, and create a modern economy and society. Their religious belief in historical progress tied nationalism and modernization to each other in Central and Eastern Europe.

THE POLISH UPRISINGS

Oppression and military arbitrariness often provoked spontaneous revolts, sometimes no more than unorganized eruptions of deep desperation by hopeless and humiliated peoples. The most steadfast resistance and agitated reaction to foreign domination were found in Poland, a medieval great power that had preserved its independence up to the early eighteenth century. The numerous Polish nobility, Poland's "political nation," proudly cultivated the "golden freedom" of their Rzeczpospolita, or "noble republic," and jealously guarded their economic, social, and political privileges. The Russian victory in the Great Northern War, however, ended an era and endangered Polish freedom: in 1717, Tsar Peter the Great gained the upper hand and imposed a Russian protectorate on Poland. "Under the Russian protectorate," Norman Davies writes, "the need for radical reform became ever more pressing; but the chances of achieving it became ever more remote" (Davies 1986, 306).

Eighteenth-century Poland was in a country in chaos. At his election, the powerless king of this "noble republic" had to sign a *pacta conventa* — "legalization of impotence," Hans Kohn called it — guaranteeing the right of the nobles to exercise the so-called *liberum veto,* permitting any member of the nobility to veto any legislation. A "formal legalization of anarchy . . . Polish liberty expressed itself not in patriotic integration, but in chaotic egotism. . . . In this chaos, tumult, and stagnation Poland had existed for so long that the conviction spread that Poland lived by disorder" (Kohn 1944, 519, 521).

In an attempt to protect the freedoms enjoyed by the nobles, the Confederation of Bar was formed in 1768 under the banner of the defense of Catholicism against Greek Orthodoxy and precipitated a bitter war against Russia, for which Poland was ill-prepared. The fighting lasted four years and ended with the first partition of Poland by the three neighboring powers, Russia, Prussia, and Austria, in 1772. This brutal awakening for the Poles generated a desperate attempt to modernize by the "four-year parliament" that convened in 1788. It culminated in the liberal constitution of May 1791, designed "to ensure the freedom of our motherland," according to its preamble. Although the constitution declared that all power was based on the will of the people, and that the members of the Sejm represented the entire nation, Poland's political regime preserved its traditional aristocratic character. Only the *szlachta* (nobility) were eligible to be members of the parliament, and political rights were restricted to those who owned real estate, which entitled burghers to participate in the political process but excluded landless gentry. Representatives of cities were only allowed to participate in the meetings, however, and had no voting rights. The serfs remained excluded from the political nation, and their conditions did not change. The only important concession granted to them was freedom of movement. The overwhelming power of the nobility was limited by the introduction of a hereditary constitutional monarchy, but the ruler's powers were further limited: he lost his right to ratify laws and appoint cabinet ministers. He was a member of the Senate but had only one vote. The crippling *liberum veto* was abolished, but decisions still required a two-thirds or four-fifths majority in the Sejm (Ring 2001, 187–90; *Materiały do dziejów sejmu Czteroletniego* 1955–69).

Even these limited reforms brought on a vicious reaction from the high nobility, who formed the Confederation of Targowce to invalidate the constitution and sought help from the tsar. Russia exploited the situation by sending in 100,000 troops, and a new partition of Poland followed. In 1793, the Polish Sejm, "protected" by Russian arms, approved this second partition and abolished the constitution, leading to a series of heroic uprisings and struggles for Polish independence.

The sequence of uprisings began on March 24, 1794, when the charismatic leader Tadeusz Kościuszko, who had been a volunteer in the American Revolution between 1776 and 1784, returned to Kraków. Instead of launching a noble insurrection, Kościuszko sought to mobilize the nation, including the urban population and peasants, formed a national militia, and proclaimed "national self-rule" and "general liberty."

By promising personal freedom and reduced labor service for the serfs in his Połaniec Proclamation, Kościuszko was able to mobilize a sizable peasant army, which defeated the Russians at Racławice on April 4. He could not, however, control the agitated masses. Revolutionary courts were established in Warsaw, and traitors were sentenced. The streets of Warsaw and Vilnius were occupied by the mob. In June, seven leaders of the Targowce conservatives were lynched. These public hangings frightened the nobility and weakened their resistance to foreign intervention. The way was open for a successful attack on Warsaw by the Prussians and Russians, which began on November 3, 1794 (Kowecki 1971).

A Prussian attack from the west was combined with a strong Russian strike by Field Marshal Suvorov from the east. On October 10, at Maciejowice, Kościuszko himself was wounded and captured. Suvorov's troops arrived in the Praga district of Warsaw, whose western sections were occupied by the Prussian army. The king was arrested and forced to abdicate. The captured leaders of the insurrection were executed or imprisoned in Russian, Prussian, and Austrian prisons (Kościuszko was freed two years later, however, by order of the Russian emperor Paul). A third partition of defeated Poland followed in 1795. The secret protocol of the Treaty of St. Petersburg stated that the "high contracting parties" agreed to "abolish everything which could revive the memory of the existence of the Kingdom of Poland . . . [which] will remain suppressed as from the present and forever" (quoted in Davies 1996, 722). Most of Poland— 62 percent of its territory, with 45 percent of the population—was incorporated into the Russian empire. Prussia occupied the western part of the country, roughly 20 percent, with 23 percent of the population, and Austria, the third victor, acquired Galicia, the southern 18 percent of Poland, with 32 percent of its population.

All these Polish territories became districts and provinces of the occupying powers. Lwów, renamed Lemberg, became the headquarters of the Austrian governor's office. Wawel, the historic royal palace of Kraków, was occupied by an Austrian garrison. German settlers arrived in Prussian Poland, where confiscated land was sold to Prussian Junkers. Poznań, renamed Posen, was germanized, and the Prussian army recruited Polish peasants for twenty-year service. The occupied eastern territories of the Polish kingdom, regarded as ancient Russian land, were organized as the western *guberniia,* or administrative district, of the empire. Polish peasants had to serve twenty-five years of military service in the Russian army. Each of the great powers introduced its own legal system. Poland, as Hugo Kołłątaj said and many Poles believed, "ceased to belong to actually existing nations." The legend was born that the wounded Kościuszko had cried, "Finis Poloniae!" when he fell from his horse.

Within two years, however, a Polish legion of 6,000 troops had been formed in Lombardy to fight for revolutionary France under the command of General Jan Henryk Dąbrowski, one of the military leaders of the defeated uprising. Generals Józef Zajączek and Karol Kniaziewicz formed Italian and Danubian legions. The spirit of struggle was kept alive. In 1806, the Polish legions participated in Napoleon's campaign and entered Warsaw. The next year, 40,000 Polish troops were fighting against Russia and Prussia under Napoleon's leadership: a kind of Polish state, the duchy of Warsaw, was created. The "Marseillaise" of Dąbrowski's Polish legion, the legendary marching song that later became the Polish national anthem, began with the famous words: "Poland is not yet lost as long as we live" (Wandycz 1974, 22–23).

Romantic Polish nationalism became a secular religion. Inspired by Adam Mickiewicz's popular national drama *Dziady,* a great many Poles espoused "sacred suffering on earth" and self-sacrifice for the national cause. They learned from the character of Konrad the poet to challenge even God, calling Him a "tsar" when He allowed suffering and injustice. Over the course of nearly three-quarters of a century, between 1794 and 1864, romantic Polish self-sacrificing heroism led to the organization of Polish legions abroad and illegal secret societies at home. Each generation triggered a new uprising.

The summer and fall of 1830 were pregnant with new revolutionary attempts: on July 28, Paris took the lead again, and, on October 14, Belgian independence was declared. This inspired the Polish revolutionary patriots to mobilize, and, on November 29, a group of conspirators set out to kill Grand Duke Constantin, the brother of Tsar Nicholas, and disarm the Russian garrison. Although their plan failed, the spontaneous formation of a national militia and a series of skirmishes liberated Warsaw, and the grand duke evacuated the country with his troops. A new chapter was opened in the Polish struggle for independence. The Polish army numbered 38,000 troops at the beginning, one-tenth of the Russian army in the country. The Sejm and the national government, appointed by the Sejm, assumed leadership in mid-December, and General Józef Chlopicki, the "dictator" of the insurrection, recruited peasants into the national army, increasing the number of troops to 57,000 by February and 85,000 by March. The ratio between the Polish and Russian armies changed from 1:10 to 1:2. The readiness to fight against the Russians increased after Field Marshal Ivan Diebitch's troops neared Warsaw in late January. The Polish army halted the Russians at Stoczek and Grochów. On January 25, the Sejm dethroned Tsar Nicholas from the Polish throne. The Polish nobility intensified the war of national independence. The uprising spread to Lithuania in March, and the rebels gained control over the entire province, except the big cities. The Polish offensive was successful in April and May.

Most of the military leaders of the uprising did not, however, believe in the possibility of a final victory. The five-member national government, headed by Prince Jerzy Adam Czartoryski, was divided between two conservatives and two liberals, while the fifth member, the left-wing Joachim Lelewel, was isolated. Both Czartoryski and the majority of the Sejm supported the national uprising but opposed social revolution and rejected the radical social reform advocated by the Left. While the national struggle went its extreme radical way, social revolution did not accompany it. The uprising, consequently, remained a struggle between the Polish nobility and the Russian tsar, especially in Lithuania and the Ukrainian provinces, where the local peasantry was strongly anti-*szlachta* and anti-Polish.

Radicalization in the summer of 1831 led to rioting in Warsaw, where a mob attacked the royal castle, killing noblemen and generals. The leadership of the uprising became even more uncertain and lost its anti-Russian radicalism. Czartoryski escaped from the capital, and General Jan Stefan Krukowiecki took over the government and army. Although the Polish forces were almost intact, Krukowiecki did not resist a new Russian offensive under General Ivan Paskievich in early September 1831, and the Russians surrounded Warsaw, ending the second uprising.

In the repression that followed, the Polish noble elite was virtually decimated. Seeking to avert further uprisings, the victorious Russians deported some 80,000 Poles to Siberia. From Lithuania and Podolia alone, more than 50,000 Polish gentry were deported. The 1815 constitution was suspended and replaced by an "Organic Statute" (1832). Poland became a part of the Russian empire. Viceroy Count Ivan Fyodorovich Paskevich Erivansky instituted a harsh dictatorship. Education, transportation, all domestic Polish issues were directed by Moscow. The Polish army was immediately disbanded; youths were recruited into the Russian army and sent to the Caucasus. Russification began: the Russian monetary system (1841), criminal code (1847), and weights and measures (1849) were introduced. Poland became a part of the Russian tariff system (1851), and Russian became the official language (1864). The institution of viceroy was replaced by that of governor-general (as in other provinces), and the country was governed as the western *guberniia* of the empire (Izdebski 1995, 83). The russification process was especially strong in the Lithuanian and Ukrainian parts of the former Polish-Lithuanian kingdom.

The most active part of the Polish elite left the defeated country, mostly for France. The roughly 9,000 Polish émigrés, two-thirds of them members of the *szlachta,* represented most of the political and intellectual elite of the country. The "national bards," including Mickiewicz, Chopin, political leaders such as Czartoryski and Lelewel, and military leaders such as General Josef Bem, all left Poland to serve the Polish national cause from abroad.

Some of them learned the lessons of failure. Mickiewicz describes the hunting, feasting, parasitic world of the Polish nobility in his epic poem *Pan Tadeusz* (1834), whose hero liberates his serfs, unlike the real Polish nobility. Romantic poets advocated the modern concept of the nation, opposing the traditional Polish political nation of the nobility. The Left went much further to promote social radicalization of the revolution. The Polish Democratic Society (1832) announced a program of equality of the nobility and peasantry and the need to emancipate the latter. The society sought to transform the "military insurrection into a social revolution" (Brock 1977, 7). Emigrant soldiers founded the General Assembly of the Polish Emigration in London and stated in their *Akt wiary* (Declaration of Faith) in September 1834: "The sovereignty of the people is unlimited. . . . The people are infallible in their judgments and in their demands" (ibid., 10).

A radical revolutionary left wing went even further: Stanisław Worcell and Kazimierz Alexander Pułaski, for example, established the Gmina Londonska (London Commune), the "first conscious populist [movement] of Eastern Europe," in Peter Brock's words. They declared property to be "at the center of all evil which oppresses mankind at present," quoting Rousseau, and demanded a "dictatorship of the people" with "equality of property for all" (Brock 1977, 11, 17, 27).

Conservative nationalists, led by Czartoryski, dreamed, however, of an international intervention against Russia and carried on an enormous diplomatic activity from their Paris headquarters, the Hotel Lambert. Mickiewicz advocated the formation of a Polish legion and even traveled to Turkey to organize one. The majority of the Polish nobility, however, blinded by their "tribal myth," were convinced that Poland was the "defender of Europe," which was accordingly in the debt of the Poles. Not only independence but also a culture enabling it to face reality were lacking in Poland, Jerzy Jedlicki argues (Jedlicki 1999, 35, 45, 223).

Conspiratorial activity never stopped at home. Captain Szymon Konarski, an émigré emissary, established a network of underground organizations, the Zwiazek Ludu Polskiego. The center of national activity was shifted to Poznania and Galicia under the relatively less oppressive Prussian and Austrian regimes. In 1845, the Poznań Central Committee decided to launch a new uprising in late February 1846. The plan, however, was reported to the Prussian authorities, and the leaders of the conspiracy were arrested. An uprising nevertheless took place in Kraków, where about six thousand people joined and sought to mobilize the peasants. The Galician Polish peasantry, however, not without incentives from the Austrian authorities, turned against the Polish nobility. In certain districts, the majority of the manors were looted and burned and landed nobility killed. Nearly two thousand noble estates and families were affected. This failed attempt at a new uprising clearly exhibited the deep social conflicts in Polish society and the *szlachta*'s lack of understanding of social problems and their connection to the national cause.

Romantic Polish nationalism was not characterized by rational self-control. Successive generations continued the heroic but hopeless struggle for the liberation of Poland. Although the liberal Left continued to promote social emancipation of the peasants, radicalization still characterized only the national movement. A new underground national government was established, called the National Central Committee. It even collected a voluntary "national tax" in preparation for a new insurrection in 1862. On January 6, 1863, the European correspondent of the *New York Tribune* reported: "A great conspiracy is hatching in Poland which has its ramification everywhere there are Poles. An outbreak is expected" (quoted in Coleman 1934, 6). The committee decided to take the plunge without serious military preparation and proclaimed an uprising when the Russians and the puppet Polish government initiated the military conscription of twenty thousand Poles in January 1863. It rapidly recruited about six thousand volunteers, who attacked Russian garrisons and troops, but the struggle was hopeless from the start. Most of the Western world was convinced that it was actually counterproductive. Horace Greeley, editor of the *New York Tribune,* wrote: "Great and universal as the sympathy of the civilized world with the wrongs inflicted upon unhappy Poland is, the recent insurrection will be almost unanimously regretted. . . . This new outbreak, we greatly fear, will postpone the realization of the ardent national wish" (quoted in ibid., 12–13). Unlike the previous insurrections, the January uprising remained a partisan war, although militarily quite successful: fighting continued for nearly a year and a half. An underground state apparatus was set up, including a police force. However, several factors contributed to eventual defeat: military operations remained uncoordinated, Lithuania and Ukraine were not mobilized, and the peasants remained hostile to the nobility.

The historical turning point occurred in February 1864. The Russian tsar seemingly learned the historical lessons better than the Polish nobility and granted ownership rights to first the Lithuanian, then the Ukrainian and Belarusian peasantry by mid 1863. The tsar ordered preparations for major reform and the liberation of serfs in Poland in the fall of the same year. The emancipation decree was announced on February 1864. Paradoxically, the archconservative Russian empire thus played the peasant card against the Polish *szlachta,* isolated it from the peasant masses, and undermined the Polish national cause. In spite of impressive peasant participation and the mobilization of about 200,000 volunteers, the number of Polish troops actually fighting never exceeded 30,000. An overpowering Russian army, led by General Fedor Berg, proclaimed victory in May 1864. Skirmishes continued, however, until the last "dictator" of the insurrection, Romuald Traugutt, failed in his attempt to reorganize the Polish partisan army in October 1864 and was captured and hanged. The uprising, hopeless from the very beginning, finally collapsed.

FROM REVOLT TO "ORGANIC WORK"

Despite the fact that romantic heroism kept the national cause alive, Poland paid a very high price for these national revolts. As a consequence of repeated defeats, however, reason gained ground over emotion, and the majority of the Polish elite gradually realized the need for radical socioeconomic change. Romantic nationalism, which had fueled the uprisings, was slowly rejected. The poet-philosopher Cyprian Norwid, who had been ten years old during the 1830–31 uprising, and, as a young adult, drew his lessons from 1848, turned against Polish romantic messianism and, in a letter to General Jan Skrzynecki, called Mickiewicz "horrible for Poland" and denounced his "mystical heroic deeds." Norwid's *Promethidion* clearly expressed the ideas of a new generation:

> not the Tartar deed, a blood-stained bridge
> Thrown on a scaffold glowing with flames
> But daily work by love relieved
> Until the toil of toils is achieved.

Creative work to civilize the nation could lead to real progress, making martyrdom unnecessary, Norwid said. He accused romantic nationalism of being harmful and counterproductive. Poland "is a nation which is undeniably great as far as *patriotism* is concerned but which *as a society* represents nothing. . . . We are *no society* at all. We are a great national banner." Polish nationalism, in his view, served to "identify nations with tribes. Such a notion can bring us back to the barbarian hordes. . . . This is a return . . . from nationhood to tribalism." In his "The Annihilation of the Nation," Norwid argued that the Polish "unjustified [national] religion" destroyed all secular ideas (Walicki [1982] 1994, 320–32).

Norwid did not have a strong influence during his uncompromising spiritual struggle between 1848 and 1882. His ideas, however, gradually gained ground. Realizing that they had "learned how to die magnificently but never knew how to live rationally," the post-uprising generations began to value the "heroism of reasonable life," Piotr Wandycz observes (Wandycz 1974, 207). The Polish "political nation" was ready to radicalize the national struggle over more than a half century but remained blind to the need for social revolution. After repeated defeat, however, they opened a new chapter in the nation's history and started nation-building the other way around: a new concept of "organic work," or political, cultural, and economic modernization, emerged.

The leader of the Poznań "organic camp," Karol Marcinkowski, declared as early as 1842: "Education and work . . . these are the means for paving the path we seek." Continuous conspiracy and insurrections had proved as disastrous in the nineteenth century as the *liberum veto* had been in Poland before the partitions, the Galician Polish historian Józef Szujski observed in 1867. "Conspiracy is absolutely unjustified. Only normal organic work is justifiable today" (quoted in Blejwas 1984, 45). National ideas remained the prime mover of Polish politics, but in a different way. Instead of hopeless romantic uprisings, a pragmatic approach to nation-building emerged: Poles had to realize, said the Kraków newspaper *Czas*

(Time), that France's defeat by the Prussians at Sedan "should put an end to all hallucinations which for the past hundred years have cost so much blood and sacrifice . . . [it] decidedly put an end to a policy based on the West" (ibid., 76).

These were the years when Warsaw positivism emerged in the short-lived Central School. The deep disillusionment of the post-insurrection years and the influence of Auguste Comte's empirical method led to the emergence of an influential intellectual group. "The most immediate task of national work is not spreading ideas," Józef Supiński, one of the founding fathers of the movement, said in an article in *Pisma*. "Our task is the formation and education of our society. . . establishment of reading rooms and schools, the improvement of moral and material well-being. . . . [These] provide a hundred times greater guarantee for the future, than political societies" (quoted in Blejwas 1984, 73–74). Supiński used the term *praca organiczna* (organic work), which became the leading slogan and goal of Polish positivism for half a century. Heroic messianism was replaced by sober realism (Ratajczak 1992). As the spiritual leader of the positivists, Alexander Świętochwski, put it in 1873, what was required was "work at the foundations." Rejecting uprisings and foreign intervention, he declared: "It is necessary to create happiness and well-being" through commerce, industry, and agriculture (Blejwas 1984, 94). Świętochwski, Bolesław Prus, Henryk Sienkiewicz, and other influential writers and scholars strongly and successfully advocated these ideas after the devastating defeat of 1864. As Świętochwski argued in his *Political Directions* (1882): "Dreams of regaining external freedom should today be replaced with efforts to acquire an internal independence. Such an independence can stem solely from a strengthening of mental and material forces, a comprehensive national progress, linked to general development and democratization of social life." He spoke of "industrial and trade conquests" rather than military victory (Trzeciakowski 1995, 144–46).

Bolesław Prus published his novel *Lalka* (The Doll) in 1890 to propagate positivist ideas. In it, he attacked the high-living, do-nothing Polish aristocracy, with their national standard of misbehavior. Poland was burdened with antiquated values: "[L]abor stands in the pillory, and depravity triumphs! He who makes a fortune is called a miser, a skinflint, a parvenu," says Wokulski, the hero, in one of his monologues, "he who wastes money is called generous, disinterested, open-handed. . . . [S]implicity is eccentric, economy is shameful." Wokulski, a veteran of the 1863 uprising, comes from an impoverished gentry family. He becomes a successful businessman, because he can "modulate his Polishness in order to do good business." He still cultivates noble habits, buying horses and fighting duels, but in his constant monologues, he struggles against these bad traditions: "[A]m I doing all this, I who despise it?" His business dealings are motivated by romanticism and altruism, but he has to make money because it is "the sole instrument for achieving his ideals" (Holmgren 1998, 70–74, 77, 80–84).

"The cultural and economic resources of the Polish nation were as yet too underdeveloped to sustain an independent state," the Warsaw positivists believed (Davies 1986, 170). The Filomat (Philomathés) group in Lithuania and the Stańczyk group in Kraków shared the new rational approach toward nation-building through industrialization, railroad construction, trade, and urbanization. A half century of peaceful modernization followed in Poland.

Industrial development and cultural and social modernization gradually transformed the country. It took decades for the peasantry to be incorporated into the national camp at the end of the nineteenth century. The tragic abyss that separated the noble and peasant societies, however, was not properly bridged until World War I. The peasants in Wladyslaw Reymont's tale remain suspicious: "[I]t hath been so from all time: the gentry rebel and drive our folk to ruin . . . who has to pay, when payday comes? What are the people in their eyes. . . . If they had their way, serfdom would be restored tomorrow! Let the nobles tear each other to pieces: 'tis no affair of ours" (Reymont 1925, 4: 181–82).

Wincenty Witos, one of the founders of the Polish peasant party Piast, confirms Reymont's account in his memoirs: "The majority of the peasants were very concerned, fearing that once the Polish state was restored, back would come serfdom and the total enslavement to the nobles" (Witos 1964, 132). Stanisław Grabski maintained that the peasantry had been won over to the cause of fighting for independence at the end of the nineteenth century in the Polish kingdom, and between 1905 and 1914 in Galicia (Molenda 1991, 125, 130).

THE PEACEFUL CZECH NATIONAL MOVEMENT

Although close neighbors of the Poles, the Czech people acted in a totally different way. After Bohemia and Moravia were incorporated into the Habsburg empire, following the bloody defeat of the Czechs in the Battle of the White Mountain in 1620, and reduced to little more than a province of Austria, the native nobility, the Czech "political nation," ceased to exist. The Czech "revolutionaries" of the mid nineteenth century consequently had only limited goals and did not demand national independence. On March 11, 1848, motivated by the French and Italian revolutions of the previous weeks, the Czech elite, led by the moderate liberal intelligentsia, gathered at Saint Wenceslas Hall in Prague and received petitions aiming at the reestablishment of the *Staatsrecht*—that is, the independent legal status of the Czech kingdom under the Habsburg monarch. They demanded free contract between the king and the nation, equal status for the Czech language in schools and government offices, and limited self-government for the confederated Czech lands of Bohemia, Moravia, and Silesia. After the Vienna and Pest-Buda revolutions, which followed within the week, equal status for the Czech language in public life and the establishment of self-government in cooperation with the Czech National Committee formed at the Saint Wenceslas gathering were promised on April 8. The peaceful Czech rebellion soon failed, however. Within three months, a military dictatorship was established under an Austrian general, Prince Alfred Windischgrätz. There was no resistance. No one took to the streets and built barricades. The Czech demands were dismissed and buried for decades. The "revolution" was over.

The Czech attitude was diametrically opposed to the emotional heroism of the Poles. First of all, the Czech "political nation" equivalent to the Polish szlachta had been entirely eliminated after 1620, and a new Austro-Czech aristocratic landowning political elite had been created in its place. The lands of the annihilated landowning class were confiscated and given to Austrian clients of the emperor. The new aristocracy, such as Prince Schwarzenberg and Counts Chotek, Sternberg, and Kinský, were all Austro-Bohemians. The lower nobility, the gentry, the real body of the "political nation"—so important in the Polish case—totally disappeared (Melville 1998). No wonder neither the old nor the new Czech political elite sought national independence.

The romantic Czech poets, scholars, intellectuals, and other members of the emerging urban middle class who launched the Czech national movement were typically moderate. František Palacký and František Rieger, its acknowledged leaders, understood the geopolitical dimensions of their struggle. Although they wanted to be rid of Austrian oppression, they also worried about German expansionism. The year 1848 was the highpoint of decades of the German movement for national unification. The *Grossdeutsch* concept of a united Germany included the Czech lands as future parts of the German empire. Palacký and the leaders of the Czech movement accordingly decided not to participate in the Frankfurt provisional *Vorparlament,* and also boycotted the elections to the Constituent Assembly in Frankfurt.

The anti-German trend was strengthened by the fear of the substantial German minority in the Czech lands. German nationalism among Bohemian Germans developed in parallel with Czech nationalism and stood in opposition to it. In August 1848, the Bohemian German Congress in Teplitz initiated the idea of the partition of Bohemia into Czech and German parts. This initiative was, in a way, an answer to the pan-Slav idea expressed by the first pan-Slav congress, which gathered in Prague in June 1848. Although Palacký and the Czech political leaders were rather cautious regarding an unqualified unification of the "Slav nation," they advocated an Austro-Slav concept. Austria, in their view, was a crucially important bastion against German expansionism, but it had to be reorganized to assure equal rights for the Slav nations. A riot on June 12, during the meetings of the congress, initiated by Czech radicals like Josef Frič, was easily suppressed by imperial troops and made Vienna more steadfast in rejecting any Czech demands. When the Reichsrat met in Vienna and then in Kremsier in the summer and fall of 1848, Palacký gave up the idea of constitutionally unified Czech lands of Bohemia, Moravia, and Silesia, but demanded cultural autonomy and an autonomous legal status for all of them. In January 1849, he suggested the creation of a Czech unit within the monarchy, based on ethnic principles, consisting of the Czech-populated areas of Bohemia and Moravia (without the German-populated territories), together with Slovak territories from Hungary. A harsh and despotic Habsburg resistance crushed all of these attempts, however, and a new absolutist regime was introduced. The New Year's Eve patent of 1851 and the Alexander Bach regime from April 1852 on continued a ruthless germanization. Even the most minimal Czech language demands were flatly rejected.

Although it was never conceptualized by a Czech movement, paradoxically enough, Czech "organic work" in economic, social, and cultural modernization advanced strikingly during these decades. The Czech lands, politically and administratively subordinated provinces of Austria without any kind of cultural or political autonomy, flourished economically and culturally. The Czech provinces achieved by far the highest level of economic advancement in Central and Eastern Europe. Rapid and successful industrialization, social modernization, and the highest literacy rate in the region made the Czech lands more similar to the West than any other part of it. In other words, Bohemia and Moravia profited a great deal from being a hereditary province of the Habsburg empire and as a consequence enjoyed an equal status with Austria proper.

Rapid economic progress certainly contributed to the further failure of Czech national demands during the 1860s and 1870s. The boycott of the imperial Diet and Reichsrat in 1867 in favor of the reestablishment of the *státní právo,* or a *Rechtsstaat,* that is, equal legal-political status with Hungary, was again rejected. The Bohemian Declaration of August 1868 that renewed this demand generated mass rallies of support around the country. The imperial cabinet of Count Karl Hohenwart was ready to accept the concept of a "trialist" reorganization of the empire and granted cultural autonomy to the Czech people, although not equal status with Hungary, in the fall of 1871. Emperor Franz Josef, a hard-nosed defender of Austro-Hungarian "dualism," rejected the "trialist" Austro-Hungarian-Slav concept, however, and dismissed the Hohenwart cabinet. The Bohemian and Moravian representatives in the imperial Diet renewed their boycott of it. As before, such passive resistance was ineffective. It did not shake the empire, and the prosperous Czech provinces were not ready for violence. The Moravian Czechs gave up the boycott in 1873, and a split in the Czech national movement in September 1874 led to the reentry of the "Young Czechs," a newly organized National Liberal party, into parliament. In the fall of 1878, even the "Old Czech" National party joined. The peaceful Czech national movement lost momentum and dried up for several decades. "Organic work" nevertheless became more vigorous and successful than ever.

THE "AGE OF REFORMS" AND THE HUNGARIAN REVOLUTION

Around 1800, at a time when the Polish "political nation" was fighting for its liberty, and before the Czech mass movement had begun, the Hungarian noble elite embarked on its own long journey toward national independence and social reform. At the outset, these two goals were not combined, but opposed to each other. The Hungarian nobility, like the Polish *szlachta,* had set out to safeguard its own "golden freedom," provoked by the reforms in the 1780s of the emperor Joseph II, an enlightened absolutist ruler seeking to adjust to a revolutionary era (Marie-Antoinette was his sister).

What most irritated the Hungarian nobles was the abolition of serfdom. Although this did not affect personal service in labor, kind, or money, it allowed free migration, choice of obligation, marriage, and the elimination of noble patrimonial jurisdiction in criminal cases. Noble tax exemptions were not eliminated, but the nobility nonetheless felt its dominance threatened. Joseph planned to destroy its institutional fortress, the medieval county *(comitat)* organization, and replace it with ten administrative districts under royal commissioners.

The Hungarian nobility counterattacked, exploiting the centralizing and germanizing attempts of the Habsburg monarch, whom they accused of violating the traditional agreement by rejecting his oath to the Hungarian constitution, refusing to be officially crowned with the Hungarian crown, and ruling by royal edict without the Hungarian Diet. The Language Decree of 1784 made the German language compulsory in public offices and required Hungarian officials to learn it within three years (Kann 1974).

The nobility passionately proclaimed Hungarian national interests and organized national resistance, with the result that the dying Joseph II had to withdraw all of his reforms but three on January 28, 1790. Latin was reestablished as the official language of legislation and higher education, while county administrations used Hungarian. A noble-national movement emerged, led by the lower nobility. Peter ócsai-Balogh, a member of the seven-member court, drafted and circulated a constitution. Its point of departure was the broken agreement between monarch and "people." The rhetoric used the terms of Rousseau's Social Contract but translated "people," "popular sovereignty," and "national liberty" as the equivalents of nobility, noble rights, and freedom. Because of the unlawful rule of Joseph II, ócsai-Balogh announced a *filum successionis interruptum,* or interruption of succession, and declared the need for a new agreement. Hungary's king, he maintained, had to swear to govern lawfully before his coronation.

The draft clearly expressed the demands of the nobility: Hungary was an independent country, not subordinate to any other. A foreign army could not be stationed on its territory. Its administration was independent of that of the other parts of the empire. Decisions relating to war and peace were the exclusive right of the Diet. Legislation was the exclusive right of the "people," that is, the noble Diet. The king had veto power only once, but not in the case of a second resolution of the Diet. The "people" were also part of the executive power and controlled the king. Matters of state would be conducted by a senate, elected by the Diet, consisting of representatives of the lower nobility. The Diet sat every year, and its sessions could be delayed by its members, but not by the king (Mérei 1983, 49–50).

The Diet, which opened in June 1790, attempted to imitate the French Constitutional Assembly, and the delegates took an oath not to leave without a new constitution. A royal agent sent an agitated report to Vienna and warned: "A similar revolution to the French may erupt in Hungary" (Marczali 1888, 542). Nothing similar happened, however. In the summer of 1790, Leopold II, the younger brother of Joseph II and the new king of Hungary, took command, made an agreement with Prussia, and stabilized his power. He then mobilized the Hungarian peasantry against their lords, scared the "traitors" with imprisonment, and rejected all the radical demands of the Hungarian nobility, including official use of the Hungarian language. In the end, the Diet happily accepted a few concessions, such as the legal acceptance of Hungarian independence, stating that the country was "not subordinated to any other country and has its own laws and rules." The most important concession was that the monarch and the Diet had to enact legislation jointly. Hungarian language teaching was also introduced in schools (*Magyar Törvénytár* 1901).

While the nobility promoted the national cause in its own interests, Hungarian radical intellectuals who had originally espoused Joseph's reforms adopted the ideas of the French Revolution. Secret societies were established in May 1794 to achieve their revolutionary goals, but by the summer, all of the conspirators had been arrested. Within a year, their leaders, Ignác Martinovics, József Hajnóczy, Ferenc Szentmarjay, and other Hungarian "Jacobins" had been publicly executed in Buda, while others were handed down brutal prison sentences. The Habsburg empire, especially under Francis I, became a police state, with strict censorship and the suppression of any liberal-enlightened views.

The national and social causes coincided again, however, in the "Age of Reforms," during the Hungarian *Vormärz* (the 1830s and 1840s, the decades before the revolution of March 15, 1848). Linguistic nationalism and the romantic ideas spread throughout the public. Celebrated poets and artists fueled an increasingly powerful national movement. The first half of the nineteenth century, nevertheless, remained a period of permanent surrender for the Hungarian nobility and a slow inching toward minor reforms. The realization of the demand for Hungarian as the only official language of legislation and in the courts took several decades. In 1826, the Diet still demanded bilingual legislation, but the monarch allowed only the translation of laws into Magyar, Latin alone being accepted for the official text. Hungarian became the sole official language of the Diet and legislation only in 1844.

The Diet called for equal status for Hungary in trade within the monarchy, but the king rejected this at the beginning of the century. In 1841, influenced by Friedrich List, the Diet decided to introduce a Hungarian protective tariff against Austrian competition advocated by Lajos Kossuth, but the king denied its right to decide upon the issue. Kossuth initiated a social movement to promote Hungarian industrial products. The members of the established Honi Védegylet (founded in 1844), an association for protecting domestic markets, volunteered not to buy foreign merchandise and "introduce the tariff at their own threshold." The results were only partially successful, but the national idea slowly became imbued in the majority of the population, the Védegylet became a sort of national political party, and a strong national mass political movement emerged from it (Kosáry 1942).

Social legislation was similarly slow and even less conclusive. The Diet did grant peasants the right to dispose of their property at will in 1833; in the mid 1830s, the majority of the nobility rejected a proposal that remission of feudal dues be permitted by free agreement between landlord and peasant, as well as legislation initiated by the liberal lower nobility on personal freedom and property rights for the serfs. In 1836 and 1840, in the most radical reform during this period, remission was finally made possible by the *önkéntes örökváltság,* a mutual agreement between landlord and serf, and the more well-to-do peasants (mostly on the Great Hungarian Plain) liberated themselves and became owners of the land they cultivated. Small measures limiting the privileges of the nobility were also considered breakthroughs: tax exemption was suspended for the lesser nobles known as *bocskoros,* and, albeit largely of symbolic importance, nobles were subjected to the toll on the new Chain Bridge spanning the Danube between Buda and Pest. The need for general and proportionate taxation and equal rights to hold public office was discussed, but no measures to this effect were accepted or introduced.

The establishment remained intact, but the way of thinking about it radically changed. The pioneering works of Count István Széchenyi and Baron Miklós Wesselényi harshly criticized the outdated institution of serfdom. Széchenyi maintained that the productivity of wage labor was three times higher than that of serf labor. He convincingly proved that noble privileges were also counterproductive, since, among other things, they created an insurmountable barrier to the introduction of a modern credit system, a prerequisite of agricultural modernization. The burning agitation of Lajos Kossuth molded public opinion and mobilized a large segment of society in favor of the national cause and reform.

True, not only were the more radical demands rejected by the upper nobility and the royal court, but radical reformers such as Baron Miklós Wesselényi and Lajos Kossuth were tried and imprisoned for years in 1839. It took a long time for the lower nobility to recognize the need for more radical social reform. The nobility could not alone realize the badly needed reforms, Kossuth wrote in an editorial in his journal, entitled "Disappointment," in the winter of 1843. Sterile disputes, unproductive sessions of the parliament, and partial results characterized the "Age of Reforms" in Hungary. The clear recognition of the importance of basic social reforms and economic modernization nonetheless took root. Moreover, a strong and enthusiastic political camp was formed, which continued the struggle for change. Only a spark was needed for a real revolutionary explosion, and it was provided by the new revolutionary wave in Europe in 1848.

The news of the Paris revolution mobilized the hesitant Hungarian Diet, which hurriedly accepted the recommendation of Kossuth on March 3 and proclaimed the full emancipation of the serfs, who became owners of the *urbarial* plots, nearly 20 percent of the cultivated land. The landlords received compensation from the state. Compensation for another roughly 20 percent of the land was paid by the liberated peasants themselves. About 60 percent of the peasants, however, were liberated without land or with an unviable fraction of a parcel, and the noble landowning class preserved its monopoly over nearly half of the land in the country. In a few days, the radicalized program of the revolutionary "Opposition Circle" demanded freedom of the press, civil rights, proportional taxation, jury trials, and the total elimination of feudal institutions. Its "Twelve Points" demanded the establishment of an independent, representative Hungarian government and a national guard.

The revolutionary crowd took over the streets of Pest and Buda on March 15: the poet Sándor Petőfi, with 5,000 people, occupied the printing house of Landerer and Heckenast and, rejecting censorship, printed the first products of the independent press: Petőfi's "Nemzeti Dal" ("National Song") and the "Twelve Points." An increasing crowd of 10,000, later burgeoning to 16,000 people, gathered in front of the National Museum. Petőfi, who had recited his powerful "Nemzeti Dal" standing on a table in the Pilvax Café in Pest two days before, now addressed it to the assembled crowd from the steps of the National Museum:

> Rise up, Magyar, the country calls!
> It is "now or never" what fate befalls . . .
> Shall we live as slaves or free men?
> That is the question—choose your "Amen"!
> God of Hungarians, we swear unto Thee,
> We swear unto Thee—that slaves we shall no longer be!
>
> (Makkai 1996, 319)

The crowd echoed the last two lines, the refrain, six times. The date was March 15, 1848. The Hungarian revolution had begun.

A victorious revolution led to the formation of the first independent government of Count Lajos Batthány with the leading liberal noble reformers, Lajos Kossuth, István Széchenyi, József Eötvös, and Ferenc Deák. The frightened King Ferdinand sanctioned the revolutionary legislation of thirty-one articles on April 11. Feudal despotism had come to an end in Hungary.

Although the liberal lower nobility were ready to sacrifice their privileges and liberate the serfs, they were unable to go any further when it came to the land question, the remaining feudal services, such as the vine tithe, and the continued existence of the guilds and their political dominance. The franchise, decided by the parliament, excluded roughly 93 percent of the population and, consequently, the first "democratic" elections in June elected a "postfeudal" parliament: only one-tenth of the delegates belonged to the revolutionary Left, which urged more radical social legislation, while 72 percent of the elected delegates belonged to the landowning noble class. Although in April and May, local peasant uprisings and seizures of estates clearly expressed the mass demand for more radical legislation, the Kossuth-led lower nobility were basically unable to go further down the road—making only minor compromises—and turned against the mass movements. Kossuth flatly told the parliament on December 14, 1848: "Everybody who agitates against the nobility . . . is the enemy of the nation! Stirring up the people over the problem of some pasture lands or anything else . . . at this time means weakening the forces we need to defend our fatherland" (Spira 1987, 284–85).

In contrast, they were ready to go to the most radical extreme on the road of national revolution to confront the Habsburgs, mobilizing a revolutionary army against the Austrian military offensive. The Diet rejected the newly appointed commander in chief, General Count Franz von Lamberg, and when he arrived in Pest, an agitated mob lynched him. The Hungarian revolution soon turned against the Habsburg monarchy, provoked by the abdication of the somewhat mentally retarded Ferdinand on December 2, 1848, prompted by General Windischgrätz, because Ferdinand had made compromises in recognizing Hungary's revolutionary government and legislation in 1848 and was bound by his word. On January 7, the Hungarian parliament declared that it would not recognize the new Habsburg monarch, Ferdinand's eighteen-year-old nephew, Franz Josef I, until he was legally crowned and had taken his oath to the Hungarian constitution and the April Laws. This did not happen, and on

April 14, 1849, the Diet declared Hungary's independence and dethroned the Habsburg monarch. Lajos Kossuth was elected governor-president.

After having been invaded in the fall, the country launched a life-or-death military struggle against Austria. The government mobilized all available resources, printed paper money, exactly like revolutionary France, and recruited peasants into the national army, which, after Windischgrätz's initial military successes, recovered the entire country. The Hungarian revolution became the most radical and important episode of the European revolutions of 1848. "The European revolutionaries hailed the Hungarians as the Revolutionary nation par excellence" (Talmon 1960, 484).

NATIONAL MINORITIES AND THE HUNGARIAN REVOLUTION

The Hungarian radical nationalist lower nobility were unable, however, to understand that all of the nationalities of the Hungarian kingdom, Croats, Romanians, Slovaks, Serbs, and others, altogether 46 percent of the population, had similar national goals and demanded the same national rights as the Hungarians. The nationalist gentry were blinded by their national ambitions and did not recognize the existence of independent Croat and Romanian nationalities within the kingdom. They forced the various ethnic minorities to magyarize, as Kossuth had advocated in his *Pesti Hírlap,* and as the Diet's language legislation had promoted in the 1840s. Confrontation was unavoidable. Croats and Transylvanian Romanians, awakened by their romantic language reformers and national bards, revolted first.

As early as March 25, 1848, provoked by revolutionary Hungarian legislation that virtually incorporated Croatia into Hungary, Ljudevit Gaj's Croatian National party elected a "Provisional National Board." A mass meeting in Zagreb endorsed a petition demanding national independence, including an independent government, responsible only to the Croat Sobor, which was elected in May and held its first session in June. From the outset, the Sobor denied the legality of the laws of the Hungarian parliament in Croatia. Baron Josip Jelačić, newly appointed *ban* of Croatia by the emperor Ferdinand, set up an interim government, and rejected directives from Hungary. The unification of ethnically Croatian provinces thus created an administratively Greater Croatia. The Croat national movement intended to gain equal rights with the Hungarians and federalize the monarchy. However, Kossuth and the Hungarian parliament were not ready for major compromises, and Jelašić occupied Rijeka at the end of August and attacked Hungary with 40,000 troops on September 11.

A declaration, then a law (Article VII.1848), on union with Transylvania passed by the Hungarian Diet prompted an immediate response from Transylvanian Romanians. A meeting on April 24, initiated by Avram Iancu, called on all Romanians to protest and demand full equality. On May 15, a mass meeting of 40,000 in Blaj (Balázsfalva) rejected union with Hungary and adopted the slogan "Nimic despre noi fara noi!" ("No decision about us without us!"). The proclamation reformulated the famous *Supplex Libellus Valachorum* of 1791, asking the emperor, the "Great Prince of Transylvania," to grant equal national rights to the "fourth recognized nation," the Romanians of Transylvania.

Stimulated by the Transylvanian Romanian national movement, a revolutionary committee in Bucharest also announced its program and elected a cabinet that included the Golescu brothers, Nicolae Bălcescu, and Maria Rosetti on June 23, 1848. A crowd attacked and occupied the palace in Bucharest, with a death toll of seven. A Romanian revolution was in the making, and the dream of a greater Romania, among other ill-defined concepts, such as a Danube confederation and an enlarged Habsburg monarchy, seemed to be a possibility (Bodea 1998). Bucharest was, however, occupied by 20,000 Turkish troops. A Russian invasion followed, and the tsar's troops remained in the Principalities until 1851. The revolutionary attempts were defeated, and the Habsburg emperor remained the only hope of the Transylvanian Romanians. Bishop Şaguna submitted a proposal to the emperor at Olmütz in February 1849 on the "union of all Romanians in the Austrian state as a single independent nation under the scepter of Austria, and as an integral part of the Monarchy" (Seton-Watson [1934] 1963, 286). Transylvanian Romanians joined the emperor's war against the Hungarian revolution. Avram Iancu organized fifteen peasant legions, massacred Hungarians in Zalatna and Körösbánya, and burned the famous Bethlen Library in Nagyenyed.

The Slovak and Serb national minorities in Hungary also mobilized and rebelled. In the name of the Slovak nation, a group of national leaders, led by Ludevit Štúr and Josef Hurban, gathered in Liptovsky Mikulás (Liptószentmiklós) and ratified a petition to the emperor calling for an autonomous Slovakia with its own parliament, language, and educational system. The Slovak delegation participated at the pan-Slav meeting in Prague in June 1848, and several Slovak nationalists preferred the Austro-Slav idea of forming a separate Slovak grand duchy or Czecho-Slovak crown land within the Habsburg monarchy. After failed negotiations, a

FIGURE 24. Ukrainian and Jewish musicians in Austria-Hungary.
Courtesy Néprajzi Múzeum, Budapest.

FIGURE 25. A German couple in Transylvania (1910). Courtesy Országos Széchenyi Könyvtár, Budapest.

FIGURE 26. A Romanian couple in Transylvania (1910). Courtesy Országos Széchenyi Könyvtár, Budapest.

FIGURE 27. The beginnings of social mobility: the first lawyer (far left) from a well-to-do Hungarian peasant-handicraft family. Courtesy Hungarian National Museum, Budapest.

FIGURE 28. The beginnings of social mobility: laborers in Hódmezővásárhely, 1905. Courtesy Magyar Nemzeti Galéria, Budapest.

FIGURE 29. A Gypsy settlement in the woods. Courtesy Hungarian National Museum, Budapest.

FIGURE 30. Gypsy woman with pipe. Courtesy Néprajzi Múzeum, Budapest.

FIGURE 31. W. Komin-
szko, *Polish Jew Mending a
Carpet*. Courtesy Muzeum
Narodowe w Krakowie,
Kraków.

FIGURE 32. J. F. Piwarski,
*Jewish Moneylenders in
Early Nineteenth-Century
Poland*. Courtesy Muzeum
Narodowe w Krakowie,
Kraków.

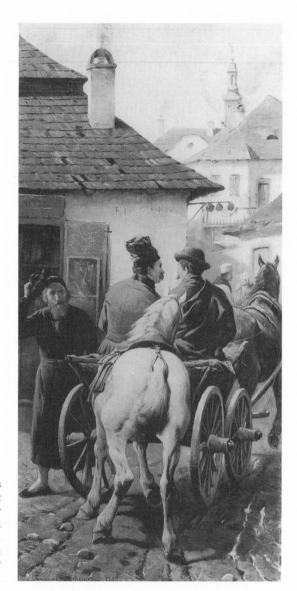

FIGURE 33. Poles and Jews. Zygmunt Ajdukiewicz, *Going to Town*. Oil on cardboard (1885). Courtesy Muzeum Narodowe w Warszawie, Warsaw.

FIGURE 34. Nicolae Grigorescu, *Jew with Goose*. Oil on canvas. Courtesy Muzeul National de Artă al României, Bucharest.

FIGURE 35. Zsigmond
Kornfeld, a Jewish member of
the Hungarian upper house,
1905. Courtesy Országos
Széchenyi Könyvtár,
Budapest.

FIGURE 36. Hassidic Jew in
the Hungarian countryside,
1900. Courtesy Néprajzi
Múzeum, Budapest.

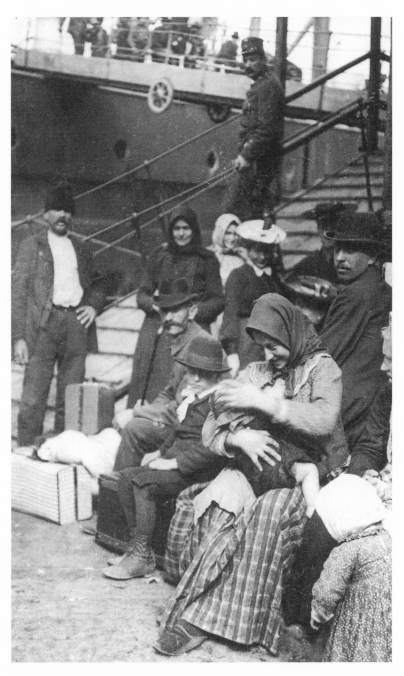

FIGURE 37. Austro-Hungarian emigrants at Rijeka, 1903. Courtesy Hungarian National Museum, Budapest.

FIGURE 38. Nicolae Vermont, *Romanian Emigrants*. Oil on canvas.
Courtesy Muzeul National de Artă al României, Bucharest.

Slovak National Council was organized, as well as military detachments, which launched three military campaigns against the revolutionary Hungarian army between September 1848 and the summer of 1849.

The Serb National Church Council also announced a sixteen-point political program in Novi Sad (Ujvidék) on March 27, 1848. On May 13, the Skupstina gathered in Sremski Karlovci (Karlovác) and declared the independence of the "Nation of Hungarian Serbs" under the emperor's rule. Their delegates, who adhered to the romantic "Illyrian" concept of South Slavic unity, arrived in Zagreb at the end of May, where they proposed a federal union of the Voivodina with Croatia. A quasi-government called the Glavni Odbor was formed, and a sizable armed force was recruited from among Serb peasant-soldiers of the military borderland, under the command of George Stratimirović. More than 10,000 partisans, led by Stefan Kničanin, joined from Serbia and attacked Hungary. On June 12, 1848, skirmishes—a "little war"—began.

The Hungarian liberal nationalists offered a broad range of human and personal liberties, but exhibited a biased assimilationist, state-nationalistic view and denied the existence of any nation in Hungary but the Hungarians. "I will never ever recognize anything other than [the] Hungarian nation and nationality under the Hungarian crown," Kossuth proclaimed to the Diet. "I know people . . . who speak other languages, but we do not have more than one nation here" (Spira 1987, 164). He was ready to fight those who did not accept this. "The sword will decide between us," he told Stratimirović when the latter made it clear that the Serbs were ready to turn to Austria for their rights (Kapper 1851).

The multinational Habsburg monarchy offered an outstanding opportunity to *divide et impera*. As a contemporary joke went: "The Austrian emperor made an alliance with the Croat king and attacked the Hungarian king." All three were, of course, one and the same person, Franz Josef I, the Habsburg emperor, king of Hungary and Croatia. The Croat, Serb, Romanian, and Slovak national revolutions in Hungary turned against the Hungarian national revolution when it became clear that their demands had all been rejected. All of these nationalities had the same aspirations as the Hungarians, but the nationalist Hungarian noble elite did not recognize their rights and regarded them as part of the Hungarian nation. A desperate suggestion from the radical Left to federalize Hungary did not gain ground, and the vain attempt to conclude an alliance—Kossuth reached agreement with the Romanian revolutionary Bălcescu on July 14, 1849—proved in vain. A proposed Danube confederation with the ethnic minorities went against the zeitgeist: it was too little, too late.

The revolutionary Hungarian army, however, was victorious, recapturing the entire country and even unsuccessfully attacking Vienna. General Windischgrätz, commander of the Austrian army, attacked from the west. Franz Josef asked for military help from Tsar Nicholas I, and Russian troops invaded Hungary from the east in June. The Hungarian army was, at last, defeated and surrounded on August 13, 1849. Former prime minister Lajos Batthány was executed, along with thirteen generals of the revolutionary army. Thousands more were imprisoned. Kossuth and many others escaped the country. An absolutist Habsburg dictatorship followed, but all the revolutionary laws, including the emancipation of the peasants and the elimination of feudal institutions, were confirmed by a royal decree of March 1853. The nationalities that had joined the emperor in defeating revolutionary Hungary, as contemporary Hungarians noted with satisfaction, got as a reward what the Hungarians received as punishment. Their political movements and struggles for autonomy or independence were also defeated.

After being defeated by Prussia in 1866, a weakened Austria reached a compromise with the passively resistant but exhausted Hungarian noble elite. The Austro-Hungarian Agreement, or *Ausgleich,* of 1867 recognized a great part of the Hungarian national demands and granted far-reaching autonomy to Hungary within the framework of a modernized "dualistic" Austro-Hungarian empire. The Hungarian elite was able to preserve its rule over the nationalities, nearly half of the population of the country, and the Habsburgs saved the monarchy and their rule over Hungary.

FROM THE BROTHERHOOD OF NATIONS
TO EXCLUSIVE, HOSTILE NATIONALISM

The Central and Eastern European national movements reached their zenith in 1848: the heroic Hungarian revolution and the Polish, Czech, Slovak, Romanian, Croat, Slovene, and Hungarian-Serb struggles signaled the turning point from a national educational-propaganda program led by enlightened nobles and an intellectual elite to a modern mass political movement. The military defeat of the uprisings of 1848 could not save the multinational empires but only prolonged their existence by a few decades. The future of independent nation-states was clearly heralded.

At this turning point, the national movements not only permeated entire nations and mobilized huge masses but acquired new characteristics. Early nationalism had meant a euphoric unification of the entire people.

Commoners and proletarians were promoted to equal citizenship and become inseparable parts of the nation, which because of the natural "brotherhood of nations" served mankind, a universalism expressed in the Polish national slogan "For our freedom and yours." "[S]olidarity within one nation," as Jacob Talmon put it, "would be extended to members of other nations. . . . Liberated nation-churches would combine into the Church universal" (Talmon 1960, 30).

In 1848, and during the second half of the nineteenth century, however, European nationalism lost these early, deeply democratic and universalist revolutionary traits. Nationalism was henceforth socially conservative and exclusive. The concept of the nation was often used against the social demands of the lower strata of society. Rulers and governments "nationalized" nationalism for their own benefit. The nation became the "center of loyalty" for the entire society, supplying "a framework of a more concrete and tangible nature than the airy heavenly cities of the world proletariat or liberated humanity. National brotherhood makes class differences irrelevant. We all fulfill ourselves in the nation" (Talmon 1960, 513–14).

The burgher middle class, which had been in the vanguard of democratic nationalism in earlier decades, now shifted to the conservative camp. Frightened by the awakened masses, the burghers ceased struggling against the ruling noble elite. They wanted rule, and turned against the dissatisfied, often organized and violent workers and peasants. The French revolution of 1848, which triggered the revolutionary wave of that year, clearly exhibited this dilemma of the revolutionary liberals. Already during the revolutionary euphoria of the February days, 12,000 people demanded the "abolishment of the exploitation of man by man" and the establishment of an "organization of labor." In the mid nineteenth century, "pauperism was the key issue of the age," and many were convinced that the "revolution will not be complete without the solution of the social question (Talmon 1960, 427, 455). Moreover, February was followed rather soon by June, when the "slave war," the uprising of the "new barbarians," the workers and urban mob, shocked Paris and frightened the propertied classes. The bloody repression of the class war "had immense repercussions all over Europe. In February, Paris gave the sign to begin the revolution; in June it provided an example of the way to liquidate it" (ibid., 174).

The German bourgeoisie, already frightened by the possibility of a social revolution before it revolted against the establishment and attempted to unite Germany, made its compromise in advance and placed itself behind the protective shield of the absolutist Prussian state and noble army. The Polish and Hungarian political nations never forgot to preserve their own "historical rights" and sought to keep control of the lower social groups, which often equated with continued domination of peasants of Ukrainian, Lithuanian, Romanian, Slovak, and other nationalities.

A switch from early universalism, deep solidarity, and the "brotherhood" of nations characterized the conservative, isolationist turn of European nationalism. The idea of the liberation of an oppressed nation helping liberate others was replaced by exclusive nationalism. Solidarity was replaced by rivalry and malice. Feelings of brotherhood gave way to xenophobic attitudes. As Konstanty Wzdulski, a pioneer of Polish anti-Semitism, phrased it, "the idea of brotherhood is a false idea . . . it has brought those societies which believe in it not gains, but losses" (Porter 2000, 166). This transformation was also connected with the "nationalization" of nationalism—that is, the manipulation and use of national feelings by governments as a weapon of *Machtpolitik* in mobilizing the nation against rival nations and scapegoated minorities.

These negative trends of nationalism emerged in 1848 all over Europe. During the "Spring of Nations," the year of thirteen European revolutions, the new forces not only bitterly attacked the establishment, but also, for first time in history, often turned against each other. In spite of universalist rhetoric on the Italian and, most of all, Polish questions, Alphonse de Lamartine, the leader of the French revolution and minister of foreign affairs, in his manifesto to Europe in March 1848, made it clear that France "comes before every other consideration." He added in May that France's "most sacred" relations with the Poles were also the "most remote and most impossible," for which France must not sacrifice her interests. "We love Poland, we love Italy, we love all the oppressed peoples, but we love France before all," he said (Talmon 1960, 473, 478). The German national struggle for unification collided head-on with the Danish and Polish national demands in Schleswig-Holstein and Poznania, respectively. The revolutionary Frankfurt parliament declared that all German-speaking people belonged to the German nation irrespective of the state in which they lived. This was a declaration of war against some neighboring countries and also a denial of Polish and other national demands in mixed-population areas. Moreover, the German revolution did not hesitate to declare a preference for "Germany's own security" and, for "healthy *Volksegoismus*," sending troops against the Danes and the Poles. The Frankfurt parliament thus clearly demonstrated that German nationalists rejected Polish nationalists' attempts to realize identical national goals.

Austrian revolutionaries dealt Metternich's regime a deadly blow but simultaneously opposed the Czech, Hungarian, and Italian national movements. Czechs nurtured pan-Slav compassion, toyed with the idea of unifying the Slavs, and felt scant sympathy for Hungarian national goals. Moreover, in proposing the unification of the Czechs and the Slovaks, Palacký, the leader of the Czech national movement, did not address the national ambitions of the Slovaks, whom he regarded as Czechs. The Poles, while emphatically opposed to Russian, German, and Austrian domination, considered Polish dominance of Ukrainians "natural." To the Hungarians, it was likewise "natural" to preserve their rule over the Romanian minority in Hungary and Transylvania, and over the Croats in subordinated Croatia. All of the nationalities of the Hungarian kingdom realized that Hungarians strongly opposed their national goals.

German, Austrian, Polish, and Hungarian assimilationist nationalism concerning peoples who lived within their states was no different from that of the West, where British and French "melting pots" amalgamated and assimilated various peoples into one single nation. They simply sought to follow the same pattern. However, it turned out to be impossible in the nineteenth century, when national consciousness emerged and nationalism became a leading trend. Nations in revolt and minority nationalities demanded their own nation-building rights. If need be, they turned against oppressors who were themselves fighting their own oppressors. Ukrainians turned against Poles, just as Croats, Slovaks, Serbs, and Romanians turned against the Hungarian revolution and, hoping to promote their own national goals, assisted the Habsburg counterrevolution.

Nationalist movements emerged all over the region and mobilized even small national groupings that wanted to establish an independent nationality. A typical example was the case of the Ruthenians (Ukrainians) in Galicia, a former province of Poland with a mixed Polish and Ruthenian population. In East Galicia, however, 70 percent of the population was Ruthenian, and this part of Galicia became the cradle of "South Ruthenian" nationalism. Here, as everywhere in Central and Eastern Europe, the national movement began as a linguistic, cultural-intellectual program. Ivan Mohylnytsky argued in his "Discourse on the Ruthenian Language" (1829) that Ukrainian was a separate branch of the Slavic languages, equal to Polish, Russian, and Czech, "just as the Ruthenian nation is equal to the other Slavic nations." During the 1830s and 1840s, Ivan Vahylevych in *Rozprawy o jezyku poludnioworuskim* (1843) spoke about a separate "South Rus" language, as did Josyf Levytsky, who published a grammar of *Galizian ruthenischen Sprache* in 1834.

Many Galician-Ruthenian nationalists considered Ukrainians to be one nation, separated into two empires. Levytsky spoke in 1831 of Ukrainians forming one nation, 5 million of whom lived in Russia, while 1.9 and 0.5 million lived in Galicia and Hungary, respectively. Bishop Iakhymovych and the Eastern Orthodox hierarchy, however, "inclined to regard the local [Galician] Ruthenians as a separate nation, different from their kinsmen in the east" (Kozik 1986, 33, 85, 111–12, 163).

In October 1848, the Holovna Rada Ruska, the national organization of the Galician Ruthenians, sent a memorandum to the Austrian minister of the interior demanding the partition of Galicia: "Poles and Ruthenians, it is clear, cannot live together in peace. The partition of Galicia is a vital issue for the Ruthenians" (Kozik 1986, 265). The Galician Poles, who gained autonomy from Vienna in 1867, reacted to Ruthenian nationalism much as the Hungarian elite did to minority nationalism in Hungarian lands when they tried to force an assimilation of Ruthenians into the Polish nation. A few enlightened Polish nobles, such as Prince Jerzy Lubomirski, argued "against a repetition of the Magyars' errors" (ibid., 334).

Nationalisms confronted one another sharply, and a "national hangover" followed the revolutionary euphoria of 1848. Xenophobic hatred and confrontation of nationalisms became stronger and stronger in Central and Eastern Europe. Romanian and Polish nationalism grew anti-Semitic. In Romania, successive governments refused to grant Jews citizenship. In late nineteenth-century Poland, a strong anti-Semitic movement equated Judaism with a mortal threat to the Polish nation.

Was such xenophobia specific to Central and Eastern Europe? "[T]he deep differences existing between the two parts of Europe . . . produced different types of nationalism—one based upon liberal middle-class concepts and the consummation of a democratic world society, the other based upon irrational and pre-enlightened concepts and tending towards exclusiveness," Hans Kohn maintains, comparing Western and Eastern nationalisms in Europe (Kohn 1944, 457).

In the Western world . . . the rise of nationalism was a predominantly political occurrence [that was] preceded by the formation of the future national states. . . . In Central and Eastern Europe . . . the frontiers of an existing state and of a rising nationality rarely coincided; nationalism, there, grew in protest against and in conflict with the existing state pattern—not primarily to transform it into a people's state, but to redraw the political boundaries in conformity with ethnographic demands. . . . [In Germany and Central and Eastern Europe] the political integration around a rational goal [in the West] was replaced by a mystical integration around the irrational, pre-civilized folk concept. [Romantic nationalism was in] violent opposition . . . to the liberal and humanitarian character of [the] nationalism of 1776 and 1789. (Kohn 1944, 329, 351–52)

Hysterical xenophobia indeed became more characteristic of the be-lated national movements of the "belt of mixed population" than in the West, which established its nation-states in an earlier period, based on a much luckier history of nation-building. In the West, István Bibó has ar-gued, peoples conquered existing states, democratizing the previously ex-clusive nation of nobles. In Central and Eastern Europe, most of the en-ergy of national movements went into destroying existing multinational imperial states. The difference between historical states and ethnic borders generated hostile relations among nationalities living together. While de-mocracy was the main vehicle of Western nationalism, it became danger-ous for the elites of the majority groups in Central and Eastern Europe. Democracy endangered national communities and strengthened separat-ism. Rising Eastern nationalism thus became genuinely antidemocratic (Bibó 1986, 191–94, 215–19).

The contrast between Western and Eastern nationalism, however, was only partly an optical illusion. French, British, and other types of West-ern nationalism also lost their early liberal humanitarian, universalist char-acteristics and turned against each other in the harsh rivalry for colonies and spheres of interest. European self-confidence and the "missionary" enterprise to enslave "uncivilized" peoples had already been condemned by Herder in his *Adrastea* (1802). Western nationalist ideology, however, became an agent of national rivalry and imperialism a few decades later during the last third of the nineteenth century. Western national self-confidence and strong belief in cultural superiority and the "white man's civilizing mission" was not better, only different, sometimes more hyp-ocritical, than its Eastern petty xenophobic counterpart. True, the West did have a great period of humanitarian and universalist nationalism around the turn of the eighteenth century. Central and Eastern Europe emerged later on the road of nation-building and reached the climax of their national development in a period when a more controversial phase of European nationalism began.

FROM RELIGIOUS TO NATIONAL
CONSCIOUSNESS IN THE BALKANS

The Balkans presents an even more specific version of nationalism and nation-building. The "national" struggle began there, paradoxically enough, well before national consciousness was born. Under Ottoman rule and in a chaotic, unorganized oppression by local warlords and robber janissary bands, spontaneous local wars erupted. Armed self-defense spread like wildfire from the early 1800s on and characterized nearly the entire century. This struggle did not in the beginning have a national character, since the Slavic peoples of the Balkans lived in a theocracy and identified themselves as Christians under Muslim rule. The armed struggle, however, soon generated strong national feelings and belated nation-building efforts.

The Balkan crisis did not, however, remain local. The rising national goals and struggles in the Balkans immediately met with cynical great power aspirations. Russia, France, Britain, and Austria all had expansionist ambitions and wanted to counterbalance one another's advances. They all wanted to gain control over the Bosporus, which was a strategic entrance to the Black Sea and exit to the Mediterranean for Russia and also for the Balkans; a passage to the Near East for Germany; a strategic base to the rear of the German states and Austria-Hungary for France; and a natural zone of expansion for Austria-Hungary. Direct great power intervention thus accompanied the national awakening in the area and helped it mature, but also subordinated the national struggle to *Machtpolitik*.

Unlike in Central Europe, where a series of doomed national struggles followed in succession, the Balkan crisis led to national sovereignty. The Balkan peoples achieved their independence and established their nation-states in the late nineteenth century, at an early stage of their national development. The window of opportunity for gaining independence was opened by the decline of the Ottoman empire, which had dominated the area for nearly five hundred years. The rigid prefeudal empire, with its extremely centralized military regime and lack of private property, began disintegrating after losing its expansionist dynamism. The turning point, which closed the era of Ottoman conquest, was the Treaty of Karlowitz in 1699. The European counteroffensive forced the Porte to withdraw and reform, generating a crisis situation during the eighteenth century. The crisis culminated in the first three-quarters of the nineteenth century. As Alexis de Tocqueville clearly recognized, "it often happens that when a people, which has put up with an oppressive rule over a long period without protest suddenly finds the government relaxing its pressure, it takes up arms against it, . . . experience teaching us that, generally speaking, the most perilous moment for a bad government is one when it seeks to mend its ways. . . . Patiently endured so long as it seemed beyond redress, a grievance comes to appear intolerable once the possibility of removing it crosses men's minds. . . . At the height of its power feudalism did not inspire so much hatred as it did on the eve of its eclipse" (Tocqueville [1856] 1978, 176–77).

The most visible sign of Ottoman decline was the progressive disintegration of the central administration. The almighty Sultan, absolute ruler and sole "owner" of all the land of the vast empire, lost control over the majority of his domain. Selim III, who rose to power in the year of the French Revolution, recognized the need for action and aimed to restore central power, but insurgent janissaries assassinated him in 1808. His successor, Mahmud II, controlled only two provinces out of the twenty-six administrative units of his empire. Local warlords, such as Ali Pasha at Ioannina in Greece and Osvan Pasvan-Oglu in Bulgaria, respectively, governed nearly the whole of the Balkans unchecked. The demoralized janissary army of 20,000–30,000 soldiers declined into an insubordinate bandit force, which brutally robbed the population, killed those who attempted to resist, and revolted against the Sultan in 1808 and in 1826, when he sought to regain control over it.

Mahmud II, the third ruler in just over a year, during the most chaotic and bloody power struggle in Ottoman history, defeated the rebels in 1826, and gradually recentralized the empire. His military reforms created a modern army and the era of disintegration and chaotic terrorism ended. Reestablished central power paved the way for reforms in the following decades. In November 1839, Sultan Abdul Mejid signed and issued a reform, the Hatti Sherif (royal mandate) of Gulhané, followed by a series of measures, commonly called the Tanzimat reforms, prepared by the Westernizing statesman Reshid Mustafa. The state administration was modernized, and new penal codes, borrowed and modified from the French system (first in 1840, then in 1858), granted equal status to all subjects, including Christians. A new commercial code was also adopted from the French system (1850).

In connection with the Treaty of Paris in 1856, which rearranged European power relations and recognized the Ottoman empire as a European partner, the Sultan issued a new reform edict, the Hatti Humayun, in February 1856, granting more autonomy to his subjects. As one of the six ethno-religious units of the Ottoman empire, the Rum-millet ("Roman nation"), which included all the Christian peoples of the Balkans, was given significant self-government under five Greek Orthodox metropolitans. Unlike the Catholic Church, "Greek Orthodoxy" was not centralized but organized along "state" lines: the Romanian, Serb, and Bulgarian Orthodox Churches were independent. The last two had actually originally been subordinated to the patriarch of Constantinople, and thus placed under Greek ecclesiastical control, but they became independent in 1831 and 1870, respectively. "These 'autocephalous' churches differ in administration, language, customs, historical legacy, and outlook," Michael Petrovich observes, maintaining that the Orthodox churches in the Balkans "acted as a surrogate state for the people who had lost political independence" (Petrovich 1980, 373, 384). "The whole tradition of Balkan national historiography," argues Paschalis Kitromilides, is "premised on the assumption that Orthodox Christianity and . . . [the Orthodox] Church played a major role in nation-building" by cementing "national identity in the years of captivity. . . . The Orthodox Church, however, as an institution of the Ottoman state remained a supranational organization. . . . The Patriarchate, through a series of acts and pronouncements of its holy synod, made official and clear its opposition to nationalism." As late as 1872, the ecumenical patriarch still denounced nationalism as "discriminating on the basis of different racial origins and languages. . . . The Christian Church . . . [is] predestined to contain all nations in one brotherhood of Christ. . . . We renounce . . . [and] condemn racism . . . ethnic feuds and dissention within the Church" (Kitromilides 1994, 178, 181).

Ottoman reforms granted equal rights to non-Muslim minorities regarding taxation, justice, education, military service, and holding public offices, and generated a secular renaissance. Within two years, Christian delegates had gained places in the Grand Council of the court. Modernization was signaled by the provincial reorganization of 1864, which created large secular administrative units called vilayets, subdivided into sanjaks, with considerable self-government and indirectly elected advisory bodies. The local native elite was strengthened. The Bulgarian *chorbaji* and the Serb *knezi* were elected by the local Christian population and acted as local native representatives of the Ottoman authorities. They worked as tax collectors and administrative agents, tried civil cases, and played an intermediary role between Ottoman officials and Christian subjects. They were also involved in trade and became rich pig traders in Serbia, a small, emerging elite, which played an important role in the armed uprising against Ottoman rule.

Although the 1830–60 Ottoman reforms attempted to modernize, consolidate, and preserve Ottoman rule in the Balkans, they proved to be counterproductive and fueled a Balkan national awakening. Spontaneous revolts against early nineteenth-century Ottoman disorder, local despotism, and extreme exploitation were gradually transformed into a national struggle for independence. All the religious and secular local self-governing institutions and their leaders, the local elite, played an important role in the nation-building to come.

The first major uprising erupted in the *pashalik* of Belgrade under unchecked janissary rule in February 1804. Faced with janissary terror, the native population declared their loyalty to the Sultan and turned to him for help. The Sultan sent a message to the janissaries, threatening to mobilize the Serbs (as had already occurred in 1798, when Serb peasants, mobilized and armed by Pasha Hadji Mustafa, had massacred the janissaries). Several armed groups of Serbian peasants under local priests and knezi attacked small janissary garrisons and began liberating the countryside, but they lacked coordination. As a preventive blow, the janissaries began to liquidate the local knezi in an attempt to preempt a potential Serb attack. The seventy-two victims were beheaded and their heads were staked on the citadel of Belgrade. One of the knezi, George Petrović, popularly called Karadjordje (Black George), escaped and emerged as a charismatic leader of the uprising. He was an illiterate peasant who had joined the Austrian army in 1787 and got military experience as a sergeant of the *Freikorps* during the Austrian campaign in western Serbia. Karadjordje's well-organized forces became decisive by capturing several citadels in Belgrade in March 1804. He ruthlessly recruited Serb peasants: as Aleksa Nenadović, one of the rebels, noted in his memoirs: "*Gospodar* George will send his men secretly through the villages and whomsoever they find at home they will kill him and break him on the wheel and burn his house." In two months, his army counted more than 30,000 men. The Serbs did not revolt against Ottoman rule, but against local robber rulers. In fact, the "insurgents" acted in the name of the Sultan, who legitimized the rebellion. "The leaders of the uprising appealed not to any nascent desire for a revival of Serbian independence," Lawrence Meriage concludes, "but to their loyalty to the sultan" (Meriage 1987, 60, 62). They did not aim for independence but at the restoration of Pasha Hadji Mustafa's orderly regime and the expulsion of the janissaries. The Serb guerrilla army was very successful, partly because of assistance from Serbs from Hungary, as well as from the Russian tsar, who sent arms and officers. Karadjordje turned out to be an excellent strategist. As a *buljukbasa,* the head of a Serb militia unit under Hadji Mustafa, he triumphantly attacked Belgrade in December 1806 and had liberated all the main Ottoman fortresses in Serbia by the summer of 1807. Vuk Karadžić, an eyewitness to the uprising, recognized the turning point in the struggle in 1807:

Up to now the leaders had told the people that they were not fighting against the Turkish Sultan, but rather they were fighting at the Sultan's command against the Janissary rebels and irregulars; not now [in the beginning of 1807], when they killed a vezir of the Sultan and had baptized Turkish women and children in and around Belgrade and Šabac, this could no longer be said nor believed, but instead . . . [they said] we can't fight the Turkish Empire alone . . . give us a tsar who will take our part. (*Monumenta Serbocroatica* 1980, 327, 329)

In March of that year, the Serbs declared independence. The Serb cause at that point became a part of a major international conflict: Sultan Selim's effort to form an alliance with Napoleon provoked an immediate Russian ground offensive and British naval attack. The Sultan attempted to pacify Serbia by accepting Serb demands and offering autonomy. Russia, however, stepped in. The intervention was urged by a few sophisticated Serb leaders, such as Metropolitan Stevan Stratimirović, Bishop Jovan Jovanović, and Archimandrite Arsenije Gagović, who worked out plans for a Slavo-Serbian empire and presented it to the tsar in St. Petersburg as early as November 1803. Adam Czartoryski, the tsar's Polish foreign minister, welcomed the idea (Meriage 1987, 64–66). Pushed by several local leaders, the overambitious Karadjordje, as Karadžić noted in his report, realized that without foreign assistance and guarantees, he would be unable to stabilize his power. He accepted the Russian offer, which promised more than the Sultan's: total independence with a Russian guarantee. The Palucci-Karadjordje Convention concluded with Russia in July 1807 also called for Russian military and economic aid, arrangements for garrisons in towns, and appointment of Russian administrators in Serbia.

The international setting dramatically changed, however, during the days when the Serb-Russian deal was being negotiated. A transitory Russian-French agreement (the Treaty of Tilsit), followed by an armistice with the Sultan in August 1807, freed the hands of Sultan Selim and left Serbia on its own. Although the Russian-Ottoman war was renewed, it ended in the spring of 1812 with the Treaty of Bucharest, which Tsar Alexander ratified on June 23, 1812, the very day Napoleon's army invaded Russia. Karadjordje turned to Napoleon, but international assistance did not come from France either. An overpowering Ottoman military force of three armies launched a deadly attack on three fronts in Serbia in July. In early October, Karadjordje escaped to Austria, followed by 24,000 Serbian troops. The Sultan recaptured Belgrade and regained control over the pashalik at the end of 1813.

The enforced Ottoman rule could not endure for long. Janissary terror continued, as well as spontaneous local revolts. One of them, in 1814, led to a bloody massacre of more than two hundred Serb rebels. In April 1815, the *oborknaz,* or grand knaz of three districts, Miloš Obrenović, an enemy of Karadjordje, who had obediently collaborated with the Sultan and even helped to repress the spontaneous peasant revolt, decided to head the revolt and achieved four sudden victories against Ottoman troops. The Porte tried to pacify the Belgrade pashalik as soon as possible to avoid a new attack by Russia, which after Waterloo lacked military commitments in the West and had a renewed interest in the Balkans. Obrenović, an illiterate peasant, emerged as a prominent member of the local Serbian administrative-merchant elite. He proved to be an outstanding diplomat. Unlike Karadjordje, he did not want to build upon Russian promises but accepted the offer of Marasli Ali Pasha in November 1815. The agreement was enforced by an imperial decree, appointing Obrenović supreme knaz of the pashalik, granting amnesty to the rebels, and allowing the Serbs to retain their arms. It also authorized the creation of the Skupstina, a state assembly, a national chancery, and a quasi-court and administration. Tax collection became a Serbian task, although the pashalik continued to pay tribute to the Sultan, and the Ottoman administration and garrisons remained intact in the country. Obrenović stabilized his position within the empire and against any potential rival: as a gift to the Sultan, he sent him the head of Karadjordje, who had returned to Serbia in 1817 but was immediately assassinated.

Although the compromise granted much less than full autonomy to Serbia, Obrenović skillfully exploited the international situation, and Serbia gained more autonomy in the years to come. An opportunity arose when a Greek secret society, the Philikē Hetairia (Society of Friends), started by Greek merchants in Odessa, prepared a general Balkan uprising with Russian patronage. The ideal place to start was the Romanian Principalities, with their extremely weak Ottoman military presence and a so-called Phanariot Greek regime representing the Porte. The *hospodar* (lord) of Moldavia, Michael Soutsos, was himself a member of the Hetairia. The organization successfully invited Alexander Ypsilantis, son of a former hospodar of Wallachia and general of the Russian army, to command its forces. The planned uprising could count on the already ongoing peasant revolt of Tudor Vladimirescu, himself a member of the Hetairia. In the spring of 1821, Ypsilantis's troops entered the Principalities. The timing was excellent, since Istanbul was preoccupied with a war against the insubordinate warlord Ali Pasha of Ioannina in Greece. The revolutionary attempt failed, however. Russia remained cautious and did not act, while Ottoman troops—despite the 1802 agreement with Russia, which forbade them to enter the Principalities without Russian consent—invaded. The local population, which traditionally hated the Greek Phanariot proconsuls of the Porte and ecclesiastical and financial overlords, remained passive or even hostile to the Greek military action. Even Tudor Vladimirescu betrayed the rising and engaged in negotiations with the Porte until the Hetairia kidnapped and executed him in May (Cărăbis 1996). Ypsilantis's "sacred Battalion" suffered a devastating defeat at the Battle of Dragasani. Ypsilantis fled to Austria, and the revolt collapsed within a few weeks.

Although the grand plan for an organized Balkan revolution failed in the Principalities, a spontaneous Greek uprising followed in the Peloponnesus in the summer of the same year. Massacres of Turkish and Greek communities in bloody partisan warfare resulted. The impenetrable mountainous area proved to be ideal for the rebels, who gradually, by the summer of 1822, gained control over the entire Peloponnesus, several islands, and Athens. The "Hellenic Republic," with its own government and declared constitution, became undefeatable. Sultan Mahmud II, in a last bitter attempt, mobilized Mohammed Ali, pasha of Egypt, to launch a naval attack against the Peloponnesus. Although the Egyptian troops landed successfully and the Ottoman army recaptured Athens, a combined British, French, and Russian armada destroyed the Ottoman-Egyptian fleet in Navarino Bay in August 1827. A Russian ground invasion crossed the Danube and reached the Balkan Mountains in 1828 as part of the allied design. The Ottoman defeat was accomplished. The signing of the Convention of Akkerman (1826), the Treaty of London (1827), and, finally, the Treaty of Edirne (Adrianople) in September 1829 guaranteed significant Russian expansion around the Black Sea and gave autonomy to large areas of the Balkans. The Sultan had to recognize the independent Greek kingdom in July 1832.

Miloš Obrenović did not risk participation in the planned Balkan uprising (unlike Karadjordje, who joined the Hetairia and was ready to participate, which motivated his return to Serbia in 1817). He nevertheless masterfully capitalized on the Ottoman defeat. In August 1830, the Sultan granted full autonomy to Serbia and recognized Obrenović as hereditary prince. Serbia had to pay an annual tribute in a lump sum, spahi landowners had to relinquish their estates, Serbian jurisdiction was recognized, and Ottoman garrisons disappeared from the country, except along the border. Serbia de facto became an independent state.

Through tactical exploitation of Balkan crises and repeated international diplomatic and military interventions against the Ottoman empire, Serbia gradually achieved full independence over the next four decades. The milestones on the road to full independence were the late 1862 and the early 1867 agreements between Prince Michael Obrenović, Miloš's son and heir, and the Porte. In the summer of 1862, an isolated confrontation between the Ottoman garrison and the Serb population in Belgrade provided an excellent opportunity to call for an international conference in Istanbul. The Porte had to agree to withdraw its troops from Serbia, aside from the Belgrade citadel and three other fortresses. In 1866, during the uprising against Ottoman rule on the island of Crete, Prince Michael was again able to mobilize the great powers and forced the Sultan to evacuate Serbia. The last Ottoman troops left the country in early 1867. Yet Belgrade's annual tribute to the Sultan, and the Ottoman flag over the Belgrade citadel, signaled the lack of full Serb independence.

Inspired by the Italian unification, Prince Michael developed the ambitious "Yugoslav" idea, with a central role for Serbia as the Piedmont of the Balkans. Through a series of agreements—with Romania in 1865 and 1868, with Montenegro in 1867, and with Bulgaria and Greece in 1867—Michael organized a Balkan League and prepared a coordinated revolt against the Ottoman empire. The plan failed, and Michael was assassinated in the summer of 1868.

Like the Serbs, the Bulgarians also continually rebelled in self-defense against the intolerable Ottoman kleptocracy, joining invading Russian armies as volunteers in 1806, 1811, and 1829. In 1834 and 1835, uprisings occurred in Tirnovo and along the Serbian border. In 1841, revolts spread across the country from Niš to Kirk-Kilissa and Shimla. In 1849–50, Vidin became the center of warfare, with 10,000 rebels. Bulgarian revolutionaries also attempted to establish alliances with neighboring nations. In 1866, a joint Bulgarian and Romanian uprising and union was planned, followed by an agreement with Prince Michael of Serbia in 1867 to organize a common Bulgarian and Serbian uprising and establish a "Yugoslav kingdom." All these plans, however, failed, as did a proposal—inspired by the Austro-Hungarian Compromise of 1867—to form an Ottoman-Bulgarian state with the Sultan as tsar.

Romantic Bulgarian writers and freedom fighters such as Georgi Rakovski, Lyuben Karavelov, Vasil Levski, Hristo Botev, Stephan Stambulov, and George Benkovski praised self-sacrificing struggle and glorified the mystique of dying for the fatherland. Botev wrote:

> He who falls in freedom's fight
> Dies not—he's mourned
> By earth and sky, nature and beast,
> And singers remember him in songs.
> (*Monumenta Bulgarica* 1996, 463)

A spontaneous anti-Ottoman uprising in Bosnia-Herzegovina in the summer of 1875 resulted in renewed hostility to Ottoman rule throughout the Balkans. "[C]orpses were seen floating down the Save . . . horrors took place a day or two after we reached Sarajevo," a pair of English woman travelers reported. "More than one-third of the whole Christian population fled over the frontier out of Bosnia into the neighboring lands. . . . The number of those who have perished . . . is unreckoned" (Mackenzie and Irby 1877, 30, 35). In June 1876, bowing to strong popular sentiment, Serbia declared war on Turkey, followed a few weeks later by Montenegro. Although Serbia mobilized one-sixth of its population, it suffered a devastating defeat.

A major uprising that began in central Bulgaria in May 1876 was met with unimaginable reprisals by the Turks. The "Bulgarian Horror," as British journals and politicians called the massacre of several thousand Bulgarians—a British consular report spoke of the murder of 12,000 people—outraged the Western public and offered an excellent opportunity for the great powers to intervene again in pursuit of their century-old goal of pushing the Ottoman empire out of Europe. After the failure of diplomatic solutions, the Austrian-Russian agreements of Reichstadt (1876) and Budapest (1877) cleared the road for Russian military intervention. A Russian army crossed the Danube, reached Shipka Pass in June 1877, invaded Bulgaria, and liberated Sofia in January 1878, realizing the dream of the Bulgarian romantics. Petko Slavejkov, one of the leading national poets, welcomed the Russian troops with a poem:

> Kin defends kin
> Brother perishes for brother . . .
> Hurrah! Let's shout aloud
> "Welcome to our land!"
> Hurrah! Good luck
> Tsar, our savior.
>   (*Monumenta Bulgarica* 1996, 419)

Bulgaria de facto (but not yet de jure) became independent. The Treaty of San Stefano between Russia and Turkey in March 1878 created an autonomous Bulgarian principality under an independent prince, which included most of Macedonia and the lands between the Danube, the Black Sea, and the Aegean. Both the neighboring Balkan countries and the Western great powers opposed this territorial arrangement, however, and in July 1878, the Treaty of Berlin revised it. The autonomous Bulgarian principality was pruned to one-third of the territory it had been given at San Stefano, keeping only the area north of the Balkan Mountains. South of the mountains, Macedonia and the newly created autonomous Ottoman province of East Rumelia were returned to the Ottoman empire, albeit with different statuses.

Bulgaria adopted a liberal constitution and invited a German prince, Alexander of Battenberg, a nephew of the Russian tsar who by marriage was also related to the British royal family, to be its king. Alexander, after the popular uprising in East Rumelia in 1885, peacefully united the two parts of Bulgaria, and won a war against Serbia, which wanted to halt the enlargement of Bulgaria. He was forced to abdicate in 1886, however, and was replaced by another German prince, Ferdinand of Saxe-Coburg-Gotha in 1887.

Bulgaria's borders and the unresolved Macedonian question gave rise in the years that followed to a series of further confrontations with its neighbors, and the country achieved full independence in the midst of this turmoil only in 1912. Ever since San Stefano, the dream of a Greater Bulgaria had remained a burning issue on the nationalist agenda.

As another consequence of the Treaty of San Stefano, Serbia regained full independence. Numerous Serbs nevertheless remained outside newly independent Serbia, mostly in Bosnia-Herzegovina, in the so-called military borderland and Voivodina, and in Austro-Hungarian Croatia. The creation of a Greater Serbia and the unification of all Serbs in a South Slav, or Yugoslav, nation remained to be accomplished.

In 1878, Romania also gained full independence. This was the work of the European great powers. Local rebellions in 1821 and 1848 had been easily suppressed by the Porte. The former, connected with Alexander Ypsilantis's failed revolution, and led by Tudor Vladimirescu, did not even briefly challenge Ottoman rule in the Principalities, and the Iaşi uprising in early 1848 was also immediately crushed. Another revolt that June in Wallachia led to the formation of a revolutionary government, which declared: "All lands inhabited by Romanians should be called Romania and form one state." With Moscow's consent, however, the Turks easily suppressed the revolt, which had, L. S. Stavrianos says, "an *opéra bouffe* quality"; all it did was demonstrate the existence of an "embryonic nationalist spirit" (Stavrianos [1958] 1963, 348–49).

Although the great powers could not agree on how to resolve the Romanian question, at the Paris Congress in 1857, they called for elections to be held in the Principalities to test the desire for union. These had to be nullified, because the results were falsified, but new elections that fall finally expressed the strong commitment of the population to create a united Romanian state, albeit under Ottoman suzerainty. Between May and August 1858, the congress met again in Paris, with Napoleon III act-

ing as the chief advocate for Romanian national interests (Iordache 1987).
In spite of the opposition of Istanbul and Vienna, the congress abrogated
the Russian-imposed Règlement Organique and proclaimed the United
Principalities of Wallachia and Moldavia, each under its hospodar, with
separate but equal national assemblies, a supreme central commission, and
a joint court of appeal. The Sultan retained suzerainty, but the great powers guaranteed the autonomy of the Principalities. The Paris Congress also
recommended land and social reforms along Western lines.

Was Napoleon III trying to play a Napoleonic role by defeating rival
great powers at the diplomatic table and redrawing the map of the Balkans
approved by the Vienna Congress in 1815? Or was he seeking to create a
buffer state allied with France between the Russian and Ottoman empires?
Probably both. His actions, in any case, served Romanian national interests. Without making any significant internal revolutionary-military
contribution themselves, the Romanians thus became independent.

In January and February 1859, the Moldavian and Wallachian assemblies elected Colonel Alexander Cuza as hospodar, creating a union at least
in the person of the ruling prince. Austria, which was at war with France
at the time, was not in a position to oppose the choice (Cojocariu 1995).
Although no charismatic national leader, Cuza tactfully persuaded the Sultan to combine the two parliaments and cabinets, thus uniting the two
Principalities de facto in the spring of 1861. In December of the same year,
the union was officially declared.

Romania was inching toward full independence in a peaceful way. In
February 1866, a coup removed Cuza and the Romanian political elite invited Prince Karl of Hohenzollern to the Romanian throne. The king-
select, a twenty-seven-year-old Prussian officer, was a cousin of the king
of Prussia (on his father's side) and a relative (on his mother's side) of
Napoleon III. He arrived in Bucharest in May 1866 and was soon recognized by the great powers. Romania accepted a new constitution based
on the democratic Belgian model. The Sultan's suzerainty, however, was
preserved for more than a decade longer (Iacob and Iacob 1995).

In 1878, as a result of the Treaty of San Stefano, Romania became fully
independent, but Romanian nationalists considered this success to be only
partial. The dream of unifying all the territories with Romanian populations into a single Greater Romania, according to the Daco-Roman concept, remained unfulfilled. Transylvania, the cradle of Romanian national
consciousness, Bukovina, and Bessarabia, all of them with mixed populations, and in some cases with a Romanian majority, remained parts
of neighboring empires. To incorporate these areas into the Romanian
nation-state continued to be a demand on the national agenda.

Paradoxically enough, Bosnia-Herzegovina, which prompted the liberation of Romania and other Balkan nations, did not gain its independence, but was instead annexed by Austria-Hungary and remained a part of it until the end of World War I. Under Habsburg rule, Bosnia-Herzegovina achieved the greatest modernization and economic growth it had ever known, but nationalists were not satisfied.

Albania, the last among the Balkan countries to achieve independent statehood, did so in 1878. Albanians, most of them Muslim, belonged to the military elite of the Ottoman empire and did not revolt against it until the uprisings in other Balkan countries, the Russian-Ottoman war, and the Treaty of San Stefano threatened their existence. Since territories inhabited by Albanians, but considered to be Ottoman, were given to neighboring Serbia, Montenegro, and Bulgaria, a few Albanian intellectuals, among them the Frashëri brothers, founded the League for the Defense of the Rights of the Albanian Nation. In June 1878, delegates from various parts of the country gathered together in Prizren, formed the Lidhja e Prizrenit (League of Prizren), worked out the Kararname, a resolution that refused to give up territories to Serbia, Montenegro, and Greece, and called for autonomous status for Albania within the Ottoman empire. In 1880, a provisional government was set up and extended its authority to include Kosovo. In 1899, one of the Frashëri brothers, Sami, published his vision in a book entitled *Albania—What Was It, What Is It and What Will Become of It?* "As long as Turkey in Europe survives, we wish to remain under its sovereignty and we will never wish to be separated from it," he wrote. But he also recognized that the empire was in ruins: "It is a dead man and, however much we may love the deceased, we must put him under the earth" (quoted in Elsie 1995, 247). A series of nation-building steps followed, including language reform and establishment of an alphabet, as recommended by the Bashkimi (Unity) literary society at the Monastir Congress in 1908. The Balkan war against the Ottoman empire in 1912 made it clear that, together with the Turks, the Albanians might be the absolute losers. The political elite therefore decided to leave the sinking Ottoman ship and demanded full independence. The Congress of Valona in November 1912 declared Albanian independence and, according to the Balkan pattern, Prince William of Wied, a German captain, was invited to rule the country. The borders were still unclear, since a great proportion of the Albanians lived in Serbia and Macedonia. Whether to establish Greater Albania with all the Albanians, or a smaller independent state with a part of the Albanian nation, remained undecided. An internationally accepted independent status for Albania was granted only after World War I.

Although all the Balkan nations gained independence during the last third of the long nineteenth century, none of them was able to unify the entire nation. The Greater Romanian, Greater Bulgarian, Greater Serbian, and Greater Albanian dreams required major border corrections and led to immediate confrontation among the Balkan nations, with plans for new wars both against the failing Ottoman empire and against each other. The Serbian-Bulgarian war of 1885, the new Bosnian crisis in 1908, and the two major Balkan wars of 1912–13 were all part of this struggle to realize unfulfilled nationalist agendas, which even more fatefully guided the Balkan nations when they joined either the Entente or the Central Powers in 1914.

— — —

Between 1794 and 1914, triggered by romantic nationalism and the idea of freedom, a series of uprisings, revolutions, wars, and reforms signaled national awakening and the long task of nation-building in Central and Eastern Europe. They went hand in hand with attempts to overturn the establishment and adopt modern Western ideas and institutions—in short, to join Europe. Although most of the revolts and revolutions were defeated, compromises granted important elements of autonomy or at least introduced Western-style legal and institutional systems and opportunities for modernization. Several peoples were able to establish independent nation-states and introduce modern, Western constitutions and political structures. Although the struggle for an independent modern state often failed, there were significant partial successes. Some of the most important prerequisites of nineteenth-century modernization were belatedly created. Serfdom and noble privileges were abolished, and free access to land, modern property rights, modern legal systems based on the Code Napoléon, parliamentary institutions, elections, modern courts with equality before the law, and other basic elements of Western parliamentary and market systems were introduced. These were major steps toward the *état de droit* that, as Rousseau phrased it, "places the law above men" and embodied a movement "from status to contract."

In Central and Eastern Europe, however, all of the newly created laws and institutions were controversial, often formally granted but essentially strongly limited. As Friedrich Hayek warns: "[T]he possession of even the most perfectly drawn-up legal code does not, of course, insure . . . [what] the rule of law demands; and it therefore provides no substitute for deeply rooted tradition." Friedrich II's Civil Code in Prussia in 1751 and the Napoleonic codes of 1800–1810 established the rule of law but did not automatically guarantee the reign of law. In Germany, "the constitution had been given, the *Rechtsstaat* proclaimed, in fact the police state continued" (Hayek 1976, 195, 199).

Western institutions were introduced in Central and Eastern Europe only partially and after at least a century-long delay. The "deeply rooted traditions" of a democratic society were totally lacking, and the power of the authorities remained intact. *Leges* (laws) could not replace *privi-leges* (Hayek 1976, 194–95), and the regime remained basically uncontrolled. Several major elements of the Western system, such as the existence of a strong nation-state with a modern bourgeois society and a real representative parliamentary democracy, were entirely lacking.

However, even partial realization of the requirements of the dual economic and political revolution of modernity had tremendous historical importance. The peoples of Central and Eastern Europe, who were shifted to the periphery of the emerging modern world system between the sixteenth and eighteenth centuries, had begun their journey on the Western road to modernization.

CHAPTER 4

ECONOMIC MODERNIZATION
IN THE HALF CENTURY
BEFORE WORLD WAR I

THE IMPACT OF WESTERN INDUSTRIALIZATION

THE INDUSTRIAL REVOLUTION affected all of Europe. The crucial concepts of modernity and progress were closely linked with railroads and industrial construction, which generated passionate patriotic feelings. Modernity became a central goal and a national program, and the economic modernization that resulted from failed revolutions and successful reforms from above in the second half of the nineteenth century, partial and circumscribed though it was, created a footing—reasonably firm in some countries, but unstable in others—for the nations of Eastern and Central Europe to join the economic rise of the West.

Meanwhile, an unlimited Western market for food and raw materials provided a major incentive to modernize old export sectors and create new ones, increasing their output in the region. The industrializing West grew from 45.1 million to 162.4 million people (i.e., by 360 percent) between 1800 and 1913 and multiplied its imports by leaps and bounds. Until the 1770s, British imports increased by 1 percent annually. Between 1800 and the 1860s, the annual growth rate of imports reached 5 percent. The value of British imports jumped from $118 million to $3.8 billion (U.S.$ 1913) between 1800 and 1913. More than one-quarter of these imports consisted of agricultural products (Deane and Cole 1967). French imports increased sevenfold between 1830 and 1913, and 7 percent of these imports were of grain and flour. Roughly 17 percent of Holland's and 12 percent of Switzerland's imports were grain and flour in 1913 (Kindleberger 1962). Food and raw materials remained dominant in world trade throughout the nineteenth century. Between the 1870s and 1913, according to Simon Kuznets's calculations, these items accounted for roughly 63 percent of international trade. Meantime, world food and raw materials trade remained largely an intra-European business. The handful of Western European industrialized countries imported roughly two-thirds of the world's food exports during the half century before the war (Kuznets 1967). Even though the percentage share of world trade generated outside Europe climbed from 33 percent to 38 percent over the period, world trade in general remained mostly a European issue. In other words, a dramatically increased Western market opened tremendous export possibilities for the agricultural countries on the periphery of Europe. The greatest potential for expanding world trade was thus the trade between industrialized Western Europe and the agricultural and raw materials–producing Mediterranean, Scandinavian, and Central and Eastern European countries. European exports between the 1860s and 1913 reached an annual average increase of 2.8 percent, while some of Europe's agricultural exporters had a 4 to 5 percent annual increase. The value of exports, according to Paul Bairoch, reached 4 percent of the aggregate European GNP in 1830. This share increased to 14 percent by 1913 (Bairoch 1973).

THE IMMIGRATION OF WESTERN
ENTREPRENEURS AND SKILLED WORKERS

The railroads and mechanized plants financed by agricultural exports were often directly serviced by Western managers and artisans, who played an important role in peasant countries with limited entrepreneurial and technological experience, notwithstanding that their numbers never exceeded a few thousand. Even in Bohemia, the most advanced area of Central and Eastern Europe, the first industrialists and engineers moved in from the West. The first major industrial firm in Bohemia, a mechanized textile factory in Pottendorf, was founded by an Englishman, John Thornton, in 1801, and the first modern sugar factory in Zidlochovice was established by a French entrepreneur, Florentin Robert, in 1837. Edward and James Thomas, two brothers from Britain, and their partner Thomas Bracegirdle, who was from Leeds, founded machine-building plants at Liberec, Prague, and Jablonec. In 1830, three British engineers, David Evans, David Thomas, and William Jones, introduced modern puddling techniques at the Vitkovice ironworks. George Woodward, an English mechanic, built a flax-spinning mill in Velké Losiny, and John Stapleton and Samuel Dicky introduced wool-spinning machines in Moravia in 1802. Two Württemburgers, Jan Reiff and H. A. Luz, established the machine-building industry of Brno at the beginning of the nineteenth century. "By far the greater proportion of the entrepreneurs in the machine-building industry in Bohemia and Moravia in the early XIXth century were foreigners, especially Germans and Englishmen," Arnošt Klima observes. "Amongst the great entrepreneurs of the first half of the XIXth century there were no Czech names" (Klima 1991, 156–57).

It is small wonder that a great many pioneering industrialists, technicians, foremen, and skilled workers in the industrializing countries of the region originated abroad. A Swiss, Abram Ganz, founded the first major Hungarian iron and engineering company in 1844, and the company reached new heights under the leadership of the Bavarian Andrew Mechwart after 1867. The Swiss Haggenmacher and Austrian Dreher families established the Hungarian beer industry. A Bavarian, Otto Steinbeis, founded the first Bosnian sawmill and pulp factory (with 10,000 workers) in 1893, and the Moravian entrepreneurs Münch and Schumpeter established Serbia's first modern woolen factory in Paraćin in 1882.

Thousands of Western foremen and skilled workers were employed in Central and Eastern Europe during the first stage of industrial development. More than one-quarter of the skilled labor force of the Budapest engineering industry consisted of German-speaking workers from Germany, Austria, and Bohemia in 1880. The first workers' weekly in Hungary, *Arbeiter Wochen Chronik,* was published in German. German and Czech foremen trained and directed the local workforce in the Paraćin mill in Serbia, where even around the turn of the century, one-quarter of the employees were foreigners. In Serbia's textile industry, even at the beginning of the twentieth century, nearly 20 percent of the skilled labor force was foreign (Palairet 1997, 294–95).

THE INTERNATIONALIZATION OF THE EUROPEAN ECONOMY

Transportation of goods and the movement of people became much easier: the leading countries of the continent, interested in the markets and raw materials resources of the unindustrialized areas, began building an unbroken European transportation network. Railroads soon connected the most remote areas of the continent to the core, and rural areas to local industrial centers. After the first railroad line in the world was built in Britain in 1825, construction gained momentum all over the continent. By 1850, 23,500 kilometers of track had been laid; by 1870, nearly 105,000 kilometers; and by 1910, more than 362,000 kilometers (Woytinsky 1925–28, 2: 34–35). During the first two-thirds of the century, the European peripheral areas had only very short lines and hardly any network. In 1870, only 31,000 kilometers of rail lines existed in the European peripheral areas, less than half of the length of those at the core. From the 1870s on, however, the peripheral areas' rail network grew more than fivefold. Before World War I, the peripheries' network was as long as the core's (Berend and Ránki 1982, 98).

The poor countries of Central and Eastern Europe were unable to cover the vast expenses of railroad and industrial construction, and Western banks and investors mostly financed it. The inflow of foreign capital, partly direct foreign investments, for building railroads, opening mines and banks, and founding industrial firms, became the prime mover of economic modernization in the area. The volume of exported capital from the core countries increased from $2 billion in 1850 to $46 billion by 1913 (Kuznets 1966, 324). During that period, until 1913, 26 percent of this amount was invested within Europe. Britain lost interest in European investment in midcentury, with the result that only 5 percent of British investment in 1914 was in Europe (Jenks 1927), but French and German investors preferred the European continent, and 28 percent of French and 52 percent of German capital exports were channeled to Central and Eastern Europe (Cameron 1961; Hartner 1980).

The fringe of an unprecedented European prosperity carried the sleepy, stagnant, unindustrialized countries along. In this respect, Europe was, indeed, "one technological community. . . . Despite internal differences in the timing of change . . . shared the fact of change and must be treated as an interconnected whole" (Jones 1981, 46).

Central and Eastern Europe thus became a part of a "globalized" European economic system. Especially after John Stuart Mill's *Principles of Political Economy* was published in 1848, free trade became an inseparable part of the zeitgeist. International organizations were established and institutionalized free trade. Britain became the main champion and framer of a new European world system: during the 1840s, the British parliament repealed the export duties on industrial goods and raw materials, then eliminated the Corn Law and the Navigation Act. Imports became duty-free, and foreign ships were allowed to enter British ports. Tariff revenues were replaced by other sources of income in Gladstone's budget in

1860. Britain became a free-trade country and soon made laissez-faire an international system. The breakthrough occurred in 1860, when Britain and France signed the Cobden-Chevalier Treaty, which introduced the "most favored nation clause." Commercial concessions secured by one country were automatically extended to other trade partners. Consequently, a multilateral free-trade system emerged. All the multinational empires introduced free trade and practically forced their oppressed nationalities to join in.

Newly independent Balkan countries were also forced to join: under international agreements, Serbia remained bound by the provisions of the Habsburg-Ottoman Treaty of 1718, which imposed a 3 percent tariff on imports from the Habsburg empire. The Berlin Treaty of 1878 expanded Bulgaria's 1860–62 treaty with the Porte, retaining an 8 percent duty on all Bulgarian imports. The country could not introduce an independent trade policy until the mid 1890s. Romania was bound by its treaty with Austria-Hungary until the mid 1880s and could not introduce protective tariffs.

Trade relations were further internationalized by various "global" institutions and a unified monetary system made possible by the adoption of the gold standard. Britain, again, was the pioneer in introducing the gold standard as early as between the 1770s and 1810s. The International Monetary Congress in Paris in 1867 generated a strong movement to join: most of the Western European countries introduced the system in the 1870s, and Austria-Hungary and Russia joined in the 1890s. Currencies became convertible and exchange rates remained stable during the entire period (Kenwood and Lougheed 1971). International economic connections were strengthened by global European institutions such as the International Telegraph Union of 1865, internationalization of the Rhine, Po, Danube, and Elbe during the 1860s, the Metric Standard International System and International Postal Association in 1875, international copyright and patent laws, adopted by most of the European countries throughout the 1880s, and other measures (Pollard 1974).

Free trade, an internationalized monetary system, and internationalized economic connections thus became dominant in the period when modernization of Central and Eastern Europe actually began in the 1860s. The countries of the region, mostly parts of huge empires, evidently adopted the concept of export-led industrialization as their modernization strategy. They sought to export as many traditional agricultural items and raw materials as possible to their industrialized neighbors and the West to increase their incomes and develop the modern industrial and service sectors of their economies.

CORE-PERIPHERY RELATIONS AND
ECONOMIC NATIONALISM IN THE MAKING

The rising interconnection between Central and Eastern Europe and the West, however, can be interpreted as a core-periphery interrelation (Wallerstein 1974), and not merely as an integrated system "where change in one cell tended to communicate to the remainder," as E. L. Jones puts it. The Central and Eastern European periphery, in this relationship, was dependent on the core: "[I]ts foreign trade, balance of payments, and production development [were] tied to, influenced by and subordinated to the core countries. The relationship is fundamentally an unequal one and benefits the core. It is often destructive of the periphery; but it can also be an inducement to development, serving—under appropriate conditions— to lift the area from its peripheral position" (Berend and Ránki 1982, 9).

The core-periphery relation was partly, but not exclusively, interpreted as an east-west (and north-south) link within Europe. The division of labor between highly industrialized and agricultural regions was not solely a world phenomenon or even a macro-European one. This relation was endlessly reproduced on the regional level. The core-periphery pattern was replicated between rising industrial metropolises and the unindustrialized agrarian regions within each country. Budapest and Bucharest versus the backward Hungarian and Romanian countrysides, respectively, epitomize this pattern. In several cases, advanced and backward regions coexisted and cooperated in the very same countries. The Italian north and south and the German east and west illustrate this configuration.

In many respects, a core-periphery type of division of labor emerged in the framework of the common market of multinational empires. In the Russian empire, paradoxically, the occupied and politically subordinated Polish, Finnish, and Baltic provinces on the western rim became industrial suppliers of the more backward agricultural, but extremely large, Russian imperial market. St. Petersburg and Moscow, huge urban centers on a European scale, formed the core of a backward empire. The huge nearby market of Istanbul played an important role in the development of the infant Bulgarian handicraft industry. The imperial division of labor thus played a determinant role in the economic development of the interrelated regions of the empires.

The Habsburg empire reproduced the classic East-West economic relationship between the industrialized western and agricultural eastern provinces of the same empire. An Austrian-Bohemian core and the Hungarian, Galician, Bukovinian, and Bosnian-Herzegovinian peripheries developed the well-known core-periphery type of division of labor. More-over, as one of the European great powers, the Habsburg empire, with its vast and relatively developed market, also became a quasi-core for neighboring peripheral Balkan countries such as Serbia and Romania.

The complex core-periphery relations generated an early appearance of—using a twentieth-century term—economic nationalism, or, regard-ing the pre–World War I decades, as Thomas David and Elizabeth Spil-man term it, "proto-economic-nationalism" in Central and Eastern Eu-rope (David and Spilman 1999). Quite a few influential politicians in the region advocated protectionism and state interventionism rather than a laissez-faire, noninterventionist free-trade policy. The Hungarian radical reformer Lajos Kossuth, who, until early 1841, had attacked both the Aus-trian tariff policy and the customs border between Austria and Hungary and urged the introduction of free trade, later that year changed his mind and became an advocate of Hungarian protectionism. He was strongly influenced by the German economist Friedrich List, who published his *Das nationale System der politischen Ökonomie* (The National System of Po-litical Economy) in 1841. List maintained that whereas free trade was ad-vantageous for Britain (and for advanced core countries), latecomers to industrialization (peripheral countries) had to protect their fragile in-dustries and economies with protective tariffs until they caught up.

List's theory became extremely popular in Central Europe: Richard Cobden, the British signatory of the Cobden-Chevalier free-trade treaty, noted in his diary during his trip to Vienna in the mid 1840s: "Dr. List . . . the champion of the protective system and 'nationality' . . . had obtained such influence in the public mind that professors of political economy could not advocate free-trade in their lectures to the youth" (Cobden 1994, 153).

Kossuth argued for industrialization and protectionism from late 1841 on. Using List's metaphor, he declared: "Without industry, a nation is a one-armed giant." He compared the economic relations between Austria and Hungary to the relationship of the innkeeper and the barrel: the for-mer could tap the latter freely. After a royal veto thwarted an initiative in the 1843–44 session of the Hungarian parliament to introduce protective tariffs "to defend the development of industry" (Mérei 1983, 907), Kos-suth initiated a social movement to introduce the tariffs "at everybody's doorstep." In October 1944, the Országos Védegylet (National Protec-tive Association) was established. Those who joined committed themselves to buy only Hungarian and to boycott foreign industrial products (Kosáry 1942). The Hungarian nationalist elite thus turned to import substitution and protectionism instead of an export-led industrialization policy.

The emerging Central and Eastern European nations often turned to state interventionism and self-help movements, characteristic elements of economic nationalism, to counterbalance the lack of independent economic and tariff policy. Prince Drucki-Lubecki, minister of finance in Congress Poland during the 1820s, was one of the initiators of economic modernization through state intervention: the foundation of the Towarzystwo Kreditowe Ziemskie (Land Credit Society) and Bank Polski (Polish Bank) was followed by the creation of state-owned industry. Bank Polski established and owned industrial enterprises on behalf of the Polish government: state ironworks were established, for example, in the Kielce region, along the rivers Bobrza and Kamienna (Jedlicki 1964). Taking advantage of limited autonomy, the Polish kingdom also imposed high protective tariffs in 1823, which remained in force until the end of the 1840s (Szlajfer 1991, 124–25). In later decades, when autonomy was withdrawn by Russia, a Polish movement analogous to the Hungarian Országos Védegylet sprang up to boycott foreign products and buy Polish industrial goods as a substitute for protective tariffs, with the slogan "Swój do swego po swoje" (Everyone should get [buy] things only from their own [people]) (David and Spilman 1999, 20).

During the severe agricultural crisis in the closing decades of the nineteenth century, "proto-economic-nationalism" with protective tariffs and state intervention for industrialization became widespread in the region. Most of the countries defected from the free-trade camp and introduced protective tariffs. Austria-Hungary was among the first in 1874 and did so again, more effectively, in 1887 and 1906. The 1887 tariff provided for an average of 15 to 30 percent ad valorem duty on imported goods. The 1906 duties ranged between 10 and 40 percent and were even higher for 260 specific items. Russia introduced its first protective tariffs as early as 1868 and increased them in 1891, 1893, and 1900. Bulgarian tariffs in 1894 increased protection more than threefold. Romania, after its treaty with Austria expired, introduced protective duties, which averaged 10–15 percent, in 1886. These were raised in 1904 and again in 1906, up to 25 percent of the value of imported goods. Serbia introduced protective tariffs in 1906. The Central and Eastern European countries were not alone: Germany (1879 and 1902), the United States (1890 and 1897), and Spain, Italy, and France followed the same trend. By World War I, only Britain, Holland, and Denmark remained committed to free trade.

More effective state intervention for promoting industrialization was carried out by a series of "industry promoting laws" in Hungary. While the tariff system of Austria-Hungary forcefully protected the empire's market for Hungarian agriculture, the Hungarian elite sought substitutes for tariff protection against Austrian-Bohemian industrial competition in the Hungarian market. The solution was found in the 1881, 1890, 1899, and 1907 laws on industrial promotion, which provided tax exemptions, preferential railroad rates, and direct subsidies for establishing new factories or enlarging old ones in Hungary. During the 1880s, the state paid annual subsidies totaling 126,000 crowns overall. This amount increased to nearly 500,000 during the 1890s and to more than 1 million in the early twentieth century. Altogether nearly a thousand new factories were established with state assistance between 1882 and 1913, and the Ministry of Commerce was authorized to buy shares of state-supported factories (Berend and Ránki 1955, 48–52). "The law on industrial promotion at least partially substitutes for the means that an independent tariff policy would otherwise provide," a contemporary analyst observed (Krajcsi 1907, 1). At the peak of state support between 1900 and 1913, state subsidies alone represented nearly 6 percent of industrial investments in joint-stock companies in the country.

Similar legislation assisted industrialization in the Balkan countries. The Romanian parliament in 1887 enacted a law authorizing direct government assistance to promote industry, providing exemption from taxes and tariff duties for fifteen years, subsidizing transport costs, and offering free building sites for industrial companies. More than 830 firms of the existing 1,150 enjoyed state subsides before the war (Hitchins 1994, 191). In Serbia, the 1893 and 1898 laws granted duty-free imports of machinery, raw materials, and semifinished products, and also tax exemptions or reductions for firms employing more than 50 workers. In 1910, nearly a quarter of the firms in operation took advantage of state assistance. In Bulgaria, a series of laws—in 1894, 1897, 1905, and 1909—provided similar state assistance for industrial firms, surpassing 4 percent of total industrial investments (Gerschenkron 1962).

By adjusting to the free-trade system and either following export-led industrialization policy or gradually using "proto-economic-nationalist" measures of protective tariffs and state intervention for promoting industrial development, Central and Eastern Europe emerged on the road of economic modernization.

THE EARLY INDUSTRIALIZATION OF AUSTRIA
AND THE CZECH LANDS

The development of the countries of Austria-Hungary was determined most of all by the interrelationship among the various regions and provinces of the Habsburg empire, the fifth greatest power in Europe, which functioned as a core region. These characteristics were mostly owing to the impressive industrialization of the western, Austrian-Bohemian provinces, which closely followed Western Europe after a delay of a few decades.

A modernizing Habsburg empire, in pitched competition with Prussia, turned toward important internal reforms. During the second half of the eighteenth century, the enlightened absolutist rule of Maria Theresa and her son Joseph II laid the groundwork for capitalist transformation along Western lines. The imperial edict of 1728 significantly increased import duties. The tariff on coarse woolen cloth, for example, was 100 percent ad valorem. The loss of Silesia to Prussia in 1742 provided an even stronger incentive to introduce mercantilist policies, and, at the same time, to promote Bohemian industry. A general patent had already restricted the guilds in 1731, and these feudal institutions were significantly weakened and later abolished by Maria Theresa and Joseph II. In 1775, the queen eliminated all internal tariffs and introduced a united national market throughout the empire, except for Hungary. Internal tariffs were also abolished in Hungary in 1784, although because the noble tax exemption was preserved, Hungary remained outside the imperial common market. Between 1783 and 1796, Bukovina and Galicia also became part of the integrated imperial market. Some parts of the empire joined during the nineteenth century: Tirol and Vorarlberg in 1875 and Istria and Dalmatia in 1880.

Maria Theresa followed the French mercantilist policy and defended the imperial market through high tariffs, in general, one-third of the value of imported goods, and import quotas to encourage infant domestic industries. The traditional French mercantilist idea of achieving a high foreign trade surplus by curbing imports of "nonessentials" and increasing domestic output and exports as much as possible was combined with the special Central European concept of *Kameralismus,* which focused on the rise of *consumatio interna,* domestic consumption (Bauer and Matis 1988, 268). Accordingly, the Habsburg policy of self-sufficiency protected the Hungarian market for Austrian-Bohemian industry through a 30 percent tariff on foreign products as opposed to a 3 percent tariff on Austrian-Bohemian ones. Inasmuch as Hungary was not a part of the imperial common market until the mid nineteenth century, tariffs were assessed on its agricultural exports to Austria. In the interests of imperial self-sufficiency, however, Hungarian exports were granted tariff exemptions from time to time (Pribram 1907; Eckhart 1922).

From the 1770s on, free industrial enterprise was authorized. In 1773, for example, cotton printing became a free industry and the paralyzing shackles of the medieval guilds were loosened. According to mercantilist practice, Maria Theresa attracted Western industrialists with tax exemptions and state loans for newly established industrial firms. After 1754, the state itself also founded industrial enterprises—including the empire's largest textile factory in Linz—in imitation of the classic Colbertian *manufactures royales*. Maria Theresa undermined serfdom through her regulations on the legal status of peasants and their obligations. On crown estates, the so-called Raab system introduced annual cash rental payments instead of traditional dues and labor service. In 1781, Joseph II abolished serfdom, which granted freedom of mobility and employment, at least in Austria and the Czech lands. Peasants were allowed to marry, leave the estate, and learn a skill. Peasant dues were transformed into rents of 17 percent of annual income. In addition, all land was taxed at the level of 12 percent of gross income. "As a result of reform legislation in 1785 and 1789," David Good observes, "the capitalist bases of Habsburg agriculture were laid" (Good 1984, 34).

In the early nineteenth century, modern technological education was also established. The Prague Technical Institute, established in 1807, and the similar Vienna Institute of 1815 were modeled on the French École Polytechnique. Various state interventions and legislation, including the introduction of modern patent law in 1810, modified in 1820 and 1832, gradually created a business-friendly environment.

Exploiting state assistance, landowning aristocrats often became the first industrialists, among them Maria Theresa's husband, Franz von Lotharingen. The early textile manufacturers in the empire, Count Bolza in Kosmonosy-Josefuv Dul, Count Haugwitz in Namestí, Count Wallenstein in Horni Litvinov, and Count Kinský at Sloup, well illustrate this widespread phenomenon. Count Bouquoy's glass manufacture at Graz, Count Salm's and Count Thurn und Taxis's sugar factories on their Bohemian estates, the Vitkovice ironworks belonging to the archbishopric of Olomouc, and the Ostrava coal mines of Count Larisch and Baron Wilczek are also good examples. Large-estate industry founded by aristocratic entrepreneurs mostly processed the raw materials resources of the estates, such as minerals, wool, wood, and agricultural products. "Only in those cases," concludes Arnošt Klíma, "where production remained closely linked with landed property, as in the case of coal or iron-ore mining, did the nobility maintain an entrepreneurial function in the 19th century" (Klíma 1991, 157).

The role of the landed aristocracy in proto-industrial activity was not only a Bohemian phenomenon but also a peculiarly Central and Eastern European form of early manufacturing. These aristocratic "industrialists" were secure and well protected from the urban guilds. Moreover, they did not have to pay taxes and produced a variety of raw materials themselves—mostly agricultural products for processing, but also minerals, wood, leather, and wool. They also had a great number of serfs, who constituted a free workforce for performing unskilled labor such as producing charcoal for ironworks, transporting raw materials and products, and working in flour mills and breweries. In Peter Zrinsky's ironworks in Croatia in the mid seventeenth century, for example, some two hundred serfs performed unskilled jobs. During the eighteenth century, several Hungarian, Croat, and Polish landowners established industrial firms, exploiting the raw materials of the land they owned. Mines, ironworks, food-processing plants, and woolen mills were established.

Count Sándor Károlyi established one of the first noble manufactures, a woolen cloth factory in Hungary, in 1722. The Esterházys and Pálffys followed. Even Maria Theresa's consort established textile (1743) and ceramics (1749) factories in Hungary. All of these, however, failed and were closed later in the century. This situation hardly improved until the mid nineteenth century. A similar phenomenon characterized eighteenth-century Poland: a great part of the 338 factories were established by landed aristocrats in Urzecze, Nalibok, and Korzec. Around the royal estates in Grodno, Antoni Tyzenhaus, the top manager of the estates, established industrial firms based on serf labor. "[I]ndustrial plants on the manorial estates, based on serf *robot,* were short-lived in Poland," Jerzy Topolski notes (Topolski 1982, 192).

Bohemian-Moravian "feudal" industrialization during the second half of the eighteenth century, however, differed from that in Hungary and Poland in one major respect: the putting-out system enabled landed aristocrats to base their enterprises on traditional peasant cottage industry. Landless peasants and smallholders—that is between one-quarter and one-half of all villagers—made their livings by wage work. Population growth was certainly a factor in industrial development: by 1789, the number of inhabitants per square kilometer in Bohemia-Moravia had increased to 55. People living on mostly unfertile land had to turn to piecework done at home to earn a living. Besides population pressure stimulating industrialization, Bohemia gradually began to profit from its political hardships: being an integrated province of the Habsburg empire, the Czech lands enjoyed the advantages of the industrialization promoted by the Habsburg court. Moreover, Austrian, Silesian, and German merchants played an important role in introducing the *Verlag* system, which integrated the rural population, working in their own homes, into organized capitalist industry.

Arnošt Klíma lists a series of examples. One obvious one is the textile factory at Linz, in Upper Austria, which depended in part on Bohemian domestic industry, employing nearly 12,000 spinners working at home in 1773, which had increased to 16,000 by 1790. A network of agents supplied the spinners with flax and transported the yarn to the central plant.

Austrian merchant capital played a comparable role in the case of the Viennese merchant J. M. Schmidt, who established a woolen-goods manufacturing center in southern Bohemia in 1769. Within six years, 1,400 spinners were working for Schmidt's factory at home, and only 300 were actually employed at the mill. An official who traveled through northeastern Bohemia in 1756 reported that yarn collectors and linen merchants were buying up the yarn and linen from the whole area to send to Silesia, most of all to Greifenberg (Klíma 1991). According to Klíma's figures, in eighteenth-century Bohemia, a great number of peasants, especially the landless ones—the so-called cottage owners—whose sons could not inherit their land, became wage employees working at home. Approximately one-quarter to one-half of the villagers worked in the *Verlag* system, and as many as 80 percent in the mountainous areas of northern Bohemia.

Between 1780 and 1798, the number of employees in the Czech textile industry doubled to nearly 700,000 people in Bohemia, Moravia, and Czech Silesia, out of 4 million inhabitants. Textiles employed more than 80 percent of workers; iron, glass, and other industries were less important (Půrš 1960). In contrast to the entirely agricultural eastern provinces of the monarchy, with a 90 percent agrarian population, Austria and Bohemia had only a 75 percent agricultural population in 1790.

The early decades of the nineteenth century, especially the 1820s and 1830s, were a period of accelerating textile boom. According to John Komlos's calculations, the leading cotton industry grew 3.7 percent annually between 1784 and 1803, but by more than 11 percent annually between 1826 and 1835, and by 8.5 percent a year between 1835 and 1847 (Komlos 1983, 99). In the main textile centers of the empire, 435,000 spindles were in operation in 1828. This number had more than doubled by 1841. In the Bohemian heartland, notably in Liberec, 355,000 spindles were in operation. In Lower Austria, the number of spindles surpassed 388,000. During these decades, a third textile center emerged in Vorarlberg, which produced 14, 6, and 4 percent of the output of the Austrian spinning, weaving, and printing industries, respectively (Good 1984, 51).

The first modern machines were introduced as early as 1797 by the Leitenberger Company; and in 1801, the Pottendorf works emerged as the first mechanized factory in the country, but mechanization remained sporadic. Austria and Bohemia's combined capacity of 20,000 horsepower in 1840 amounted to only half that of Germany and Belgium, less than a quarter of France's, and hardly more than 3 percent of Britain's. Although more than half of the steam engine capacity was used in the textile industry, hand spinning remained dominant until 1840, and two-thirds of the production was done in traditional small-scale units. Although it employed hundreds and even thousands of workers, the new large "manufactory" of this period was a transitory, pre–Industrial Revolution "proto-factory," to use Herman Freudenberger's term (Freudenberger 1977). Weaving—with the exception of the most modern, Swiss-established Vorarlberg center—was done by hand in cottages. The woolen industry was even less modernized. In the Liberec textile center, of the 3,000 looms in operation, only 40 were mechanized in 1841. In the Brno center, five-sixths of the woolen production was delivered by guilds in 1850. Spinning remained mostly done by hand in the woolen industry until the 1880s.

Textiles represented 41 percent of industrial output in 1841, and food processing another 21 percent. Coal mining began to rise after 1830, when output reached 180,000 tons. That increased to 880,000 tons by 1850. Coal consumption, however, did not surpass 43 kg per capita in that year, a fraction of the 800 kg and 170 kg per capita coal consumption of Belgium and Germany, respectively. With its 8.8 kg per capita output, the iron industry was stronger than its German counterpart (7.3 kg) in 1850, but during the first half of the century, it grew far more slowly than textiles: at one-third the rate between 1826 and 1835, and one-half between 1835 and 1847 (Brusatti 1973; N. T. Gross 1971; Komlos 1983).

Based on contemporary statistics, factories produced two-thirds of the Habsburg empire's industrial output in 1841, nearly seven-eighths of it in the western provinces—that is, Austria and the Czech lands. The eastern provinces, including Hungary, remained far behind and produced only one-eighth of the empire's industrial output. This has sometimes led to an oversimplified equation of the Austro-Bohemian industrial advance with British progress during the Industrial Revolution (Půrš 1960), which is clearly refuted by the low degree of mechanization and the still dominant putting-out and "proto-factory" systems in the Habsburg empire. From around the turn of the century through the 1830s, instead, a belated "first or preparatory phase" of industrialization took place in Austria and the Czech lands, which might be termed "a successful proto-industrialization" or "industrialization before the industrial revolution" (Mendels 1972; 1982, 74).

Proto-industrialization in the western provinces of the Habsburg empire, led by the monarchy's consistent mercantilist-*kamaralist* state policy, generated agricultural prosperity in the eastern provinces, most of all in Hungary. While grain consumption stagnated at around 175–77 kg per year, grain production, inspired by export potential, increased from 28 to 67 million hectoliters, or by 139 percent, in Hungary and Croatia between 1789 and 1841 (Komlos 1983, 55, 61). The rising industry in the western provinces and the agricultural prosperity in the eastern parts of the monarchy were closely interrelated. The division of labor in the empire had a mostly positive effect on both parts of the monarchy, but mutual stimuli could not eliminate the separation and disparity of the various ethnic-national regions (Berend and Ránki 1987, 399–40).

Economic development was helped by a continuous reform process, especially after 1848. The liberation of serfs and abolition of noble privileges, free access to land, introduction of modern property rights, the establishment of the common market of the monarchy, extensive railroad construction, and the foundation of a modern banking system facilitated the modernization of the entire empire from the mid nineteenth century onward. On that very basis, prepared by the proto-industrialization of the previous decades, true industrial takeoff began to accelerate in Austria and the Czech lands between 1860 and 1880.

During this second phase of industrialization, food processing emerged as the new leading industrial and export sector. Textiles, formerly the leading sector in Austrian-Czech early industrialization, could not cope with strong Western competition, but food processing could. Sugar-beet refining boomed in Europe during the Napoleonic wars, but temporarily collapsed again when the continental blockade was lifted and cane-sugar imports resumed. From the 1830s and 1840s on, however, French and German technology spread and the first sugar-beet refineries were established in Moravia. In 1837, the Belgian Florentin Robert moved to Moravia and established the first modern sugar-beet refinery in Zidlochovice. By 1861–62, 130 sugar refineries were in operation and produced more than 80,000 tons of raw sugar in Austria and the Czech lands. Moreover, Austrian entrepreneurs founded about a dozen sugar refineries in Hungary from the early 1850s onward. The dramatic increase in sugar-beet production provided the raw materials for a rapidly growing number of factories. Most important, a revolutionary innovation boosted the Austrian-Czech sugar industry: Julius Robert, the son of the pioneering founder of the Zidlochovice factory, invented a new diffusion technology that immediately transformed the industry and inspired the rise of a new branch of engineering as well. Within a decade, over a hundred sugar refineries had introduced this new, much more efficient technology. Large modern factories appeared. The average output per factory rose from 1,000 tons in 1871 to 6,500 tons in 1913. The sugar industry became the most modern and strongest branch of Austrian-Czech industry. More than 82 percent of the huge production capacity of the empire was located in Bohemia-Moravia. Output multiplied from 80,000 tons in 1848 to 1,783,000 tons by 1913. After Germany and Russia, Austria-Hungary became the third-largest producer in the world. In 1860, the monarchy became self-sufficient in sugar, and by 1913, 60 percent of the output was exported. The sugar industry, delivering nearly 10 percent of total exports in the 1910s, remained the leading industrial export sector of the monarchy until World War I.

Lower Austria and Bohemia were at the center of a strong, modern, export-oriented brewing industry that developed in these decades. In 1851, nearly three thousand traditional small breweries produced 5.6 million hectoliters of beer. In 1913, roughly one thousand large factories with modern English technology produced more than 20 million hectoliters of beer. Plzen, Budweis, and Schwechat emerged as legendary centers and international brands. Aside from domestic consumption, the brewing industry also became an export sector, although the value of its exports reached only one-tenth that of the sugar industry.

Food processing's percentage share of Austrian-Czech industry increased from 11 to 35 percent between 1865 and 1880, while during the same period, the role of textiles decreased from 41 percent to 33 percent (N. T. Gross 1973, 274).

The great spur of the *Gründerzeit,* or era of promoterism, around 1870 was interrupted by the great depression of the decade that followed. After 1880, however, a Rostowian takeoff followed (Rostow 1963). The Industrial Revolution arrived in Austria and the Czech lands. Coal, iron, and steel production illustrate the breakthrough of industrialization. The foundation of the Österreichische-Alpine Montangesellschaft in 1881 constituted a symbolic milestone. Anthracite production jumped from 4.8 million tons to 27.4 million tons, and iron and steel output soared from 0.3 to 1.7 million tons, a nearly sixfold increase, between the mid 1870s and the early 1910s. The centers of coal mining were located in Doubrava, Silesia (46 percent), Kladno, Plzen, and Ostrava in the Czech lands (41 percent), while the increasing output of lignite was extracted mostly in

Bohemia (83 percent). The Skoda works employed six thousand workers, and the Maschinen- und Waggonbau-Fabrik employed nearly four thousand before the war. The field of engineering grew by 9 percent annually during the twenty-five years before World War I.

Once again, the leading sector of successful Austrian industrialization, the modern mechanized textile industry, expanded rapidly. Between 1880 and 1913, the number of cotton spindles—60 percent of them in the Czech lands—increased from 1.6 million to 4.9 million. Cotton consumption per capita (6.2 kg) surpassed the French (5.4 kg), and approached the levels of Belgium (6.6 kg) and Germany (6.8 kg). The paper industry quadrupled production during these decades. The special boom in the consumer goods industries was based on the enormous market of the agricultural eastern part of the empire: more than 78 percent of the cotton goods and nearly half the woolen production of Austrian-Czech industry was sold in Hungary. As a consequence, the net industrial production of Austria-Bohemia increased by four times from 1.0 to 4.2 billion crowns (in constant prices) between 1880 and 1911. Per capita output trebled. One quarter of industrial output was produced by the textile industry, another quarter by food processing, and one-fifth by the iron and steel and engineering industries (Fellner 1916).

The western provinces of Austria-Hungary became industrialized. As in Western European countries, the workforce shifted from agriculture to industry: 60 percent of the population in Lower Austria, 52 percent in the Czech lands, and 46 percent in Lower and Upper Austria combined worked in industry, while the agricultural population declined to roughly 35 percent of the workforce (Milward and Soul 1977). GDP in the Austrian and Czech territories was 80 and 44 percent higher, respectively, than the monarchy's average. Bohemia-Moravia produced 56 percent of the industrial output of the hereditary provinces of the empire. Its industrialized western half made Austria-Hungary Europe's fifth industrial power, with 6.3 percent of the continent's industrial output. The empire was also fifth in coal, iron, and steel production, and sixth in textile manufacture.

The Austrian and the Czech lands emerged as an industrialized regional core with agricultural peripheries within the monarchy and in the neighboring Balkan countries. No other country or area of the region could repeat that example. The core-periphery interrelationship, however, initiated the modernization of the backward agricultural provinces of Austria-Hungary and also, at least in part, of the neighboring areas of Central and Eastern Europe. The European regional and local cores exhibited a pull effect because of their markets, investments, and other stimulating inputs. The long nineteenth century was a period of building modern infrastructure, banking, education, the realization of a belated agricultural revolution, and—in the relatively more advanced Central European countries—also the beginning of industrial development.

RAILROADS AND BANKS:
MODERNIZATION WITH FOREIGN INVESTMENTS

The advanced areas required mass transportation to gain easy access, not only to markets, but also to the food and raw materials of the unindustrialized areas. Modern transportation, first of all railroads, arrived in Central and Eastern Europe rather early. The Habsburg empire's first, 53-kilometer-long railroad, on which horse-drawn trams plied between Linz and Budweis, was opened in 1832, and the first company to use steam engines, the Kaiser Ferdinand Nordbahn, linked Vienna with Bochnia, Galicia, in 1836, financed by the Vienna Rothschilds. The first part of the line between Vienna and Brno was opened in 1839. The state bureaucracy prepared a central long-term plan for railroad construction in 1841, focusing on the extension of the Nordbahn and the building of the Südbahn. In the mid 1840s, the Vienna–Prague track was laid and the first part of the Vienna–(Buda)Pest line was opened.

The appearance of the railroad received an enthusiastic reception. In the romantic age, it was not simply a means of transportation, but the symbol of speed, modern technology, progress, and culture. Poets, painters, and musicians celebrated railroads all over Europe. After the first, 40-kilometer-long railroads were opened in Hungary, the national poet, Sándor Petőfi declaimed:

> Railroads by the hundreds, by the score!
> Keep building more and more!
> Cover the world with railways
> As the earth is covered with veins.
> They are the veins of the earth,
> Civilization pulsing through their girth.
> They carry far and wide
> The very juices of life.
>
> (Petőfi 1985, 701)

By 1854, 2,617 kilometers of railroad had been laid in the Habsburg empire. In that year, a new law guaranteed 5 percent interest on the fixed capital of railroad companies who received concessions to build. A huge railroad boom followed. By 1867, 6,430 kilometers, by 1873, 15,597 kilometers, and by 1913, 44,748 kilometers of rail lines were in operation in the monarchy. Their length increased by more than seven times between 1867 and 1913, creating a railroad density similar to that of the West. In the six most advanced European countries, the ratio of rail lines to land area was 1 kilometer to 10.1 square kilometers, while in the Habsburg empire, it was 1 to 13.5. The ratio of rail lines to population was 9 kilometers per 10,000 inhabitants in both cases.

This extensive railroad construction led to an unexpected railway boom in the agrarian part of the empire as well. Nearly half of the empire's lines were built in Hungary, so that railroad density there became somewhat more developed than in Austria. Agrarian Hungary had a railroad network density ranked sixth in Europe, ahead of Germany, Holland, and France. However, while the ratio between length of lines and land area was 1:10 in Bohemia and Hungary and 1:8 in Austria, it was only 1:28 in Galicia, and 1:100 in Dalmatia. Nevertheless, backward though they were, the railroads of the easternmost provinces of Austria-Hungary were still at a higher level than those in various neighboring countries. Bosnian railways—calculated by kilometers of passenger travel per head—were, for example, twice as developed as Serbia's (Palairet 1997, 233).

The Russian empire, having learned the lesson of the Crimean War, initiated a considerable railroad construction program. "Without railroads and mechanized industry, Russia cannot be secure within its boundaries," Russia's minister of finance said. "Its influence will decline in Europe to a degree irreconcilable with its international prestige and historical importance" (Laue 1969, 7). Between 1860 and 1913, nearly 70,000 kilometers were built, the second-largest network in the world, which also connected occupied Poland and the Baltic region to the empire and to the world. The first line in Polish territory was built between Wrocław and Myslowice in 1847. The Warsaw–Vienna line was opened in 1848. In the Polish kingdom, however, railroad construction lagged behind. In 1862, only 635 kilometers of track existed, but by 1887, more than 2,000 kilometers had been laid, connecting Warsaw with Kiev, Moscow, and St. Petersburg. The industrial centers of Lodz and the Dabrawa Basin were linked by rail, and four lines connected the kingdom with Prussia and Austria. All in all, Poland had a sparse network of railroads, although surpassing the railroad density of Bulgaria, Greece, and Turkey. The Baltic area was first linked with the empire by a line to Riga.

In the Balkans, railroad construction was meager. The poor, newly independent Balkan countries had had little money available and to some extent no real economic need to build railroads. Their traditional economies, mostly subsistence farming, did not spur the introduction of modern transportation. Great power interests, needless to say, did. With the Vienna Conference of 1883 and the Berlin Agreement, united Germany, anxious to enlarge its sphere of interest in the Balkans, and nurturing colonial aspirations, initiated the building of the Orientalische Eisenbahnen, or Berlin–Baghdad line. All the Balkan countries committed themselves to completing their own section of the line by 1886: the line between Belgrade and Niš; from Niš to Pirot and Zaribrod to the Bulgarian border; from Vranje to the Turkish border; from Zaribrod through Sofia to the Turkish border; from Belovo to the Bulgarian border; and from Salonika through Mitrovica to the Serbian border. Between 1860 and 1880, altogether about 2,000 kilometers of railroad were built in the Balkans, and 1,300 kilometers in Romania. Between 1880 and 1914, however, a further 6,000 kilometers were completed. Greece had 1,600; Romania 3,500; Serbia 1,000; and Bulgaria 2,100 thousand kilometers before World War I. The 460-kilometer-long Serbian and 697-kilometer-long Bulgarian sections of the international Orientalische Eisenbahn's Berlin–Istanbul line were those countries' main railroads; in Serbia, only another 400 kilometers of branch lines were built before World War I (Berend and Ránki 1982, 96–97).

For the rest, one can hardly speak of rail networks in the prewar Balkans. According to Michael Palairet's calculations, rail transportation produced 8.9 million dinars of value-added national income in Serbia, and 16.2 million in Bulgaria, whereas cart and packhorse transportation produced 34 and 77 million dinars, respectively (i.e., four to five times more). "After the main lines had been completed (1888) it was expected that the Balkan states would build branch networks. They did little of the kind . . . Balkan governments regarded the railway as a facility of the administration rather than as a provider of economic services. . . . The impact of these railways was barely felt before World War I" (Palairet 1997, 328–30).

In the mid 1870s, two Englishwomen in Ottoman Bosnia traveled by horse-drawn coach, there being only a "fragment of modern railway, lying detached and unconnected on the Bosnian plains. Along this railway, without beginning and without end, a train used to run once a day each way, conveying a ludicrously small average of goods and passengers." Between Salonika and Monastir, they also noted "trains of patient horses carrying iron from Cardiff and cotton from Manchester to the markets of inland towns" (Mackenzie and Irby [1867] 1877, 3, 91).

Romania, however, was an exception. The first, 70-kilometer-long line, financed by British investors, connected Bucharest to Giurgiu in 1869. The agricultural products of the central plain could thus be transported to the Danube ports and hence to the Black Sea. By the early 1870s, a British-Austrian consortium completed the Lemberg–Cernauti–Suceava line. In 1872, the German Bleichröder group opened the Roman–Galaţi–Bucharest–Pitesti line, and by 1880, the Ploiesti–Predeal line was added, providing connections to the Hungarian railway system. In 1874, connections to the Russian system were also established. By 1880, 1,300 kilometers were in operation. By 1914, 2,250 kilometers were in place (Hitchins 1994, 199). Prewar Romania had the largest railroad system in the Balkans.

Railroad density in the Balkans reached only one-fifth to one-quarter of that in Western Europe. The backward Balkan railroads, however, transported only one-sixteenth to one-thirty-second of the goods carried in the West. Romania's more advanced network transported one-sixth of the volume of goods relative to track of Western Europe. Railroads in the area mostly served great power interests but undoubtedly contributed to domestic economic development.

Capital-intensive railroad construction was financed mostly by Western investors, not only because of poor domestic capital accumulation and insufficient internal sources, but also because Western interests initiated the work. In the Habsburg empire, foreign investments played an important role at the early stage of modern economic transformation, especially in building a modern infrastructure. Up to 1900, 6.9 billion crowns in foreign investments were channeled into the monarchy's economy. Roughly 6.4 billion crowns, 93 percent of the total, were concentrated in two areas: state loans and railroad investments. Railroad shares were mostly sold abroad (72 percent). The western, advanced provinces, however, soon became capital "exporters" to the less developed eastern provinces. Some 4.7 billion Austrian crowns were invested in Hungary, for example, and nearly 1 billion in the Balkans.

More than two-thirds of Austrian investments in Hungary (which were partly German in origin) between 1867 and 1913 supported railroad construction. Russian railroad construction was almost entirely (94 percent) a foreign business until 1880. Foreign participation decreased to less than half after the turn of the century. Nevertheless, in the prewar period, foreign money financed three-quarters of Russian railroad investments. The Deutsche Bank financed the Orientalische Eisenbahnen in the Balkans, although the French Banque Impériale Ottomane also contributed to the construction of the 660-kilometer-long line east from Salonika.

In most cases, newly founded local banks also contributed to railroad investments. The modern banking system in Central and Eastern Europe, however, was created mostly by foreign investments. In advanced Austria-Bohemia, a genuine early banking system emerged during the first half of the nineteenth century. Aside from the Austrian National Bank (1816), private banks were founded, such as the Arnstein und Eskeles bank, and others by Salomon Rothschild, Georg Sina, and Samuel Wodianer. The first real modern banks of the Crédit Mobilier type in the Habsburg empire, the Niederösterreichische Escompte-Gesellschaft and the Österreichische Creditanstalt, appeared in Vienna in the 1850s. Between the 1860s and 1880s, the Boden-Creditanstalt, the Wiener Bankverein, and the Länderbank followed. The most important Bohemian credit institution, the Živnostenska Banka pro Cechy a Moravu, was established in 1868. Only one-fifth of the shares of these big banks were in foreign hands, mostly German, in 1900 (*Tabellen zur Währungsstatistik* 1902).

The situation was entirely different in the agrarian areas and countries. In Hungary, modern credit institutions hardly existed in the *Vormärz* period. Traditional private credit and, from the 1830s on, small local savings institutions chiefly served the economy. The very first banks—the Pesti Hazai Első Takarékpénztár and the Pesti Magyar Kereskedelmi Bank—appeared in the early 1840s. The Austrian National Bank opened a branch in (Buda)Pest in 1851. Modern banking, however, was instituted only after the Austro-Hungarian Agreement of 1867: the Vienna Rothschilds established the Magyar Általános Hitelbank (1867), and the Anglo-Österreichische Bank and the Franco-Österreichische Bank founded the Anglo-Magyar and Franco-Magyar Bank in 1868 and 1869, respectively. Austrian financiers established the Magyar Általános Földhitel RT (1871).

From 1880 on, a reorganized banking system played an important role in financing the economic modernization of Hungary. At that time, the leading role was played by the Pesti Magyar Kereskedelmi Bank, a partner of the Viennese Wiener Bankverein, which had a 40 percent share in the bank's Hungarian businesses. In 1867, the Hungarian banks' total capital was 29 million crowns, and in 1913, 2.6 billion, but they controlled up to 6.7 billion. Altogether, 55–56 percent of the shares of the leading Hungarian banks were in foreign hands, including the 45–46 percent in Austria, around the turn of the century.

Similarly, 60 percent of the capital of the four biggest Russian banks and 45 percent of the capital of Russia's ten largest banks were in foreign hands, mostly French, but partly German (Crisp 1967, 227). The same was true in Russian Poland. The leading financial institutions, such as the Bank Handlowy (1870) and the Bank Dyskontowy (1871), were established by the big financiers of the country, Kronenberg and Epstein, but were closely connected with the French Crédit Lyonnais and the German Deutsche Bank, respectively.

The origins of Romanian banking go back to the late 1860s, when, after the unification of the two Romanian Principalities, a new national monetary system and a new currency, the leu, were introduced. The first private banks, notably the Marmorosch Bank, the Creditul Funciar Rural (1864), and the Creditul Urban Bucuresti (1874), were founded. Prince Cuza also granted concessions to foreign—British, French, and Austrian—financial groups, who founded the Banca Romaniei (1865) (Pintea and Ruscanu 1995). The most important step in creating a modern banking system, however, was taken with the foundation of the Banca Nationala a Romaniei by private Romanian financiers and the state (with a one-third share) in 1880. The amount of its loans increased from 66 million to 1,073 million lei between 1891 and 1914 (Axenciuc 1995). By 1914, 215 banks were in operation in Romania, but nine of them—four of which were in foreign hands—controlled 70 percent of total resources (Hitchins 1994, 197–98). The German Disconto Gesellschaft, Länder Bank, and Deutsche Bank and the French Crédit Mobilier provided more than 60 percent of the capital of these leading Romanian banks. French banks also introduced modern Bulgarian banking: the Banque Générale de Bulgarie, the Crédit Foncier Franco-Bulgar, and the Banque des Balkans were founded by leading Paris banks (Berend and Ránki 1987, 604, 607).

In Central and Eastern Europe, foreign capital thus played a decisive role in building a modern infrastructure and banking system, major elements of economic modernization. Capital from the more advanced West served the creation of an economic sphere of interest by opening up cheap food and raw materials resources and paving the road for a developed market. In certain circumstances, in an appropriate domestic economic environment, the process also helped the modern transformation of the importer countries on the periphery.

The volume of exported capital began to soar during the last third of the nineteenth century, exactly the period of major modernization efforts in Central and Eastern Europe. Between 1850 and 1870, exported capital increased from $2 billion to $6 billion, while between 1870 and 1913, it jumped to $46 billion (U.S.$ 1913). Britain, France, and Germany provided more than three-quarters of the total. However, unlike Britain, France and Germany preferred European investments and channeled more than half of their capital exports to Europe, including Central and Eastern Europe: 28 percent of French and 52 percent of German capital exports went to this region. Roughly half of the French capital consisted of state, municipal, and public loans, partly for railroad construction, while another 15 percent went directly to railroad building, and 10 percent for the extracting and processing industries.

In the case of Hungary, domestic capital accumulation reached roughly 22 billion crowns. Investments totaled approximately 17 billion crowns, of which 6.8 billion came from foreign (including Austrian) sources. Roughly 40 percent of all investments in Hungary thus came either from the western provinces of the monarchy or abroad during the half century before World War I (Berend and Ránki 1979, 77).

Capital exports to the Balkans before the war reached almost U.S.$1.3 billion, nearly 3 percent of total foreign investment worldwide. However, only 3 to 5 percent of this amount was in the form of direct investments in the extracting and processing branches. A great portion of the foreign capital was used for building up a new state apparatus. Roughly 20 percent of Romanian loans went for military purposes, and 40 percent of Bulgarian loans served deficit financing. By World War I, Serbia had received twenty-six foreign loans. Ten were used for repaying loans, another eight went to military expenditures, and only eight loans, less than one-third of the foreign credits, constituted economic investment. As a consequence, most of the Balkan countries, where the payment of interest swallowed up nearly one-third of the public revenue, were unable to repay the huge amount of the loans and became insolvent: Serbia in 1895 and Bulgaria in 1901. "Every independent state can buy enough rope to hang itself if it is willing to pay the price," Herbert Feis comments sarcastically (Feis 1965, 263).

Some investors favored raw materials, and of the small Western industrial investment in Serbia, 40 percent went into their extraction. The largest amount, U.S.$5–6 million, was for copper and iron-ore extraction. The most sensational investments in raw material extraction, roughly $80 million, were channeled into the Romanian oil fields, among the richest in Europe at that time. After the 1895 mining law was enacted, foreign investors were allowed to develop the Romanian oil industry. Between 1903 and 1914, the German Steua Romana, Standard Oil's Romano-Americana, and Royal Dutch-Shell's Astra Romana controlled 94.5 percent of the Romanian oil industry. Other industries were also mostly foreign-owned: gas and electricity (95.9 percent), sugar (94 percent), metallurgy (74 percent), and forestry products (69 percent) (Hitchins 1994, 188, 193). More than 80 percent of Romanian industry before World War I was established by foreign investments.

Direct foreign investments played an important role in modernization in Russia and in the eastern parts of Austria-Hungary. In 1913, 2.1 billion rubles out of total foreign investments of 7.6 billion rubles—roughly one-quarter of Russia's total capital—were channeled into industry. As a consequence, half of all industrial investments and more than 80 percent of mining and smelting investments came from abroad. "Unfortunately, our country is poor," the Russian finance minister, Count Sergei Witte, wrote in a memorandum to Tsar Nicholas II in 1900, "[and] there is no other way to develop our extraordinarily backward industry except through the direct cooperation of foreign capital" (Laue 1969). A quarter of all the industrial firms in Poland were in foreign hands, but they employed 54 percent of the industrial labor force and produced 60 percent of industrial output, Witold Kula notes (Kula 1947, 33). Before the war, similarly, a quarter of all industrial investments in Hungary came from Austria and the West. In modern fields such as engineering and the iron, steel, and chemical industries, foreign participation reached 30 to 44 percent (*Magyar Statisztikai Évkönyv* 1915, 123–24). One-third of industrial investments in Bosnia were initiated by the Austro-Hungarian *Landesregierung,* or provincial government, which established the Gewerkschaft Bosnia to extract the country's rich mineral deposits and founded tobacco factories (Palairet 1997, 218, 220). Bosnian industrialization was thus initiated from abroad. Foreign capital inflow stimulated Central and Eastern European economic transformation by providing additional investments equivalent to one-quarter to one-third of domestic capital formation, by creating the basic network of transportation and banking, and also by initiating mining and processing. Dependence on foreign sources varied from country to country, as did the role of foreign ownership and its positive or negative consequences. In some cases, such as the Austro-Hungarian monarchy and the Russian empire, foreign investments played a stimulating role, giving an "initial push" to the domestic economy, while in other cases, such as, for example, some of the Balkan countries, it resulted in paralyzing dependence and the creation of isolated "foreign enclaves" within the preserved traditional economic environment. Nonetheless, various degrees of modernization were all connected with foreign capital investments in Central and Eastern Europe.

THE BELATED AGRICULTURAL REVOLUTION

Building railroads and founding banks, when combined with the previously introduced domestic reforms—liberation of the serfs, free access to

FIGURE 39. The organizing committee for the 1896 millennium celebration in Hungary. Courtesy Magyar Nemzeti Múzeum Történeti Fényképtára, Budapest.

FIGURE 40. Nicolae Grigorescu, *Romanian Great Boyar.* Oil on canvas. Courtesy Muzeul National de Artă al României, Bucharest.

FIGURE 41. Hungarian gentry playing cards, 1908. Courtesy Magyar Nemzeti Múzeum Történeti Fényképtára, Budapest.

FIGURE 42. Bureaucracy and army: the Bornemissza brothers (1905). Courtesy Hungarian National Museum, Budapest.

FIGURE 43. The Radziwiłł palace, Poland. Courtesy Muzeum Historyczne Miasta, Warsawy, Warsaw.

FIGURE 44. The Orlicí palace in the Czech lands. Courtesy SPN Pedagogicke Nakladelstvi, Prague.

FIGURE 45. Esterházy
Castle, Hungary.
Courtesy Magyar
Nemzeti Múzeum
Történeti Fényképtára,
Budapest.

FIGURE 46. Miklós
Barabás, *A Romanian
Peasant Family Go to
Market.* Courtesy
Magyar Nemzeti
Galéria, Budapest.

FIGURE 47. Shepherds in Hortobágy, Hungary. Courtesy Néprajzi Múzeum, Budapest.

FIGURE 48. Dance party in a middle-class Budapest home around 1900. Courtesy Hungarian National Museum, Budapest.

FIGURE 49. Soma Orlai Petrich, *Village School* (early nineteenth century).
Courtesy Magyar Nemzeti Galéria, Budapest.

FIGURE 50. Gymnasium (high school) in Brno, 1860s. Courtesy SPN
Pedagogicke Nakladelstvi, Prague.

FIGURE 51. The New York Café, one of Budapest's 300 coffeehouses. Courtesy Budapesti Történeti Múzeum Kiscell, Budapest.

FIGURE 52. Vincent Morstadt, *Wenceslas Square* (1830). Courtesy SPN Pedagogicke Nakladelstvi, Prague.

FIGURE 53. Wenceslas Square in 1870. Courtesy SPN Pedagogicke
Nakladelstvi, Prague.

FIGURE 54. Prague in 1911. Courtesy SPN Pedagogicke Nakladelstvi, Prague.

FIGURE 55. Kolozsvár-Cluj, 1860. Courtesy Fővárosi Szabó Ervin Könyvtár, Budapest.

FIGURE 56. Mosque in
Belgrade around 1900.
Courtesy Muzej Grada
Beograda, Belgrade.

FIGURE 57. Mosque in Plovdiv,
Bulgaria. Courtesy Bulgarian
Academy of Sciences, Center for
Architectural Studies, Sofia.

FIGURE 58. Mosque in Sofia, 1882. Courtesy Bulgarian Academy of Sciences, Center for Architectural Studies, Sofia.

FIGURE 59. The bazaar in Mostar, Bosnia-Herzegovina. Reprinted from Amir Pašić, *Islamic Architecture in Bosnia and Hercegovina* (Istanbul: IRCICA, OIC, 1994). Courtesy Research Centre for Islamic History, Art, and Culture of the Organisation of the Islamic Conference, Istanbul.

FIGURE 60. The Çarşi in Gjirokaster, Albania. Reprinted from Machiel Kiel, *Ottoman Architecture in Albania, 1385–1912* (Istanbul: IRCICA, OIC, 1990). Courtesy Research Centre for Islamic History, Art, and Culture of the Organisation of the Islamic Conference, Istanbul.

FIGURE 61. Charles Doussault, *A Street in Bucharest* in the 1830s. Reproduced from Florea, *Romanian Art*, 10. Courtesy Meridiane Publishing House, Bucharest.

FIGURE 62. Modernizing Belgrade. Courtesy Muzej Grada Beograda, Belgrade.

FIGURE 63. Modernizing Sofia. Courtesy Bulgarian Academy of Sciences, Center for Architectural Studies, Sofia.

FIGURE 64. Greek Orthodox monastery in Bulgaria. Courtesy Bulgarian Academy of Sciences, Center for Architectural Studies, Sofia.

FIGURE 65. Parliament building, Budapest, 1910. Courtesy Magyar Fotografiai Múzeum, Budapest.

FIGURE 66. Subway construction, Budapest, 1895. Courtesy Budapesti
Történeti Múzeum Kiscell, Budapest.

FIGURE 67. Hungarian village, 1900s. Courtesy Museum of Hungarian Architecture, Budapest.

land, and the creation of modern state institutions — provided the minimal requirements for capitalist transformation in the region. Virtually all of the achievements of the eighteenth-century agricultural revolution were belatedly introduced in most parts of Central and Eastern Europe between 1850 and 1913. Modern transportation directly connected the traditional food-producing regions with Western and imperial local markets. The expanding and virtually unlimited markets of rapidly industrializing Western Europe (including the western provinces of Austria-Hungary) became accessible. Railroads provided the link to export markets, as well as facilitating the importation of modern tools and machinery, while banks provided loans for investment and trade.

In Austria-Hungary, agricultural modernization was preceded by the transformation of the landed estates of the nobility. After the liberation of the serfs, roughly 30 percent of the land remained in the hands of former noble owners in Austria, one-third in Bohemia (owned by 151 families) and one-quarter (owned by 73 families) in Moravia. In Hungary, this share surpassed half of the land. The estates of the Princes Schwarzenberg, Lichtenstein, and Esterházy remained quasi-empires. After losing the free serf labor and tax exemptions, however, they emerged as modern capitalist estates. Because the liberation of the serfs with their fief land was compensated for, the big estates received huge financial resources for modernization. Prince Schwarzenberg received 3.7 million crowns, and two Lichtenstein princes 3.2 million crowns. Altogether, the former noble owners of the big estates in the hereditary provinces received 450 million crowns in compensation. During the first decade after 1848, 17 million forints were paid to Hungarian landowners.

Financing became abundant, however, only as a result of the emergence of a modern credit system. Mortgage credits in Austria-Bohemia and Hungary increased from 2.2 billion and 0.1 billion crowns in 1858 to 13.4 billion and 2.8 billion in 1907, respectively. Mortgage loans for landed estates reached 40 to 50 percent of land value in early twentieth-century Hungary and Austria-Bohemia. Capital was thus supplied.

Labor reserves were virtually unlimited. More than half of all Hungarian peasants were liberated without land or with tiny parcels, insufficient to support whole families. Austria-Bohemia was not much better off in this respect. A large proportion of the landless peasantry and the increasing peasant population — 39 percent of the agricultural population of Hungary, 36 percent in Bohemia and Moravia, and 30 percent in Austria — became wage laborers on big estates.

More efficient wage labor and independent peasant farming, especially in Austria, Bohemia, and in the Hungarian Great Plain, were introduced hand in hand with the basic accomplishments of the Western-style eighteenth-century agricultural revolution. The most important innovation was the introduction of a modern crop-rotation system in place of the ancient two- and three-field rotation system, with spring and fall crops each on one one-third of the land, while the remaining one-third remained fallow, which dominated agriculture in the region until the 1850s and 1860s. Adopting modern crop rotation meant a four- to seventeen-round (Norfolk) crop rotation. Wheat, barley, and other traditional crops were rotated with legumes, turnips, clover, sainfoin, alfalfa, ryegrass, peas, beans, and so on. This scientific system not only preserved but also enriched the soil, thanks to the nitrogen-fixing mechanism of the legumes. As a consequence, the amount of fallow land radically declined: in Hungary, from 22 percent in 1871–75 to only 10 percent in 1901–5; in Bohemia-Moravia from 22 percent in 1848 to 1 percent in 1908; and in Upper Austria from 14 percent in 1867 to 9 percent at the end of the century. One does not see a similar change in Galicia and Dalmatia, where the percentage share of fallow land remained almost unchanged and the traditional three-field crop rotation was preserved.

The modern rotation system was combined with innovations such as canalization, drainage, manuring, and new methods of soil conservation and management. In 1896, 18 kg of manure was used per acre in Hungary, enough to manure every ninth year. In the early twentieth century, artificial fertilizers also came into use: 17 kg per acre in Austria versus 5 kg per acre in Hungary in 1907. This amount increased nearly five times before the war.

Selected improved seeds, new, more efficient crops, and the beginning of mechanization all improved performance. The primary machine of the age, the steam engine, did not lead to the mechanization of agriculture, except for threshing, which became fully mechanized in the hereditary provinces and 90 percent mechanized in Hungary by the early twentieth century. The number of steam threshers per hectare, however, was only about one-tenth that in Germany. Steam plows were much less successful, although their number increased from seven to a hundred and fifty-nine on large Hungarian estates during the second half of the century. Heavier, steel-tipped plows, horse-drawn carts in place of ox-wagons, and sowing and harvesting machines increased productivity from ten- to fifteenfold. In 1902, only 233,000 estates out of the existing 2.8 million used animal-powered machines, while 38,000 used steam engines. Thus, altogether 9 percent of the estates introduced modern technology in Austria-Hungary.

Regional differences were tremendous: in Bohemia, 49 percent of the estates used machinery, but this included all of the estates larger than 5 hectares (Tremel 1969). On the other hand, only 511 steam engines were in operation in Galicia, so only one out of every 1,973 estates used one (in contrast with the western provinces, where one in every 342 estates did). Dalmatian subsistence farmers did not use machinery at all; moreover, five or six families together generally owned a single plow and a couple of draft animals.

The area under cultivation was enlarged and yields significantly increased. The yield of wheat, for example, in the hereditary provinces of Austria-Hungary increased by one-third between the first half of the 1870s and the first decade of the twentieth century, from 9.7 quintals to 12.6 quintals. Within this average, the Bohemian-Moravian yield per hectare was as high as 16.8 quintals, and the Austrian yield was 13.3 quintals, while Galician and Bukovinian yields were 11.6 quintals. Hungarian yields increased from 9.7 to 12.6 quintals during the same period. Grain production in Austria-Hungary, as a consequence, increased from 100.4 million quintals in 1844 to 138.1 million quintals by 1875–84, and to 217.6 million quintals by the prewar decade. While the output of the hereditary provinces increased by 74 percent, Hungary's output increased by more than one and a half times. Hungary emerged as the grain supplier of the empire: 60 percent of the arable land was given over to grain, half of this to wheat. Sugar-beet production, the empire's leading export industry, increased nearly threefold, from 22 million to 64.3 million quintals, in Austria-Bohemia, and nearly four times, from 6.7 million to 31 million quintals, in Hungary between the early 1870s and 1910s.

Replacing the traditional pasturing and grazing of animal stock also revolutionarized animal husbandry. The eighteenth-century agricultural revolution saw the introduction of stabling and stall-feeding, using a great variety of fodders, such as turnips, clover, and alfalfa, produced by the modern crop-rotation system. Peasants were no longer forced to slaughter a large proportion of their stock in late winter for lack of grazing. Scientific research also led to breed improvements: milk cows instead of oxen, meat pigs instead of fat pigs. In Hungarian animal husbandry, the traditional working oxen, the *magyarszürke,* constituted 78 percent of the stock in 1884. By 1911, however, the ratio of that breed had declined to 30 percent, behind imported, improved Swiss breeds. The cattle and pig stocks of the monarchy increased by two-thirds, and their value doubled, between 1850 and 1910. In Austria-Bohemia and the other hereditary provinces, there were 387 cattle and 123 pigs per 1,000 inhabitants. In Hungary, the figures were 335 cattle and 288 pigs.

Land tenure was similar in Poland and Romania to that of Austria-Hungary. The tsar's radical land reform in the final stage of the Polish uprising in March 1864 (altogether 4.4 million hectares went to nearly 700,000 freed serfs) affected only 40 percent of the land. However, between 1864 and 1890, peasant property increased by 8 percent to 43 percent of the total available land, while the share of noble estates dropped from 46 to 30 percent. All peasant obligations and landowners' control of villages were liquidated.

Unlike those in Hungary, Polish big estates were not the prime movers of agricultural modernization. Although mechanization of large estates had begun even before 1864, with the appearance of threshing machines, reapers, and the steam plow, "up to the 1880s, landowners had little incentive to engage in costly methods of intensive farming," Piotr Wandycz notes (Wandycz 1974, 200). Nor did they have the financial resources, since the tsarist regime punished the Polish nobility, especially the gentry, the pillar of Polish resistance, by paying only 64 million rubles in compensation for the land given to the peasants, while collecting nearly twice that in land taxes from the landowners.

Most of the peasant farmers continued traditional farming. One-third of the peasant estates were much smaller than two hectares and unsuitable for market production. Moreover, land reform postponed the consolidation of peasant estates, leaving them scattered in various small strips, not unlike the medieval village communes. The peasant economy preserved the three-field rotation system and continued subsistence farming. The only progressive sector was the more well-to-do peasants, who increased their landholdings following bankruptcies among the gentry, which led to a large proportion of newly created small farms. Landlessness, partly caused by insolvency, but mostly by very rapid population growth, actually quadrupled during the quarter of a century after land reform. However, only 30 percent of the estates were larger than nine hectares. On average, yields increased only by 10–25 percent, and agricultural output increased between 50 to 100 percent in the case of the main crops, before the war. Grain output more than doubled; potato output increased by four times between 1861–70 and 1911–13 (Kochanowicz 1995, 127). Unlike in Hungary and some of the eastern provinces of Austria-Hungary, agriculture did not become an export sector in Poland, but served to supply the rapidly increasing domestic market: the population of the country increased fourfold during the nineteenth century, more than doubling just between 1850 and 1900.

In the united Romanian Principalities, in terms of the Paris Treaty (paragraph 46), serfs were liberated and all feudal services were abolished in 1864. The landed estates of the monasteries, one-fourth of the landed area of Wallachia and one-third of that of Moldavia, were secularized, and all the 1.8 million hectares of land, cultivated by peasants, was granted to 468,000 families. The former serfs, *clacasi,* and free peasants, *razesi* and *mosneni,* however, owned only 30 percent of the agricultural land: 250,000 out of the 650,000 former serfs received no land at all or got only very small parcels; 85 percent of the peasants either had no land at all or had very small parcels, not enough to support a family. On the other hand, estates larger than 100 hectares, only 0.6 percent of the total number of estates, numbering at most five thousand large estates, occupied 55 percent of the agricultural land in Romania. Boyar and state estates together contained roughly 70 percent. From the eighteenth century on, a peculiar leasing system emerged. The peasants were obliged to lease from the big estates, and more than half of the estate land was leased out by the mid nineteenth century. In 1866, the law on agricultural contracts made five-year contracts obligatory. The government enforced it and violators were fined, imprisoned, or drafted into the army. "The eventual result was the establishment of a system of rural servitude that is often compared unfavorably with the feudal era," Paul Michelson writes (Michelson 1987, 113).

The big landowners, the boyars, collected their rent via *arendaşi,* lessee managers, nearly half of whom were Jewish and some others of whom were Greek grain merchants. The arendaşi subleased the land to peasants through an exploitative sharecropping system, often in exchange for half of the crop. The land reform of 1864 actually strengthened this system. Around the turn of the century, the system included 2.3 million hectares out of a total 3.8 million, including 60 percent of the area of the big estates, but 73 percent of estates larger than 3,000 hectares. The peasants, besides paying rent for the rented land (money and/or produce), were also obliged to work for the landlord or arendaşi, and provide *plocoane* ("gifts"). In addition to boyar and arendaşi exploitation, the central government and the county *(judeţ)* also robbed the peasants. The 1882 law on tax collection granted 3 to 9 percent of collected revenues to the tax collector. Consequently, taxes "in some parts of the country amounted to 80 percent of the peasants' total annual production" (Hitchins 1994, 176). The Land Law of 1889 permitted the sale of 1.2 million hectares of state land to decrease land hunger, but many of the new owners soon became insolvent. Peasants, however, could not leave the village. The Rural Law made their land inalienable. This kept the nearly landless peasants in the villages and permitted the boyars to impose whatever conditions they wanted, creating a "monstrous regime," as Henri Stahl calls it, in the decades before the war (Stahl 1980, 89). Robert Seton-Watson calls these years "the Golden Age of irresponsible landlordism"; "in some respects the peasant found himself as much exploited, as fatally tied to the soil, as in the vanished days of serfdom" (Seton-Watson [1934] 1963, 369).

Nothing had changed in Romania for centuries: peasants in the mid nineteenth century still used wooden plows, often without moldboards, or even just wooden hoes; the ground was not cleared, merely plowed twice, lengthwise and crosswise, and crop rotation was unknown (Stahl 1980, 53). At the beginning of the twentieth century, mechanization made its very first steps: only 4,600 steam threshers and 12,500 sowers, hardly more than half and one-quarter of the Hungarian figures, respectively, were employed in the Romanian fields (Serban 1914, 10). Latifundia were cultivated with primitive technology by peasant smallholders using their own livestock and implements. The term "latifundia fallow field" was used of the big estates (Stahl 1980, 92). Market opportunities, however, inspired a massive increase in cultivation. This process had already begun in the first half of the century, when the land under tillage nearly doubled in Moldavia. Seminomadic transhumant animal husbandry was rapidly replaced by land cultivation after 1860: arable land then represented only 20 percent of the total, but it had increased to 47 percent by 1906.

The land area devoted to grain in Romania increased from 2.5 million to 5.2 million hectares during the half century before World War I. The medieval exploitation of peasants on this increased land area led to a dramatic increase in output, although modern methods were hardly used, and there were no significant increases in yields—from 9.6 to 11.6 quintals of wheat per hectare over these fifty years. The newly cultivated land, which amounted to 86 percent of the country's arable land, was used for grain. Wheat and corn output increased from 672,000 and 912,000 tons to 2,223,000 and 2,666,000 tons, respectively: nearly a fourfold increase for wheat and a threefold increase for corn between the 1860s and 1910s (Axenciuc 1996).

The failure of the Balkan countries to introduce the revolutionary methods of modern agriculture was connected with the Ottoman legacy: absence of a landed nobility and of privately owned big estates; peasant smallholdings as the basic unit of production; and a certain commitment to egalitarianism (Todorova 1997, 172). The greatest obstacle facing the adoption of Western agricultural methods was, however, the South Slav land-tenure system, the "institution of universal peasant landownership"

(Palairet 1997, 308), with extremely small and overpopulated plots of three or four hectares. Ottoman land, including the market-oriented Serbian and Bulgarian *chifliks,* was confiscated and sold; sometimes, it was bought by a community and divided. The *zadruga,* a South Slav version of the medieval village community, with collective property, large families, and common communal work *(moba* and *pozaimitza),* survived into the twentieth century. The Serbian law created a special inheritance system for members: "Relationship in the house communion gives right of inheritance before even a higher degree of relationship out of the communion. The rights of an adopted member precede in respect of inheritance even those of blood relations without the house communion" (Mackenzie and Irby [1867] 1877, 2: 330). This and other forms of village communities, of course, played a positive role in clearing woods and expanding cultivated land. The organized collective work of the peasantry within the communities, using primitive technology, definitely helped the transition to agriculture from a pastoral economy. However, the zadruga was in permanent decline after the mid to late nineteenth century, when the 1844 Civil Code allowed its dissolution, which happened in most cases after 1878. An egalitarian community tradition, however, was strengthened by state regulations, which did not permit total pauperization of the peasants. Laws of 1860 and 1861 prohibited foreclosure on basic farm instruments, draft animals, and one hectare of land. Foreclosure for nonpayment of taxes was also forbidden (Stavrianos [1958] 1963, 261). Illiterate Balkan peasants with noncapitalistic communal attitudes could not adjust to modern requirements: "Foreign visitors and government officials called it laziness, ethnographers associated this behavior with the 'heroic' values of pastoral society, and intellectuals sidestepped the issue by referring to the 'pre-capitalistic' attitudes of the Balkan peasantry," Michael Palairet observes (Palairet 1997, 311).

The small parcels were largely incapable of producing for the market and supplied only family consumption. Balkan subsistence farming—in the best of cases, only one-third of farm produce was sold at market—remained traditional and incapable of structural and technological change. Nearly one-third of Serbian peasant farms had no draft animals, and 40 percent of them had no vehicles. Only one of ten farms in Bulgaria and Serbia in 1900 had an iron plow. "[I]ntensive crop cultivation and stock raising failed to materialize in any of the prewar Balkan states," say Lampe and Jackson (1982, 183). Owing to the rapidly growing population, agricultural productivity—that is, output per member of the farm population—consequently decreased, and it represented only 72 percent of the level of the early 1870s in Serbia and 62 percent in Bulgaria in the 1910s. "Grain agriculture never reattained the productivity of the late Ottoman period," according to Palairet (1997, 186).

Was there an absolute failure of agricultural modernization? Not at all. Around the turn of the century, major structural changes emerged. The most important advance in Balkan agriculture was renewed cultivation of plains and valleys thanks to the rapid transformation from transhumant animal husbandry, which had offered the only safe way of life for centuries in the Balkans. The cultivated area increased from 5.6 million to 8 million hectares, by 43 percent, in Bulgaria in less than a quarter of a century before World War I. In Serbia, the cultivated area was 0.39 million hectares in 1867, and 0.55 million hectares in 1889, but 1.05 million hectares in 1905, an impressive increase of nearly 270 percent. Serbian peasants cut down one-third of Serbia's forests in twenty years around the end of the century, thereby increasing the area of arable land. The woodlands formed the basis of pig raising, and the pig stock consequently diminished from 1.3 million in 1866 to 0.9 million head by 1890, a drop of nearly one-third. The role of livestock and animal products declined from 45 percent to 36 percent of Serbian farm output in consequence of the great transition from seminomadic animal husbandry to arable farming. Stockraising still remained very important: the roughly 400 and 600 cattle and 200 and 1,000 pigs per 1,000 inhabitants in Romania and Serbia, respectively, constituted a much higher density than was found in the rest of Europe.

The decline in the traditional pastoral economy was compensated for by grain and garden crop production, which increased by two and three times, respectively, between the early 1870s and 1910s. In Bulgaria, wheat and corn production doubled in the same period. Altogether, the Balkans became a major grain-producing area: wheat and corn output in Romania and Serbia, on the one hand, and Bulgaria, on the other, increased by three times and by one-third in the two decades around the turn of the century, reaching 37 million and 35 million quintals, respectively, in the early twentieth century. The grain economy became the most important sector of the Balkan economy. Technological backwardness was partly counterbalanced by higher manpower input. Given favorable climatic and soil conditions, output per unit of land was comparable to the world average: the Romanian 1.29 tons per hectare topped the European average (1.28), while the Bulgarian 1.06 and the Serbian 0.88 tons per hectare outmatched North American (0.98) and Argentinian (0.66) levels.

Agricultural modernization thus encouraged important export sectors, mostly a cereal monoculture. At least half of the cultivated land was given over to grain, producing 20 percent of the entire European output. Even the mostly subsistence-farming Balkan countries participated in international trade.

THE EXPORT SECTORS AND THEIR SPIN-OFF EFFECT

Foreign trade exploded in the nineteenth century. The value of world exports at constant prices totaled U.S.$7.3 billion (in 1990 dollars) in 1820, and jumped to $56.2 billion, then to $236.3 billion by 1870 and 1913, respectively (Maddison 1995, 236, 239). Europe's exports increased by an unparalleled annual 2.8 percent during the last decades of the century. Foreign trade expansion was one of the most characteristic features of the age. It was precisely between 1870 and 1913, when world trade increased fourfold, that Central and Eastern Europe became a factor in it. Capitalizing on the geographical proximity of the area to the European core and its phenomenal rise in import needs, Central and Eastern European countries expanded their exports faster than the European average. Bulgaria increased its exports by 5.3 percent annually between 1880 and 1910, the Russian empire by 4 percent, Romania and Serbia by 3.3–3.4 percent, and Hungary by 3 percent (Bairoch 1973). Before World War I, Central and Eastern Europe contributed roughly 16 percent of European trade, while the Scandinavian and Mediterranean countries' trade combined totaled only 12 percent.

Exports consisted of a few agricultural products, primarily grain. Hungarian agricultural exports increased by more than twelve times, from U.S.$30 to $381 million (1913 dollars) between 1850 and 1913. Hungary, which exported two-thirds of its wheat in processed form as wheat flour, became one of the biggest global wheat and wheat-flour exporters, with 2.6 percent of the world's wheat, and 24 percent—second behind the United States—of world wheat-flour exports. Until the end of the nineteenth century, 70 percent of the wheat-flour exports went to Western Europe, while 30 percent went to the western provinces of the empire. After the turn of the century, however, the Western European market was virtually conquered by American wheat flour, and Hungary's exports were reoriented toward Austria-Bohemia, which "imported" nearly 98 percent of Hungary's exports in the 1910s.

Romania exported half of its wheat and 40 percent of its corn production and became the fourth-biggest grain exporter in the world.

Wheat exports, more than 60 percent of total exports, represented 8.3 percent of the world's wheat exports. In the early 1860s, Serbia exported no grain, but by 1880, 20,000 tons, and by 1912, 210,000 tons were exported, mostly from the Danube and Sava ports. Around the turn of the century, more than one-quarter of Bulgarian and 13 percent of Serbian grain went to exports. Grain represented roughly 70–71 percent of Romanian and Bulgarian exports and one-third of Serbian exports (Lampe and Jackson 1982, 169).

Livestock exports continued to play an important role in the Balkans' trade. Serbia's per capita production of pigs and cattle ranked first and second in the world, respectively. Livestock and animal products remained the number 1 export until the end of the nineteenth century, representing roughly 40 percent of total exports. By the early twentieth century, however, this share dramatically declined to one-fifth of total Serbian exports. A similar trend characterized the export of prunes. During the 1880s, peasants harvested the fruit from the plum forests of northern Serbia and dried the plums in homemade mud-brick stoves *(pusnica)*. This cottage industry produced one-quarter of total Serbian exports. As a consequence of agricultural transformation and growing grain farming, prune exports dropped to 10 percent of Serbia's total exports by the 1890s. Besides grain, Bulgaria also produced and exported tobacco, which did not require sophisticated processing. Tobacco leaves were dried in the sun, then cut up. Roses, rose oil, and certain garden products also offered some export possibilities. Almost all of the Central and Eastern European countries, however, lacked the necessary diversification in exports. The five leading export items of these countries, all of them agricultural products with low market elasticity, represented 75 to 80 percent of exports. Very few nonagricultural products were available for export.

The Austrian-Bohemian provinces of Austria-Hungary, of course, adhered to a rather different model. Because of their successful industrialization and the industrial-agricultural division of labor between the western and eastern parts of the empire, processed industrial products dominated exports. The most important Austrian-Bohemian export to Western European markets was, however, sugar. Roughly 60 percent of production was exported, accounting for nearly 10 percent of total exports in 1910. Beer followed a distant second, with only 10 percent of the value of sugar exports. The most important market for the rapidly developing Austrian and Czech industries at the turn of the century, especially for the leading sectors, textiles, iron, and engineering, was the agrarian half of the empire: Hungary and the other unindustrialized eastern provinces. More than 78 percent of cotton products, 62 percent of woolen products, 57 percent of clothing, and 56 percent of silk products were sold in Hungary in 1910. Around the turn of the century, 85 percent of Hungarian textile consumption was satisfied by Austrian and Czech products. This share declined to 70 percent before the war. In the case of Galicia, Bukovina, Dalmatia, and Bosnia-Herzegovina, Austrian-Czech industrial products flooded and dominated the entire market (Schwartz 1913; Hertz 1917).

While Austria-Bohemia was the dominant core of Austria-Hungary, Poland, at the western rim of the Russian empire, was repeatedly and bloodily defeated militarily, brutally oppressed politically, and much less industrialized than Bohemia. However, in 1851, Poland became a part of the Russian tariff system, sheltered by Russian protectionism, which closed the huge market to Western goods in 1877. The extremely large Russian empire was more backward than Poland. This situation opened a great opportunity for Polish industry. Meanwhile, the Polish elite gave up their repeated attempts at armed uprising and turned to "organic work." Bolesław Prus's novel *Lalka* (The Doll) expressed and promoted this change. The main hero, Wokulski, a nobleman who participates in the 1863 uprising, is imprisoned, exiled, and then, dissatisfied with his own traditional "Polishness," turns to business and becomes a highly success-ful businessman. "In relying on the power of money, Wokulski comes to wield it as the sole instrument for achieving his ideals" (Holmgren 1998, 71). In the new environment, and with this new attitude to business, Poland could indeed exploit unlimited export possibilities. Poland's ex-port goods to Russia were almost entirely industrial products such as tex-tiles, coal, and iron. Polish foreign trade rocketed: in 1850, its value was 16 million rubles, by 1880, 246 million, and by 1910, 1,213 million. Between 1890 and 1910, trade nearly trebled. In 1864, one-quarter of Polish in-dustrial output was exported to Russia. By 1900–1910, this share had in-creased by two-thirds. According to Andrzej Jezierski, nearly 80 percent of the 515 million rubles in Polish exports to Russia were textiles and iron goods in 1910. The textile and iron industries exported 80 percent and 40 percent of their products to Russia, respectively. Agricultural and animal products, on the other hand, constituted less than 12 percent of Polish ex-ports (Jezierski 1967, 52–162; Kochanowicz 1995, 131, 134).

Export possibilities triggered relatively rapid industrialization. Between the 1870s and 1910, the number of industrial workers increased more than fourfold, and industrial output eightfold (Kula 1947, 42). Poland's ex-tremely rich, high-grade coal resources offered a great opportunity for establishing an important export sector: coal output increased from 0.9 to 6.8 million tons, nearly sevenfold between 1878 and 1913. Raw materials extraction, however, inspired processing as well. Traditional iron-ore mining was modernized and an efficient iron and steel industry was established. Steel output increased from 0.1 to 4.6 million tons between 1854 and 1903. Around Warsaw, modern engineering industries produced transport and farming machinery. The value of the output of the Warsaw machine-building industry increased by sixfold between 1864 and 1880 (Kochanowicz 1995, 133). Mining, iron, steel, and engineering industries embodied one-fifth of industrial production in 1910. The textile industry became the leading export sector, however. Nearly half of all industrial workers were employed in textiles, and they produced almost half of the country's total industrial output (Kostrowicka et al. 1966, 218).

Although rapid growth of the domestic market was, as Ireneusz Ihnatowicz and Andrzej Jezierski stress, important for the development of the Polish industry, especially textiles, the unique industrial development of Poland was based on exports to the booming Russian market: after the elimination of internal borders in 1851, Polish industrial output increased threefold in twenty years. During the next twenty years, production quadrupled again. Around the turn of the century, Poland produced 40 percent of the Russian empire's coal, 23 percent its steel, 20 percent of its textiles, and 15 percent of its iron, and Polish per capita industrial production was twice that of Russia.

In Hungary, industrial exports accounted for only about 37–38 percent of total exports. Two-thirds of Hungarian exports fell into the category of processed food, mostly wheat flour for the western provinces of Austria-Hungary. The role of wheat flour in Hungary's exports to Western Europe diminished dramatically, however, from 34 percent in 1880 to 9 percent in 1910, while sugar (12 percent), processed wood products (9 percent), electric bulbs, and engineering products began to play a more important role (Berend and Ránki 1974).

Hungary and Poland profited from the increase in agricultural and raw materials production. Both countries had safe, guaranteed markets within the empires to which they belonged. Additionally, prices were higher than world market prices. During the last quarter of the nineteenth century, when world grain prices dropped by nearly one-third because of American competition, Hungary enjoyed a 30 percent price increase for grain in the protected market of Austria-Bohemia. These markets opened very early in the mid nineteenth century, and the rapid agricultural growth, 2 percent annually for half a century, soon generated massive investments in grain processing. The first modern mechanized flour mill, Pesti Henger-malom Társaság, was established in 1838, but the real *Gründerzeit,* the age of boosterism, began in the 1860s. The great grain merchants who sold the products of the Hungarian estates in Austria-Bohemia soon realized that the best place to invest their accumulated capital was the mill indus-try, which, at this early stage, paid about 50 percent interest, potentially doubling one's assets in two years. By 1867, fourteen joint-stock export mills were in operation, and the horsepower of the flour-mill industry in-creased thirteenfold in a decade. Unique prosperity followed the Austro-Hungarian Compromise of 1867. One-third of the newly founded joint-stock companies were flour mills. By 1866, the big Budapest export mills were grinding 50,000 tons of wheat annually, and by 1879, 430,000 tons. At the end of the century, their output was valued at 646 million crowns and embodied more than 44 percent of Hungary's industrial production. By 1913, the output of Hungary's food-processing industries had doubled again, but it now constituted only 39 percent of the country's industrial production. Hungary built up the world's second-largest flour-mill in-dustry, behind the United States. Unlike Russia and Romania, which ba-sically exported their huge grain harvests unprocessed, Hungary processed two-thirds of its exported grain.

The impressive spin-off effect generated by the dramatically increased agricultural production and exports went far beyond processing grain. The flourishing flour-mill industry offered a good market for the domestic en-gineering industry. In place of the traditional millstones, for example, the innovative engineers of the spectacularly rising Ganz Company introduced patented cast-iron-roller milling, a major technological improvement that contributed to the boom in the flour-mill industry. Rolling mills soon became an export item in and of themselves. Starting with the relatively small Röck, Schlick, Vidats, and Ötl works, Hungarian companies pro-duced everything from plows to threshing machines; and they were joined, after 1900, by the largest, the Austrian-English firm of Hoffer, Schrantz, Clayton & Shuttleworth. In 1912, the Kühne Machine Factory sold its first tractors as well. Domestic production could not cover the entire demand, but, at the beginning of the twentieth century, it met at least half of it.

Industrial production for agriculture and food processing was not the only spin-off. Another important impact was the growing domestic cap-ital accumulation from the grain trade and from processing, which led to investments in various branches of industry. Two examples may illumi-nate this process. Two Jewish merchant houses, the Weiss and Deutsch families, founded their fortunes on the grain trade with Austria, and were among the first investors in the flour-mill industry. The Deutsch family—later Baron Hatvani-Deutsch—pioneered the Hungarian sugar industry. Adolf B. Weiss, a former village pipe maker turned grain merchant and flour-mill owner, established the richest bourgeois dynasty in the country. His two sons, Berthold and Manfred, later Baron Csepeli-Weiss, founded the first canning factory in the country in 1884. Military contracts inspired them to produce products other than food for the army, a guaranteed buyer, and munitions were an obvious choice. The factory moved to remote Csepel Island, south of Budapest, where, by the early twentieth century, Hungary's largest iron and steel and engineering companies employed 5,000 (during World War I, 30,000) workers. The grain trade and milling industry thus provided an opening to other branches of industry. Agricultural prosperity and exports became a source of further industrialization and structural changes.

The same kind of spin-off effect evolved from railroad construction. As we have seen, Austrian and other foreign investors in Hungary financed railroads. During the 1850s and early 1860s, virtually everything needed to build them was imported, from rails to locomotives. Extensive railroad construction, however, created a huge and flourishing market for domestic entrepreneurs. The Austrian railroad and shipping companies first sought to open Hungarian coal mines so that a nearer and cheaper supply could replace coal from Bohemia. Austrian transportation companies opened anthracite sources in the country, in Pécs and Stájerlak-Anina, and Resica-Domán in southern Transylvania. At the last site, the Austrian State Railway Company began the extraction of iron ore as well and built up a significant iron- and steelworks. Hungarian entrepreneurs soon joined: in 1852, the Rimamurány Iron Works Co. was formed from three smaller companies. The Ganz Co.'s main product in the 1850s, based on a technological innovation, was the cast-iron railway-carriage wheel. By the 1880s, the company produced railroad tracks as well. By the end of the century, five large companies produced 28,000 pieces of railroad tracks during the 1890s, twice as many as had been produced in the previous decade. In 1873, the Hungarian State Railway Company founded the Magyar Államvasúti Gépgyár (MÁVAG), which during the first quarter century of its existence built a thousand locomotives, and subsequently won a gold medal at the Paris world exhibition in 1900. During the second half of the nineteenth century, Hungary, unlike the Balkan countries, was able to supply and expand its large network of railroads with coal, rails, and locomotives without imports (Berend and

Ránki 1974). Domestic capital accumulation, an entrepreneurial attitude, and a rapidly growing, skilled, educated labor force thus generated spin-offs that included structural changes and the beginnings of industrialization from the agricultural boom and the external influence of railroad investments.

Additional factors such as cheap labor, and weak oversight of working conditions, made the Hungarian and other Central and Eastern European industry more competitive. According to the Hungarian industrial and labor statistics report of 1901, the work day exceeded ten hours in 71.2 percent of the factories (*Üzemi és munkás statisztika* 1901, 96). The statistical report of 1910 registered the characteristics of an early capitalist factory system: of 4,835 factories, only 109 had bathrooms with showers, and only 75 had cafeterias (ibid. 1910). At one textile factory, "in one year," reported the government's industrial inspector in 1910, "one quarter of the female workers got tuberculosis" (*Iparfelügyelöi jelentés* 1910, 895).

The Balkan countries could not generate industrial development. Aside from a few unprocessed agricultural products, their only nonagricultural export items were unprocessed raw materials. Extraction began around the turn of the century in Romania and Serbia. The discovery of rich Serbian copper resources enticed French investors to open mines. Roughly 40 percent of industrial investments were channeled into mining before the war. Output, however, was not yet significant. Romanian oil played a much more important role. One of Europe's richest oil fields was discovered in Romania during the 1860s, but extraction could not begin before 1895, when a new mining law enabled foreign investment. The big German banks, headed by the Deutsche Bank, rushed into the business, followed by Royal Dutch Shell and Standard Oil. Between 1901 and 1914, Romanian oil production increased from 298,000 tons to 1.8 million tons, and the country became the fifth-largest producer in the world. Next to grain, unprocessed crude oil was Romania's second most important export, accounting for 12 percent of total exports before the war (Lampe and Jackson 1982, 264). The crude oil was processed mostly abroad, and Romania still imported refined oil.

From the 1870s and 1880s on, the peasant cottage industry that had supplied most of the demand for industrial consumer goods was gradually replaced by large-scale industry; flour mills and sugar refineries produced one-third of Romania's industrial output (Iacob 1996). Timber and oil extraction were responsible for more than 36 percent, while other branches hardly existed: textiles and metallurgy each represented 8 percent. Altogether 54,000 small and medium-sized enterprises were in operation in early twentieth-century Romania. Six large joint-stock companies controlled 40 percent of industrial capital stocks. Industry produced only 17 percent of the national income (Hitchins 1994, 161, 192–93).

Austria-Hungary and the Russian empire were almost self-sufficient and offered the most important single market for the Czech lands, Hungary, and Poland. The Balkan countries were both part of a large European division of labor and also connected and integrated into a neighboring imperial unit: during the 1870s and 1880s, Romania had a one-sided trade connection with Austria-Hungary and more than one-third of its exports were sold there. By the early twentieth century, however, the share of the Austrian-Hungarian market had dropped to 10 percent, while Belgium, Britain, and France absorbed more than half of Romanian exports. Serbia, on the other hand, remained highly dependent on Austria-Hungary during the 1870s and 1880s. Nearly 90 percent of Serbian exports were sold in the neighboring empire. Although this overwhelming share had declined significantly by the early twentieth century, 40 percent of Serbian exports still went to Austria-Hungary in 1911. Germany, however, emerged as a major partner, buying 25 percent of total Serbian exports. Independent Bulgaria remained dependent on Ottoman markets for a while: 44 percent of the country's exports were still sold there at the end of the 1880s. This share, however, declined to one-quarter by the early twentieth century, and to 16 percent in 1911, while Belgium, Britain, and Germany bought more than half of Bulgaria's export products. Central and Eastern Europe became an integral part of the European economy, and exports were the driving force of modernization. The central question, however, is whether "the countries of [the] area had become trapped in the role of raw material [and food] exporters, or rather, would be able to go on from there to build up a suitably developed economic structure" (Berend and Ránki 1982, 119).

The Balkan countries, with their monocultural grain economies, had very little chance. Grain and raw material prices declined by one-third during the last third of the nineteenth century. In addition to their lack of export diversity and the "complementary" role of their economies, tied to much stronger partners, the Balkan countries' technology for processing plums, tobacco, and even grain and hogs was rather primitive. Some of these products were processed in a traditional cottage-industry style, financed and marketed by merchants. Most important, however, the dominant subsistence farming and lack of sufficient capital accumulation created strong obstacles to adjusting to the demands of the world market. In addition, the social environment of bigoted, strongly communal, and illiterate peasant societies, without a significant middle-class or entrepreneurial culture, overseen by a corrupt military-bureaucratic elite, hampered the ability to adjust. Domestic preconditions for a spin-off effect were and remained rudimentary in the Balkans.

The Balkans, as well as the entire Ottoman empire, also had to cope with devastating competition from the advanced Western countries. The Anglo-Ottoman Treaty of 1838 fixed duties, eliminated monopolies, and led to an impressive increase in imports of cheap foreign goods, especially until the 1860s. The Industrial Revolution in the core countries thus at least temporarily destroyed the traditional guild and cottage industries in the Ottoman periphery. Deindustrialization had a long-lasting effect and could not be overcome before the last third of the century (Keyder 1991, 166–68).

As a consequence, agricultural modernization and radically increased exports could not generate structural changes in the economy. Romania—like Russia—continued exporting 98 percent of its significant grain production without processing. Unlike in Hungary, a modern flour-mill export industry was not created. Serbia—unlike Denmark—continued exporting live and slaughtered pigs and cattle, without introducing milk or meat processing or producing more sophisticated products, with lower prices as a result.

This internal weakness played the primary role in a series of defeats in trade wars and competition for markets. Austria-Hungary introduced prohibitive tariffs against Romanian hogs in 1882 and launched a trade war between 1886 and 1889. Romanian exports to Austria-Hungary, as a consequence, dropped from 34 percent to 7 percent from 1881–85 to 1886–90. In 1895–96, the empire closed its markets to Serbian hogs on a veterinary pretext, cutting Serbian pig exports to Austria-Hungary by half. This measure was repeated in 1906 and led to the five-year-long "Pig War." Serbian exports to Austria-Hungary dropped from 86 percent to 28 percent from 1901–5 to 1906–10. In 1896 and 1906, the empire virtually closed its borders to cheap Balkan grain, which was imported by big Hungarian flour mills to mix with high-grade Hungarian grain, decreasing the cost of production. The special *őrlési forgalom,* or milling customs-reimbursement system—a virtually tariff-free import system in which for every 70 kg of wheat flour exported from 100 kg of imported grain, the state repaid the import tariff—was first restricted, then entirely abolished (Berend and Ránki 1953, 250–51). The Balkan grain exporters thus lost one of their most important markets. For various reasons, the Balkan countries often lost their markets from one decade to the other: Bulgarian exports to the Ottoman empire dropped from 44 to 29 percent between 1886–90 and 1891–95, and Romania lost a great part of its British market—its exports declined from 54 to 19 percent—between 1886–90 and 1896–1900 (Lampe and Jackson 1982, 174).

Romania's rich oil resources might have offered greater opportunities for a major spin-off effect in structural changes in the economy. In reality, this did not happen. Although the high price elasticity and marketability of crude oil could have initiated the development of processing and established a modern chemical industry, the foreign investors, Royal Dutch Shell, Standard Oil, and the German banks, extracted the crude and transported it to their own countries. In 1915, they built a pipeline to the Black Sea. Domestic processing hardly developed: only 41 million lei was invested to build refineries—mostly on the eve of war— out of the more than 400 million lei invested in the oil industry. Romania's second-largest key export sector thus remained an isolated enclave with no major impact on the transformation of the national economy; in H. W. Singer's words, it was "an outpost of the economies of the more developed investing countries" (Singer 1950).

The northernmost and southernmost provinces of Austria-Hungary, such as Galicia and Bosnia-Herzegovina, experienced economic trends similar to those in the Balkans. Galicia's monocultural potato plantations and low-quality beef cattle served only the export market (mostly to the western provinces of the empire). The same was true of the newly discovered rich oil resources. The Drohobycz and Polanka oil fields were exploited by international companies, and their output increased in a spectacular way: Galicia produced 1.2 percent and 5 percent of the world's oil output in 1900 and 1909, respectively, and became the third-largest oil producer in the latter year, but production was not processed domestically (Topolski 1982). Bosnia-Herzegovina, liberated from centuries of Ottoman occupation, and immediately occupied (1878), then annexed (1908) by Austria-Hungary, did not have the necessary domestic economic, social, and cultural forces to generate structural changes and industrialization from agricultural and raw material production and exports along Polish and Hungarian lines. Foreign investors were not attracted to the area, mostly because of its lack of infrastructure and educated labor. In the late 1860s, plums remained the province's most valuable product, and only one man in a hundred could read (Mackenzie and Irby [1867] 1877, 1).

Bosnia, however, had rich resources: wood, coal, rock salt, and metals. The Austrian Landesregierung, headed by Count Benjamin Kállay, continued a committed "civilizing mission" according to the most enlightened colonial policies and initiated an embryonic semi-industrialization process (Palairet 1997, 217–37). Like the other Balkan countries, Bosnia was characterized by subsistence farming, and the literacy rate did not surpass 12 percent of the population in the early twentieth century. However, the empire's railways connected the province with Hungary and with the sea at Fiume (Rijeka), and state investments developed raw material extraction and semimanufactured processing branches. By 1907, nearly one-third of Bosnia's industrial capacity (in terms of labor force) was created by fully or partially state-owned companies. All significant mineral resources were provided to the Gewerkschaft Bosnia and Varaser Eisenindustrie A.G. Large chemical factories were founded at Lukavac and Jajce. Long-term concessions initiated a private forestry and timber industry and granted a de facto monopoly—more than two-thirds of cutting rights—to two companies. The Bavarian Otto Steinbeis established his sawmills at Dobrljin and Drvar and employed 10,000 workers. The timber industry soon became the leading branch of Bosnia's infant industrial sector. Steinbeis expanded his business and built pulp mills in 1907. State-generated industrialization focused on export-oriented businesses: 86 percent of the industrial labor force was employed by export industries, which produced mostly semimanufactured products. During Bosnia's quarter of a century of Austrian rule, annual industrial growth surpassed 12 percent, leading to a higher rate of industrialization than that of the other Balkan countries: by 1910, more than 17 percent of the active population worked in large-scale industry, compared to 14 percent in Russia, 5.5 percent in Serbia, and only 3.5 percent in Bulgaria. Wage levels surpassed Serbian and Bulgarian wages by one-fifth and one-third, respectively. With only 21 percent of the population of Bosnia, Serbia, and Bulgaria combined, Bosnia-Herzegovina had about 54 percent of the region's large-scale industry (Palairet 1997, 237).

Bosnia's introductory structural changes, however, left most of the traditional sectors intact. The two largest industries, clothing and food processing, remained almost entirely small-scale. In 1907, more than 25,000 out of a total of 29,000 industrial establishments did not employ workers at all, and nearly 4,000 others had only two employees on average. Only 187 firms represented large-scale industry. Small-scale handicraft industries, including the proto-industrial textile branches, collapsed as a result of competition from Austrian industrial products. On the whole, Bosnia-Herzegovina's transformation remained extremely fragile. The province, like most of the unindustrialized countries of the Balkans, exhibited a dual economic structure: the export sectors formed isolated enclaves within the Bosnian economy as a whole, while all the rest remained traditional and deeply backward.

Domestic consumption of industrial products was partly covered by the traditional cottage industry of peasant families. Clothing, shoes, and even furniture, home appliances, and instruments were often made at home or by local handicraft industries. The bulk of the demand for machinery, industrial consumer goods, and transportation equipment, especially in urban centers, was satisfied by imports. The overwhelming majority of imports consisted of processed industrial products. In the case of the eastern and southern provinces of Austria-Hungary, Austrian, Bohemian, and partly Hungarian industrial products flooded the domestic markets. In Romania and Bulgaria, roughly half of total imports originated from Austria-Hungary and Germany, one-fifth to one-quarter from France and Britain. More than two-thirds of Serbia's imports came from Austria-Hungary and Germany. Serbia could finance its imports from its export incomes, but Romania and Bulgaria ran huge trade deficits.

Impressive increases in agricultural and raw materials exports generated higher imports, growth rates, and incomes but had little effect on the transformation and structural changes of the Balkan economies. Galicia, Bukovina, Dalmatia, and Bosnia-Herzegovina remained overwhelmingly agricultural- and raw materials–producing areas without a significant spin-off effect or the beginning of industrialization.

REGIONAL DIFFERENCES

Central and Eastern Europe exhibited extreme regional differences. In terms of industrialization and per capita income, the region's western rim—Austria and Bohemia-Moravia—approached Western European levels. On the other hand, the Balkans and the easternmost and southernmost provinces of Austria-Hungary remained unindustrialized and had the lowest per capita income levels in Europe (see table 2). Hungary and Poland, although remaining basically agricultural, demonstrated an impressive beginning of industrialization and, in terms of per capita income level, stood in between the western and eastern rim countries of the region (Milward and Soul 1977; Berend and Ránki 1982).

Austria-Hungary's GNP was only three-quarters that of the advanced economies of Western Europe. Within Austria-Hungary, however, the Austrian-Bohemian lands surpassed the empire's average by roughly 60

TABLE 2 *The Occupational Structure of Central and Eastern Europe, 1910 (percentage of population)*

	Agricultural	Industrial
Austria	35	46
Bohemia-Moravia-Silesia	34	51
Hungary	64	23
Poland	63	24
Galicia and Bukovina	73	18
Dalmatia	83	9
Croatia	79	13
Romania	75	10
Serbia	82	7
Bulgaria	75	10

SOURCE: Iván T. Berend and György Ránki, *The European Periphery and Industrialization, 1780–1914* (Cambridge: Cambridge University Press, 1982), p. 159.

percent and were approaching the Western level, while Hungary reached only three-quarters of the empire's average, and Galicia hardly exceeded half that level (Österreichisches Institut für Wirtschaftsforschung 1965, 31). GNP in Hungary and Poland stood at 56–58 percent that of Western Europe, while the GNP of the eastern and southern provinces of Austria-Hungary and the Balkan countries hardly surpassed 40 percent of that mark (Bairoch 1976a, 279).

Economic modernization experienced significant successes in Central and Eastern Europe. Modern economic institutions were established, a belated agricultural revolution profoundly increased output and exports, modern railroads connected the area to other parts of the continent, and income levels rose conspicuously. In some of the countries, especially in the Austrian-Bohemian territories, industrialization broke through, and the area followed the historical structural changes of the West. In others, such as Hungary and Poland, structural changes began transforming the countries' economies, but they remained far behind and could not join the club of the industrialized West. Their success was painfully limited. Most of the countries of the region had dual economies. Witold Kula speaks of the "co-existence of asynchronism" between "mechanized industries and . . . industries which were technologically obsolete. We deal with a harmonic association of large-scale industry with petty-commodity production. These phenomena cannot be explained by the 'lagging behind' approach. Their character turned out to be a lasting one" (Szlajfer 1991,

113, quoting Kula 1983, 75). The coexistence of the traditional and modern, of a preindustrial rural economy alongside industrial cities, turned out to be a lasting characteristic of Central and Eastern Europe.

The eastern and southern provinces of Austria-Hungary and the Balkan countries, however, did not even reach this duality. The phase of modern structural changes remained a distant goal in the overwhelmingly agricultural and raw materials–producing countries. Despite its economic progress and advances, the region humiliatingly failed to modernize.

CHAPTER 5

SOCIAL CHANGES

"Dual" and "Incomplete" Societies

INDUSTRIALIZATION AND SOCIAL RESTRUCTURING
IN THE WEST

REVOLUTIONS OR RADICAL sociopolitical reforms and industrialization caused dramatic changes in traditional societies. The nobility, the former leading elite, lost its privileges and had to adjust to a new capitalist market economy. Its "natural" political and military power was eliminated or severely weakened. A new elite emerged in the form of the banking and industrial bourgeoisie, representing an overwhelming economic power. A similar transformation took place in the lower layers of the society: the peasantry became free, and its numbers and proportion in society rapidly decreased. The peasantry, which had made up two-thirds to three-quarters of the population of agrarian societies, began to disappear. Britain's radical social transfiguration epitomized the future: by the early twentieth century, the agricultural-peasant population had faded to just 5 percent of Britain's population. France, Germany, and other Western European countries remained far behind Britain, but the trend was the same. The real disappearance of the peasantry was only complete fifty to seventy years later, during the second half of the twentieth century.

The majority of the rural population shifted to industry and became blue-collar workers. Most of them worked in big factories. They formed a relative majority of the new society, often more than one-third, and in some cases even more than 40 percent, of the population. In mid-nineteenth-century Britain, at the height of this spectacular transformation process, Karl Marx and Friedrich Engels described the propensity for social change and predicted the emergence of a polarized class society with an ever smaller and richer bourgeoisie accumulating the wealth. At the other pole, they placed the growing number of exploited industrial proletarians lacking all "means of production" and accumulating nothing but poverty (Marx and Engels [1848] 1988).

In reality, however, nineteenth-century Western class society—in the sense that the *philosophes,* Marx, and Max Weber used this term—changed remarkably after 1870. A striking new phenomenon appeared: the rise of a modern middle class. An army of white-collar service workers and bureaucrats emerged, including a new professional layer of teachers, lawyers, medical doctors, journalists, and entertainers. Although it would be nearly a century before they became a majority in the advanced societies of the West, this growing middle class was the most rapidly expanding social group around 1900.

Two layers became visibly different within a new entrepreneurial elite: a financially and socially higher-ranked upper middle class, and a steadily expanding modern lower middle class, including bureaucratic and professional groups. This bourgeois middle class and the working masses characterized nineteenth-century Western society. The former nobility had to adjust to the new situation. The landowning aristocracy went through a gradual process of *embourgeoisement.* The former middle class, most of all the lower nobility, the gentry, with smaller landed estates, and the privileged urban patrician class became déclassé and virtually disappeared into the various layers of the new society.

This new, "ideal typical" social pattern, using a Weberian category, did not, however, break through entirely in the West before World War I. Arno Mayer clearly recognized the "importance of the modern forces that undermined and challenged the old order." He rightly argued "that until 1914 the forces of inertia and resistance contained and curbed this dynamic and expansive new society within the *anciens régimes* that dominated Europe's historical landscape" (Mayer 1981, 6). The nobles retained much of their wealth and status and dominated strategic economic stations, while compensating for their loss by moving into key positions in the new armies and state bureaucracies. They learned to adapt and renew themselves, preserving their interests by a gradual *embourgeoisement.* The *grands* bourgeois, the "aristocratizing barons of industry" in Britain, France, and Germany, imitated the ways of the nobility, built mansions on their country estates, and assumed aristocratic poses and lifestyles. The old elite, in Joseph Schumpeter's words, remained a *classe dirigente* in "active symbiosis" with the rising bourgeoisie (Schumpeter 1955). If the aristocratic establishment was not yet passé in most of nineteenth-century Western Europe, it remained vigorous in Central and Eastern Europe, which did not start to transform itself along Western lines until the last third of the century, and then only in piecemeal fashion. The absence of successful industrialization and the preservation of agrarian economies buttressed the role of the noble elite and perpetuated the status of the peasantry, still somewhere between two-thirds and more than three-quarters of the total population.

A modern working class accounted for only one-tenth to one-fifth of the population. Although the traditional nobility lost its privileges, it preserved economic power through ownership of 40 to 50 percent of the land. Nobles continued monopolizing political power. The emerging bourgeoisie remained small and much less influential than its Western counterpart. It could not, and did not even try to, share political power with the traditional elite of the region. Similarly, a modern middle class hardly emerged; the traditional gentry middle class preserved its social status. There was thus a special "symbiosis" between the old and new social strata, which coexisted in a unique "dual society."

The least industrialized Balkan countries were the former provinces of the Turkish empire that became independent in the 1860s and 1870s, which long continued to bear the marks of Ottoman rule and remained wholly peasant societies, with neither a modern working class nor a modern middle class. The most peculiar feature of the Balkan societies, however, was the almost total lack of a national elite as a proprietor class or a politically dominant layer. The former landowning military and political elite had consisted of the occupying Turks, and, to a much lesser extent, of converted, "Ottomanized" Bosnian, Albanian, and Bulgarian elites, subordinated to the Sultan. After the liberation of the Balkan countries led to the disappearance of the bulk of the previous elite, Balkan societies were left "incomplete," "eliteless" societies. The gap began to be filled by members of the military and bureaucratic classes of the newly independent countries, but these soon followed the Ottoman pattern and became rich by exploiting the opportunity to hold office. Urban and rural peasant-merchants also became a substitute bourgeois layer and part of an emerging elite.

Just as in economic modernization, social transformation remained partial and unfinished in Central and Eastern Europe. "Dual" and "incomplete" societies represented both the dominant traditional characteristics and the new elements of a rather sluggishly modernizing society. While in the West, a new society started to replace the old, in Central and Eastern Europe, old and new lived in parallel, but the new was unquestionably subordinated to the old.

THE DUAL SOCIETY: THE SURVIVAL OF THE NOBLE ELITE

Between 1848 and the 1860s, the serfs were liberated, noble privileges were abolished, and feudal institutions were mostly eliminated. Nonetheless, C. A. Macartney exaggerates the decline of the old elite when he characterizes the aristocracy of Cis-Leithania, the Austrian-Bohemian region of Austria-Hungary (i.e., on the Austrian side of the river Leitha), as no more than a decadent relic of the past:

> By 1890 the direct power of the aristocracy was a shadow of what it had been in 1848. . . . They formed a tight little clique in which everyone knew everyone else . . . and spent their time in gambling, horse-racing, exchanging scandal and seducing other people's wives and daughters . . . [others] shut themselves up on their country estates, which they formed into . . . a dream-world which had been reality in the eighteenth [century]. (Macartney 1968, 620)

Although several elements of the above description are true, especially regarding the parasitic lifestyle of the old elite, the old nobility in reality remained the dominant social class even in the most advanced western provinces of Austria-Hungary. The reform measures did not threaten the socioeconomic command of the noble elite. Unlike in Western Europe, big estates continued to dominate in the Czech lands, Poland, Hungary, Croatia, Bosnia-Herzegovina, and Romania. Because the reforms were introduced from above either by the old elite itself or by the absolutist governments of the Habsburg and tsarist empires, they were socially extremely cautious. Even the most radical reforms carefully salvaged the leading positions of the old elite and preserved "law and order."

Large noble estates continued to occupy from one-third to one-half of the land in these countries. Around the turn of the century, big estates in Austria took up 8.7 million hectares, 29 percent of the land. A few hundred families of the high aristocracy *(Hochadel)* owned at least one-fifth of the land. In Bohemia, 151 families owned nearly 1.5 million of the province's 5.2 million hectares. One-quarter of Moravia's land was in the hands of seventy-three noble families. Moreover, post-1848 legislation introduced the *fidei-commissum,* the legally institutionalized entailed landed estate, a clear continuation of privileged feudal property. At the turn of the century, *fidei-commissa* occupied roughly 2.2 million hectares of land in Cis-Leithania. Big estates occupied 35 percent of the land in Poland, 40 percent in the Czech lands, 45 percent in Hungary, and 50 percent in Romania. The aristocracy thus preserved the basis of its economic power. Moreover, the aristocrats relatively easily transformed their estates from low-efficiency feudal manors to modern, more productive capitalist enterprises. Their income increased, because output grew about threefold, and, thanks to extensive railroad construction, they gained easy access to the market.

After customs barriers were lifted between Austria and Hungary in 1851, competition from Hungarian agriculture caused serious trouble for the Austrian-Bohemian landed nobility, which skillfully adjusted to the new situation by reducing the land under cereals and focusing on cash crops, mostly sugar beets, supplied to their own sugar refineries. Similarly, they modernized their forestry management and integrated production with the timber and paper industries. Consequently, a somewhat modernized aristocracy held strong positions in modern industry as well. Three-quarters of the distilleries, two-thirds of the sugar refineries, and nearly 60 percent of the breweries—that is, the leading branches of Czech industry—belonged to magnates in late nineteenth-century Bohemia. More than 400,000 workers, day laborers, foresters, and so on, worked for the Bohemian nobility.

Aristocrats also had a strong grasp on political power. They monopolized the innermost circles of the court of Emperor Franz Josef and filled the leading positions of high state bureaucracy: even in the early twentieth century, 40 percent of the top positions in the Ministry of the Interior, nearly half of the heads of departments at the state railways, and all the heads of the state governorships, the *Statthaltereien,* were aristocrats. They were strongly overrepresented in the Herrenhaus, or upper house of the Reichsrat. The *Hochadel* families were granted hereditary seats by the emperor, who also made lifetime appointments for more than 150 top representatives of the old elite. It was only at the end of the period under discussion, in 1907, that the introduction of universal male suffrage radically changed this situation. Until the introduction of general military service, aristocrats as a rule held at least the rank of major or captain in the army, and they monopolized its upper ranks as well.

The economic and political positions of the Hungarian aristocracy were even stronger. At the beginning of the twentieth century, fewer than four thousand people, 0.2 percent of the landowners, owned 32 percent of the land. One-fifth of the land belonged to the biggest estates. The "preserved" feudal type of property, ninety-two *fidei-commissa* (sixty of them were sanctioned by the emperor between 1867 and 1912), covered 35 percent of the country (*Magyar Statisztikai Évkönyv* 1913). In 1905, more than 150 aristocrats had important positions on the boards of leading Hungarian banks and industrial firms (*Magyar Pénzügy* 1905). Legislation in 1886 granted life membership in the upper house to every male adult member of an aristocratic family (with the rank of count or baron). Half of the prime ministers and more than one-third of all cabinet ministers in Hungary between the Austro-Hungarian Compromise (1867) and the Great War came from aristocratic families. The highly exclusive electoral system of the country granted the right to vote to only 6 percent of the population, including all noblemen. Small wonder, then, that 58 percent of the deputies came from noble families, 16 percent of them from the aristocracy (Mayer 1981, 173).

The Romanian boyar class, although it lost its privileges in 1864, preserved its economic power. The *mosierime,* the large landowners, some 2,000 families, owned three million hectares, 38 percent of the arable land. Later, they were able to enlarge their estates: the Land Law of 1889 authorized the sale of state-owned estates, amounting to 1.2 million hectares of land, and the bulk of it, as Robert Seton-Watson noted, "passed into wrong hands," that is, to the landlords. "The country was but a big estate, administered like an estate—a complex of latifundia in which private law is public law, the inheritance of landed wealth is the inheritance of power in the State," said the prominent Romanian writer Michai Eminescu (quoted in Mitrany 1930, 24). Romania was, indeed, characterized by "irresponsible landlordism" (Seton-Watson [1934] 1963, 368–69). When the country became independent, the Romanian "political nation" was composed entirely of the propertied class of 4,000 voters, whose franchise was based on wealth and position. Their number was approximately equal to the upper-level bureaucracy.

The new constitution of 1864 introduced nearly universal male suffrage, but with the severe restriction of a collegial electoral system under which the propertied class directly elected 80 percent of the deputies, while the majority of the population, the entire peasantry and other lesser taxpayers, elected the remaining 20 percent via delegates. The upper chamber was entirely occupied by the landowning and top bureaucratic elite (Michelson 1987, 27, 72, 138). In Romania, the big "landowner was himself the law" (Seton-Watson [1934] 1963, 389).

The situation of the nobility in partitioned Poland was somewhat different. The *szlachta,* the Polish nobility, was by far the largest noble elite

in Europe: probably 20 to 25 percent of ethnic Poles, by some calculations, and 10 percent of the overall Polish, Lithuanian, and Ukrainian population of the kingdom. In principle, the entire *szlachta* had equal rights
and privileges in the "noble democracy," leading public posts were not
hereditary, and the titles of "baron" and "count" did not exist. In reality,
however, the noble elite formed three distinct layers. The first consisted
of landed nobles with serfs. At the end of the eighteenth century, only
roughly 40,000 nobles had more than ten serfs. Some fifteen families,
among them the Radziwiłłs, Czartoryskis, and Potockis, which had accumulated exceptional wealth and power, acquired the title of prince and
virtually ruled the country, forming a real Polish grand aristocracy, totaling fewer than 2,000 people. *Szlachta* with ten to twenty serf families made
up about 8 percent of the nobility, or around 25,000 people. Finally, about
a third of the *szlachta* had around ten serfs. The largest number, however,
belonged to the two lowest levels of nobility: the peasant-nobles, with
small parcels of land they cultivated themselves, and the landless nobility
who served the landed nobility and rich urbanites in various posts. This
latter group numbered from 400,000 to a million (Korzon 1897–98, 159–
61; Ring 2001, 69–95).

Although the *szlachta* preserved economic power and most of their
landed property, their privileged position had been undermined. In Congress Poland, established under Russian rule after the 1815 Congress of
Vienna, the Polish nobility enjoyed local self-government at the provincial *(guberniia)* and district *(uezd)* levels, held assemblies, and elected administrative and judicial functionaries every three years. Polish law and
aristocratic institutions were abolished after the failed uprising of 1830–31,
however, when the constitution of 1815 was replaced by an "organic
statute" (1832) that made Poland a part of the Russian empire and excluded
the Polish nobility from political power. Conversely, substantial autonomy was granted under Habsburg rule in neighboring Galicia in 1867,
when the province became one of the seventeen *Kronländer*, with a Sejm
Krajowy (Galician Diet) dominated by Polish nobles (Izdebski 1995,
80–85).

The survival of the old elite was not, however, limited to the preserved
economic and political power of the aristocracy. The lower layers of the
nobility, the gentry and the so-called petty nobility, who cultivated small
parcels of land and lived as peasants, also preserved their noble privileges.
Unlike the high aristocracy, the gentry were hit hard by the emancipation
of serfs, which deprived them of the pillars of their noble existence: a free
labor force and tax exemptions. The ongoing changes, including the un-

bearable competition of modernized large estates and the possibility of losing their heavily mortgaged lands, undermined the economic position of a broad layer of the Central and Eastern European gentry. In this situation, the agricultural depression of the 1870s and 1880s was a mortal blow for them.

As a consequence, the gentry gradually lost their landed property and became landless. In Hungary's Sáros County, 170 landed gentry families were recorded in mid eighteenth century, for example, but the 1895 census registered only 34. Landowners with estates of 200 to 1,000 cadastre yokes, or 114 to 570 hectares (a cadastre yoke was defined as the amount of land that could be plowed with a yoke of oxen in a day), were considered to belong to the gentry in Hungary. The number of these landowner families decreased from 30,000 to 7,000 during the second half of the nineteenth century. The Polish gentry, the most numerous gentry class in the world, was virtually eliminated as a landowning class. Moreover, in response to their leadership in the fight for independence, the Russian government deliberately launched devastating attacks against them. Between 1836 and 1861, the authorities carried out a "legitimation" of the Polish nobility by limiting the number of privileged estates. The status of the petty nobility—roughly 250,000 people—was not confirmed, thus eliminating them from noble status. As a consequence, the number of the Polish nobility in the Polish kingdom under Russian rule dropped from more than 300,000 to nearly 50,000. In Prussian Poland, their number decreased by 40 percent during the nineteenth century.

The bulk of the Hungarian, Polish, Czech, and other Central and Eastern European gentry—at least two-thirds in real terms—became déclassé. In a modern society, they would have lost their traditional positions in the political-economic elite of their country and have become either proletarians, service workers, or professionals, as often happened in the western provinces of the Habsburg empire, in Austria proper, and partly in Bohemia, where the *embourgeoisement* of society advanced the most.

That was not, however, the case in most of Central and Eastern Europe. The déclassé gentry found compensation in occupying prestigious positions in the new state bureaucracy and army. Although financially bankrupt and mostly with relatively low incomes, they were thus still able to preserve their status in the ruling new bureaucratic and political elite.

In the case of Hungary, the preservation of the gentry's power through absorption into prestigious and often lucrative state positions has been well documented by Andrew C. Janos in his portrayal of the "politics of backwardness" (Janos 1982, 108–11). After the Austro-Hungarian Compromise of 1867, especially during the 1870s and 1880s, the government of Kálmán Tisza (1875–90) built up a huge state bureaucracy, partly to rescue the declining gentry and create a haven for them. The 16,000 civil servants inherited from the Austrian administration had doubled by 1875 and then increased to more than 60,000 by 1890, and to 120,000 by 1910. Roughly 3.5 percent of the labor force was employed in the civil service. "No other age in Hungarian public life came to be so completely identified with the gentry as were the years of Kálmán Tisza's premiership" (ibid., quoting Lippay 1919, 98). As a consequence, 57 percent of the Hungarian state bureaucracy was of gentry origin in 1890. In the office of the prime minister and in the Ministry of Interior, they made up two-thirds of the employees. Although this extremely high representation somewhat decreased during the next quarter of a century, it was still 46 percent in 1910. Between 1875 and 1918, 61 percent of the employees in the prime minister's office, 64 percent in the Ministry of Interior, and 38 percent in the Ministry of Commerce were members of the gentry; altogether, they occupied 48 percent of the positions in the four most important ministries (Berend and Szuhay 1979, 141–42).

The gentry continued to play a decisive role in the political arena: between 1887 and 1910, more than 48 percent of the representatives in the Hungarian parliament belonged to the gentry. Janos identifies 27 percent of the representatives as public employees and another 22 percent as attorneys (ibid., 110–11, 138).

The joint Austro-Hungarian army offered another possibility for preserving elite positions. According to Karl Kandeelsdorfer's calculations in 1896, nearly 29 percent of the officer corps belonged to the nobility. István Deák's innovative calculations—based on a random sample of 64 officers—show that 20 percent of the officers were noblemen in 1870. Of them, 45 percent belonged to the old and 55 percent to the new service nobility, that is, families of newly ennobled officers and state bureaucrats. Although more than three-quarters of the officer corps of nearly 18,000 career officers were of German nationality, approximately 10 percent were Hungarian, 5 percent Czech, 2.5 percent Polish, and 2.4 percent Croat. The Hungarian National Guard offered a better opportunity for the gentry than the joint army: in 1869–70, when the Honvéd army was created, 60 percent of the newly appointed officers were from gentry families, and another 14 percent were aristocrats.

It is true, however, that the heavy overrepresentation of the gentry and the nobility at large gradually declined. Roughly 90 percent of the high-ranking generals of the joint Austro-Hungarian army were noblemen in 1859. Their number decreased to 41 percent by 1908 and to 25 percent by 1918. The gentry contingent of the officer corps of the Hungarian Hon-véd army also declined from 60 to 39 percent between 1870 and 1881 (Deák 1992, 161–63, 183).

The genuine political "home" of the gentry, however, was county administration. In Somogy County, for example, between 1867 and 1910, nearly two-thirds of the 79 top administrative officials were recruited from the gentry, while only 2 percent of them belonged to the aristocracy and well-to-do landed gentry. The case of Somogy County was not unique: nationwide, two-thirds of the leading county bureaucracy was from the gentry (Berend and Szuhay 1978, 141–42).

The parliament, the state and county bureaucracy, and the army could not, however, absorb the entire déclassé gentry class. Twice as many impoverished gentry sought to occupy state offices as were actually employed during the last third of the century. Of 400 gentry families in Somogy County and 600 in Sáros County, only 50 and 49, respectively, found prestigious positions in these institutions. A great many became managers on big estates or went into professional fields and became judges, attorneys, journalists, and even teachers.

The Romanian déclassé gentry also found a safe refuge in the public offices of the central administration and in the *judeţe*. At the beginning of the twentieth century, more than 100,000 people—2 percent of the population—were employed thus. Half of them occupied lower positions, with incomes hardly better than that of a salaried worker. Only 1 percent of them, the higher echelons, earned a middle-class income, but social status, power, respect, and the possibility of earning substantial additional income came with the office.

Throughout, even the lowest layer, the petty nobility, struggled to maintain at least the decorum of noble status. Both the Hungarian *bocskoros nemes* ("bemoccasined noble," squireen) and the similar Polish *szlachta zasciankowa* ("nobles behind the walls," because of their habit of living together in exclusive communities) were in real terms peasant-nobles who cultivated their own small pieces of land and whose children served landowners on manorial estates. Petty noblewomen ("household misses") served in manor houses. The peasant-*szlachta,* the "middle brothers," as aristocratic mentors called them, were addressed as *pan* and *pani* (lord and lady), they shook hands and were asked to sit down. In the petty noble villages, symbolic etiquette and outfits were preserved to demonstrate noble status: families used pompous language and aristocratic manners. Their houses had porches and, if possible, a piano inside. Women wore gloves and short mantles lined with white fur and carried parasols. "In dress and manners, the landowners' patterns were obligatory for the petty nobility" (Chamerska 1996, 78).

Władysław Reymont's Nobel prize–winning *The Peasants,* an encyclopedic novel about Polish peasant life, describes the "nobility of Rzepki," the people of a noble-peasant village, as very poor but pretentious people, who had "only a bag and a bundle, one cow for five and one cap for three." When these noble peasants arrived at a district peasant meeting, "they came all in one band, taciturn, looking down and askance at everyone they met. Their womenfolk, dressed like manor-people, very much pranced out, walked in their midst, and were treated by them with the utmost courtesy" (Reymont 1925, 2: 89–90).

In Central Europe, the elite of the noble establishment thus hung onto their permanently weakened positions. The gentry remained the foundation of the "historic middle class" and influenced the manners, attitude, and national self-consciousness of virtually the entire society. Their habits were considered "national characteristics." The newly ennobled bureaucratic-military elite, and even part of the intellectual elite, totally assimilated into the gentry and enthusiastically adopted their lifestyle and manners. Old and new nobility thus amalgamated.

The preservation of the old noble elite was only partly the consequence of the semisuccessful modernization of the economy and society. The old elite imposed themselves on the society by clinging to their landed estates and military-bureaucratic positions. Their role was legitimized for the society by the process of failed, incomplete nation-building. The lack of independent statehood, combined with conflicting claims by mixed nationalities within and without state borders, led to a strong, aggressive, and traditional representation of national identity. Military virtue and experienced leadership acquired special significance. People wanted a leading elite that represented national continuity, an asset when statehood and nationhood were lacking and required verification.

The uncertain future of independent nationhood and the troubled relations among all the neighboring nations and minorities created "political hysteria" in the region (Bibó 1986). In this environment, where historical and ethnic-linguistic borders did not meet, the old elite could reincarnate and reestablish their legitimate power as the national leadership. In István Bibó's assessment, the noble elite were totally out of step with realities. They were accustomed to making unreasonable demands and to formulating policy based on what they wanted, rather than on what could be accomplished, thus disengaging policy from a rationale of cause and effect. In this deformed political culture, the irrational inclination of the noble elite to propagate historical and national myths became a source of strength and charisma. The people of the region sought to live in these myths and wanted to believe that national independence and the unification of the entire nation would automatically resolve all the country's unsolved and painful political, economic, and social problems.

The prevalence of myths actually prepared the way for the rise of a national intelligentsia, partly emerging from the déclassé gentry, but also from commoners. The national intelligentsia consisted of prophet-poets, writers, historians, linguists, ethnographers, teachers, and priests, those who cultivated the distinctive national culture and were able to substitute the missing national continuity and strengthen national self-confidence. They represented, or even produced, evidence of deep national roots and historical rights against the existing multinational state formations and rival nations. Culture acquired eminent political importance, although this did not lead to its flourishing but rather to its overpolitization (Bibó 1986, 215–26). The old elite found a crucial new function to legitimize their power. A great part of this elite, however, the historical gentry middle class, became totally anachronistic and collided head-on with the new requirements of the modern age of capitalism and democracy.

Late nineteenth-century realist writers of the region often wrote about the declining, parasitic, passé, but still dominating gentry. Chekhov focused on the twilight of the old nobility. His heroes loiter in manor houses and mansions in the countryside and are unable to change their lives and start working. A vain nostalgia for action substitutes for deeds. Real human dialogues are supplanted by the "nihilism" of empty monologues, real human relations by empty illusions. That was also the world of Stanisław Wyspiański, a Polish contemporary of Chekhov's, who sought to destroy the Polish myth. In his *Wesele* (Wedding, 1900), the historic mission of the noble intelligentsia, the typical embodiment of the declining gentry, is a wedding with the "people," a symbolic mission to create national unity. Deed, here too, is only a pseudo-action. The impossibility of a dialogue between the two social layers is even linguistically expressed: the peasants speak a mountain *(goral)* dialect, the noble intelligentsia, the literary language. Their declamations are empty, pathetic words. The Poet meets his hero, an armored knight—the natural personification of the nobility—and finds the armor empty. The "Wedding" symbolizes the replacement of deeds by daydreaming. The spirits who appear have consciousness but are unable to act (Spiró 1986).

The Hungarian Kálmán Mikszáth also said a nostalgic-critical farewell to the Hungarian gentry. In his *The Gentry* (1897), he presents the world of Sáros County, a place of "hallucinations," where "small men are great lords." The event, here too, is a wedding at which once-illustrious families create the illusion of their lost wealth. The best food and wine are served; the guests arrive in elegant carriages, wearing diamonds. They gamble with nonexistent fortunes at the card table. When the celebration ends, the jewels and carriages are taken back to their real owners. Everything was pretense, and everyone returns to a simple office the next morning.

In one of Mikszáth's last novels, *A Noszty fiú esete a Tóth Marival* ([1908] 1912) (The Young Noszty's Affaire with Mary Tóth), a poor gentry family, the Nosztys, plot for young Feri Noszty to seduce the daughter of a millionaire businessman, Mihály Tóth, to make their marriage unavoidable. The conspiracy is assisted by Baron Kopereczky, squire of the fictitious Bontó County. "Well, you have to see the power of the family [as being] like a fortress withstanding the decay of centuries," Kopereczky's brother-in-law, old Noszty, explains. "It has walls, bastions, towers, [but] alas, it also has cracks in the walls. . . . This fortress needs attention all the time, its weaknesses have to be supported, the cracks have to be repaired, sometime a strap of iron is needed to hold it." The Tóths represent modern middle-class virtues in contrast to the corrupt gentry world of the Nosztys. The plot comes to grief because of the resistance of Mihály Tóth. The young Feri Noszty shrugs its failure off, saying: "The world is quite large. There are many more girls. . . . The main thing is, anyway, health and a little luck at the card-table" (quoted in Czigány 1984, 237, 240–41).

The noble elite preserved their old manners and value system, a kind of a "feudal anticapitalism," although, like the Nosztys, they often sought to find "a strap of iron" in mésalliances, marriages with rich commoners, to hold together their ruined "fortresses." At the same time, however, they rejected modern values and looked down on business as ungentlemanly. This rigid antibusiness attitude emerged mostly during the seventeenth and eighteenth centuries and evolved into a "national characteristic" during the nineteenth and even twentieth centuries.

Maria Bogucka sheds light on the Polish gentry's attitudes from the seventeenth century to the early twentieth. In 1623, a representative of the gentry, one Stanisław Zaremba, accused the merchants ("keen bloodhounds") of "demoralizing society by importing luxury goods" and by their "tricks and intolerable profits." He characterized townsmen as enemies who "are destroying and impoverishing Poland and robbing her wealth while enriching foreign countries and themselves." Jan Jurkowski, a teacher in Pilzno in the early seventeenth century, versified:

> Let yeomen till land, grow wheat for the daily bread
> Let women count profit from spinning a fine thread
> Let merchants have gold, let the Jew count his treasure
> You stick to [a] soldier's prize, your only measure.

An early twentieth-century writer echoed this attitude: "Genuine nobility is a peculiar power and a genuine nest of virtue, fame, dignity and integrity. . . . Nobility soars up high with the eagles." Bogucka concludes that according to these views, "engaging in urban occupations was shameful and dishonest by their very nature" (Bogucka 1993, 99–110).

The gentry rejected the idea of trade or even of marketing their own products. When, in a pamphlet published anonymously in 1880, Jósef Ignacy Kraszewski recommended modern commerce as the road to nation-building, *Głos szlachcica polskiego* ("The Voice of a Polish Gentleman") responded in vitriolic tones, calling Kraszewski a "grave digger of his own class," who "lived according to the customs of their forebears, and not the customs of shopkeepers." The gentry rejected "the worship of the golden calf and utilitarianism" since they were "the exclusive heir to the entire historic national past . . . Religion, Motherland, Family and Tradition." Jan Ludwik Poplawski went even further in his *Głos* (1887) when he stated: "Today, we have already begun descending to the level of the Jews . . . we will soon turn completely into a nation of profiteers and traders" (quoted in Jedlicki 1999, 218–19, 280).

Strikingly similar attitudes emerged in Hungary. The mid-nineteenth-century Hungarian historian Mihály Horváth said that in previous centuries, "the common opinion . . . at least that of the noble classes . . . biased by prejudice . . . cherished the most absurd ideas concerning commerce." Zsigmond Pál Pach has masterfully analyzed the changed mentality of the Hungarian nobility, which engaged in trade (like their English counterparts) in the sixteenth century, but turned against it during the seventeenth and eighteenth centuries. Baron Lőrinc Orczy expressed this view in a poem in 1780:

> Heated debates rage among us,
> Does shameless trade befit the Magyars?
> For it may indeed corrupt our morals,
> Say, where do you think it might lead us?
> In counties Zemplén, Szabolcs, Ung and Bereg
> Much money, food and wine fill all the cellars.

Need we more? Should our lives be disconcerted?
So that more money might stuff all our purses?

All this influenced the entire society, including the peasantry, and led
to the emergence of an anticapitalist national character (Pach 1994, 150–51,
155–56). Gyula Szekfű, a leading Hungarian historian of the first half of the
twentieth century, hailed the "anti-commercial and anti-capitalist talents
of the Hungarian race"; according to him, history proved that "the principle of trading and production for profit disagreed with the Hungarian
nature. . . . [B]ourgeois characteristics were quite far from the mental habit
of Hungarians, nobility and peasantry alike. . . . Undoubtedly, the Hungarians may be listed among those peoples that have the least inclination
to develop in a capitalist direction" (Szekfű 1920, 291; 1922, 81–82).

The same "anti-capitalist character" was "diagnosed" for the Romanians by the mid-nineteenth-century Romanian economist-statistician
D. P. Martian, who criticized his countrymen for lacking the entrepreneurial spirit needed for economic modernization (Michelson 1987, 30).
"[E]ducated Romanians have shown a tendency to avoid following a
commercial career, leaving this field of activity to alien elements . . . the
country . . . is thus deprived of the opportunity of building up an independent middle class," the English author G. C. Logio noted a century
later. This attitude also had a toxic impact on business morale. Logio describes the Romanian view that "elusion of obligations is a mundane affaire and a fashionable art which should be cultivated assiduously" (Logio 1932, 115, 118).

The aristocratic establishment thus survived, not only by virtue of the
preservation of the old noble elite, the principal role of the big estate, and
the determinant position of the gentry as the backbone of the "historic"
or "gentleman middle class" *(történelmi* or *úri középosztály),* but also because of the elite's conservative "feudal anticapitalist" values and attitudes,
which penetrated the society and figured as Polish and Hungarian "national characteristics."

The most visible feature of the gentry's attitude was a "gentlemanly"
lifestyle, maintaining the pretense of old noble wealth by spending much
more than the never-enough income earned at an often-mediocre office
job. "Ah, if I could only afford to live the way I live" was a typical Hungarian remark, reported by John Lukacs's mother (Lukacs 1988, 91). This
irresponsible lifestyle led to heavy indebtedness and invited corruption as
a means to fill the huge gaps in family budgets. Connections to relatives
of the upper nobility, the advantage of having a "historic" name, and offices

with access to lucrative "gifts" became an inseparable part of the gentry's way of life. Business activity, entrepreneurship, and thrift were thought ungentlemanly and even shameful. The moral outlook of the gentry was thus the antithesis of Max Weber's Protestant ethic. This "anticapitalist" character was regarded as an "elegant" national pattern to follow.

DUAL SOCIETIES: THE EMERGENCE OF A NEW ELITE

In parallel with partial economic modernization, especially from the mid to late nineteenth century on, a new entrepreneurial, bourgeois elite and a modern middle class slowly and gradually began to develop. Coexistence of the old and new elites under the unquestioned political and social leadership of the old elite was a hallmark of the dual society.

The modern new business, service, and intellectual elites formed a rather thin layer in Central European societies. Cis-Leithania, the rapidly industrializing Lower Austria, and Bohemia-Moravia-Silesia were exceptions. In contrast to the situation in other countries of the region, the majority of the population there left agriculture and relocated in industry, commerce, and services. In Lower Austria and Bohemia-Moravia-Silesia, 60 and 52 percent of the population, respectively, worked in the new nonagrarian sectors. In the strong industrial and service branches of the economy, a nearly Western type of bourgeoisie and middle class emerged. The self-conscious Czech-speaking merchants, industrialists, and intellectuals of Prague envisaged their own club, the Měšťanská Beseda, as early as 1844, and the institution was inaugurated in January 1846 (Sayer 1998, 82–83). Vienna and even Prague became important financial centers. The Wiener Bankverein, the Creditanstalt, the headquarters of the Vienna Rothschilds, and the Živnostenská Banka of Prague and their affiliates developed strong positions in the Balkans. The Austro-Czech textile, sugar, iron, and engineering industries supplied the entire empire and several neighboring countries besides. A strong financial and industrial upper middle class, an army of clerks and employees in the business sector, and white-collar workers in services and professional fields made up between one-fourth and one-third of Vienna and Prague society, respectively.

During the nineteenth century, more than 1,000 prominent Austrian and Bohemian bankers, industrialists, and merchants were ennobled (Mayer 1981, 111). This was a clear sign both of the strength of the modern business elite and of its assimilation into the aristocratic establishment. Characteristically, the numerous Austrian-Bohemian bourgeoisie and middle class still remained politically weak compared to the old elite and did not even seek to gain direct political power. The Austrian and Bohemian societies, although nearest to their Western counterparts, still exhibited the characteristics of the dual society.

The eastern half of the empire did not see a similar rise of a modern middle class. By 1869, in Hungary, shortly after the Ausgleich, independent entrepreneurs in banking, industry, trade, and transportation, including the so-called petit bourgeois shopkeepers and artisans, white-collar workers, and intellectuals, numbered roughly 600,000 people. In other words, the emerging upper and lower middle class represented only about 8–9 percent of the country's workforce. By 1910, their number had almost doubled, to nearly 1,100,000, which embodied nearly 15 percent of the workforce.

The wealth and importance of these newly emerging social layers, however, surpassed their number. Although Hungary's Gross Domestic Product increased more than threefold during the half century before World War I, the contribution of agriculture declined from nearly 80 percent to just over 60 percent. Modern industrial and service branches produced nearly 40 percent of domestic product before the war (Berend and Ránki 1979, 65, 77). The top 150–200 bourgeois families, who owned and ran much of Hungarian banking, industry, transportation, and trade, accumulated vast wealth, comparable to that of the landowning aristocracy. The leading financial groups centered around the Pesti Magyar Kereskedelmi Bank (Commercial Bank) and the Magyar Általános Hitelbank (Credit Bank). Leó Lánczy, Fülöp Weiss, Ferenc Chorin, Adolf Ullmann, and the Kornfeld, Manfréd Weiss Herzog, and Deutsch families were familiar names among the "about fifty people at the top of Hungarian banking and industry," Jenő Varga observed; they "controlled about 20 percent of the capital and nearly half of the net income" of these sectors (Varga 1912, 10). By providing mortgage credits for landowners, a highly indebted class, they also acquired their share of the income from the landed estates. Moreover, the financial-merchant elite bought up one-fifth of the landed estates over 200 cadastre yokes (114 hectares).

The growing number of medical doctors, teachers, journalists, entertainers, and corporate clerks made up only a small fraction of the society. They became very important in the rising cities, most of all in the capital city, however, where they formed a large and influential urban middle class. The largest segment of the business middle class consisted of hundreds of thousands of shopkeepers, a great many of whom ran village general stores and pubs. Tens of thousands were tailors (20 percent of them self-employed), shoemakers (9 percent), and butchers and bakers (23–24 percent). Most of them were small-business people, partly from premodern times.

An extremely fragile middle class emerged in Romania, where, even before World War I, three-quarters of the population still worked in agriculture. In 1900, 78 percent of the people were still illiterate. Even so, a small but rich and influential bourgeoisie and merchant class emerged. The big taxpayers consisted of more than 10,000 entrepreneurs, 1,300 lawyers, 150 engineers, and 42 bankers in 1903–4. They were concentrated in Bucharest, the rapidly growing capital city, where their main strength lay in banking. The Banca Agricolă, Banca Românească, and the Banca Marmorosch Blank were their strongholds. Romania's significant role in world grain exports generated the largest incomes for the bourgeoisie engaged in trade (Zeletin 1991). They were, however, totally excluded from public life and political power. Moreover, because of their Jewish origins, a great number of them were also unable to gain citizenship. Nevertheless, their wealth, combined with the widespread corruption that became an organic part of the social and political life of the country, opened a path into high politics for them. A large part of the Romanian lower middle class remained traditional artisans. Around the turn of the century, 166,000 families made a living in this way.

Another part of the old-fashioned, early-modern type of petite bourgeoisie, lower-middle-class merchants in Romania's quiet, dusty little cities, originally small shopkeepers, innkeepers, and moneylenders in villages, became rather well-to-do by selling the products of the big estates. As their most lucrative role, they became *arendaşi*, leaseholders, or middlemen between the absentee boyars and the peasant renters. By 1900, more than half of the land of the big estates (above 500 hectares), and three-quarters of the largest estates (over 3,000 hectares), was leased. On average, an *arendaş* leased 700 hectares, but, mostly in Moldavia, gigantic estates were leased: the Fischer Trust, founded in 1890, leased nearly 238,000 hectares.

The economic power of the thin but strong modern bourgeoisie and their command of communication, education, culture, and also of business bureaucracy made the rising middle class bountiful partners for the old elite. Nevertheless, they could not compete with the political and administrative power and social prestige of the landed nobility and gentry. They looked for political representation and connections among the old elite and sought to put themselves on an equal footing with the nobility by buying noble ranks. About three hundred business people acquired patents of nobility, roughly one-tenth of them even attaining baronial rank in Hungary. The nouveaux riches rushed to buy estates—not so much for economic advantage as for status—and built mansions in the country-side. The effort to assimilate, however, could not change their social status. They remained second-class citizens or even noncitizens, outside the body of the nation. The old noble elite looked down on them and rarely toler-ated their company.

THE "JEWISH QUESTION"

One of the most important factors leading to exclusion, aside from the persistence of the aristocratic establishment and its values, was the non-indigenous origin of the new business and middle-class elite. In the rigid framework of noble society, social mobility was extremely slow or nonexis-tent. The déclassé gentry could preserve their role in the sociopolitical elite by holding bureaucratic positions in the state and county apparatus and in the army. Even if they became intellectuals, a transformation that began in the first half of the nineteenth century, the landless gentry oc-cupied state-related positions. Lawyers, the majority of gentry intellec-tuals, did not engage in private practice or business law but became judges and prosecutors, part of the bureaucracy. Downward mobility hardly ex-isted. The same was true of upward mobility, since the newly liberated serfs, although free peasants, were still excluded from the body of the na-tion. Uneducated and alien to the urban environment, the vast majority of them could not merge into the rank and file of the middle class.

As a consequence, a gap characterized the middle layers of the former noble societies. This gap was filled by nonindigenous elements: Greeks, Germans, and, most of all, in the second half of the nineteenth century, Jews. They were strongly urban and traditionally business- and education-oriented. When the need arose and possibilities opened up for business and intellectual positions, they appeared without competition, yearning to occupy these fields.

Greeks played an important role in Romania, where the century of Pha-nariot rule up to 1821 had established their pivotal power. By represent-ing the Ottoman Porte, the "closed caste" of the Phanariots, as the histo-rian Nicolae Iorga (1933) characterizes them, formed the leading group of the political and business elite, although their significance declined steeply after Romania gained independence. The Greeks' role was also im-portant in Hungary, especially in the early stage of capitalist transformation, but it decreased, especially after Greece became independent in 1830, when a great many Greek businessmen repatriated.

The traditional German-speaking patrician layer, the founders of a great number of Hungarian cities and townships, who played a pioneering role in early capitalist business activity, mostly turned toward intellectual and professional positions and rapidly assimilated, becoming Hungarian nationalists during the nineteenth century and an organic part of the rising middle class (Szelenyi 1998).

Partitioned Poland faced a different destiny. Germans became the backbone of the entrepreneurial and middle class in Prussian Poland, where these groups became very strong. Although two-thirds of the population of Russian Poland and Galicia engaged in agriculture up until World War I, in Poznania, this share was only 42 percent. Nearly 60 percent of the population of Prussian Poland worked in industry and services. A deliberate germanization, however, strengthened the German elements in big business and in various middle-class positions. "There were hardly any Poles among [the] greater industrialists, bankers, or traders," Piotr Wandycz says. Only 28 percent of traders were Polish. Polish participation was stronger in small-scale industry. Nearly half of the entrepreneurs were Polish in Prussian Poland, but only a few employed more than 200 workers in the 1880s (Wandycz 1974, 230).

In Prussian Poland, where the total number of the Jews had dropped to 2.5 percent of the population by 1900, they did not play a leading part in the middle class, but in Russian Poland and Galicia, where nearly one in ten inhabitants was Jewish, their role was pivotal. In the big, modern cities Warsaw and Lodz, the industrial and administrative centers of the country, where the entrepreneurial middle class was most concentrated, 33 and 30 percent of the population was Jewish, respectively (Śliwa 1997). Together with Germans, they were strongly overrepresented among the big banking and industrial bourgeoisie. Several families established their wealth through army contracting at the end of the eighteenth century and the beginning of the nineteenth. The majority of the registered 156 war contractors in Warsaw were Jewish merchants (Kosim 1986, 105, 130). One of them, Szymon Rosen, who settled in Warsaw in 1795, began business as a moneylender and continued as an army contractor. During the 1830s, he ran a leading commercial firm. His son Mathias graduated from the Warsaw Lyzeum, and became one of the pillars of the modern entrepreneurial class in Poland. Leopold Kronenberg became the richest financier and industrialist. Most of the business magnates, the Kronenbergs, Rosens, Epsteins, Natansons, Rotwands, Lilpops, and Wawelbergs, were either Jews or Germans. A xenophobic attitude emerged, characteristically expressed in 1880 in *The Jews, the Germans, and Us,* a popular pamphlet by Jan Jeleński, a right-wing radical (Jedlicki 1999, 279). The Germans, however, soon assimilated. "These Szlenkers, Temlers, Szweds, Pfeifers . . . Lilpops, Strassburgers are already blood from our blood," a contemporary Polish baroness wrote one of her friends (Kolodziejczyk 1986, 244).

The Jews, on the other hand, remained in many respects outside Polish society and were considered alien, and sometimes inimical. The positivists, represented by Bolesław Prus, recognized assimilated Jews as Poles, since "Jewishness does not so much refer to descent and religion, but rather to darkness, pride, separatism, laziness, and exploitation." A few years later, however, Roman Dmowski and Jan Popławski rejected assimilation as an "intrusion of Jewishness into the midst of the nation," saying that Jews remained foreign to Polish society because they could not "understand or feel its aspirations and interests" (quoted in Porter 2000, 163, 228). Jews, nevertheless, occupied more and more middle-class positions in the country. Among the merchants, especially small retailers, Jews became an absolute majority: 65 percent of shopkeepers in Warsaw were Jewish at the end of the nineteenth century. They also played an important role in the growing, but still small, intellectual stratum (Wróbel 1991).

The majority of the Romanian entrepreneurial and middle class was Jewish. Modern commerce was naturally concentrated in cities and towns, which, unlike the Romanian peasant countryside, were strongly Jewish. In 1900, 40 percent of the urban population—some 280,000 people—were Jews engaged in commerce and handicrafts (Rosen 1995). "They gained control over much of the trade, industry, and finance. In time they even acquired a foothold in agriculture by leasing the large estates of absentee landlords" (Stavrianos [1958] 1963, 484).

The Jews were also the most important nonindigenous element in Hungary, where their number rapidly increased tenfold and reached 5 percent of the population in the nineteenth century. One-third of them were beggars, peddlers, and workers until 1848 (Hanák 1992). The other two-thirds, legally excluded from various activities and landownership, were innkeepers, small merchants, shopkeepers, and artisans. They easily adjusted to the economic booms that followed after 1848 and in 1867. True, in 1910, 30 percent of the Polish Jews and more than 32 percent of the Hungarian Jews were lumberjacks, skilled workers in printing and other industries, day laborers, and domestic servants. However, roughly 80 percent of the industrial magnates were Jewish around World War I.

In this environment, the ideal of a native "gentleman" entrepreneur emerged. In 1791, Józef Wybicki published his didactic novel *Mysli polityczne o wolnosci cywilnej* (The Gentleman Turned Citizen), portraying impoverished Polish gentry who move to the city to open a factory. "[I]n our recent romances, engineers were idealized as heroes; they made fortunes, they were loved, they [had] noble characters," the enlightened Polish modernizer and writer Bolesław Prus remarked a few decades later (quoted in Jedlicki 1999, 57, 194). Prus himself introduced tradesmen heroes, however, in his *Lalka* (The Doll), in 1890. Wokulski, although a successful businessmen, is also a philanthropist. Money for him is always a means, not a goal. The idealized déclassé gentleman, a freedom fighter of the 1863 uprising turned capitalist, offered a model for a new Polish attitude (Holmgren 1998). In 1870, Mór Jókai, the most popular writer of nineteenth-century Hungary, similarly idealized the hero of his *Fekete gyémántok* (Black Diamonds), a late romantic daydream about a model entrepreneur, a veteran of the 1848 war of independence, who is socially sensitive, wants to raise up his workers to be small businessmen and co-owners, and struggles against bad foreign investors and their local agents (in this case, the Church). Jókai's larger-than-life hero, Ivan Berend, a patriot, inventor, and sportsman, embodied the nonexistent type of modern Hungarian gentleman-turned-businessman.

In fact, 54 percent of self-employed people were Jewish in Hungary in 1910, and more than 36 percent of the Jews became self-employed in industry, trade, and transportation. More than 20 percent of the Jews worked as clerks and employees in banking, industry, and other fields, or in the free professions. Their share among clerks and employees in banking and trade was more than 53 percent, and in industry, 43 percent. Nearly half of the medical doctors, 45 percent of lawyers, 42 percent of journalists, 38 percent of private engineers, and 23 percent of actors were Jewish in 1910 (Katus 1992, 97–98, 101–3). This highly urbanized population played hardly any part in agriculture. More than 73 percent of the Jews worked in industry, handicrafts, commerce, and banking, and another 11 percent in communications and the free professions. An indigenous, patriotic gentleman-entrepreneur was lacking in Central and Eastern Europe.

The "Jewish question" arose in Austria and to some extent in Bohemia as well. In the Czech lands, unlike in Poland, Romania, and Hungary, the Jewish minority was relatively unimportant. In 1850, only slightly more than 75,000 Jews lived in Bohemia, a number that increased to nearly 86,000 by 1910. These numbers represented only 1.7 and 1.3 percent of the contemporary population of Bohemia, respectively. True, the emancipation of Jews occurred relatively early there; they gained the right to own landed property in 1841. Marriage and residence restrictions were lifted in 1848. Full legal emancipation was granted in 1867. A strong Jewish assimilationist movement was established in the very same year to "spread love of the homeland and of the mother tongue among Czech Jews." In 1900, 54 percent of the Bohemian Jews used Czech as an everyday language. In Moravia, where the number of Jews was higher and some autonomy was granted them, the Czech-speaking layer constituted only 17 percent of the Jews.

Regardless of the relatively small number of Jews, anti-Semitism followed a familiar pattern. Two years after the legal emancipation of Jews, Jan Neruda, the leading writer in the country, wrote in his pamphlet *Pro starch židovský* (On the Jewish Fear): "The question is not the emancipation of the Jews, but rather emancipation from the Jews, so that we might be able to free ourselves from the exploitation of one's fellow man." Rudolf Vrba accused the Jews of dominating industry, banking, and the press, and demanded state control of banks and the stock market. He also urged banning Jewish immigration and removing Jewish students from public schools. Czech nationalism looked upon the mostly German-speaking Jewish minority as a reserve of German nationalism, a germanizing element, the enemy of the Czech nation. In 1892, the Svůj k svému (Each to His Own) movement launched a boycott campaign against Jewish shops. During the 1897 anti-German riots in Prague, besides attacking and destroying German stores, coffee shops, and the German Theater and *Schulverein,* the mob also smashed the windows of synagogues in Královské Vinohrady and in Žižkov. The "December storm" was a major trauma for the Jews: "The carefully constructed plans and cherished hopes . . . lay strewn along the sidewalks of Prague and tens of smaller communities together with the shards of glass and broken furniture of Jewish homes and shops" (Kieval 1988, 21, 69, 72–73).

Although an indigenous bourgeoisie was much stronger there than in Hungary, Poland, and Romania, Jews still played a profound role in Cis-Leithanian business and among the ranks of the emerging middle class. According to William McCagg's pioneering calculations, Jewish participation in Viennese public institutions, including the National Bank, the Chamber of Commerce, and the Stock Exchange, grew from 25 percent in 1858 to 60 percent in 1913. Their real foothold, however, was in banking, where their participation reached 37 percent in 1858 and had increased to nearly 50 percent by 1913. In Austria, Bohemia-Moravia, Galicia, and other non-Hungarian parts of the monarchy, as of 1917, Jews accounted for 30 percent of the directors of industrial stock companies and 41 percent of industrial magnates, defined as directors of seven or more companies (McCagg 1992, 73, 78). In 1910, Jews were well represented in banking (15 percent). Among the Jews paying the highest taxes, 32 percent were in trade and 33 percent in industry. Prominent Jewish manufacturers such as Leopold Pollack von Parnegg, Max Mandl, Isidor Mauthner, and the Brunner family played key roles in the leading Austro-Bohemian textile industry (ibid., 85–86).

Ethnic-religious divisions thus deepened the symbiosis and conflict between the surviving aristocratic establishment and the emerging modern society. The influence of the rising modern elite was profoundly weakened by its strong nonindigenous contingent.

INCOMPLETE SOCIETIES

"Incomplete" societies were strikingly different from dual societies. The societies of the newly independent Balkan nations emerged without a traditional elite because their own elites had been physically eliminated or driven from these countries centuries earlier by the occupying Ottoman power. Instead, an alien elite, the Greek Phanariots in the Romanian Principalities, and pashas, agas, spahis, âyans, and derebeyis in the other Balkan areas, ruled the countries. Due to the peculiar Ottoman system, where instead of private landownership, the state's (i.e., the Sultan's) land and income were managed by an appointed bureaucratic-military elite, the latter constituted the Balkans' political-economic and military "nobility."

This alien bureaucratic class was joined by domestic Serbian, Bulgarian, Bosnian, and Albanian pseudo-elites. The subordinated native elite consisted, first of all, of the village and *knezina* chiefs who served as middlemen between the Ottoman authorities and the local population. Maria Todorova speaks of a "lack of continuity of political elites in the Balkans (Todorova 1997, 171). Balkan towns comprised an Ottoman nucleus, the *çarşija,* with a small group of assimilated merchants, artisans, and moneylenders. "Those few Serbs who do live in towns as tradesmen dress as Turks and live according to Turkish customs . . . during revolts and wars they either shut themselves up with the Turks in cities or run away to Germany," Vuk Karadžić said in the early nineteenth century (quoted in Halpern and Halpern 1972, 12).

After gaining independence, the new states rushed to build huge bureaucracies and armies. "The new political class which carried out the revolution in Serbia was made up of many *hajduks,* of some intellectuals, and of the 'better people, who were able to feed and arm two, ten, or twenty serving companions'. . . the *gazdas,*" Traian Stoianovich says (Stoianovich 1963, 311). The hajduks, bold popular fighters and outlaw heroes, now became important elements of the new "governing class." The extremely small educated class also gained important ground in the mostly illiterate countries. In countries of mass illiteracy (70–80 percent), the few educated men were badly needed in state administration and business.

The formerly subordinated native elite and the new military, administrative, and educated leaders followed the Ottoman tradition of exploiting bureaucratic offices to get rich in a few years. The leading writers of the age in Bulgaria targeted this phenomenon. Ivan Vazov, in his *Toj e mlad, zdrav, inteligenten* (He Is Young, Healthy, Cultured), satirized the rush for bureaucratic sinecures. His antihero, a young man with every advantage, refuses to consider any employment outside the bureaucracy. Anton Strasimirov's drama *Kasta* (1908) bitterly attacked the corruption of government officials (Moser 1972, 103, 173). The new national elite centered on the city. Their number was limited. Including all the settlements with more than 2,000 inhabitants, that is, cities and large villages together, only 9 percent of Montenegro's, 10 percent of Serbia's, 13 percent of Bosnia-Herzegovina's, and roughly 20 percent of Bulgaria's population lived in towns. Serbian figures for 1910 illustrate the overwhelming predominance of the peasantry in these countries. At that time, 5 percent of the population was employed in public offices and professions and 4 percent in trade. Some 7 percent of the country's inhabitants worked in industry, mostly in handicrafts. Even in Bosnia-Herzegovina, which reached a higher degree of industrial development than Serbia and Bulgaria together, more than 25,000 out of 29,000 industrial establishments "used only the labour of their proprietors" (Palairet 1997, 229). In the Balkan countries overall, only 1 percent of the active population was employed in large-scale industry.

During the last two or three decades before World War I, an important new social group emerged as part of the new national elite, the well-to-do peasantry. These decades were characterized by an increased fragmentation of peasant landed estates. Big estates did not exist in most of these countries, and at the turn of the century, 97 percent of Serbian peasants had only small properties, insufficient for marketing produce. Nearly 60 percent of the peasants owned fewer than five hectares of land, and less than 4 percent owned more than twenty hectares (Tomasevich 1955,

206). This thin layer of successful rich peasants became village merchants and moneylenders. They sent their children to school and became an integral part of the new elite. In his social drama *Parvite* (1907), Petko Todorov bitterly attacked this village elite who wielded economic and political power. In a symbolic gesture of social justice and unification, Milka, the daughter of the rich *corbadzi* of the village, leaves her family to join Dimitar, the teacher and leader of popular forces (Moser 1972, 177).

The Balkan societies, which had lacked their own elites and been "incomplete" during Ottoman times, thus began establishing native bureaucratic-military-merchant elites.

THE LOWER LAYERS OF DUAL AND INCOMPLETE SOCIETIES: PEASANTS AND WORKERS

The duality of traditional and modern characterized both the upper and lower layers of the Central European dual societies. Not only did the position and status of the old elite remain in place, but the overwhelming majority of the peasantry also endured. Their "disappearance" distinguished the West, although only in Britain did this actually occur. In continental Western Europe, the peasantry remained a significant minority, and its upper layers merged into the ranks of an ever-growing middle class.

In Central and Eastern Europe, the reduction of the peasantry in the active population had hardly begun. Well-industrialized Austria-Bohemia was an exception. Peasants constituted only 34–35 percent of the population of Upper and Lower Austria and Bohemia-Moravia-Silesia in 1910. Although illiteracy had not disappeared, it was no longer perpetuated: as early as 1880, 95–99 percent of school-age children attended schools. The western provinces of Austria-Hungary approached the Western European standard.

The peasantry, however, constituted between two-thirds and three-quarters of the population in the other countries of Central and Eastern Europe, including the eastern part of Austria-Hungary. In Poland and Hungary, where the percentage of peasants in the population decreased from 70–80 percent to 62–64 percent between the 1860s and 1910s, modern social transformation had at least begun. In Galicia and Bukovina, 73 percent of the active population still worked in agriculture in 1910; in Dalmatia, 83 percent; and in Croatia, 79 percent. In Romania, this proportion was 81 percent in 1860 and 75 percent in 1910. These figures were typical of the Balkans in general: the peasantry constituted 82 and 75 percent of the Bulgarian population in 1860 and 1910, respectively, and 89 percent and 82 percent in Serbia in the same years. Traditional peasant societies continued to predominate.

They suffered from the overwhelming presence of the big estates. "We village folk are pressed together as fish caught in a net: the manor-lands, stretching out on all sides, squeeze the life out of us," Reymont's hero complains. "Ye cannot throw a stone but it falls on the manor-lands . . . and ye are taken to the court—sentenced—fined—imprisoned." In winter, "famine was looking in at the byres . . . warm meals were served only once a day; and people went to the miller in ever-increasing numbers to borrow a few bushels of flour that they were to pay for [with] later work. . . . Others went to Yankel, begging him to lend a screw of salt, or a quart of groats, or a loaf of bread" (Reymont 1925, 2: 269, 252–53).

Peasant life did not change much during the century: there was solid continuity in everything from working methods to eating habits and entertainment, lifestyle, and all the superstitions of the peasantry. In a story by Ivan Vazov from the 1870s, an old Bulgarian peasant woman takes her sick grandson to a monastery in search of a cure. "'The devil take you! What businesses have you here, Iliitsa?' The monk asked impatiently. 'My grandson is ill. . . . Where is the old abbot? . . . I want him to read over my grandchild.'. . . 'What can I do for him if he's ill!' The monk angrily muttered. 'You can do nothing but God can do everything'" (*Balkan Range* 1976, 109).

Although emancipated, peasant majorities still remained excluded from political society in their nations. With one insignificant exception, peasants did not have voting rights and could not influence politics on their own behalf. In Poland under tsarist rule, this possibility did not exist at all; in Hungary, only 6 percent of the people had voting privileges. In Romania, out of 5 million inhabitants, only 20,000 people gained direct voting rights.

This exclusion was connected to the educational level of the peasants. At the end of the nineteenth century, 70 percent of the population of Poland remained illiterate. The figure for unskilled workers and day laborers from villages rose to 75–80 percent. Although from the 1880s on, secret teaching societies, sometimes called "flying universities," were organized by patriotic educational activists to cultivate Polish language, history, and religion, they rarely reached the countryside. According to Anna Zarnowska's striking figures, only 20 percent of school-age children in Warsaw—the "city of illiterates," as it was called—attended primary schools in 1880. The percentage had increased to only 25 percent by the start of World War I (Zarnowska 1996, 139, 142, 144). "In Vola," says one of Reymont's peasants, "there is a school, which my children attended for three winters running. What is the result? They cannot even read in a prayer book. Devil take such teaching!" (Reymont 1925, 1: 220).

The Hungarian educational situation was much better. Maria Theresa had taken the first important steps toward modern mass education in 1774. Her *Ratio Educationis* made compulsory the establishment of schools in every village and parish. However, in 1868, the year József Eötvös's modern school act introduced free, compulsory elementary education, 68 percent of the population was still illiterate. Before World War I, this figure decreased to 33 percent—that is, every third adult did not know how to read or write. The implementation of the law was also incomplete. Around the turn of the century, only 82 percent of school-age children attended primary schools. By the start of the war, nearly 90 percent were enrolled.

The schooling situation was much worse in the eastern and southern provinces of Austria-Hungary: of 6 million inhabitants of Galicia in 1886, more than 4.8 million were illiterate. In 1910, 59 percent of the population remained illiterate, and nearly 70 percent of school-age children did not attend schools (Himka 1988, 59–60, 64). In Dalmatia, Bukovina, and Bosnia-Herzegovina, respectively, only 67, 36, and 15 percent of school-age children attended school. The great majority of the population in the countryside lacked basic reading and writing skills. The conditions in the latter provinces approached those of the Balkans as a whole. Until the mid nineteenth century, virtually the entire population, roughly 90–95 percent, was illiterate. During the last quarter of a century before World War I, schooling made impressive progress in Romania. At the time of unification, Moldavia had no public primary schools at all, and Wallachia had 1,635 rural primary schools. The law of 1864 introduced compulsory four-year elementary education, but was not effectively enforced. Twenty years later, only 27 percent of school-age children were enrolled in the countryside. New school laws at the turn of the century resulted in important improvements: in 1900, only 40 percent of school-age children were enrolled in schools, but by 1909, the number had reached 61 percent. The reality, however, remained stark because of poverty and ignorance: fewer than two-thirds of the officially enrolled students attended school. At the turn of the century, only 11 percent of the rural Romanian population was literate, compared to the 40 percent in urban areas (Ronnas 1984, 227–32). The literacy rate of the rural population over eight years of age had increased to 33 percent by 1912 (Hitchins 1994, 171).

When two British women traveled from Pristina to Vuchitern in Serbia in the 1860s, they visited a school that was, as they described it, "a little low den, with earthen unsmoothed floor, and a few broken benches." When they learned from their guide that none of the Albanian girls they met who "studied" at the school could read or write, they asked: " '[T]hen what is it that you do learn there?' 'To say our prayers.'. . . 'Can you understand these prayers?' 'No.'" In another place, they visited a school where Serbian girls studied to "read Serbian and Old-Slavonic, and write a little. 'That is all that we can teach them,' explained Katerina, the teacher, 'for it is all we know ourselves'" (Mackenzie and Irby [1867] 1877, 277, 279, 404). Around the turn of the century, the illiteracy rate decreased to 79 percent in Serbia, but education was still in its infancy.

In Bulgaria, the first schoolbook in modern Bulgarian appeared in 1824, the first secular school was established in 1835 in Gabrovo, and girls' schools were opened in 1857 and 1862 in Stara-Zagora and Gabrovo, respectively. By World War I, however, only half of the school-age generation was enrolled in schools (Peeters and Zlatanoff 1909, 22, 33, 35, 211–17). The illiteracy rate stood at 72 percent of the population. Even a little elementary education made people "learned" and respected. Hadji Gencho, protagonist of a story by Luben Karavelov, one of the founders of modern Bulgarian fiction, typically justifies postponing a decision by saying: "I must ask Naiden, too, because Naiden, you know, is a learned and clever man — seven years he has studied" (*Balkan Range* 1976, 69). Even by the early twentieth century, in the best cases, only one-third of the population was literate (Berend and Ránki 1982, 56–58).

Persisting patterns of rural life in the Balkans were clearly signaled by the slowly disintegrating village communities. In Romania in 1864, roughly one-third of the peasantry was concentrated in free villages (*răzeși*) and so-called mixed villages. The land of these free villages, and of some of the mixed villages, was owned by the entire community and administered by the *obştia,* an assembly of all the adult members of the community, men and women alike. Ownership was granted on a first-come basis. If somebody cleared the woods, the land belonged to him. In the most archaic cases, such as the town of Cîmpulung in 1846, when a ruling was published, peasants did not have unequal and hereditary shares of the communal land. The entire property and its revenue belonged to the community. In other cases, there was unequal and hereditary distribution of land within the community. Local policing and jurisdiction were also the assembly's responsibility, as was the collection of taxes, exacted from the village as a lump sum, which the obştia then divided among the households. These village communities practiced an ancient type of pastoral and agricultural combined economy. The life of the village was largely tied to the forests. They raised animals and from time to time cleared sections of the woods and cultivated small pieces of land. According to Henri Stahl, it was a kind of "itinerant agriculture"—a vast pastureland, sprinkled with enclosed islets for cereal crops among the pastoral enclosures, both periodically moved. Even the plains remained basically pastureland. The community did not cultivate more than from one-fortieth to one-third of the arable land and did not even use plows until the second half of the nineteenth century. Such communities survived into the early decades of the twentieth century, especially in the hilly and mountainous regions (Stahl 1980, 37–54, 77, 211).

In South Slav rural areas, traditional large families of three generations and relatives, sometimes as many as from sixty to eighty or more people, worked together in household units called *kuca* or *zadruga*. The leading intellectual of Serbian national revival, Vuk Karadžić, gave an excellent description of this institution: "The Serbs live mainly in *zadrugas*. In some houses there are four or five married men. There are as many *vajats* [sleeping quarters] as there are married men, and the house itself is only for communal eating and the place in which the old women and men sleep. . . . Every household has a *staresina* [headman] who governs and guides the household and all its property" (quoted in Halpern and Halpern 1972, 16). From this report, we know of zadrugas with thirteen married couples, but in 1863, in Orasac, the largest household had twenty-three members. In later decades, however, successive divisions of the zadruga took place. A great number of married couples established their own households. Mutual help, nevertheless, continued: *moba,* or collective cultivation of corn; *pozajmica,* mutual help with harvesting and other forms of labor exchange; and *sprega,* reciprocal loans of livestock, equipment, and even cash (Halpern and Halpern 1972, 43, 52–53).

Half of the Romanian landed peasant families owned fewer than 5 hectares of land, and a further 14 percent owned 5 to 10 hectares. Thus nearly a million families lived in very poor conditions. The vast majority of such Balkan poverty plots of less than 10 hectares were able to sell only a marginal portion (in the best case, 20 percent) of their products. Some 89 percent of Serbian and 86 percent of Bulgarian peasant economies in the early twentieth century practiced what was essentially subsistence farming. The deep poverty, lack of political rights, and immobility of the illiterate peasant masses did not change much.

Not only were the peasantry's numbers unquestionably dwindling, especially in Austria-Hungary and Poland, but many of the liberated peasants were beginning to be transformed into urban workers. Most of these peasants in transition came from the landless peasantry—39 percent, for example, in Hungary, where those with too little land to make a living (1–3 hectares) made up roughly 30 percent of the peasantry. Their rank and file was supplemented by new generations of landed peasant families who either could not inherit land or, because of the large number of children, inherited only small fractions.

A great many of these peasants became wage laborers, who at a minimum sought seasonal work. In Ludmila Podjavorinská's novel *The Woman,* the Slovak peasant Stephan Zatko works "until Christmas loading beets into the railroad wagons. After Christmas he took various jobs, ice-quarrying or wood-cutting, or . . . 'propping the wall' in the city while waiting for one merchant or another to hire someone to carry a sack of flour or sugar. . . . At dawn he had to take the one-hour walk into the city in bone-biting cold. At dusk he came home, happy if he had earned some forty or sixty farthings." A large part of the peasantry had to leave the villages and look for work as harvesters on big estates. The female heroine of the same novel, Iva, "had gone to the harvest three years ago. . . . The farm agent transported the hired men and women out somewhere to the Hungarian Lowland" (Podjavorinska [1909] 1976, 158, 148). Others looked for jobs in railroad construction, water regulation, and building work in the growing cities. During the second half of the nineteenth century, grandiose earthworks, waterworks, and railroad construction offered job opportunities for unskilled peasants all over the region. Some of them were employed by industrial firms as seasonal workers in flour mills, sugar refineries, and breweries, which needed a relatively large number of seasonal workers during the peak period of three or four months around fall.

Roughly 14 percent of the Romanian peasantry, about 200,000 families, were landless and became wage laborers. The number of poor smallholders, however, was much larger: in 1900, 472,000 peasant households, 40 percent of the total, had no draft animals at all (Hitchins 1994, 170). The number of Romanian peasants who left the land to make their livings as wage earners remained much lower than in Poland and Hungary because of the obligatory contractual work introduced by the 1866 law. According to the law, which the police and army enforced, peasants had to contract with a landlord or arendaş, leasing a piece of land for payment in kind and labor service. This system was highly exploitative and bound peasants to the land, blocking their mobility.

Nearly half of the peasants in Poland and Hungary during much of the time period under discussion left their homes and gradually adjusted to the new workers' lifestyle. Some of them moved to cities and became unskilled industrial workers. This kind of mobility was also characteristic in the western provinces of Austria-Hungary. In 1900, 30 percent of the peasant population of Austria and 36 percent of that of Bohemia became agricultural wageworkers.

Altogether only about one-third of the peasants had enough property to remain independent farmers. In Hungary, only 10 percent of the peasants became well-to-do and acquired quasi-middle-class status. Their number was less than 3 percent in Romania, where 36,000 peasant families owned farms of 10 to 50 hectares, altogether nearly 700,000 hectares, or 18 percent of all peasant lands.

The native peasantry, in many cases, was confronted with landowners and employers of different ethnic groups. In Poland and Hungary, peasants often worked for Jewish entrepreneurs. Various minority groups, such as Ukrainians in Russian Poland and Galicia, worked on Polish big estates. Slovak peasants in northern Hungary and Romanian peasants in Transylvania worked for Hungarian landlords. Romanian peasants in the Romanian kingdom had to make contracts with the mostly Jewish arendaşi. The role of the nonindigenous bourgeoisie and middle class generated class-based ethnic conflicts in most of the countries in Central and Eastern Europe. The social conflicts and sharp polarization of nineteenth-century societies that in the West led to the formation of Marxist workers' parties, mass trade unions, and class confrontation surfaced as ethnic-religious confrontation and hostility in Central and Eastern Europe.

The most dramatic embodiments of this social conflict were a mid-nineteenth-century jacquerie in Galicia and an early twentieth-century one in Romania. In western Galicia, in 1846, peasants slaughtered 728 landlords and destroyed 474 manors (Himka 1988, 24). The Romanian peasant uprising was a consequence of the exploitative agricultural system, a special mixture of serfdom and capitalism, unique in modern Europe. As David Mitrany puts it, the landlords and renters enjoyed all the advantages, while the peasants suffered all the disadvantages of both systems (Mitrany 1930, 80). The Romanian peasants, who had long tolerated subhuman living conditions, erupted in a bloody revolt in March 1907. Thousands of peasants turned against their boyar landlords, but most of the absentee estate owners were invisible to them. Their real anger and brutal hostility were directed against the well-known middlemen, the Jewish renters, and often against Jewish shopkeepers and moneylenders. The uprising developed into an anti-Jewish pogrom, beginning in Botoşani and expanding to include all of Moldavia, and then Wallachia. A peasant army attacked Galaţi, and four thousand peasants marched on Bucharest. They burned Jewish houses and killed thousands of Jews, frightening the entire regime. At last, in April, 120,000 troops suppressed the uprising and killed about 10,000 peasants (Seton-Watson [1934] 1963, 386–87). Ethnic-religious hostility was widespread, however, and fueled extreme nationalist, right-wing populist movements and ideas all over the area.

The duality of the society in its upper layers was also clearly visible in the lower strata. While the traditional, slowly disintegrating peasant majority was preserved but excluded from political society, a modern industrial and service working class also appeared. Its numbers surpassed those of the peasants only in Austria-Bohemia: 52 percent of the Bohemian-Moravian-Silesian and 46 percent of the Upper and Lower Austrian working population were employed in industry, trade, and transportation. Small wonder that late nineteenth-century Czech realist literature produced the first working-class writings in the literature of the region. Jan Neruda, the "Czech Dickens," reported the atmosphere of the first May Day celebration in Prague: "With a peaceful yet iron step there marched on the *First of May,* 1890, endless and boundless legions of workers' battalions. . . . It was a mighty march, irresistible, as when the waves of the ocean rush forward. . . . Red badges, red neckties . . . [the] color of the world socialist movement . . . the colors fly today over the heads of those who fight for full social equality" (Neruda 1983, 211–12). Petr Bezruč's self-conscious proletarian voice in his *Silesian Songs* ("I am a hideous pitman just sprung from the mine") is equally unique:

> Ye lords of the mines below;
> The mines flare and reek, and there comes a day,
> A day when we'll take what we own.
> (Bezruč [1909] 1929, 186, 188)

The proportion of industrial workers did not surpass 23–25 percent in Poland and Hungary, 19 percent in Galicia and Bukovina, 13 percent in Croatia, and 9 percent of the active population in Dalmatia. In Romania, only 28,000 workers were employed by industrial firms, mostly small-scale, in 1860. The number increased to 200,000, or 10 percent of the active population, by 1913, and roughly half of them worked in big industrial firms with at least 100 workers (Constantinescu 1960). The emerging modern industrial working class remained connected to the villages. Keith Hitchins rightly stresses that unskilled Romanian urban workers "usually preserved their links to the village and continued to obtain a part of their income from agriculture" (Hitchins 1994, 163). The same was true all over Central and Eastern Europe.

Illiteracy among workers, male and female alike, was high: 54 percent and 56 percent of male and female workers, respectively, were illiterate in Poland around the turn of the century. The proportion of illiterates among unskilled workers and day laborers reached 75 percent among men and 80 percent among women (Zarnowska 1996, 139).

Roughly half of the industrial workforce of Central and Eastern Europe worked in small-scale industries before World War I. These workers—half members of the family, half servants—more closely resembled workers prior to the Industrial Revolution than modern factory workers, who hardly existed at all in these incomplete societies, which preserved their peasant character. Of the 7 to 10 percent of the industrial population of the Balkan countries, only 1 percent worked in modern big factories, while the others were traditional artisans. This extremely small group of workers was essentially all male. Women were scarcely permitted to leave the household.

Like the upper layers, the traditional and modern lower strata of society in Central and Eastern Europe differed ethnically. The traditional layer of the upper stratum was indigenous, but the modern layer was strongly recruited from nonindigenous members of the society. Here, too, the lack of mobility and proto-industrialization in the previous period caused a shortage of trained, skilled urban workers. As documented earlier, a great part of the skilled workers were German, Bohemian, and Jewish. In 1910, 43 percent of the foremen and 44 percent of the workers in Hungarian industry did not speak Hungarian. Roughly 30 to 35 percent of the Jewish population of Poland and Hungary became workers around the turn of the century. "Nearly half of the organized masses of the workers who moved to industrial centers were recruited from non-Hungarian ethnicities," the early twentieth-century Hungarian historian Gyula Szekfű observes (Szekfű 1920, 324).

The distinction between indigenous and nonindigenous was both feeble and overpoliticized. The so-called native or national groups were in reality mixtures of various ethnicities themselves. They had moved to and settled in these countries during the previous centuries, assimilating into the dominant ethnic groups. Slavs and Germans, for example, mingled with Hungarians and Romanians all over the Austro-Hungarian empire. Various kinds of Slavic peoples—Poles and Ukrainians, Serbs and Croats—also intermixed. Irrespective of whether they had lived in the country for several generations or were relatively freshly settled new im-

migrants, unassimilated groupings of Jews, Germans, and other nationalities were *considered* nonnative and treated accordingly. When the Jewish innkeeper sides with the Poles in an argument between Polish and German peasants in a pub, one of Władysław Reymont's peasants shouts:
"'What, a Jew to side with our folk! Who ever heard of such a thing!' . . .
'Yea, I am a Jew,' said the innkeeper, 'but . . . born here as you were, as
my father and grandfather were too! . . . Am I not, then, one of you?'"
(Reymont 1925, 3: 283). He was, indeed, no doubt, not considered to be
one of them.

THE DEMOGRAPHIC REVOLUTION

During the nineteenth century, Europe's modern social transformation
from a traditional agricultural society into an industrial one was inseparable from the population explosion. The population began to grow rapidly in the eighteenth century, and its growth rate increased from 0.5 to
2 percent annually during the nineteenth. Birthrates in Western Europe
decreased from 36–38 births per 1,000 inhabitants in the 1780s to 25–30
births by 1910, as a consequence of rapid urbanization, increased educational level, and drastic changes in lifestyle and environment. Death rates
declined even more dramatically. A better food supply and advances in
medical practice, including the elimination of medieval diseases such as
cholera, plague, and smallpox, sharply reduced mortality after the 1740s.
The death rate declined from 34–35 deaths per 1,000 inhabitants to 14–20
during the century. Life expectancy at birth jumped from twenty-five to
fifty years in Western Europe.

The "demographic revolution," as the French demographer Adolphe
Landry called it (Landry 1934), led to a population growth unparalleled
in history. During a single century, population increased fourfold in
Britain and nearly doubled in France. Western Europe altogether saw a
population increase of 360 percent. Did this impressive demographic
change generate the Industrial Revolution because traditional agricultural
economies could not feed the radically increased population? Or, conversely, did the revolutions in industry and agriculture lead to the demographic changes? This "chicken or egg" type of question has been answered
in contrasting ways, and the demographic revolution has been interpreted
either as the cause or a consequence of the Industrial Revolution.

In Central and Eastern Europe, the causal connection between the two
phenomena is much less ambiguous than in Western Europe. In that part

of the continent, the demographic revolution clearly preceded the process of industrialization. Revolutionary changes did not transform the economy until the last third of the nineteenth century. Internal economic factors thus did not induce or reinforce any radical change in demographic trends. However, while the population of the European core increased three and a half times, the population also trebled on the peripheries of the continent between 1800 and 1914. Furthermore, the intracore and intraperipheral variation of population growth rates was also comparable: Britain's fourfold, Holland's threefold, and France's less than twofold population growth was mirrored by Russia's more than fourfold, Poland's more than threefold, the Balkans' and Hungary's twofold, and Mediterranean Europe's less than twofold population increases (see table 3).

Population growth had a slower start in Central and Eastern Europe during the first decades of the century. The population of the Habsburg empire, for example, increased by 5.3 percent between 1800 and 1820, but by 9.1 and 9.6 percent between 1880 and 1890 and 1890 and 1900, respectively. Between 1830 and 1910, annual population growth in most of the countries of Central and Eastern Europe surpassed both that in Britain (0.80 percent) and Europe as a whole (0.82 percent). Russia grew at 1.13 percent per year, Romania at 1.02, Serbia at 1.08, and Bulgaria at 1.87 (Bairoch 1976b, 283).

Despite the absence of an industrial revolution in Central and Eastern Europe, a demographic revolution did occur there. However, the factors generating rapid population growth were radically different from those in the West. Marriage customs, for instance, changed significantly in Western Europe. Based on a comparative demographic analysis, John Hajnal has differentiated Western European and Eastern European marriage patterns, separated along a dividing line from Trieste to St. Petersburg. In Western Europe, as a consequence of rapid urbanization, industrialization, and changing lifestyles, more people remained unmarried and people married at a later age than previously. In contrast, marriage customs remained almost unchanged in Eastern Europe, which was characterized by earlier marriage and a higher marriage rate (Hajnal 1965). Between 1778 and 1895, only 3.5 percent of the women in Hungary who died at the age of 50 and over were single. Only 10 percent of the young women between the age of 25 and 30 were unmarried in Hungary, while this number was 35 to 50 percent in Western Europe. Marriage rates in 1910 were much lower in Western Europe—fifteen to sixteen marriages per 1,000 inhabitants—than in Hungary (eighteen marriages) or in Serbia (twenty marriages). Furthermore, people married five or six years earlier in Eastern Europe. In Hungary in the second half of the nineteenth century,

TABLE 3 *European Populations, 1800–1910 (in millions)*

	1800	1850	1880	1910	1910 as % of 1800
European Core	45.1	100.4	124.7	162.4	360.1
Scandinavia	5.0	7.9	10.7	13.7	274.0
Mediterranean Region	30.5	43.6	49.3	59.5	195.1
Russia	35.5	68.5	97.7	160.7	452.7
Poland	9.0	—	16.9	29.0	322.2
Hungary	9.3	13.8	15.7	20.9	224.7
Romania	(2.0)	3.7	4.6	7.0	189.2
Serbia	(0.2)	0.9	1.8	2.9	322.2
Bulgaria	—	—	2.8	4.3	153.6

SOURCE: Carlo Cipolla, ed., *The Emergence of Industrial Societies* (London: Collins/ Fontana Books, 1973), 747–48.

women's modal age at marriage was eighteen, and that of men was twenty-three (Andorka 1994, 318). In Serbia, from the 1880s up to the mid twentieth century, the overwhelming majority of men and women married between the ages of sixteen and twenty-seven (Halpern and Halpern 1972, 26).

Birthrates and death rates exhibited major dissimilarities as well. The most visible difference was the almost unchanged birthrate in Eastern Europe. While birthrates sharply declined from 36–38 to 25–30 per 1,000 in Western Europe, in Eastern Europe, they at most decreased only from 35–40 to 36–37 per 1,000 inhabitants, and they remained at the previous level in the Balkans throughout the nineteenth century. In Hungary, the birthrate declined slightly, to 36 per 1,000 inhabitants. In Romania, the figure was 43; in Bulgaria, 41; in Serbia, 38; and in Russia, 46 (Armengaud 1973, 56). This situation can be interpreted as a consequence of the preserved rural-agricultural society and lower level of education.

Imported improvements in health care, especially vaccination and the progressive elimination of medieval diseases such as smallpox, plague, and cholera, were the real reason for the population explosion in the hardly changed economic environment of Central and Eastern Europe. Widespread water regulations also halted malaria.

In the Habsburg empire, Maria Theresa followed the modern Western European model by introducing her *Normativum Sanitatis,* the basics of a modern health system. The Hungarian Public Health Act of 1876 followed the Western European pattern of registration of deaths and investigation of cause of death. Sanitary norms were established for housing, schools, shops, and institutions. Prevention became the duty of public authorities. Medical practice was regulated, and childbirth became much safer. Cities and settlements with more than 6,000 inhabitants were required to employ medical doctors; small villages jointly employed a *körorvos* (district physician) who treated the poor free of charge. State food inspection, first aid, and ambulances were also introduced (Matle-kovits 1898).

Some form of public health regulation was established all over the region. Health services reached from one-quarter to one-half the Western level in terms of number of medical doctors and hospital beds by the end of the nineteenth century. There were 34 and 39 medical doctors per 100,000 inhabitants in Germany and France, respectively. The Austrian-Bohemian level matched this standard (35 doctors), while the Hungarian level remained somewhat below it (23 doctors). The number of hospital beds in Hungary stood at half the Austrian-Bohemian level. Transylvania had 15 doctors per 100,000 people; Bukovina and Galicia, 12; and Croatia and Russia, 9 (Katus 1979, 1129).

The results of the imported agricultural revolution were equally important. Better food supply, improved nutrition, and a halt to famine had a significant impact on population growth. In Kiskúnhalas, Hungary, demographic crises in 1679, 1709, and 1739 reversed the entire population increase every thirty years (Melegh 2000, 278). Famines and epidemics also caused a dramatic increase of death rates in Bohemia—from 30 to nearly 40 per 1,000—during the last two decades of the eighteenth century. Calculations based on the 1777 census show death rates above 40 per 1,000 in Hungary, which climbed to 49 per 1,000 in 1784 (Gyula Benda 2000, 131). The famines of 1788–89 and 1816–17 in Hungary caused 100,000 deaths, and cholera killed a quarter of a million people in 1831 and 1873. In Romania, severe drought and famine in the countryside in 1873–74 and smallpox and cholera epidemics in urban areas in the same decade were probably the last "medieval" scourges. In Poland, great epidemics dissipated from the late eighteenth century onward.

As a result, death rates began to decline, although they remained at higher levels than in Western Europe: the death rate decreased to about 25 per 1,000 inhabitants in Hungary, 26 in Romania, and 30 in Russia, as compared to 14–18 deaths per 1,000 in Western Europe. This more moderate decline, and an even more moderate decline in the birthrate, was enough to generate high population growth.

Declining death rates led to higher life expectancy. During the last decade of the eighteenth century in Keszthely, Hungary, 62 percent of the population died by the age of 19, while 20 percent lived at least to the age of 50. In the mid nineteenth century, these percentages changed: 55 percent and 25 percent, respectively, died before the age of 19 and lived after 50. Those who reached adulthood could expect to live at least until the age of 40 to 50 (G. Benda 2000, 133, 143). A more impressive improvement followed. Although the average lifespan remained 10 to 20 years shorter than the Western European average of 50, it increased substantially: at the beginning of the twentieth century, the average lifespan of Hungarians was 39 years; that of Russians, 31; and that in the region as a whole, 30 to 40. These figures represented a 10- to-20-year increase compared to the beginning of the century. In the early nineteenth century, life expectancy in the north Hungarian township of Eger was 20.7 years, and in Csongrád County, only 16.6 years, mostly because of the extremely high rate of infant mortality. Between the mid eighteenth and mid nineteenth centuries, every fourth or fifth newborn died before the age of one (Á. B. Lukács 1977; G. Benda 2000). Average life expectancy hardly surpassed 20 years anywhere in early nineteenth-century Central and Eastern Europe.

The demographic revolution not only preceded economic modernization in the region but served as a major stimulus to it. Instead of 25–30 million inhabitants at the beginning of the nineteenth century, the region had to feed 70–75 million people in the early twentieth century, with proportionately more adults than before. The traditional economy was unable to accomplish this task. Higher productivity in both agriculture and industry was badly needed. The "imported" demographic revolution forced economic modernization.

The situation resulted in the emigration of a part of the increased population to the New World. During the century after 1820, about fifty million Europeans emigrated, three-fifths of them to the United States (Hatton and Williamson 1998, 533). First of all, there were those who were landless and could not find employment elsewhere. More than two-thirds of the emigrants from Austria-Hungary were peasants. When the great wave of European emigration began, from the first decades of the nineteenth century to 1850, more than three-quarters of European emigrants to the United States were from Britain, and another 17 percent from Germany. Between 1850 and 1880, 82 percent of the emigrants were still British and German. By then, however, emigration had started from Central and Eastern Europe, and 2.5 percent of the European emigrants were from Austria-Hungary. From 1880 on, the peripheral regions of the continent became the main source of European emigration: in 1880, 45 percent of the emigrants were Scandinavian, Italian, and Central and Eastern European. By 1890, this percentage had increased to 72 percent, and by the early twentieth century, to 80 percent. During a third of a century, between 1880 and 1914, 24 percent of European emigrants left from Italy, 13 percent from the Iberian Peninsula, and 6 percent from Scandinavia. Roughly one-quarter of the emigrants originated from Central and Eastern Europe, including Russia. The share of the latter was relatively low, only 9 percent of the total (Ferenczi and Wilcox 1929–31).

The massive emigration absorbed one-fifth to one-quarter of the population increase in the Central European region. At the end of the century, the migrants were mostly young male adults. Between 1868 and 1910, three-quarters of the immigrants entering the United States were between the ages of 15 and 40. Two-thirds were male (Hatton and Williamson 1998, 536). The bulk of the population of the region, however, remained immobile: in Croatia, 75 percent and 71 percent still lived in the place of their birth in 1880 and 1910, respectively. The corresponding figures for Hungary were 75 percent and 69 percent (Dányi 2000, 31). Emigration from the Balkans remained insignificant. Deep poverty, lack of mobility and information, and the surviving communal society blocked the road to mass emigration. However, political turmoil and the foundation of independent nation-states led to mass emigration of Muslims to Istanbul, Anatolia, and other Ottoman territories: during the last three decades of the nineteenth century, more than a million Muslims departed from the independent states. This wave of emigration continued during and after the Balkan wars (Todorova 1997, 175). Even from Russia, more than 90 percent of the emigrants belonged to various minority groups—Jews, Poles, Finns, Lithuanians, and Germans—who left the empire mostly because they had been persecuted and oppressed.

Immigration did not play a significant role in European population movements. The overwhelming majority of emigrants sought a new life overseas. Russia, a frontier country with huge empty lands in the east, attracted 4.2 million immigrants, two-thirds of them European, but the other Central and Eastern European countries did not experience mass immigration during the nineteenth century. The only massive inflow of population was the immigration of hundreds of thousands of Eastern European—Russian and Polish—Jews into Romania and Hungary. According to Robert Seton-Watson, at the beginning of the nineteenth century, only about 2,000 Jewish families lived in the Romanian Principalities. By 1859, the number of Jews had increased to more than 127,000, and by 1900, to between 300,000 and 400,000 (Seton-Watson [1934]

1963, 347–49). At the time of Joseph II's Edict of Toleration, issued for Hungarian Jewry in 1783, Hungary's Jewish population was about 80,000. By 1825, following the partition of Poland and the annexation of Galicia by the Habsburg empire, this number had increased to nearly 250,000. In 1910, nearly 1,000,000 Jews lived in Hungary (Silber 1992, 3, 10).

Tens of thousands of skilled workers from Germany, Austria, and Bohemia also settled all over Central and Eastern Europe. A few thousand engineers, managers, and entrepreneurs found new homes in these countries too. The number of immigrants was limited, but their role in these societies became crucially important.

FAMILY AND GENDER RELATIONS

As described in Frédéric Le Play's classic six-volume study, *Les Ouvriers européens,* preindustrial familial relations changed drastically in nineteenth-century Western Europe. The continuity of age-old relationships was undermined by industrialization, factory work, and urbanization. More and more women started working outside the family. More people remained unmarried, married much later, or moved from the traditional village family home to cities and small urban dwellings. The old-style *famille souche,* or stem family, of three generations—the parents, their married eldest son and his wife and children, and his unmarried siblings, living under the same roof—gradually disappeared. The new family structure became the nuclear family, two generations, parents and children, living together. Birth control, although still confined to coitus interruptus, significantly limited the number of children. Traditional village families of from twelve to thirty people were rapidly replaced by small families of from five to six (Le Play 1877–79).

New research has, however, strongly challenged this view. Michael Mitterauer and Reinhard Sieder speak of the "myth of the large preindustrial family" and prove their statement mostly using English family statistics: the mean household in Britain consisted of around five people throughout the seventeenth, eighteenth, and nineteenth centuries. In preindustrial Amsterdam (in 1755), the average family size was roughly three people; in Vienna in 1890, about five (Mitterauer and Sieder 1982, 27–28). "The mean size of co-resident groups remained remarkably constant at about 4.75 persons per household across Northwestern Europe from the seventeenth to the early twentieth century," Wally Seccombe observes (Seccombe 1992, 236). The Central and Eastern European family structure differed markedly from that of Northwestern Europe. John Hajnal speaks of "two kinds of pre-industrial household formation system," the Northwest European type being characterized by late marriage, relatively few married couples, and a high proportion of servants in the family, whereas in Eastern Europe (and elsewhere), large joint households dominated (Hajnal 1983). The difference between Western and Eastern European demographic patterns, with a Trieste–St. Petersburg dividing line, was thus undoubtedly reflected in family structures.

Russian "family communes," consisting of from thirty to forty people "under the rule of a stern patriarch," have been broadly studied (Czap 1983, 106). Mitterauer and Sieder present the figures for Rjazan province, Russia, in 1814: nuclear families were only one-third of the total, while nearly 60 percent were three-generation families, and a further 7 percent comprised as many as four generations. In Lithuania, at the end of the eighteenth century, 64 percent of families were grouped around two or more married couples. In Croatia, Bosnia, Serbia, Albania, and Bulgaria, nineteenth-century extended families often comprised from twenty to thirty and in some cases as many as eighty people (Mitterauer and Sieder 1982, 29–30). In Orasać, Serbia, single-couple families made up only 2 percent of the population in 1863 (Halpern and Halpern 1972, 28).

On the western rim of Central and Eastern Europe, the situation indicates a kind of transitory situation, with strong regional differences within Bohemia and Hungary. In various parts of these countries, two-generation nuclear families dominated. However, in the agrarian parts of Bohemia during the second half of the nineteenth century, extended families continued to function where the married young couple had to accept the unmarried adult brothers and sisters of the head of the household to keep the land together. In early twentieth-century Slovakia, there was "a pronounced tendency toward a common family household economy involving several marital couples—the parental couple with married sons and married brothers and sisters" (Horská 1994, 104–5).

"Patriarchal life is dominant . . . the villagers usually still live together; in some villages, there are families with thirty or forty members under one roof," a mid-nineteenth-century ethnographer wrote of north Hungarian villages (Pap 1865). According to the newest research, in thirteen villages in the same area and period, hardly more than one-fifth of the families were nuclear two-generation families. Nearly three-quarters of the families consisted of grandparents, their married son and his wife and children, and married brothers and sisters, on average twelve, but in some cases as many as twenty-nine people. Ethnographic monographs also

record families of from forty to sixty people (Dányi 1994, 394, 398). However, in the northern Slovak areas, as reflected by the mid-nineteenth-
century census of the small village Szőlősardó, 40 to 50 percent of the
families were nuclear two-generation families, with an average of three
children (Heilig 2000, 241).

The traditional large, three-generation family was preserved in most
of Central and Eastern Europe, albeit with striking regional differences
and with a gradual change in later decades. Patriarchal relations also survived and changed only slightly. The master, the paterfamilias, no longer
governed all the relatives of the large family, including his wife, adult children, and their spouses. However, male domination was preserved, and
women were not yet liberated in either society or the family. All over Europe, women were second-class citizens who had to obey their husbands.
They remained less educated, highly subordinated, and dependent within
the family.

Although women were paid less (they earned only half what men did,
according to Anna Zarnowska [1996, 139]), female labor nevertheless
gradually led to the erosion of the old patriarchal relations. "Marriage lost
its character as a property transaction. . . . Parental and community
influence . . . declined" (Seccombe 1992, 235). Women became more independent. They also became better educated, and female intellectuals began to play a role. The struggle for women's political rights flooded turn-
of-the-century Western Europe, and, although European women gained
voting rights only in Finland and Norway before World War I, women's
suffrage became widespread after the war. Only the beginnings of these
changes appeared in the peasant societies of Central and Eastern Europe,
which remained bound to the old functions of the family.

In Western European societies, the preindustrial family was above all
the basic context of the organization of work, but its classic functions also
included the protection of its members, the socialization of children, and
the management of leisure. In nineteenth-century Europe, all these functions of the family eroded. The "functionless family" gradually led from
domination within the "rigidly hierarchical institution to a partnership
of individuals. Members of the family . . . gained greater independence
and the right to live their own lives" (Mitterauer and Sieder 1982, 88).

Among peasants in rural Central and Eastern Europe, the family remained an important—and in some cases, the dominant—form of the organization of work throughout the nineteenth century. Socialization and
acculturation of children remained mostly a family responsibility. In some
backward areas of the Balkans, among Albanian and Montenegrin fami-

lies, even the archaic "judicial" function of the family, the duty of blood revenge, survived. As a consequence, the hierarchical structure of the family was not strongly challenged either. The head of a large rural family was its unchallenged master, and his wife, children, and even married sons and their wives and children, as well as the unmarried members of the family, worked together. A marriage did not mean the establishment of a new household. The division of labor within the family was strict and traditional. The "manager," in many cases, the "dictator," of the household was the patriarch, who ordered and controlled all the activities and work. The male adults worked in the fields, repaired and sometimes even made the tools, did construction work, and transported goods. The female folk did all the household work, including spinning, weaving, and making clothing, especially in the winter. They also had a major role in tending and milking the animals and assisting in the fields. Small children also had a role and had to work in the family household. The traditional patriarchal family remained nearly unchanged in rural areas.

The first signs of transformation appeared during the second half of the nineteenth century: birth control led to a decline in the number of children born to a family to four or five. In some areas, a "one-child system" was practiced, mostly to keep the small parcel of family land intact (Vasary 1989). "We do not make beggars," peasants in Ormánság said in justification of early birth control, explaining: "One parcel, one child" (Andorka 1978, 94–95). Families thus began to shrink.

An even more important factor was the beginning of urbanization and the emergence of an urban lifestyle and family characteristics more similar to the Western European pattern. These new phenomena remained marginal and influenced the lives of only 10 to 25 percent of the population in the various countries of the region. Moreover, the industrial working class, like the traditional peasantry, remained a male-dominated society. The foremen and the vast majority of skilled workers were male, as were the unskilled workers who did most of the jobs requiring physical strength. A good worker did not allow his wife to take a job. The life of a miner's wife was, in fact, extremely similar to a peasant woman's life in the household, including keeping some animals in the backyard.

However, the partial success of industrialization in some Central European countries produced the first modern female workforce. In Poland, 24 percent of the industrial workers were female. Up to 33 percent of unskilled workers and day laborers, and 78 percent of service workers, were women. As many as 46 percent of all textile workers were female, and three-quarters of all women industrial workers worked in textiles before the war (Zarnowska 1995, 123–24). In Hungary, food processing employed 28 percent of female workers, and textiles and clothing another 33 percent. Women were mostly employed in unskilled jobs and in all made up 25 percent of the industrial labor force in Hungary in 1910 (*Üzemi és munkás statisztika* 1910).

"We like to say that employment has freed millions of women, but this freedom is only ostensible; the reality is different . . . [because women work for wages that] are insufficient to properly support them" the Yugoslav-Czech Milan Fric wrote in his *O ženskej otázke* (On the Woman Question) (Fric [1907] 1991, 161). That was definitely true. Wage differences conserved gender hierarchy, especially because statistics did not count unpaid domestic work done by women as a contribution to GDP. "The new material basis of patriarchal authority became the male control of the primary wage. . . . Industrial capitalism brought limited gains to younger single women and setbacks to married women of the working class" (Seccombe 1992, 244–45). The appearance of women working independently of the family in cities and towns, and of two-generation families with from four to five children, signaled the first changes in patriarchal dominance in Central and Eastern Europe.

Hierarchical, male-dominated family life nonetheless remained a kind of "natural law." Very few had the courage to question or attack this social injustice. Moreover, male domination was often brutal, and physical abuse of women and children was an everyday phenomenon. "Who eats her husband's bread must do her husband's will," peasant women said. In Reymont's Boryna family, although Yagna "defended herself tooth and nail . . . daily the yoke grew heavier. . . . Many times she had wanted to return to her mother, but the latter . . . threatened to send her back . . . by force. . . . She lived in continual terror, oppressed by such a sense of injustice . . . that she often wept for the whole night" (Reymont 1925, 2: 260).

Budapest was perhaps the most Western European city in Central and Eastern Europe, but there too, as John Lukacs notes, "around 1900 masculinity and virility were still very dominant; the supremacy of the male was unquestioned and unquestionable, sometimes to the detriment of feminine sensitivities." Inequality was also given linguistic expression. Rather than saying *a férjem,* "my husband," a Hungarian woman generally called her husband *az uram,* "my master," or "my lord" (Lukacs 1989, 106).

Wayne Vucinich describes the Balkan situation for women in much darker tones. Women were "generally treated as inferior beings." Muslim and Christian women alike lived in social isolation [and] deferred to men with blind subservience . . . the man rules with absolute authority, and the wife obeys him slavishly . . . [women] eating separately with the children and, when on a trip, walking laden with freight several steps behind their husbands. . . . The treatment of children (especially female) with indifference and inhumanity is also traceable to Ottoman influence. The children were brutally exploited for the labor power, particularly girls[,] who married young and became "someone else's fortune." The children were taught to serve their parents. . . . They were put to work in their teens and subjected to iron discipline. (Vucinich 1963, 92)

The woman's situation was considered to be "natural" and did not generate complaints for a long time. The gentry's "benign patriarchalism" in Poland gave the highest respect and esteem to women. During the 1820s, in her *Pamiątka po dobrej matce* (Legacy of a Mother to Her Daughter), Poland's first recognized woman writer, Klementyna Tanska-Hoffmanowa, although demanding equal recognition for women, who play an equal role in the social division of labor, denounced women's education: "Women certainly have less need to possess knowledge . . . study should not be an aim. . . . To know how to make her husband happy, to make his life pleasurable, to bring up their children properly, to find new . . . ways of pleasing everyone: that is the system of education for a woman" (quoted in Phillips 1999, 207).

"[B]y existing human rights and standards [a woman is] . . . not even a human being but just a thing," Eliza Orzeszkowa asserts, however, in her novel *Marta*. In the early twentieth century, Polish women's rights advocates, such as Iza Moszczenska, flatly rejected the concept of "benign patriarchalism," arguing that in spite of obligatory aristocratic codes of distinctive politeness to them, women were still the "slaves of their men folks" (quoted in Pietrow-Ennker 1992, 1–7, 21).

The education of women, a main factor of equality, languished during the entire century. Illiteracy, as was noted earlier, remained high throughout the region. Girls in many cases were not even considered to be worth educating. In late nineteenth-century Romania, only 27 percent of school-age children in the countryside were enrolled. Girls, in a telling illustration of male domination and the general mentality, were almost entirely neglected: only 13 percent of enrolled students were girls. When official enrollment increased in subsequent decades, the same general mentality kept girls out of school: two-thirds of all eligible students attended schools, but only slightly more than half of the eligible girls attended. Female illiteracy, even at the turn of the century, remained nearly absolute: only 3 percent of rural and 7 percent of the total female population could read and write (Ronnas 1984, 227–32). In Poland around the turn of the century, illiteracy remained very high even among female industrial workers: 56 percent of them could not read or write. Illiteracy reached 80 percent among female unskilled workers. Among service workers, only one-third of the male workforce was illiterate, but nearly 70 percent of female service workers could not read or write (Zarnowska 1996, 139). The situation was not altered by the admittance of the first few women to universities in 1900 (Homola-Skapska 1992, 82).

Toward 1900, however, a vanguard group of women, especially writers and other intellectuals, raised their voices for women's education and equality, and Polish women in particular expressed ambitious educational aspirations (Szwarc 1993). Early feminist voices were also heard in the Czech lands. A series of female realist writers illustrates this new trend. Božena Němcová demanded "public acknowledgement of a woman's right of self-determination" as early as in the mid nineteenth century. Her follower Karolina Svetlá, the daughter of a Prague merchant and wife of a professor, "insisted on the right of education, the free choice of occupation, and the social usefulness of women" (Novák 1976, 164, 183). Female writers denounced the lack of equal education and rights for women (Rudinsky 1991). In the backward Slovakian part of Hungary, Elena Maróthy Soltésová's *Potreba vzdelanosti pre ženu* (The Need for Women's Education) took aim at middle-class men:

[T]he majority only want their wife to be beautiful, charming . . . and devoted to them body and soul. . . . They require her to have only social skills . . . they follow their own pleasure and see a woman as only an object for themselves. . . . The other [lower-class] group of men . . . believe that a woman exists . . . for her material use. They want first of all a housekeeper and . . . helpful labor . . . so that to the lower classes a wife is really a beast of burden ordered to work without rest. . . . Any sort of education . . . is a disadvantage, not a benefit . . . a husband is the ready-made enemy of his wife's education through his conviction that it leads her away from her duty. (Soltésova [1898] 1991, 134–36)

Milan Fric, the male feminist quoted above, demanded "giving women rights equal to men's in every respect, and emancipating women's morality from slavery to men's passion" (Fric [1907] 1991, 159). Feminist revolt went beyond the demand for education and even equal rights. Under a characteristic title, *Vzpoura* (Rebellion, 1901), Božena Viková-Kunetická, later the first female member of Czechoslovakia's parliament, expressed aggressive feminism, attacked monogamy, and launched a "dark and noisy revolt . . . not only against rigid social conventions, but also against emotional and moral components within the author's own personality" (Novák 1976, 244–45).

These were rare voices. The "Women Question" had scarcely been addressed. The liberation of women was by and large tabled for a future agenda. Half of society, the female population, was totally dependent on the other, male half. This subordination was even more brutal and naked among the lower strata of the society.

THE GROWTH OF TOWNS AND CITIES

The separation of the traditional and the modern, and the beginning of real social change, occurred first in the newly emerging, rapidly growing cities. City and countryside were two different worlds all over nineteenth-century Europe. The antagonism of these two worlds, however, was incomparably sharper and more hostile in Central and Eastern Europe than in Western Europe, where the majority of the population became urban at the beginning of the twentieth century. Rising modern metropolises increased in population: London, for example, went from 1.1 million inhabitants in 1800 to 2.7 million by 1850, and then to 7.2 million by 1910. Paris had 0.5, 1.1, and 2.9 million inhabitants in 1800, 1850, and 1910, respectively. This miraculous growth of the capitals was accompanied by the development of several other large cities: Manchester, Glasgow, and Liverpool increased in population roughly tenfold between 1800 and 1910, and each had more than 0.7 million inhabitants at the beginning of the twentieth century. Besides Paris, Marseille and Lyon grew fivefold and each had roughly 0.5 million inhabitants in 1910. Besides Berlin, with its more than 2 million inhabitants in 1910, Hamburg, Cologne, Leipzig, and Munich also became large cities, with from 0.5 to 1.0 million inhabitants.

Central and Eastern Europe could not follow the breathtaking pace of Western Europe's urbanization. The growth of some towns and cities there was nevertheless quite rapid. In Hungary, 1.1 million people lived in towns with more than 20,000 inhabitants in 1870. Their number increased by nearly three times during the four decades ending in 1910, when it reached 3.1 million. The total population in Serbian towns with more than 2,000 inhabitants was 28,000 in 1834 and 310,000 in 1910. Unlike Western Europe, where the absolute majority of the population already lived in cities before World War I, Central and Eastern Europe remained highly rural. The Czech lands were the only exception: 16 percent of their population lived in towns with more than 2,000 inhabitants in 1843, but this increased to 43 percent by 1900, and became more than half of the entire population before World War I.

The share of the real urban population (in cities with more than 20,000 inhabitants) in Hungary increased from 7 percent to 17 percent between 1870 and 1910. Counting the entire population of settlements with more than 2,000 inhabitants, Poland had an urban population of 15 percent at the end of the eighteenth century, which increased to 33 percent by 1910. Serbia's "urban" population was 4 percent in 1834 and 11 percent in 1910. Romania, Bulgaria, and Bosnia-Herzegovina had urban populations of 17, 18, and 13 percent, respectively, in the early 1910s. Thus, a small segment of the population in the region—one or two people out of ten—lived in towns even before the war.

The typical industrial city was rather rare in the region. Lodz, the "Polish Manchester," and Plzen, Brno, and Moravská-Ostrava in the Czech lands were exceptions. Ostrava, the coal and iron center of northern Moravia, grew nearly sevenfold, to 150,000 inhabitants, during the last three decades before the war. The population of Plzen jumped fourfold, to 100,000, by World War I. Brno grew to 180,000 inhabitants.

The capital cities, Prague, Budapest, Warsaw, and in some respects, Bucharest, became both modern industrial centers and the administrative, transportation, and cultural nuclei of their countries. Prague had only 150,000 inhabitants in 1851, but the number had increased to 225,000 by 1910. Around the old city, however, new, modern suburbs sprang up. Karlin, Smichov, Žižkov, and Vinohrady concentrated more people than in Prague proper. Altogether, when Greater Prague was administratively constituted after the war, the city had nearly 677,000 inhabitants (Sayer 1998, 85, 177). Warsaw had 100,000 inhabitants both in 1800 and in 1850, but the stagnant city flourished during the second half of the century: its population increased to 252,000 by 1880, and to 856,000 by 1910, when it became the eighth-largest city in Europe.

Budapest's development was exceptional, comparable only to the American miracle: in 1800, three small cities, Buda, Pest, and Óbuda, on both sides of the Danube River, had altogether 54,000 inhabitants. By 1850, the three cities had 140,000 inhabitants. Population took off after the Austro-Hungarian Ausgleich of 1867 and the administrative unification of the three cities in 1873: Budapest's population doubled, then doubled again during the next two decades. By 1880, Budapest had 370,000 inhabitants, and by 1910, 880,000. From 1870 on, a series of industrial suburbs began to encircle the capital city: Ujpest, Pesterzsébet, Kispest, Pestszentlőrinc, Csepel, and other small adjacent settlements grew from

100,000 inhabitants in 1900 to nearly 200,000 by 1910. Although administratively they remained independent until 1949, in practice they merged with and became part of Greater Budapest, with 1.1 million inhabitants, the seventh-largest city of Europe.

Bucharest emerged as a small settlement but grew rapidly from the late nineteenth century on. Though its growth was much less spectacular than that of Prague, Warsaw, or Budapest, by the turn of the century, the Romanian capital had 276,000 inhabitants. By 1910–12, the population was more than 341,000.

Modern Western-style metropolises thus developed but remained isolated islands in rural Central and Eastern Europe. Moreover, urban settlements remained estranged from peasant societies. A great proportion of the urban population was German and Jewish. Nearly half of Prague's population was German-speaking in the mid nineteenth century. Eduard Hanslick described this situation: "Aristocracy and bourgeoisie, the whole cultivated middle class in Prague, spoke only German, and knew only as much Bohemian as enabled them to make themselves understood by domestic servants." He also mentioned Czech-language performances at the Prague Theater (Ständetheater) "at around 4:00 in the afternoon, three hours before the German performance was due to begin. . . . One sent one's domestic servants to these Bohemian performances; none of our circle ever went to them" (quoted in Payzant 1991, 39). German-speaking inhabitants assimilated rapidly, however, so that by 1880, only 22 percent of the population spoke only German. By World War I, the figure had dropped to 7 percent. Budapest's case was similar: in 1850, 80 percent of the population spoke only German. The Buda city authorities ended their contract with the German Theater in the city in 1870, and the Pest authorities did so in 1880. The Budapest stage was thus "de-Germanized" (Freifeld 1999, 168). The German-speaking population of the city dropped to 54 percent by 1873, and to a marginal 4 percent by 1900. Germans made up 51 percent of the population of Temesvár (Timisoara), 30 percent of the inhabitants of Brassó (Brasov), and altogether 21 percent of the population of the Transylvanian Hungarian cities in 1900 (Ronnas 1984, 100, 341). In the Moldavian part of the Romanian kingdom, 39 percent of the urban population was Jewish. In Bucharest, and in Romania in general, 35 percent and 32 percent of the urban population, respectively, were Jewish and German at the turn of the century (ibid., 96). In Budapest, which the anti-Semitic mayor of Vienna, Karl Lueger, called *Judapest,* one of four inhabitants was Jewish, in contrast to the country as a whole, where one out of twenty was Jewish. Unlike Warsaw, Budapest, and Bucharest, which had massive Jewish minority populations, Prague remained an exception.

Although 22 percent and 33 percent of Bohemian Jews lived in Greater Prague in 1880 and 1910, respectively, the share of the Jewish minority in the city remained rather low: 6.3 percent in both 1869 and 1910 (Kieval 1988, 13).

The social structure of the capital cities reflected a different world from the agricultural peasant countryside. Budapest was home to 54 percent of the industrial workforce of the entire country. Half of the city's population consisted of industrial workers. In 1890, 40,000 workers marched and celebrated May Day, responding to the call of the Social Democratic International. In 1912, the first confrontation between the industrial workers and the police force, "Bloody Thursday," illustrated the strength of the labor movement. Two-thirds of the intellectual and white-collar workers of the country were also concentrated in the capital city. Literacy was substantial: only 9 percent of Budapest's population remained illiterate, mostly old people and young peasant housemaids serving middle-class families. In the country at large, more than one-third of the population was illiterate. Bucharest also reflected this contrast: around the turn of the century, only 15 percent of the country's population was literate, while 63 percent of Bucharest's population could read and write.

The new metropolises mimicked their Western European counterparts. The spectacular reconstruction of Paris under Napoleon III offered an attractive example. Similar grandiose construction works were initiated in Vienna, Prague, and Budapest. The famous Ringstrasse and the spectacular new public buildings at the end of the century, and the first shocking modern apartment houses and villas erected in the early twentieth century, transformed Vienna into a modern European capital city.

During the reconstruction of Prague between 1885 and 1903, whole areas, including the old Josefov district and the Jewish ghetto, were destroyed in the name of slum clearance. Most of the seventeenth- and eighteenth-century baroque buildings, symbols of the Counter-Reformation, were demolished. Various neogothic and neorenaissance public buildings formed the modern "Golden Prague." The new National Theater, the "little golden chapel on the Vltava," was opened in 1881, then, after a fire, reopened in 1883. The former Horse Market, renamed Wenceslas Square, was crowned by the new neorenaissance National Museum in 1890. The major squares were decorated with important national statues: the foundation of the Jan Hus monument was laid in 1903; the statue of the patron of Bohemia, Saint Václav, was completed in 1913 (Sayer 1998, 99, 100–102). A vivid, flourishing fin de siècle Prague emerged (Wittlich 1992).

Budapest gained the status of a European metropolis during the three decades before World War I. The Nagykörút and Kiskőrút, the two Ringstrassen, and the crossing main boulevards, the Sugár út (later Andrássy út), ending in the monumental Hősök tere, and Rákóczy út, created a new city structure. New public buildings, most of all, the enormous neogothic parliament building on the bank of the Danube, the Opera House, and the headquarters of the Customs Office, the spectacular new Danube bridges, the Margít híd, Ferenc József híd, and Erzsébet híd, decorated a real European capital. At the millennium celebration in 1896 of the arrival of the Hungarian tribes in the Danube valley, Budapest inaugurated the Continent's first subway line, two kilometers long, and a network of electric streetcar lines. The city became a railroad center, with ornate railway stations: Gustave Eiffel built the West station. Large parks, the Városliget, Népliget, and Margitsziget, and the Dunakorzó, created elegant, popular public spaces in the rapidly growing city. The Hungarian capital became one of Europe's most beautiful and representative metropolises.

In the proud, impressive cities, full of the symbols of national revival and grandeur, a strongly Western European, cosmopolitan lifestyle developed. Like Paris and Vienna, Budapest in 1900, with its 600 coffeehouses, some of them open twenty-four hours a day, also became a capital of coffeehouse culture. In 1894, Alajos Hauszman, the architect who rebuilt the royal castle, built one of the most elegant coffeehouses, whose cosmopolitan name, New York, was symbolic. Writers and journalists had their favorite coffee shops and *Stammtisch* (the same table reserved for the same group of people), where they read the newspapers. The coffeehouse became their study and its tables their desks. Some of them even received their guests there (Lukacs 1988, 148–51).

The capital cities had vivid cultural lives. When the British statesman Richard Cobden visited Vienna in the mid nineteenth century, his program self-evidently included visits with Prince Metternich, Count Moritz Esterházy, and Baron Rothschild, as well as to the opera for a performance of Rossini's *Guillaume Tell* (Cobden 1994, 152–55). Upper-middle-class families kept boxes at the opera in Vienna, Prague, and Budapest. The inhabitants of Warsaw in 1830 already had their choice of seven newspapers. During the second half of the century, a "theater mania" flooded the city. To see every single performance became chic (Wapinski 1994, 154).

The emerging big cities differed not only from the traditional peasant countryside but from sleepy, second-rate little towns of the kind condemned by late nineteenth-century realist Czech writers for narrow-mindedness and prejudice, whose very air, said Svatopluk Čech, was "poisoned with hate, envy and jealousy-gossip . . . hired assassins of old women wait behind every corner" (quoted in Novák 1976, 241). Some towns, however, preserved their traditional agricultural life. In 1910, Debrecen, on the Hungarian plain, with its 90,000 inhabitants, was, for example, still by and large just a "big village."

The Balkan towns, including the capital cities, although home to most of the thin modern social strata, consisting of the new bureaucratic and merchant elite of these countries, also remained typical quiet small towns. Before World War I, the largest of them, Sofia, had a population of 100,000; Belgrade had 90,000 inhabitants; Sarajevo, 52,000. In the 1870s, in the most "urbanized" Balkan country, Bulgaria, only seven towns had more than 15,000 inhabitants. The Balkan cities, which had a long tradition dating from antiquity, had been incorporated into the Ottoman system and subordinated to the state. Guilds were restricted, but state sanctions and protection offered certain advantages for the producers. Cities, however, never gained an autonomous role in the Ottoman empire (Todorova 1997, 173). Unlike the modern Central European metropolises, the Balkan cities preserved their oriental townscapes. Raina Gavrilova presents a brilliant description of this world. The narrow, mostly unpaved, interwoven streets do not serve for lively traffic but "discourage the entrance of outsiders" and "control the access to different [religious] zones with[in] the town." The quiet, green residential areas with gardens and orchards were totally separated from the modest town center. The *çarşi*, the main street, a continuation of the intercity road, served as a business street, in some cases enlarged to a district by a few neighboring streets or blocks, mostly roofed. All the merchants and artisans had their shops here, the owner sitting in front. The barbershop, tavern, coffeehouses, the "clubs of the Orient," and the public buildings—inns or caravansaries *(hanlar)*, public baths, and courthouses—were all located on the çarşi. Taverns and coffee shops *(kahvehanelar)*, patronized only by well-to-do adult men, were the center of an otherwise nonexistent social life, where all the important problems were discussed and decided. In the small township of Strumitsa, Bulgaria, with 10,000 inhabitants, there were thirty-one coffeehouses. When postal service was introduced, the mail was also delivered to the coffeehouse. At the end of the century, a new institution, the *chitalishta* (reading rooms) were added to these central institutions. Women and girls gathered at the *shadravan*, the large public fountain in the middle of the city, to chat, gossip, and meet boys.

The small, slow Balkan cities preserved their oriental characteristics for most of the nineteenth century. Only the capital cities and bigger towns around the turn of the century became somewhat "European." That was the time when European suits and hats, *alafranga (á la française)*, began replacing folk costumes and Turkish dress. High tables and chairs also started to supplant the *sofra*, or low, round table, surrounded by cushions on the floor. The first courageous men and women started walking side by side on the street. The "Europeanization" of the previously Ottoman Balkans gradually changed the costumes, attitudes, and lifestyles in the slowly growing cities (Gavrilova 1999).

Sofia, Belgrade, and some of the smaller, "second-ranked" cities gradually became middle-sized, still slow and quiet, but visibly European cities. Unlike the Central European capitals, however, they did not become home to modern workers. In Belgrade, only 3,800 industrial workers were employed in 1908 (Halpern and Halpern 1972, 48). As a rather visible and symbolic factor of Europeanization, all the Continent's main architectural trends appeared. In Belgrade, the classic architecture of the 1830s and 1840s was followed, especially between 1850 and 1880, by neoromanesque, neogothic, and neorenaissance structures, and around the turn of the century, by an eclecticism drawing on local color—Serbian traditions—and Serbian-Byzantine architecture. A series of major public buildings were erected in these styles: the neorenaissance National Theater and the Old Court by Emiljan Joksimović; the monumental neorenaissance National Bank by Konstantin Jovanović; and the Belgrade Cooperative and the Serbian Academy of Arts and Sciences building by Andra Stefanović (with Nestorović, then with Djordjević). All of the leading Serbian architects studied in Budapest, Vienna, or Munich. In addition, more than fifty Western architects worked in the city during the second half of the nineteenth century. The most characteristic public buildings and the entire city landscape imitated the style of the world's capitals (Mladenović 1995, 222–23, 233). The Balkan capitals and several other smaller cities lost their oriental character and became more European.

Budapest, Warsaw and Prague, and, to a lesser extent, Bucharest, together with their industrial suburbs, became modern working- and middle-class cities with highly literate populations. Ethnically, socially, and culturally, these big cities portrayed a transformed, modern, cosmopolitan world. They signaled the future. The present, however, was the traditional countryside, with its overwhelming peasant society. Central and Eastern Europe might have begun social modernization but, even at the end of the period under discussion, on the eve of World War I, they stood at the beginning of a long, rough historical road toward Western European modernity.

FIGURE 68. Preziosi Amedeo, *Bucharest Fish Market* (1869). Watercolors and pencil on paper. Courtesy Muzeul National de Artă al României, Bucharest.

FIGURE 69. Market in a Slovak township. Courtesy Hungarian National Museum, Budapest.

FIGURE 70. Lajos Deák-Ébner, *Poultry Market*. Courtesy Magyar
Nemzeti Galéria, Budapest.

FIGURE 71. Old service "industry": Slovak glazier, 1895. Courtesy Slovenské Národné Múzeum, Etnograficke Muzeum, Martin, Slovakia.

FIGURE 72. Slovak peasant plowing, around 1900. Courtesy Hungarian National Museum, Budapest.

FIGURE 73. Mihály Munkácsy, *Making the Butter.* Courtesy Magyar
Nemzeti Galéria, Budapest.

FIGURE 74. Hand-cranked mill in Martonos, 1901. Courtesy Néprajzi Múzeum, Budapest.

FIGURE 75. Romanian woman weaving, 1908. Courtesy Néprajzi Múzeum, Budapest.

FIGURE 76. Hungarian peasants working in the field. Courtesy Museum of Hungarian Agriculture, Budapest.

FIGURE 77. Early nineteenth-century sugar factory in Nagyszeben, Hungary. Courtesy Magyar Tudományos Akadémia Történettudományi Intézete, Budapest.

FIGURE 78. Károly Lotz, *Towing a River Boat.* Courtesy Magyar Nemzeti Galéria, Budapest.

FIGURE 79. Building the first Transylvanian railroad in the 1860s. Courtesy Magyar Tudományos Akadémia Történettudományi Intézete, Budapest.

FIGURE 80. Construction work. Courtesy Magyar Nemzeti Múzeum Történeti Fényképtára, Budapest.

FIGURE 81. Horse-drawn tram in Budapest, late nineteenth century. Courtesy Hungarian National Museum, Budapest.

FIGURE 82. Ironworks in Reşiţa (Resica), Transylvania, early twentieth century. Courtesy Magyar Tudományos Akadémia Történettudományi Intézete, Budapest.

FIGURE 83. Láng Engineering Co., Budapest (1903). Courtesy Magyar Tudományos Akadémia Történettudományi Intézete, Budapest.

FIGURE 84. National Bank, Bucharest. Reproduced from Florea, *Romanian Art,* 22. Courtesy Meridiane Publishing House, Bucharest.

FIGURE 85. Mihály Munkácsy, *Strike*. Courtesy Magyar Nemzeti Galéria, Budapest.

FIGURE 86. Working-class apartment building, Budapest, 1910. Courtesy
Budapesti Történeti Múzeum Kiscell, Budapest.

CHAPTER 6

THE POLITICAL SYSTEM

Democratization versus Authoritarian
Nationalism

SOCIOECONOMIC CONDITIONS and the burning, unsolved national question had lasting political consequences in Central and Eastern Europe. The preserved agrarian character of its peasant societies, lack of industrialization and urbanization, and unfinished nation-building in the region in comparison with the western half of the continent all influenced political institutions and practice alike. The political elite and intellectuals had faith in progress, however, and believed in the possibility of learning from the most successful countries, adopting their institutions, and changing their own destiny and history. The main goal of the nations of the region was to join "civilized Europe" (i.e., Western Europe), and this objective equally penetrated the economic, cultural, and political arenas. No doubt, the introductions of modern constitutions and a parliamentary system were strongly influenced by Western European examples. Political parties also often imitated their Western European counterparts.

Despite the attempt to follow Western Europe, however, the result was something different. Modern democracies emerged only in the industrialized, rich core of the continent, where strong, well-established, self-confident nation-states existed. The unindustrialized countries, struggling for independent nationhood, were unable to follow this road. Both the states and the governments were traditionally autocratic and remained authoritarian, with an autocratic interpretation and practice of law and civil rights. Unable to realize their national dreams, people became frustrated and militantly hostile toward the "enemies of the nation," whether oppressor great powers or rival oppressed nationalities living in the same area. Fundamental nationalism penetrated politics and became the leitmotiv of foreign policy. Aggressive expansionism, police terror, and military conflicts characterized endless attempts to unify the entire nation or create an indivisible "nationalizing" nation.

The bulk of the population was excluded from the political body of the nation under these authoritarian regimes throughout the nineteenth century. Around the end of the period, however, limited, but still partially successful socioeconomic development awakened both an important part of the oppressed peasants and the emerging and geographically concentrated working class. This paved the way for radicalization and revolt. As an inseparable feature of the politics of modernization that either failed or enjoyed only partial success, radical right- and left-wing populism emerged and heralded future revolutions.

THE POLITICAL LEGACY OF AUTOCRATIC RULE

The historic road toward democracy has been paved only in those countries that emerged in early modern times as the rich core countries of the nineteenth-century world system. As Barrington Moore says in his often-quoted work on the *Social Origins of Dictatorship and Democracy,* the "contract as a mutual engagement freely undertaken by free persons, derived from the feudal relations of vassalage . . . constitutes a crucial legacy to modern Western . . . free society." In these countries, "a rough balance [emerged] between the crown and the nobility, in which the royal power . . . left a substantial degree of independence to the nobility . . . [as] a decisive precondition for modern democracy." However, the most important development, Moore maintains, is the commercial revolution in agriculture and "the ways in which the landed upper classes and the peasants reacted to the challenge of commercial agriculture." A successful bourgeois transformation paves the way for political democracy.

The lack of these historical factors, the weakness of towns and town dwellers, the reintroduction of serfdom, and the "manorial reaction" to the advance of commerce blocked the road to attaining the prerequisites of modern democracy in Central and Eastern Europe. The socioeconomic and political development of these countries thus created the "social origins of dictatorship" (Moore 1966, xvii, 415, 417).

Together with far-reaching medieval and early-modern roots, nineteenth-century failures of industrialization and social modernization were the source of further serious negative political consequences. The continued role of the landed nobility, the emergence of a pervasive bureaucratic-military elite, and the weakness of modern burgher and well-to-do peasant elements in the surviving uneducated peasant societies created formidable hurdles on the road to parliamentary democracy.

The lack of a viable, unified nation-state, and the seemingly insurmountable obstacles to creating one in an age of exalted nationalism, was, however, the crucial impediment to democratic development. An existential fear for the national community penetrated the societies of Central and Eastern Europe. All these countries, with their ethnically mixed populations, had lost their independence between the fifteenth and eighteenth centuries and been incorporated into vast multinational empires. During the nineteenth century, all of the elites of the Central and Eastern European peoples, and, under their influence, gradually the peasant masses as well, reacted strongly against their oppression by foreign powers. Were the Balkan peasants in the Ottoman empire or the Czechs and Poles in the Habsburg and Russian empires, respectively, really more oppressed than ethnic Russians in the Russian empire or ethnic Serbs in independent Serbia? Probably not. However, even well-to-do middle-class Czechs suffered national humiliation because they could not use their mother tongue in offices. Poles could not tolerate the fact that the official language of Poland's public schools was Russian. Slovaks and Romanians felt like second-class citizens in Hungary. Moreover, in the age of nationalism, all socioeconomic pains were interpreted as consequences of foreign oppression. People believed it, just as they believed that the "imagined" national community was indeed an existing strong community and that they had to give their supreme loyalty to it, had to live and die for it. Even if their oppression was, at least partly, only imagined, it thus became a very real political factor in nineteenth-century Central and Eastern Europe.

In this political framework, nationalities began to fight for independence from the Ottoman, Russian, and Habsburg empires. Unlike in Western Europe, where nations emerged within the boundaries of existing states, state and nation were not coterminous in this region. In addition, subordinated nations, jumbled together in the "belt of mixed population," became rivals in competition for the same goal: national independence. As a consequence, they confronted one another and often collided head-on. Central and Eastern Europe became a hotbed of hostile, fundamental nationalism.

Reaching the ultimate goal of independence, which was realized in most parts of the Balkans only at the end of the nineteenth century, did not lead to the erosion or disappearance of national hatreds. On the contrary, the strengthening of the nation-state and the efforts to unite the entire nation in an area of highly mixed populations permanently fueled further national goals. The struggle for autonomy and independence against germanizing Austria and russifying Russia in the Czech lands and Poland, the attempt to assimilate non-Magyar nationalities and create an "indivisible Magyar nation" in multiethnic Hungary, and the concept of creating a Greater Serbia, Greater Croatia, Greater Romania, and Greater Bulgaria by incorporating neighboring fellow nationals and the territories in which they lived led to permanent confrontation and warfare within the multinational empires and also among newly independent nations.

In István Bibó's analysis, this historical environment nurtured the desire for strong government. It revitalized and legitimized the unquestioned leading role of an autocratic monarch, the noble elite, state bureaucracy, and army, "saviors of the nation." The longing for a strong nation-state, which might be able to cure all burning national, social, and economic ills, nurtured romantic nationalism throughout the nineteenth century. Romantic idealization of prophet-intellectuals and the longing for charismatic, all-powerful leaders to lead the people to the Promised Land created an atmosphere conducive to authoritarianism. The romantic idea of self-sacrificing struggle for the nation was translated into combat against "enemies of the nation": oppressors, aliens, minorities, and rival neighbors. Deformed, interrupted national development led both to chauvinism and to autocratic, authoritarian regimes and policies (Bibó 1986, 330–43).

All of the dominating empires in nineteenth-century Central and Eastern Europe had inherited the tradition of an autocratic, aggressive, expansionist bureaucratic and military state machine. Wars over neighboring territories characterized the entire century. Accordingly, patriarchal, highly bureaucratic centralized states that embodied fundamental nationalism, conservative institutions, brutal political subordination, patronage, clientalism, and corruption were the main features of the politics in the area. Paradoxically, after having gained their freedom from autocratic and oppressive multinational empires, the formerly subordinated nations followed the only pattern they knew and built up similarly authoritarian, corrupt, bureaucratic states.

"What emerged in Eastern Europe between the end of the eighteenth century and roughly the middle of the next was the autocratic, centralized state run by a more-or-less despotic ruler with the help of a steadily growing bureaucracy," Peter Sugar sums up. "The next fifty years, roughly the second half of the nineteenth century, saw the gradual weakening of the power of the autocrat, but not the diminishing of authoritarian rule in Eastern Europe." The emerging Western democratic great powers had a strong influence on the entire continent and often played a direct role in influencing political institutions in Central and Eastern Europe. Newly autonomous countries in the region introduced Western-style constitutions and legal codes. "[T]hat the inhabitants were considered citizens, that parties were permitted, that parliaments functioned, that rulers became 'constitutional monarchs' are also clear indications of the influence of the Western model. Yet, all these changes" were only a pseudo-transformation "at best skin deep; under this thin layer of Western veneer the reality remained unchanged" (Sugar 1999, vi, 9–10, 12).

There was not merely a marked difference between adopted Western European law and Eastern European reality. East of the river Rhine, as László Péter has attested, "an autocratic principle of the law" remained characteristic during the nineteenth century. "This difference in the presumption of the law between the two parts of Europe had momentous consequences. While in western Europe where the law was silent, the citizen was said to be free, in the legal systems beyond the Rhine, the opposite prevailed: where the law was silent [i.e., did not expressly protect individuals and social groups], . . . it was the state authorities who were . . . 'free' . . . [and] could lawfully issue decrees and act at their own discretion in matters which interfered with the individual and the group" (Péter 1997–98, 12–13). The government extended its authority to the sphere of civil rights and preserved the right of supervision over associations, banning those considered to endanger the security of the state. In Hungary, assemblies were also supervised, and permission was often refused if the meeting was not thought "advisable" by the authorities. If a gathering "deteriorated into subversive agitation against . . . public order," it was disbanded, if need be by force. Individual rights, in these systems, were concessions from the government. The autocratic principle of law obstructed the freedom of the citizens and remained an "active ingredient of the legal-political order" in the region (ibid., 18–28).

Western freedoms and rights were only partially granted in the united German Reich (Wehler 1973) and post-Ausgleich Austria-Hungary too, but matters were even worse in other parts of Central and Eastern Europe. In the crucial time of transformation, the political destiny of Central and Eastern Europe was still strongly determined by the three autocratic powers that had dominated it throughout the sixteenth, seventeenth, and eighteenth centuries.

OTTOMAN AUTOCRACY AND BALKAN AUTHORITARIANISM

The Ottoman empire ruled the Balkans for half a millennium. Its supreme ruler, the Sultan, governed according to the Şeri (shari'ah), the unchangeable Sacred Law of Islam, which regulated all aspects of life and did not leave much room for secular laws. The Sultan's administrative authority was unlimited, however, and he had the power of life and death over his subjects. He was served and assisted by a bureaucratic-military elite, recruited originally from trained slaves who advanced on the basis of merit. This system was later replaced by open, institutionalized bribery. During the later centuries of the empire, the entire state administration was built on corruption: tax farming became pervasive, and concessions were sold to the highest bidders. Office-holding was considered an investment for high returns. "Bribery is the beginning and root of all . . . tyranny . . . the most vast of evil," stated Mehmed Pasha, the treasurer of the empire in the early eighteenth century. Bribery gave "permission from the government for every sort of oppression" (Stavrianos [1958] 1963, 120).

Two British travelers, describing the situation a century and a half later, observed:

Next in authority to the Turkish governors comes the town-council, or medjlis. . . . In former days . . . the Christians had only to bribe him [the governor] in order to secure a certain amount of protection. Now-a-days, the governor must still be bribed, but . . . all the medjlis must be bribed too. . . . The only chance is to play the foreign governor and the local Mussulmans against each other, but it is a dangerous game. (Mackenzie and Irby [1867] 1877, 257)

Expansionism was the essence and driving force of the regime. It had a religious basis. Holy war and colonization were the dynamic elements in the Ottoman conquest, Halil Inalcik maintains ([1973] 1994). The Ottoman empire, which included present-day Syria, Egypt, Iraq, Algeria, and Tunisia as well as the Balkans, united the Sunni Middle East. When further expansion became impossible, the decline of the regime began, starting in the sixteenth century and closely linked to the emergence of the Atlantic economy and the Industrial Revolution. The empire lost its dynamism and potential for expansion, and the European great powers imposed their will upon the Sultan, who was forced to open hitherto closed frontiers. The Treaty of Adrianople (1829) mandated freedom to navigate the Danube and the Black Sea and paved the way for Western commercial penetration. The Anglo-Ottoman commercial agreement of 1838 went much further, imposing a free-trade system. Reforms to adjust to the new situation became unavoidable in Istanbul. Attempts at reform around the turn of the century aimed at recentralization, based on a reorganized army and state. European-type reforms followed in the 1840s and 1850s, but they came too late and served to undermine the regime rather than change it. The *Tanzimat* reforms gradually introduced new institutions: the Land Law of 1858, for example, allowed private claims on abandoned land. Even foreigners were allowed to own private farms in 1867. Agricultural output significantly increased: between 1848 and 1862, it doubled, and then doubled again up to 1914. At the same time, agricultural exports increased elevenfold. In spite of these achievements, the rigidity of the system, including the primacy of state ownership of land, was preserved. Ottoman rule in the Balkans remained autocratic right to the end: notwithstanding efforts to recentralize the empire and transform its superstructure, it remained essentially unchanged, and the decline became unstoppable (Adanir 1982, 150–52). The Porte began to lose ground and gradually had to withdraw from large Balkan territories, mostly between the 1860s and World War I. The withdrawal passed through various transitory stages, however, before the Balkan nations gained independence during the 1870s and 1880s.

The Ottoman legacy is a broadly discussed topic. According to Maria Todorova "the creation of autonomous and independent Balkan states was not only a break with but a rejection of the political past. This is evident in the attempt to substitute new European institutions for the Ottoman state institutions." On this basis, she maintains that "Ottoman legacy was insignificant" in the independent Balkans as far as political institutions were concerned (Todorova 1997, 170). This may be true in a literal sense, but the imported Western institutions were fitted into Ottoman traditions, which also molded Balkan attitudes and mentalities. The Ottoman political legacy was thus ultimately decisive in the newly established autonomous, then independent, states around the turn of the century.

In Romania, the road to independence, after a decade of a kind of Western European protectorate over the Romanian Principalities, was opened in 1866 with the election of a constituent assembly. The constitution of 1884 was modeled on the Belgian constitution of 1831 and reflected modern Western democratic values. The architects of transformation believed in a spectacular change: Romania, the Bucharest newspaper *Steaua Dun-*

ării proclaimed, would be a true "Belgium of the East" (Hitchins 1994, 19). Civil liberties and freedom of association and the press were legally protected.

Form and substance, however, were essentially different. The regime remained highly authoritarian. First of all, political rights were granted to only a small part of the citizenry. "Politically the peasantry was an almost negligible quantity," Robert Seton-Watson writes ([1934] 1963, 357). Although the Romanian electoral system formally granted universal male suffrage, in reality the bulk of the population was excluded from the political nation, because the electors were divided into three uneven categories. College I consisted of people with large landed property (with an income of at least 1,200 lei). This group represented 1.5 percent of the eligible voters but elected 41 percent of the representatives. College II required the payment of a yearly tax of 20 lei, and included professionals and primary school graduates, who altogether constituted 3.5 percent of the voters but elected 38 percent of the representatives. In other words, 5 percent of the voters chose 79 percent of parliamentarians. College III, 95 percent of the voters, elected the remaining 21 percent of the representatives, but in two different groups: the first, which consisted of 4 percent of the voters, either had to have landed property with a higher income level or be schoolteachers or priests, regardless of income. All the remaining 91 percent, all the poor and uneducated masses of voters, belonged to the second group and had only indirect votes: fifty of them elected a single elector. In the upper house, or senate, 1 percent of the electorate voted in 55 percent of the senators. A second well-to-do group, also 1 percent of the voters, selected the remaining 45 percent of the senators, while 98 percent of the electorate did not have the right to send delegates to the senate (Eidelberg 1974, 15–16).

The king, not parliament, formed the government. Elections were controlled by the government through the minister of the interior's appointments of the prefects of the *judeţe* (counties). They "left no device unused in order to ensure a government victory, and afterwards the mandates of numerous opposition deputies and senators were invalidated" (Hitchins 1994, 96). Small wonder, then, that the government always had an absolute majority in the parliament and both chambers became obedient ratifying bodies. A telling example: in the 1883 elections, the governing Liberal party gained more than 91 percent of the votes.

In real terms, the government's responsibility to the parliament became a mere formality. Counties and communes were not allowed to make their own decisions; the central bureaucracy determined their budgets and policies. The judiciary, in practice, was subordinated to the executive and legislative branches of power. State and Church were not separated. The Jews, roughly 5 percent of the population, were excluded from citizenship (Welter 1989). In his 1879 address to parliament, King Carol warned: "The Great Powers demand that we should adapt ourselves to the ideas prevalent in civilized states, before they admit us into the European family of states." A parliamentary commission, however, declared: "[T]here are no Romanian Jews and never were, but only such as were born in the country, but are assimilated neither in language nor customs and do not aspire to be" (Seton-Watson [1934] 1963, 350–51).

Romania introduced a two-party system, consisting of the Partidul National Liberal and Partidul Conservator. Although both Liberals and Conservatives experienced some factionalism for a while, the parties consolidated and dominated the political arena until the war (Căpreanu 1994). A few personalities played leading roles and monopolized power. The Conservatives were more closely connected with the landowning classes and were ardent defenders of land tenure, the agricultural character of the country, and, consequently, free trade. The Liberals were based in the urban middle class and advocated agricultural modernization, state interventionism, protection, and industrial development. More important, however, both parties sought unrestricted political power and were authoritarian once in government, enriching their clienteles (Stan 1995). As prime ministers, the Conservative Lascăr Catargiu, during the first half of the 1870s, and the Liberal Ion Brătianu, during the 1880s, exercised authoritarian, "virtually dictatorial power." The Brătianu family established a leading political dynasty in the country: in 1908, Ionel Brătianu, the son of Ion, became the leader of the Liberal party and prime minister. He would be the dominant figure in national politics for two more decades.

Besides exclusive and corrupt party politics, authoritarian practices found favor with another important political player, King Carol. After Philip of Flanders, the brother of the king of Belgium, declined the Romanian throne, Ion Brătianu persuaded Prince Karl of Hohenzollern-Sigmaringen, an officer in the Prussian army and son of a former prime minister of Prussia, to accept it. Prince Karl, a foreigner in his new country, did not have much power in domestic politics during his first years of rule after 1866 but strongly aspired to it (Pascu 1996). In November 1870, he tried to convince the great powers that Western European political institutions were inappropriate in unindustrialized Romania, which lacked a strong middle class. He proposed revision of the Paris Treaty (1856) to favor a "powerful regime" under a king wielding autocratic authority, in which a council of state and senate, appointed by him, would play merely advisory roles. This attempt failed.

Crowned King Carol of Romania (r. 1881–1914) after the country gained full independence, Karl realized his goal in a different way. Using his constitutional authority to appoint and dismiss ministers and governments, he successfully manipulated power. The parties and politicians grew dependent upon him, and Carol strengthened his role by frequently changing governments, replacing Liberals with Conservatives and then switching back again. Moreover, he could take advantage of the existence of various factions in both parties (Neagoe 1995; Hossu 1995). In the course of eight years after 1899, for example, he dismissed and appointed five governments. In this exclusive political system, the tactical division of the small political elite and the ability to exploit their rivalries guaranteed a key role for the king. The leading parties and the king both used the "spoils system" of political corruption. Carol's role was unquestioned in military and foreign policy issues (Scurtu 1988). The king's personal authority in foreign policy matters is clearly exhibited by the crucial alliance with the Central Powers in 1883, which he personally arranged without discussion in parliament or even by anyone but a few insiders. Carol kept the only copy of the treaty in his private safe. Only upon its renewal in 1892 did the king have to inform his minister of foreign affairs, and then, two months later, the prime minister, of the existence of the treaty. Parliament and the public, however, were not even informed about its existence until the war. Autocratic rule was nevertheless somewhat limited by the freedom of the Romanian press and the presence of a parliamentary opposition. More important, the great powers' behavior always limited the rulers' freedom of action.

Bulgaria, similarly under the tutelage of the great powers under the terms of the Berlin Treaty, enacted a Western-style liberal constitution at Tirnovo in 1879. Universal male suffrage, parliamentary power in a one-chamber system, and civil liberties were guaranteed. The next day, Alexander von Battenberg, a German prince related to both the British and Russian royal families, was elected prince of Bulgaria. The young soldier-prince was dissatisfied with the democratic constitution. The scenario was strikingly similar to the Romanian one. "The present constitution is not suited to the country. It places the person of the Ruler in continual opposition to the National Assembly . . . the people lack the most elementary requisites for constitutional life . . . I wish . . . the necessary authoritative powers . . . [to defend] the interest of the State," Prince Alexander complained (Koch 1887, 70–72). He did not hesitate: following a coup on

May 9, 1881, he dismissed the government and demanded extraordinary powers for seven years. Parliament, "elected" under overt and strict military control, unanimously accepted Alexander's demands in July: the prince became a dictator. In the delicate international situation of the country, resistance to Russian patronage, however, led to the restoration of the previous Tirnovo constitution in short order (Manolova 1989). Moreover, in August 1886, a military coup—the kidnapping of the prince from the palace—led to his abdication.

This time real power was concentrated in the hands of Stefan Stambolov, the hero of the unification of Eastern Rumelia and Bulgaria, whose National party gained an absolute majority at the October elections of 1886. Three commissioners were sent to Western Europe to find a new prince. Finally, Prince Ferdinand of Saxe-Coburg-Gotha accepted the Bulgarian throne and was crowned in August 1887. During the first years of his rule, Stambolov dominated the political arena of the country. "He believed that the end justified the means, and he never hesitated to employ force and even brutality in order to have his way," L. S. Stavrianos writes. "[H]e remained a peasant—rough, impatient, and offensively blunt. . . . His critics accused him of instituting a reign of terror" (Stavrianos [1958] 1963, 435, 437).

King Ferdinand, however, outsmarted Stambolov, who served as prime minister between 1887 and 1894. Using political manipulation, intrigue, and political bribery, the king gradually became the master of the country. He believed that "every man has his price," which in Bulgarian politics turned out to be true. The political elite were allowed to grow rich so long as they "remained faithful servitors of the throne" but were ruined if they ceased to serve (Seton-Watson [1934] 1963, 358–60). Government officials were blackmailed by a law threatening prosecution if they possessed "more than they ought." Although Stambolov, as usual, won 90 percent of the vote in the 1893 elections, Ferdinand dismissed him within a few months and refused to give him a passport when he wanted to go abroad. Within a year, the former almighty prime minister had been murdered and brutally mutilated in the street. The police did not even make an effort to find the assassins.

The Bulgarian two-party system lost its importance. Both the Liberal and Conservative parties were in the hands of the king, who frequently appointed and dismissed officials. The Constantine Stoilov cabinet governed between 1888 and 1889, followed by the Vasil Radoslav cabinet for another two years, and then by Stoyan Danev for two more years. Corruption, clientelism, and concentration of power in the hands of King Ferdinand characterized the politics of Bulgaria. Ferdinand rebaptized his son Boris in the Greek Orthodox faith to strengthen the position of his dynasty (Stoianov 1989).

Serbian politics was defined by wars, coups, and assassinations. Exploiting the Bosnian crisis, autonomous Serbia declared war on the Ottoman empire in the summer of 1876. Although Serbia was immediately defeated, Russian intervention and great power politics at the Treaty of Berlin (1878) led to its territorial enlargement and recognition of full Serbian independence. Prince Milan Obrenović became king of Serbia (1882). The political arena was characterized by the rivalry between the Austrophile Progressive party, connected with the Obrenović dynasty, and the Russophile Radical party, linked to the exiled Karadjordjević dynasty. "From 1882 on, Serbian political parties . . . gradually ceased to distinguish between issues of . . . democratization and modernization on the one hand and the national 'mission' of all-Serbian unity . . . on the other," Ivo Lederer writes (1969, 407).

The 1869 constitution, which was enacted after Prince Michael Obrenović had been assassinated, established autocratic rule in Serbia. Unlike most of the other countries of the region, it granted a liberal franchise, but strongly limited the role of the Skupstina (parliament), which did not have the right to initiate laws or modify government bills. The government was not responsible to the Skupstina and could legislate provisionally and promulgate budgets by decree. The prince, who had the right to appoint and dismiss governments, thus had the upper hand. This was illustrated when the Radical party won the 1883 elections. King Milan refused to appoint a Radical government and formed the Conservative Hristić government instead. Brute force and murder often settled the contest between the political elite and the king. The question was not one of democratic or autocratic rule, but rather of who would exercise authoritarian power.

After losing his war against Bulgaria in 1885, King Milan tried to gain public support by introducing a liberal constitution (1889), which guaranteed democratic institutions and rights. He could not save his throne, however, and was forced to abdicate in favor of his thirteen-year-old son, Alexander. In four years, the young king dismissed the governing regents, abolished the liberal constitution in favor of the previous autocratic one, made himself commander in chief of the army, brought in laws restricting freedom of the press and of association, and harshly attacked the opposition Radical party. When this party, with the support of an almost revolutionary opposition, won a majority at the July 1901 elections, agitated mass demonstrations filled the streets of Belgrade. The police callously arrested and killed demonstrators. New elections were held in an atmosphere of unbridled police terror in May 1903. The Radical party withdrew from the ballot. Accounts, however, were settled in June: twenty-eight officers invaded the royal palace, killed the royal couple, and threw their bodies from the palace windows. The conspirators also killed the prime minister, the minister of interior, loyal officers, and two brothers of the queen. The old parliament, not the newly elected one, restored the liberal constitution and elected the exiled Peter Karadjordjević king of Serbia (Subotić 1992). In September 1903, the Radical party, led by Nikola Pašić, won a majority of the seats and, for the first time in Serbian history, established a constitutional government with democratic freedoms.

Although the first signs of peasant representation in politics and more constitutional rule narrowed the huge gap between democratic forms and authoritarian substance in prewar Balkan politics, the short period of autonomy and independence was characterized by a lack of "pluralism of economic, political and ideological power. . . . All power was concentrated in the hands of those who managed the government. . . . [The de facto political systems were] centralized autocracies dominated by narrowly recruited bureaucracies" (Sugar 1999, vi, 13–14). Real parliamentary democracy remained lacking, and there was a serious deficit in civil liberties.

THE "NATIONAL MISSION" OF EXPANSION
TO UNITE THE NATION

Although the "national mission" of a government strengthened and united the nation, it also legitimized authoritarian rule. In Bulgaria, for example, the main nationalist goal subsequent to the Treaty of Berlin (i.e., after July 1878) was the liberation of "all Bulgarian territories"—that is, Eastern Rumelia, Thrace, and Macedonia—and the reestablishment of the Greater Bulgaria of the Treaty of San Stefano (March 1878). This nationalist program became the basis of an alliance between the king and the army.

Macedonia was claimed by Greece and Serbia in addition to Bulgaria. A Central Macedonian Revolutionary Committee was formed in 1893, which established the Internal Macedonian Revolutionary Organization (IMRO), led by two schoolteachers, Damian Gruev and Gotse Delchev. Armed bands launched constant attacks on the Turks in Macedonia in preparation for a general uprising in 1903. When it came, this was put down by an Ottoman army, which in the process destroyed two hundred villages, killed thousands, and forced thirty thousand refugees to flee into Bulgaria.

In 1908, however, the so-called Young Turks seized power to renew the empire; Austria proclaimed the annexation of Bosnia-Herzegovina; and Bulgaria declared full independence. The turmoil spawned the formation of a Balkan League of Bulgaria, Serbia, and Greece against Turkey in 1912. In a few weeks, the First Balkan War led to a spectacular allied victory and the conquest of most of Turkey in Europe. The Treaty of London sanctioned this result in May 1913. Bulgarian forces occupied eastern Thrace, and Greek and Serbian troops liberated Macedonia. In June, however, in a major miscalculation, the Bulgarians attacked Serbian and Greek troops to conquer Macedonia, starting the Second Balkan War. Exploiting the opportunity, Romania and Turkey attacked Bulgaria from the north and east, while the Greeks and Serbs did so from the south and west. After a humiliating defeat for the Bulgarians, the Treaty of Bucharest (August 1913) gave the largest parts of Macedonia to Serbia and Greece, while Romania took southern Dobrudja and Turkey regained much of Thrace, including the city of Edirne (Adrianople). The dream of a Greater Bulgaria, which had permeated the history of independent Bulgaria for a third of a century before World War I and generated almost continual warfare, faded away.

Serbia was more successful in realizing the dream of a Greater Serbia. The entire Serbian political elite espoused the goal of all-Serbian unity under the banner of Srpstvo. After the country had won its independence, the central goal of Serbian politics was the territorial acquisition of Macedonia and Bosnia-Herzegovina. Serbia also established connections with Serbs in Dalmatia and the Voivodina, and with South Slavs in the Habsburg empire. The guiding principle of Serbian politics was to play the role of a "Balkan Piedmont" and liberate all South Slavs from Ottoman and Habsburg rule. All of the leading political parties, from Jovan Ristić's Liberals to Nikola Pašić's Radicals, shared this mission. This led to permanent warfare, a military campaign in Bosnia in 1876, a war against Bulgaria in 1885, and participation in the two Balkan wars of 1912–13.

Serbian nationalism was genuinely mixed, then, later gradually transformed from Great Serbianism into Yugoslavism. Uniting all the Serbs within and without Serbia or uniting all the South Slavs (i.e., the Yugoslav idea) was the leitmotiv of Serbian politics during the entire nineteenth century. Ilija Garašin's *Načertanije* (The Program), his 1844 program for Serbian national policy, and Vuk Karadžić's *Srbi svi i svuda* (Serbs All and

Everywhere) already exhibited this mixed concept of Great Serbianism and Yugoslavism. Ivo Banac interprets these as expressions of Great Serbianism, "the purpose of which was to assimilate the vast majority of Catholic Croats and all Bosnian Muslims" (Banac 1984, 80). Many Serbs, however, envisaged a South Slavic nation. That was also true of the Croats, who also blurred the concepts of Croat and South Slav nations when, in the new program of the party of Croatian Right, they declared in 1894: "[W]e want to unite the entire Croat nation, which lives in Croatia, Slavonia, Dalmatia, Fiume, Bosnia and Herzegovina, and Istria, into one single state within the Habsburg monarchy" (Kemény 1956, 2: 288). They naturally sought to incorporate the Serbs who constituted a quarter of the population of Croatia proper into the Croat nation.

These overlapping and conflicting national ambitions were amalgamated in the Illyric concept of Yugoslavism. Its initiators were mostly Croats and Serbs outside Serbia. From language reformers in 1800 to politicians and idealistic national movements in 1900, proponents of South Slavism called for the unification of Serbs and Croats. The Dalmatian Frano Supilo and the Croat Ante Trumbić initiated a meeting of leading Croat and Serb politicians at Fiume (Rijeka) in 1905, where the Hrvatsko-Srpske Koalicije, which became the majority party in Croatia, was created and a common plan of action was agreed on (Gross 1960).

After the annexation of Bosnia-Herzegovina by Austria in 1908, various ultranationalist and paramilitary organizations—Slovenski Jug, Narodna Odbrana, Mlada Bosna, and the dramatically named Ujedinjenje ili Smrt (Unity or Death)—were founded in Serbia with the central goal of the creation of a united Yugoslav state. The Croat political elite, which originally advocated autonomy and a "trialist"—Austrian, Hungarian, Slav—reorganization of the Habsburg monarchy, gradually lost confidence in the emperor. After 1907, Croatia was governed by absolutist methods. The Sabor (parliament) did not sit, and the new *banus,* Slavko Cuvaj, ruled autocratically. In March 1912, this state of affairs was institutionalized: Franz Josef suspended the Croat constitution, along with freedom of assembly and of the press, and the *banus* became a royal commissioner. Under the banner of revolutionary Yugoslavism, young Croat nationalists attempted to assassinate Cuvaj, and then the newly appointed *banus,* Baron Ivo Skerlecz. The Serb victories in the two Balkan wars fueled Yugoslav ambitions and hopes of a war against the Habsburg empire.

The legitimacy of the authoritarian regime in Romania was guaranteed by a continuous struggle for independence and the call for a "Romania for the Romanians." Such slogans were common in the Balkans, and similar goals were proclaimed in Bulgaria and Serbia. In Romania, however, the call was aimed, not only at foreign tutelage, but also at "aliens" within the country, especially Jews, who, partly because of heavy immigration from the east during the nineteenth century, had grown to be 5 percent of the country's population. "Chauvinism with particularly strong anti-Semitic overtones became an integral part of the national creed. . . . In fact, nationalism became synonymous with anti-Semitism for Romanian politicians," Stephen Fischer-Galati observes (1969, 385–86). Virtually alone in Europe, Romania refused to grant citizenship to Jews almost up until World War I.

An unparalleled early twentieth-century jacquerie, a spontaneous peasant uprising, also turned out to be the deadliest anti-Jewish pogrom of the period. The uniquely exploitative Romanian agrarian system led to an unavoidable bitter and violent peasant revolt. Unrest in the Romanian countryside became a common phenomenon. The first major uprising occurred in 1888, followed by "almost permanent tension." Local conflicts became everyday events, accompanied by strong eruptions such as those in 1892, 1894 (which spread across one hundred localities), and again in 1900. Tensions intensified between 1904 and 1906. In the latter year, various isolated outbursts signaled the coming climax (Ilincioiu 1991, 40). The last straw was the introduction a new tax of 5 lei on the peasantry in November 1906. Peasants refused to pay the extra tax and threatened tax collectors. People became extremely agitated in January and early February, the regular time for the renewal of annual contracts. Dissatisfaction erupted on the Flăminsi estate in Botoşani, northern Moldavia. This estate belonged to Dimitrie Sturdza, grandson of a former *hospodar,* who lived in Western Europe and had never seen his estate, but rented it out, mostly to the bigger arendaş company, the Fischer brothers. The peasants rejected the exploitative contract offered by the Fischer brothers and nearly lynched their administrator on February 8, 1907.

Students of Romanian social and agricultural history agree with the contemporary analyst Radu Rosetti, who maintained that the revolt was a reaction against the latifundia and contract system (Rosetti 1907). In February, the peasant unrest spread to other settlements, where peasant communities filed various petitions and sent delegates to discuss their needs. Flat-out refusals often generated violent reactions: the Maxut and Feredeeni forests were occupied, the guards were removed, and the arendaş family was expelled on February 21. Within a week, peasants from Botoşani villages clashed with army units. In early March, in Stănceni, peasants from neighboring villages attacked the town, looted and destroyed houses and shops, and were confronted by hundreds of soldiers.

Fighting continued for several days. "The ferment has spread out to nearly all communes and hamlets in the district," the district attorney reported from the Dorohoi district on March 8. "Everywhere the rebels have devastated the houses of the landlords, *arendaşi* and shopkeepers." In addition to destroying buildings and shops and abusing shopkeepers, renters, and landlords, in early March, peasants turned to lynching and killing. In the Olt district, estates and manors were destroyed, and the landlord Ion Momicenau was killed. The government sent troops under General Năsturel, who ruthlessly suppressed the rebels, either "killing the offenders or burning their houses down." "[T]he artillery fire was effective on 150 houses in Vieru and about 200 houses in Stăneşti," the prefect of Ghica wired the ministry. The peasants "demand land and justice, they pillage towns and boroughs . . . the authorities are helpless and the troops insufficient," the Russian consul-general reported from Iasi. "There are many dead and wounded. . . . The peasants [have] seized the whole of Moldavia" (Ilincioiu 1991, 54, 138, 179, 275–76).

The uprising was a desperate struggle for land and "just contracts" and against an intolerably exploitative agricultural system and irresponsible landlordism. The absentee boyar estate owners were largely invisible to the peasants, so the jacquerie was directed chiefly against the highly visible middlemen: the arendaşi, especially Jewish renters, village shopkeepers, and innkeepers, who were traditionally also moneylenders. Since roughly half of the arendaşi and shopkeepers in Romania were Jewish, the peasant revolt amounted to an anti-Jewish pogrom.

Anti-Semitism had deep traditional roots in Romania, and the populist movement that articulated the demands of the peasantry also agitated against the Jews. Three days before the uprising, a populist newspaper, *Moldava de Sus,* which had already declared in an editorial on December 30, 1906, that the "Yids" were the enemies of the Romanian people, urged a mass uprising against the Jews: "Perhaps out of impoverished ancient Moldavia, today overwhelmed and stifled by Yids, once more a man . . . will rise up and start a new hetairia against the Yids. . . . All true Romanians will give it assistance and will struggle until they have achieved such a crucial victory, so as to save our ancestral land and our race from the plague and the infernal plans of the Yids" (*Moldova de Sus,* March 1, 1907, quoted in Eidelberg 1974, 206–7). Pogroms destroyed thousands of shops and houses. Jews were beaten and killed, and thousands escaped only by leaving everything behind and taking refuge at army headquarters and in big cities.

The peasant armies frightened the entire regime and evolved to the point where not only local estates, manors, villages, and small towns were attacked but also big cities such as Galați. Four thousand peasants even marched on Bucharest. Finally, in April, an army of 120,000 troops suppressed the uprising, killing some 10,000 peasants in the process, according to Seton-Watson ([1934] 1963, 386–87).

Political anti-Semitism, channeling social dissatisfaction into the reservoir of xenophobia, gained a tremendous impetus. Leading Romanian intellectuals, such as the historian Nicolae Iorga, the economist Alexander Cuza, and the poet Octavian Goga, launched vitriolic anti-Semitic attacks. The right-wing populist Constantin Stere denounced the Jews as the embodiment of alien "plundering capital," a "parasite group," and a heavy burden on Romania. The bloody pogrom was seen as a patriotic popular outburst and a victory for the national cause (Ioanid 1992).

An equally strong factor in Romanian nationalism, part of the general trend in the Balkans, was the goal of creating a Greater Romania and uniting all Romanians. In the "belt of mixed population," various ethnic groups were hopelessly intermingled, and many Romanians lived together with Ukrainians, Hungarians, and Bulgarians in Bessarabia, Bukovina, Transylvania, and Dobrudja. Both the loss of southern Bessarabia to Russia in 1878 and the acquisition of southern Dobrudja from Bulgaria in 1913 fueled Great Romanianism and the call for the unification of all Romanians living in neighboring Transylvania, Bukovina, the Banat, Crișana, Maramureș, and Bessarabia. The main enemy, in this respect, as in the case of Serbia, was Austria-Hungary.

Transylvanian Romanians did not share the concept of Greater Romania for long. Instead, they demanded complete equality with the other nations of Transylvania, as the Transylvanian Diet in Sibiu declared in 1861. The Romanians did not challenge the unity of the monarchy. After 1867, when the Austro-Hungarian Ausgleich eliminated all hopes for autonomy and equal rights, the *Pronunciament de la Blaj,* a statement in May 1868, rejected the compromise and demanded the reestablishment of Transylvanian independence. The Romanians, however, followed the same tactic of passive resistance that other minorities had used and abstained from political activity during the last quarter of the century. National activism, of course, had little chance in Transylvania, where the franchise was so limited that out of the three million Romanians, only about 20,000 had voting rights. This number increased after 1905, but only 35,000 of 110,000 voted for national candidates in 1906. However, the Romanian National party was revitalized in 1905 and dropped the demand for autonomy from its program. More ambitious goals emerged. Aurel Popovici, in his 1906 book *Die Vereinigten Staaten von Gross-Österreich,* advocated the concept of an ethnically organized federal Austria. Many Transylvanian Romanian intellectuals shared this view and considered including an independent Romanian state in this federation (Bocşan 1998).

Authoritarian power, fundamental, violent nationalism, and the expansion of the nation-state at the expense of its neighbors thus characterized the politics of the Balkans.

RUSSIAN AUTOCRACY AND POLISH NATIONALISM

The second major player in nineteenth-century Central and Eastern Europe was Russia. The Russian principalities had emerged from under the rule of the Mongolian Tatar "Golden Horde" in the late fourteenth century and evolved into a united Russian empire, which by some accounts inherited some characteristics of the brutal Tatar system. The empire certainly rose through consistent centralization of power and ruthless subordination of the entire society. In the sixteenth century, Tsar Ivan IV, known to history as Ivan the Terrible, brutally crushed the boyars and confiscated a great part of the big estates as a basis for a military service nobility, the *oprichnina*. The huge country was strictly centralized and ruled by the tsar's government and the appointed governors of the provinces, who, from 1837 on, were subordinated to the Ministry of Interior. When a late eighteenth-century reform imposed local noble self-administration, the gentry were required to serve in various bureaucratic positions, without political rights or independence. In the mid nineteenth century, the gentry-bureaucratic service class numbered roughly 900,000 people (Starr 1972, 8). Decentralization of the tsarist regime meant only delegation of authority under central control. When the ministerial system was introduced in the early nineteenth century, the ministers reported directly to the tsar. "Autocratic power was the one unmistakable reality of Russian political life" and "favored personal authority and discretionary action over formal regulations," so that "personalized, paternalistic" rule characterized Russia throughout the nineteenth century (Pearson 1989, 19, 257).

As the "Third Rome" and leader of the Greek Orthodox world, Moscow nurtured a sense of mission and an aggressive expansionism. The eighteenth and nineteenth centuries saw consistent Russian expansion to the east, south, and west alike. Russia annexed much of Central Asia, Georgia, a great part of Armenia, the Crimean peninsula and the adjacent Black Sea region, the area north of the river Amur to the Chinese frontier, North

Sakhalin, Finland, Estonia, Latvia, and Lithuania. Autocratic Russian rule had a strong impact on Central and Eastern Europe. During the eighteenth century, Russia acquired a protectorate over Poland, and then, at the end of the century, occupied two-thirds of the country. Polish autonomy, which had existed until 1831, was eliminated after the 1830–31 uprising, and Russian Poland became the western *guberniia* of the tsarist empire.

Continual warfare with the Ottoman empire opened the gate to a further southward expansion, and the annexation of Bessarabia under the Bucharest Treaty of 1812 was an important milestone on this road. Bessarabia, with its mixed Romanian (54 percent), Ukrainian (28 percent), German, and Jewish population, was progressively russified, and in 1908 most of the land became Russian property, Russian became the official language, and power was placed in the hands of a military governor.

Russian authority was expanded to the two Romanian principalities under Ottoman rule by the Treaty of Kütchük Kainardji (1774), which guaranteed the tsar's right to intervene there. A new victory and the Treaty of Adrianople (1829) made Russia a co-ruler: Russian troops were stationed on Romanian soil, and the Russian commander, General Count Paul Kisselev, established a constitution for the Principalities. Russian troops suppressed the 1848 revolution in the area, but eventually were forced to give up their positions by European great power politics.

After having launched a new and successful military campaign against the declining Ottoman empire, Russia liberated Bulgaria and attempted to create a Russian protectorate there, or, as many thought, a trans-Danubian *guberniia*. The tsar's emissary, Prince Dondukov-Korsakov, presented a draft constitution for the country, and General Peter Parensov took command of the Bulgarian army, whose officers above the rank of lieutenant were all Russian. The colonization of the Balkans, however, failed. The European great powers, as in the case of Romania, blocked the road to further Russian expansion. Tsarist Russia, in spite of halfhearted reforms and the introduction of local semi-self-government, then a semiparliament (*duma*), did not change much during the entire "long" nineteenth century. "Up to 1917, the tsar was the father of his people, an irresponsible autocrat," Eugen Weber observes (Weber 1972, 423). "Sometimes compromises were forced upon the autocracy . . . but in Poland, [and] the Ukraine . . . Russian rule was characterized by repression, intolerance and contempt," Paul Hayes adds. "By the early twentieth century the violent overthrow of the system was increasingly seen as the only answer to autocracy" (Hayes 1992, 64, 67). Although this expansionist, autocratic Russia, with its powerful military machine, failed to conquer the Balkans, it kept a firm hold on its Baltic possessions and Poland and thus influenced Central and Eastern Europe throughout the nineteenth century.

Oppressive Russian rule generated a series of bloody revolts in occupied Poland. The courageous, if often irrational, armed revolts against Russia launched by three consecutive generations up to the 1860s were, as we have seen, later replaced by "organic work." Bolesław Prus, a leading intellectual and writer, asked in one of his weekly articles: "What is one to think of a society in which poetry obscures all other spheres of life?" (Donskov and Sokoloski 1991, 60). The successful struggle of the new, realist political forces against Polish romantic and messianic heroism led to an impressive economic and social modernization of Poland. This transformation undermined the romantic noble national resistance.

The national cause, however, was not dead at all. Based on the modernized country, it renewed and modernized itself into an integral nationalism that included an awakened peasantry. The Polish peasantry had been alienated from the nobility and hostile to the "nobles' cause" throughout decades of rebellion. As Jan Popławski wrote in the Warsaw paper *Głos,* "two nations," two separate civilizations, "the folk and the privileged" existed in Poland. Toward the end of the nineteenth century, however, after members of the "Great Emigration" and veterans of the January insurrection established the Polish League in Switzerland in 1887, a new nationalist camp emerged that not only preserved the legacy of romantic nationalism but also turned toward and sought to recruit the peasant masses. The old and new nationalisms were tightly bridged. New folk nationalists now celebrated the peasantry as the guardian of genuine Polishness.

In 1893, the league was reorganized and renamed the National League, then, in 1897, the National Democratic Movement (Endecja) by Roman Dmowski. Born to a suburban bourgeois family, Dmowski was imprisoned while a student at Warsaw University before becoming the leading ideologue and publicist of reborn Polish nationalism. Based on intense and exclusive nationalism, Dmowski, Popławski, and Zygmunt Balicki launched successful propaganda to strengthen the national spirit through their popular periodicals *Przegląd Wszechpolski* and *Polak* and a network of further education. Enamored of the Polish language and Catholicism as a basis of Polish culture, as well as of the peasantry for carrying Poland "on their shoulders," they advocated an independent Polish state. Although they shunned direct struggle and insurgence, they sought to prepare the nation for struggle. As a central factor of preparedness, they argued, the nation must revitalize its struggle, "the basis of life," Dmowski said, using the well-known social Darwinist concept. In his book *Myśli nowoczesnego Polaka,* which became "the bible of Polish nationalism" (Wandycz 1974, 291), Dmowski maintained that without struggle, a nation "degenerates morally and disintegrates." The "noble nation" loses its virtues and becomes an outdated, "feminine nation." Poland must defeat its internal enemies and guard against racial contamination, he argued, and he launched an attack on Jews, calling for strengthening the national spirit by boycotting Jewish business and "spiritually isolating Polish life from Jewish influence." He made the mass emigration of Jews, as a "final solution," a tenet of the exclusive nationalist Narodowa Demokraczja, or Endeks program. Polish nationalism henceforth, like Romanian nationalism, became inherently anti-Semitic. This was not the case before the 1880s, when "good patriots considered it vulgar . . . to reinforce anti-Jewish stereotypes or to encourage Polish-Jewish conflict" (Porter 2000, 159). The most extreme expression of Polish anti-Semitism was the crusade launched after 1881 by the magazine *Rola,* whose editor, Jan Jeleński, published proto-fascist brochures, *Our World of Finance* (1874) and *The Jews, the Germans, and Us* (1876). Jeleński and *Rola* made the concept of the struggle for national survival fashionable and advocated a ruthless tribal struggle against the Jews. One of Jeleński's close collaborators, Konstanty Wzdulski, demanded the immediate expulsion of Jews. At the end of 1881, a bloody anti-Jewish pogrom engulfed Warsaw. Two people were killed, two dozen were injured, and about a thousand families were financially ruined by looting. Soon afterwards, a thousand Jews emigrated from Warsaw to the United States.

"The main reason for antipathy toward the Jews," stated an editorial in *Głos* in 1886, "is not that they are worse or better, but mainly that they are different." Jews were perceived as a foreign body that infected the social organism. "One cannot deny," wrote an anonymous writer in *Przegląd Wszechpolski* in 1895, "that one of the most important phenomena of our life recently is the incredible increase in anti-Semitism in all spheres . . . and in all possible forms." Oppressed over centuries, Jan Popławski wrote, the Jews "have in their blood the desire for revenge . . . they want to destroy everything." Dmowski alleged that there was a well-organized Jewish conspiracy that, "according to a plan" and based on a "very well-developed internal organization," wanted to conquer Poland to create a "settlement for the Jewish nation" (Porter 2000, 164–66, 176–79, 229). The nation, he maintained, "was compelled to insulate itself behind high walls of exclusion and hostility, and the open, universalistic, idealist nation of Mickiewicz was lost," Brian Porter writes (ibid., 182).

A portion of the intellectual elite and the disaffected masses they were able to mobilize turned against enlightened romanticism. Modernization, a central element of romantic dreaming in the area, had extremely uneven results. It could not create prosperity on a scale that would enable Poland to catch up with the West. However, Poles at the end of the century had to face the destruction of patriarchal communities and the selfish ruthlessness of financial circles and the market economy. Modern capitalism lost its attractiveness for the losers. Market capitalism seemed foreign and Jewish in their eyes. German and French irrational philosophies and rightwing populism, especially the German *Völkisch* movement, offered an alternative concept: a conservative, strongly anti-Western romanticism opposed to both materialism and fin de siècle modernism. Eugen Diederichs, the eccentric, mystical right-wing editor of the German periodical *Die Tat* (The Deed), called this irrational, xenophobic, antimodernist trend the "new romanticism." It had deep roots in Central and Eastern Europe, especially among Slavic peoples. Traditionalism, rejection of the power of money, and the idealization of pure village life and the peasantry, the untouched communal society with its "inner values," the importance and supreme value of spiritual life, emotion, and instinct, paved the way for proto-fascist movements.

Besides the Jews, other ethnicities were also hated. Poland's Russian oppressors were regarded as Asiatic barbarians. "Who can deny that Moscow is the heir . . . of the Golden Horde?" Zygmund Miłkowski demanded in his *Wolne Polskie Słowo*. Lithuanians and Ukrainians were considered part of the Polish nation. Poland had a "civilizing mission" in Lithuania and Ukraine, which had "been our property for five centuries. . . . Nearly everything that has any lasting value [there] at all . . . is the result of Polish thought and Polish will." Dmowski argued that Ruthenians (Ukrainians) did not exist; they were only a "pitiful type of Pole." "Ukraine never did exist, does not exist, and will not exist." Ukrainian nationalism in Galicia was declared to be a "purely artificial creation." Instead, the Polish nationalists offered polonization, or assimilation, as an alternative (Porter 2000, 184, 223–25).

The Endeks, whose headquarters were located in Posnań and Lwów, had originally painted the Russian autocracy as the main enemy. When the tsar introduced his semiconstitutional regime after 1905, however, they argued for the reestablishment of Polish autonomy within Russia. In German Poland, Germany, with its assimilationist policy, became the main enemy.

Nationalism was a leading concept even for Polish socialism. Alongside general socialist statements, the first draft of the program of Ludwik Wariński's socialist movement in 1879 declared: "We also believe deeply that the Polish people, mobilized in the name of social-revolutionary principles, will demonstrate irrepressible strength and steadfast energy in the struggle with the partitioning governments, which have joined economic exploitation with unprecedented national oppression" (Porter 2000, 106). Unlike Dmowski's exclusive xenophobic nationalism, the other major new force of national independence, the Polish Socialist party (PPS), established from four socialist groups in 1893, advocated an "independent democratic commonwealth . . . [with] complete equality [of all nationalities] on the basis of a voluntary federation" and accepted the idea of insurrection. Rosa Luxemburg's separate Social Democratic party of the kingdom of Poland (SDKP), which became the PPS-Lewica (Left) after a 1906 PPS split, maintained that proletarian revolution in the Russian empire would automatically eliminate national oppression.

Jósef Piłsudski and the PPS-Rewolucja, or "social patriots," as Rosa Luxemburg lampooned the nationalist socialists in the PPS, argued that social progress was impossible without national independence. The homeland's independence, Piłsudski insisted, was "a condition characteristic of socialism's victory in Poland" (Brock 1969, 346–48). The son of an impoverished Lithuanian Polish gentry family, Piłsudski studied medicine in Kharkov, was deported to Siberia for five years in 1887, then became one of the founders of the PPS and editor of *Robotnik*. After another arrest in 1901, he gradually devoted himself entirely to the national cause and turned toward violent action. Although not a trained soldier, Piłsudski began preparing cadres and officers for a future Polish army for action against Russia. His paramilitary units launched various attacks during the revolutionary crisis of 1905–6, and in 1908, he moved to Galicia, in Habsburg Poland, as an outlawed terrorist, where he founded his First Brigade.

HABSBURG AUTHORITARIANISM AND CZECH NATIONALISM

Although the Habsburg empire was the most enlightened absolute power in Central and Eastern Europe, it was nonetheless unquestionably autocratic for the first two-thirds of the nineteenth century, with heavy censorship, an army of police spies, and a politically influential Catholic Church. With the revoking of the liberal constitution that resulted from the revolution of 1848, the "entire administrative system [became] purely

FIGURE 87. The Berlin Conference, 1878. Courtesy Hadtörténeti Múzeum, Budapest.

FIGURE 88. Alexander
Cuza. Courtesy Magyar
Tudományos Akadémia
Történettudományi
Intézete, Budapest.

FIGURE 89. King Carol I
of Romania. Courtesy
Hadtörténeti Múzeum,
Budapest.

FIGURE 90. Nikola Pašić,
prime minister of Serbia
before World War I.
Courtesy Hadtörténeti
Múzeum, Budapest.

FIGURE 91. Kálmán Tisza,
prime minister of Hungary.
Courtesy Hungarian National
Museum, Budapest.

FIGURE 92. King Ferdinand I of
Bulgaria. Courtesy Hadtörténeti
Múzeum, Budapest.

FIGURE 93. Hungarian gendarmes and Romanian voters, 1906. Courtesy
Hungarian National Museum, Budapest.

FIGURE 94. Emperor Franz Joseph in the uniform of a Hungarian hussar, 1898. Courtesy Hungarian National Museum, Budapest.

FIGURE 95. The Kaiserlich und Königlich Kriegsmarine's dreadnought *Viribus Unitis*. Courtesy Hadtörténeti Múzeum, Budapest.

FIGURE 96. Archduke Franz Ferdinand of Austria-Hungary and his wife, Sophie, whose assassination triggered World War I. Courtesy Hadtörténeti Múzeum, Budapest.

FIGURE 97. Serbian soldiers in the trenches, World War I. Courtesy Hadtörténeti Múzeum, Budapest.

authoritarian." As late as October 1860, Emperor Franz Josef wrote to his mother: "We shall, indeed, have a little parliamentary government, but the power remains in my hands" (Macartney 1968, 440, 499). However, unlike the Russian and Ottoman regimes, the Habsburg monarchy introduced Western European legal institutions at the end of the 1860s: censorship was abandoned, and freedom of speech, press, property, belief, and association were granted. Citizens became equal before the law, and the judiciary was separated from executive power.

The empire, nevertheless, preserved its autocratic character: "The Crown in fact emerged with its power not greatly shorn," C. A. Macartney observes; the new laws left it "in a very strong position *de jure,* and *de facto* it was even stronger." The monarch and his government claimed the right of supervision of associations and assemblies. He remained the commander of the army and had virtually no limits with respect to foreign affairs. He retained the right to veto legislation and the right to dissolve parliament. His supremacy was based on the bureaucracy and the army, the "cement" of the monarchy. Regarding Hungary, the king-emperor did not have veto power, but "the unofficial right of 'preliminary sanction' filled the gap." The monarch was entitled to appoint the prime minister of his choice and to retain him in office in the face of an adverse parliamentary majority. In Austria, the emergency clause allowed the government to enact necessary measures if the Reichsrat was not in session. These measures required a retroactive endorsement by the Reichsrat, but it was a formality, since there was no case of refusal. "The *Reichsrat* had become in fact little more than . . . an advisory body to the Crown." Although the parliament, which was elected by 5.9 percent of the population, had some control, "where . . . fundamentals were at issue, the Monarch's will was enforced, if necessary, over Parliament's head" (Macartney 1968, 561–67). "The malfunctioning of the representative system produced in practice a transfer of power to the bureaucracy. Political and administrative functions were intertwined and were not uncommonly identified as one and the same," Paul Hayes adds. A huge, self-serving bureaucracy of three million people (in 1914), preoccupied with its own advancement and preservation of privileges, grades, and ranks, became a major, authoritative player (Hayes 1992, 69).

Although less expansionist than Russia, the Habsburg empire launched various wars to maintain and enlarge the monarchy. It participated in the partition of Poland at the end of the eighteenth century and gained Galicia. In 1775, it took over Bukovina, with its mixed Romanian, Ukrainian, German, and Jewish population, and it participated in the French wars and in the struggle with Prussia to lead German unification. It fought wars to hold onto northern Italy and Hungary in the mid nineteenth century and enlarged the Habsburg domains by first occupying (1875) and then annexing (1908) Bosnia-Herzegovina. Even after the creation of the dual *kaiserlich und königlich* (imperial and royal, or *k. und k.*), system, Austria's first reaction to the 1905 electoral victory of the nationalist opposition in Hungary was to use military force. A plan called the *Lösung der ungarischen Krise durch Waffengewalt* (solution to the Hungarian crisis by military force) was prepared and discussed in the emperor's hunting mansion in Bad Ischl at a meeting chaired by Franz Josef on August 22, 1905.

In 1879, the empire became a partner with Germany in the Dual Alliance (which was enlarged by Italy in 1882 and became the Triple Alliance), an aggressive political and military agreement that was a part of war preparation. Austria-Hungary was also a pillar of the Dreikaiserbund, the alliance of the three emperors of Russia, Germany, and Austria (1881) to maintain the status quo they had created in 1815 and harmonize expansion in the Balkans.

The Habsburg empire's authoritarian character was especially clearly exhibited in its relations with the subordinated nations. Prince Felix Schwarzenberg established the concept of an absolutist, centralized state, leader of a reorganized German Confederation, in 1848. After the suppression of the revolution of 1848–49, absolute power without differentiation among subordinated nationalities was established by the Sylvester Patent of December 31, 1851. As was sarcastically noted and often quoted, those who were loyal to the Habsburgs in 1848 received the same treatment as a reward that those who had fought the empire got as punishment. In 1854, in order to create an "Austrian nation," the "nationalizing" monarchy made German the empire's only official language. After the dream of *Grossdeutsch* unification vanished in 1866, however, and Austria made its compromise with the empire's strongest nationality, the Hungarians, in 1867, Habsburg subjects fell into three separate categories: privileged Germans and Magyars; semiprivileged Poles and Croats, in Galicia and Croatia, respectively; and nonprivileged peoples, such as the Czechs (until 1910), Serbs, Slovaks, Ukrainians, Romanians, Slovenes, and Croats living outside Croatia. Roughly a quarter of the population belonged to the latter category, and another quarter to the semiprivileged group. Approximately 60 percent of Hapsburg subjects—whether German, Polish, Romanian, or Serb—had "brother" co-nationals living outside the empire, and some 40 percent even had a "motherland" nation-state not far off.

The Czech lands and Bukovina did not enjoy any important elements of political, linguistic, or cultural autonomy. The Czech national movement's traditional demand since František Palacký's Old Czech movement, which was taken up by his son-in-law, František Rieger, was the restoration of the *Böhmisches Staatsrecht*—the old constitution of the Czech kingdom as an autonomous unit within the monarchy. After 1863, following the prototype of Hungarian passive resistance during the years of absolutism, the Czechs withdrew from the Reichsrat and boycotted it for sixteen years.

A new hope rose in 1871, when Count Siegmund Hohenwart, the newly appointed prime minister, in cooperation with the Old Czech party, worked out the Fundamental Articles. The plan was to establish a Diet of the Czech Lands, so that Bohemian representatives would not sit in the Reichsrat, but would instead participate in a joint congress of the delegates of the Austrian, Hungarian, and Czech parliaments (Scharf 1996). Autonomy was planned for the Bohemian administration in economic affairs as well. A drafted nationality law would have conferred equal official status for the Czech language with the German in each district where at least 20 percent of the population spoke Czech as their native language. Government officials would have been required to speak both languages. This reasonable compromise, however, failed. Gyula Andrássy, the prime minister of Hungary, angrily defended the dual structure of the monarchy and opposed any movement toward federalism. The emperor himself preferred the structure created by the Ausgleich.

The defeat of the Old Czech concept led to the decline of the movement itself and the rise of the Young Czech movement, organized in 1874, following a break with the Old Czechs. The Young Czechs used different tactics and stressed cultural and educational programs. Aided by the flourishing Czech economy, the Matica Česká and Matica Školska patriotic societies and the sports organization Sokol developed into an increasingly radical national mass movement. The language war was not easily resolved. In Bohemia—according to the 1910 census—while 63 percent of the population was Czech, 37 percent was German. In Moravia, the Czech majority constituted 72 percent of the population, and the German minority only 28 percent. In the third "Czech land," Silesia, however, the Germans were most numerous, 44 percent, and even the Poles outnumbered the Czechs (32 and 24 percent, respectively). The Taaffe government, during the 1880s, made some concessions by reinstating Czech as the so-called external language of the judiciary and public administration, and then, as the internal language of the Prague and Brno superior courts when processing Czech cases. Prague's venerable Charles University was also divided into Czech and German units. Endless debates and various resolutions yielded no solutions. Austrian Germans who opposed the creation of a "Slav state" within the monarchy founded a pan-German party, whose Linz program proposed *Anschluss*—union—with Germany. "It was among the Germans, in reaction to the concession made primarily to the Czechs, that the first movement [that] advocated the dissolution of Austria-Hungary emerged," Peter Sugar writes (Sugar 1999, iv, 26).

The deadlock helped the Young Czechs, who turned to the "average" Czech of the rising middle class rather than to their rivals' constituency of aristocratic landowners. Under the leadership of Karel Kramář, a believer in Slav unity, the Young Czechs performed well in the 1891 Reichsrat elections, winning three times as many votes as the Old Czechs. An organized filibuster paralyzed the work of the parliament. Riots raged in Prague, and the Austrian authorities introduced a state of emergency, banned several Czech national organizations, and arrested many of their members.

Paradoxically, to preserve national oppression, the Austrian government democratized the electoral system: to counterbalance the restive Czech middle class, the number of eligible voters was tripled in 1893. The emperor appointed a Polish count, Casimir Badeni, an experienced and loyal administrator in Galicia, as prime minister in 1895. He sought to cut the Gordian knot of debate over language with a new regulation: both German and Czech would become official languages throughout the former Czech kingdom, and state employees would have to learn both languages within three years. The new effort to find a compromise led virtually to civil war; the German nationalists organized a filibuster, then even violence in parliament and on the streets of Vienna and Graz. The emperor dismissed Badeni and dropped the plan. A Czech revolt followed and paralyzed the work of the Reichsrat. Bohemia remained in a state of permanent unrest.

The political domination of the Young Czechs gradually evaporated during the 1890s and early 1900s. The enfranchisement of the lower urban and rural classes, owing partly to electoral reform in 1896, but mostly to the introduction of universal male suffrage in 1907, broadened the social base of some new parties that advocated lower-class interests, such as the Social Democratic party, the National Socialists, and the Agrarians. In the 1911 elections, the Young Czechs won only 19 seats compared to the 52 won by the Social Democrats and Agrarians combined (Oskar Krejcí 1995). However, the national question remained in focus, and the various Czech parties formed a consultative National Council in Prague in 1900.

It was in this context that the former Young Czech deputy and professor of sociology Tomáš Masarýk formed his nationalist and left-of-center Realist party in 1890. For the first time in the decades-long history of the Czech national movement, the traditional demand for the reintroduction of Czech *Staatsrecht* was rejected. Masarýk regarded it as unrealistic and advocated a democratic federal reorganization of the monarchy instead. Almost alone in the region, the new Czech national movement, with its middle-class backing, linked the national question with democracy and human rights. Masarýk was a unique national leader in Central and Eastern Europe. This highly cosmopolitan intellectual—who had a Moravian-Slovakian father, a Moravian-German mother, and an American wife—was a firm believer in the ethnic identity of Czechs and Slovaks. He maintained that the Slovaks were Slovak-speaking Czechs, while the Czechs were Czech-speaking Slovaks. Small wonder, then, that he gradually turned toward a new national concept: Czechoslovakism, the unification of Czechs and Slovaks within the monarchy. Similarly, he endorsed Serbo-Croat unity.

The Slovak national movement declined after the Austro-Hungarian Compromise of 1867. As early as 1861, at the Turčiansky Svätý Martin meeting, Slovaks demanded equality of language and Slovak as the official language in the Hornouhorské Slovenské Okolie, the "North Hungarian Slovak District," but the tactic of passive resistance and abstention from political activities between 1875 and the mid 1890s proved counterproductive. Slovak nationalism staged a comeback in the mid 1890s. The most ardent new advocate of the traditional demand for Slovak autonomy within Hungary was Father Andrej Hlinka, who established a Slovak wing of the Hungarian Néppárt (People's party) in 1896. This embryonic party became the Slovak People's party after the turn of the century and won seven seats in the Hungarian parliament in 1906. The party organized credit cooperatives, people's banks, and reading rooms, and propagandized among Slovak peasants, inter alia using anti-Semitic slogans. A Slovak intellectual group in Budapest led by Milan Hodža, a member of the Hungarian parliament, worked for universal suffrage and federal reorganization of the monarchy based on a "trialism" that included Slavs to replace the "dualist" Austro-Hungarian structure of the empire. Union with the Czechs was not, however, on the agenda among the Slovak population of northern Hungary.

Slovak students at Charles University, the youngest generation, nonetheless started the Československá Jednota, or Czechoslovak Society, and given that Masarýk was the most prestigious intellectual leader of the Czech national movement before the war, Czechoslovakism gained ground. It was popularized, moreover, by the journal *Hlas* (1898), founded by Vavro Šrobár, who was influenced by Masarýk. After 1907, all the Slovak political parties built contacts with the Czechs. In the spring of 1914, the Slovak National party, a kind of umbrella organization of all the parties, amended its program by stressing close cooperation with the Czechs and endorsing the concept of democratic federal reorganization of the monarchy (Kann and David 1984, 384).

HUNGARIAN NATIONALISM

Slovak nationalism in northern Hungary, Romanian nationalism in Transylvania, Croat nationalism in Croatia, and Serb nationalism in the Voivodina all met stubborn opposition from Hungarian nationalism. The Carpatho-Ukrainian religious movement that sprang up in the late nineteenth century and led to a mass conversion of Ukrainian peasants from Greek Catholicism to Greek Orthodoxy provides a telling example. The Hungarian authorities, worried by pan-Slavism, responded with mass arrests and charges of treason and antistate activity. At a mass trial in Máramarossziget in 1913–14, thirty-two Ukrainian peasants were sentenced and jailed.

The Hungarians were more fortunate than other peoples in the Habsburg empire with respect to the national question. Even though their 1848–49 revolt suffered both defeat and retribution, it led to the compromise of 1867. The Hungarian noble elite, exhausted by passive resistance against Austria and hungry to reassert their political domination in the country and fill lucrative public positions, were ready to negotiate. They sought to stabilize their power over the nationalities and consolidate the multiethnic state. The same was true of the emperor and his Austrian political elite, especially after Austria's defeat by Prussia in 1866 dashed its hopes of leading German unification. The Austrian-Hungarian Ausgleich of 1867 restored the constitutional integrity of Hungary and guaranteed the country quasi-independent, autonomous self-government. This found symbolic expression in the personality of Count Gyula Andrássy, Hungary's first prime minister (1867–71). As a colonel in the revolutionary army, Andrássy had fought against Austria in 1848 and was sent to Istanbul by Kossuth in 1849 to try to persuade the Porte to intervene against the Habsburgs. While in exile after the defeat of the rebellion, he had actually been sentenced to death in absentia by the Austrians in 1851.

"Today is the day of festive joy and national pride," the German-language Budapest newspaper *Pester Lloyd* proclaimed on May 9, 1867: Franz Josef had allowed himself to be crowned king of Hungary in the Mathias Church in Buda. A decade before, in 1857, the poet János Arany had "welcomed" Franz Josef with his metaphoric "The Bards of Wales," in which one of the bards tells the visiting king:

> Our brave were killed, just as you willed,
> Or languish in our gaols:
> To hail your name or sing your fame
> You find no bard in Wales
>
> (Makkai 1996, 280)

Franz Josef now had a rather different welcome. Thousands jammed the railway station to greet the emperor. A thick cordon of people lined the route and showered the royal couple with flowers. The entire political elite attended the ceremony, and Liszt's Hungarian Coronation Mass was played (Freifeld 2000, 215, 218–19). The hated butcher of 1848, whose bedroom in the Hofburg in Vienna was decorated with paintings of the major battles that had defeated the Hungarian revolution, would henceforth be the beloved father of the Hungarians.

The compromise reestablished Hungarian domination over all ethnic minorities in the country. They altogether represented half of the population that had actually allied itself with the emperor to defeat the Hungarian revolution in 1848–49. An independent Hungarian government was formed, responsible to the Hungarian parliament. The monarchy was transformed into a dual state, renamed Austria-Hungary. The Austrian emperor was crowned king of Hungary, and the most important portfolios of the government of the dual monarchy—defense, foreign affairs, and finance—became "common affairs." The joint army used German as the language of command, although small national military units, the Honvéd army in Hungary and the Landswehr in Austria, were also established. Common finances included a common Central Bank in Vienna. The three ministers of common affairs were responsible to delegates representing the two parliaments. One of the three common ministers was almost always Hungarian, and four out of eleven ministers of finance and four out of ten ministers of foreign affairs were Hungarians during the period of the dual regime.

A so-called economic compromise retained a customs union and divided common expenditures and payments of state debts according to a quota. (Three-tenths of the expenditures were covered by Hungary.) The economic compromise, including the renewed customs union, was signed for only ten years, however, and renegotiated every tenth year. Transylvania, the Voivodina, and the so-called Military Frontier, mostly populated by ethnic minorities, became integral parts of Hungary.

Relations between Hungary and Croatia were, however, regulated by a separate Hungarian-Croat compromise in 1868. It was modeled on the Austro-Hungarian system, but contained more restrictions. The franchise was even more limited than in Hungary: instead of 24 percent, only 8 percent of the adult male population had voting rights in Croatia. This situation changed only in 1910, when 32 percent of the male population gained voting rights. The compromise provided less autonomy for Croatia, since common affairs were directed by the Hungarian parliament. The king, based on the recommendation of the Hungarian prime minister, appointed Croatia's chief executive, the *banus*.

Autonomous Hungary introduced a modern European parliamentary system. The franchise was limited to about 6 percent of the population, which was not unusual at that time in Europe. This percentage, however, did not change with time. Besides, an open ballot made elections controllable by the administration. The legislative, executive, and judicial branches were each given separate powers. Liberal European institutions and legislation were introduced. Basic human rights, equality before the courts, and equal rights for all citizens, including minorities, were guaranteed. A liberal law (Law XLIV of 1868) regulated the rights of the nationalities, which were allowed to use their native languages at various local levels and in schools and were equally eligible to hold any position. Jews were emancipated. Personal freedom for minorities was thus guaranteed.

Collective national rights and representations were, however, rejected. "In Hungary there is only one, indivisible political nation, the Hungarian," declared Ferenc Deák, the father of the compromise. Consequently, the official language of legislation and government, as well as of the higher courts, was Hungarian. Compulsory free basic education was introduced (Law XXXVIII of 1868), accompanied by intensive school construction and teacher training. "[L]iberal values were not only legalized and institutionalized but also realized in practice" in Austria-Hungary, making it "the eastern border of Europe," in Péter Hanák's words (Hanák 1988, 31). The liberal generation of Ferenc Deák and József Eötvös, the main architects of the system, left its mark on autonomous Hungary.

Political practice and the autocratic principle of law, however, differed from institutionalized freedoms. The authoritarian reality of power, the most important characteristic of the politics of backwardness, was independent of constitutional and legal formalities. Hungarian governments ruled by fiat. Under Law XIX of 1869, judges were required to enforce government decrees as well as statute law and lawful custom. The authority of the government was strengthened because statutory law only partially secured personal and civil rights. A government decree of 1875 regulated the licensing of associations and the supervisory role of the authorities, including the right to disband them. A decree of the minister of interior in 1868 ordered all local authorities to "follow with attention the proceedings of meetings," and, if need be, to disband the gathering. The use of red flags at meetings and the holding of strike meetings were banned in 1874 and 1894, respectively. In 1878, a confidential circular of the prime minister ordered local authorities to permit assemblies "only if six to ten 'distinguished citizens' stood surety for the meeting" (Péter 1997–98, 17, 22, 25–27). Civil rights were thus closely controlled and limited.

Kálmán Tisza's governing Szabadelvü Párt (Liberal party), founded in 1875, was virtually unchallengeable and had a comfortable absolute majority for thirty years. In 1881, 225, in 1887, 261, and in 1910, 258 representatives out of 413 belonged to the government party. Only once during nearly fifty years in power did the government party fail to secure a parliamentary majority. When the united opposition, the Függetlenségi és 48–as Párt (Independence and 1848 party), won the elections in 1905, the emperor rejected the result and appointed the captain of his *Darabont* bodyguard unit, Géza Fejérváry, prime minister of Hungary. Parliament was surrounded by troops, mostly non-Hungarian units, in February 1906, and a uniformed colonel read a royal decree dissolving it. The former united opposition was allowed to form a government only after it gave up its major demands for an independent Hungarian army and tariff system in a humiliating compromise with the crown. In new elections in 1906, the victorious opposition used the same excessive force as its archenemies had before, resulting in thirty-two election-related deaths.

After the reestablished Liberal party regained power as the Nemzeti Munkapárt (National Work party), brutal violence marked the 1910 elections: 194 infantry battalions and 114 cavalry squadrons terrorized voters in 380 constituencies. Military force, of course, was only the *ultima ratio* to save the situation. In most cases, corrupt county administrations, subordinated to the government, closely controlled and successfully manipulated the open ballot elections. "Electoral corruption—the purchase of votes, the use of forgery, and intimidation—... became routine," Andrew Janos says of the liberal Hungarian era of the 1870s and 1880s. If need be, the authorities provoked unrest and arrested opposition voters.

The administrative bureaucracy was welded into a single, powerful machine ... "making" the elections and perpetuating the ... majority. ... The political machine emerged as the single most important actor on the Hungarian political stage. The autocratic tendencies ... were further mitigated ... by a number of habits, conventions, and quasi-institutions that operated as correctives in the absence of free competition and represented built-in restraints on the arbitrary exercise of power ... they were most effective in protecting the personal and political rights of the members of the establishment ... they were also instrumental in blunting the harshness of the bureaucratic regime towards the lower classes and the national minorities. (Janos 1982, 97–101)

Democratic institutions, such as freedom of the press and parliamentary opportunities for the opposition, also served to restrain the arbitrary exercise of power. Corrupt practices were made public, and use of the filibuster placed some limits on the majority's law-making machinery. Even the "almighty" Kálmán Tisza twice lost elections in his district. Opposition parties, although unable to win elections, played some role in Hungarian political life. The "left" opposition parties united as the Függetlenségi és 48–as Párt in 1884 to provide real parliamentary opposition. Originally, they had rejected the compromise of 1867, but they gradually came to accept it. Still, they demanded even more autonomy, including independent Hungarian tariffs to protect the country from Austrian-Bohemian industrial competition, and also called for the joint army to be divided. In the early 1880s, they formulated an alternative policy on nationalities. Lajos Mocsáry, a representative of the liberal old guard, sharply criticized forced assimilation.

This party gradually lost its anti-Austrian radicalism, however, as well as its more cooperative attitude toward ethnic minorities. It made more and more compromises and turned out to be quite similar to the government party. In order to assume power after it won the 1906 elections, the Függetlenségi és 48–as Párt gave up all its electoral demands. In parliamentary struggles, it nevertheless still often publicly unmasked the autocratic features of the regime.

The "right" aristocratic-religious opposition, which combined into the heterogeneous Egyesült Ellenzék (United Opposition) in 1878 (renamed the Moderate Opposition in 1881), did not have a genuinely independent program, but advocated a less tolerant minority policy. Political anti-

Semitism took root in Hungary around that time and followed the same course as in Austria and Germany. Wilhelm Marr's *Der Sieg des Judenthums über das Germanenthum* was published in 1873, and Győző Istóczy, who delivered his first anti-Semitic speech in the Hungarian parliament in 1875, launched a coherent anti-Semitic program, characterizing Jewry as an "attacking caste" that was flooding the country. The goal of the Jews, "a race with a national religion," Istóczy maintained, was "to conquer the European nations and, if possible, eliminate them, not by sword and fire," but through money and economic power. According to János Gyurgyák's convincing and detailed description of the birth of Hungarian political anti-Semitism in his *A zsidókérdés Magyarországon* (Gyurgyák 2001), Istóczy declared that anti-Semitism was a natural defense against pan-Judaism and Jewish world hegemony. Unless Hungary waged "a struggle of life or death," it would become "a Jewish state" in a matter of a few generations, a "new Palestine," where Hungarians would be second-class citizens. A vitriolic campaign was launched against Jewish immigration and the theory of a "Jewish conspiracy against the Christian nation" was popularized. In a speech of June 1878, Istóczy developed a Zionist concept as a solution to the "Jewish question": "the reestablishment of a Jewish state in Palestine" with national institutions and sovereignty. In the event that the legal, political struggle failed, however, "if there were no other ways and means, as the *ultima ratio,* physical strength [meaning violence and power] would matter and, in that case, it is not we who would lose." The foundation of the far-right Országos Antiszemita Párt (National Anti-Semitic party) in 1883 was an attempt to create a coalition that would rise above the existing parties, but it was unable to establish itself. It won only seventeen seats in the Hungarian parliament in 1884, and an internal crisis led to its disappearance in the early 1890s. Political anti-Semitism did not, however, remain an isolated episode in late nineteenth-century Hungary. From that time on, it had a permanent place in the political and intellectual life of the country.

In 1882, one of Istóczy's comrades-in-arms, Géza Onódy, played a central role in launching a vicious anti-Semitic campaign by reinventing the medieval blood libel, charging that a Christian girl had been ritually murdered in Tiszaeszlár. That fall, anti-Semitic atrocities led to states of emergency in several counties. In the summer of 1883, however, the religious murder trial failed spectacularly, and exposure of police manipulation resulted in a major liberal victory. The anti-Semitic atrocities that had engulfed the country were forcefully suppressed (Szász 1987, 1222–31, 1271–77).

A series of anti-Semitic writings, papers, and cartoons nonetheless sought to mobilize the population. In 1882, Károly Nendtvich's book *Die Judenfrage in Österreich-Ungarn* repeated the charge that the goal of a Jewish conspiracy was *Untergrabung und Vernichtung*—to undermine and eliminate Christian society and conquer the country for themselves. In 1894, skewering the "Judaization" of Budapest, the anti-Semitic satirical journal *Herkó Páter* dubbed the city *Juda-pest* and published a caricature of the *uj honfoglalás,* the conquest of the Danube valley by Jews in 1896.

Miklós Bartha, in 1910, developed a popular concept by distinguishing "Hungarian Jews" from the Kazárs, as he called the immigrant Polish Jews from Galicia, who had the same Mosaic religion, but, he maintained, differed ethnically from their Hungarian counterparts. *A Cél* (The Target), an anti-Semitic journal founded in 1910, launched unceasing attacks to "defend the nation." Sándor Kiss became a frontrunner in the spread of racist, social Darwinist ideas in Hungary by separating nation and race. He accused Hungarians of "racial laziness," saying that nature demanded that the race be kept alive, if necessary by rejecting equality, fraternity, and liberty. Béla Dáner, of the same group and journal, proposed the introduction of a Jewish nationality in Hungary and urged that Jews emigrate to Palestine. The maximum number of Jews Hungary could accept, he argued, was no more than 40,000–50,000.

Although its ideology and arguments were in place, political anti-Semitism did not become an integral part of Hungarian nationalism at this stage. Antiminority, assimilationist nationalism nonetheless dominated Hungarian politics. As Kálmán Tisza, the opposition leader at the time, put it in the parliamentary debate on the Law on Education in November 1868, the entire liberal Hungarian political elite of the 1860s was convinced that assimilation was in the best interest of the minorities. Under the rubric of the "indivisible unitary Magyar nation," autonomous Hungary's half century in the dual monarchy was characterized by a forced assimilation policy. Against the letter and spirit of the nationality law, minority representatives were effectively excluded from high official positions. Although in eighteen of sixty-two counties (excepting Croatia), between 66 and 96 percent of the population belonged to Romanian and Slovak majorities, the *főispán* (high sheriff) and his deputy in these counties were always Hungarians.

In 1870, although 60 percent of the population of Transylvania was Romanian, only one-third of the officials were ethnic Romanians, a proportion that had declined to 6 percent by 1891. A total of 3 to 4 percent of those appointed to positions in district courts, government ministries, university chairs, and education supervision were Romanians. Although the use of native languages was allowed in district courts by the Nationality Law of 1868, the reorganization of the judicial system in 1869 practically eliminated this right and magyarized the entire justice system. Virtually the same thing happened in primary and secondary education, where the use of mother tongues was guaranteed in the Nationality Law. In practice, however, the entire school system became the main tool of assimilation. At the secondary level, all state schools became entirely Magyar. The German, Slovak, Romanian, and Ukrainian languages were not used at all. Even the three existing Slovak denominational secondary schools were closed in 1874, and the Romanian churches were allowed a total of five secondary schools.

In 1903, only 14 secondary schools out of 190 in Hungary were non-Magyar. As Béla Grünwald stated at the time: "The secondary school is like a huge machine, at one end of which the Slovak youths are thrown in by hundreds, and at the other end of which they come out as Magyars" (Seton-Watson [1934] 1963, 400). Primary schools were partly run by minority churches. For example, in 1870, the Orthodox Church maintained 1,604, and the Uniate Church, 2,058 schools. Even in these schools, however, 18 to 24 hours of 26-hour units were reserved for Magyar education according to a 1902 ministerial decree. In 1907, a new law on education demanded spoken and written fluency in Hungarian after four years. In the end, only 20 percent of all primary schools provided non-Magyar language education, and only one-third of all minority children were taught in their mother tongue, in a country where half the population belonged to ethnic minorities (Dolmányos 1988, 640–41).

Successive Hungarian governments suppressed any national movement that threatened the indivisible Magyar national state and the dual structure of the monarchy. Their task was relatively easy, since all the ethnic minorities used the counterproductive weapon of passive resistance between 1875 and 1906. Organizations considered dangerous to Magyar supremacy were persecuted and closed down, among them the Matica Slovenska, in 1875, and the Transylvanian Romanian National party, in 1894. The most ardent advocates of Romanian, Slovak, Croat, and Serb national self-determination were persecuted, and ethnic unrest was bloodily suppressed if need be. Special jury courts were employed between 1871 and 1885 to handle press offenses. The Kolozsvár court frequently charged the Transylvanian Romanian press with "incitement of national hatred." Between 1886 and 1908, Seton-Watson notes, 362 Romanians were sentenced to a total of 134 years' imprisonment and fined about 100,000 crowns for political offenses (Seton-Watson [1934] 1963, 405 n. 1). When

Svetozar Miletić recruited volunteers in the Banat to help the South Slav cause in 1876, despite his parliamentary immunity, he was arrested (with another Serb, Kazapinović) and sentenced to five years for separatism. Aurel Popovici, a Romanian student and author of a pamphlet entitled "The Romanian Question in Transylvania and Hungary," was sentenced in 1891 to four years' imprisonment. Fifteen Romanians were sentenced to thirty-two years' imprisonment for writing the Memorandum of the Romanian National party in 1894. Three Slovak representatives in the Hungarian parliament, among them Milan Hodža, future prime minister of Czechoslovakia, were arrested and imprisoned in 1906. A show trial was arranged against Vavro Šrobár and Andrej Hlinka in the same year. When the Slovaks built a church in the village in Csernova (Černová) where Hlinka had been born and wanted him to consecrate it, the gendarmerie opened fire and killed thirteen peasants in 1907. Another show trial was held in Hajdúdorog in March 1914, when Father Mureşan and fourteen Romanians were sentenced for resisting the transfer of seventy-five parishes from the Romanian Uniate Church to Magyar control and the introduction of the Magyar language into the liturgy. The Romanian electorate was more severely restricted than the Magyar: only about 3 percent of the population of Transylvania gained voting rights. In 1910, when Romanians sought to elect their representatives, ten voters were killed. The number of minority representatives declined from 26 to 8 in the Hungarian parliament as a result. Less than 2 percent of the representatives represented half of the population, the ethnic minorities. Parliament should be unanimous in "patriotic joy" because the elections had "virtually wiped the nationalist agitators out of public life," Prime Minister István Tisza declared (Seton-Watson [1934] 1963, 428).

The Hungarian regime was nonetheless still incomparably more liberal than those of Russia and several Balkan nations. Its assimilationist policy and discrimination against minorities were not marked by terrorism, and punishments were in most cases relatively mild. The methodical magyarization and continual frustration of strongly national-minded people and institutions that sought to advance their national causes were, however, offensive and oppressive. The Magyar political elite no doubt sought to follow the English and French historical examples by assimilating other ethnicities and creating a homogeneous nation-state with a single official language, but this was doomed to fail in the age of nationalism. The Romanian nationalist Aurel Popovici expressed the feeling of ethnic intellectuals when he called Hungary "a Bastille of nationalities."

Forced assimilation did not work at all. Although, according to Péter

Hanák's calculations, the share of the "Hungarian" population increased by nearly 8 percent during the last three decades of the *kaiserlich und königlich* system, 30 percent of that increase (a million people) was the result of assimilation. Most of this figure was attributable to Germans (400,000) and Jews (200,000) in urban areas. The homogeneous and closed Romanian and Slovak peasant communities, however, preserved their languages and identities. Between 1880 and 1910, the numbers of the Hungarian-speaking minorities doubled, but still only 22 percent of the minority peoples spoke Hungarian (Hanák 1988, 414–18).

Authoritarian power and overwhelming nationalism were thus everywhere dominant in Central and Eastern European politics. Autocracy was self-evident in militarized states, especially in the case of the Ottoman and Russian empires, where war was a commonplace activity of the state machine. It was also a natural legacy in noble societies where the landed aristocracy and gentry preserved economic and political power. The situation was basically the same in the formerly "incomplete" Balkan societies, where a newly emerged military-bureaucratic elite took over. These closed elites monopolized the right to elect representatives and determined who was elected. By the early twentieth century, only 5 to 7 percent of the population had voting rights, representing mostly rich landowners and bureaucrats. The leaders of the bureaucratic-military elite had almost unlimited, practically uncontrolled authoritarian power. The poor and uneducated bulk of the population was excluded from politics.

Nationalism was the triumphant political mainstream that legitimized authoritarian regimes. These trends characterized politics in the region of unfinished nation-building. Nationalism motivated oppression, assimilation, and political and armed conflict both among nationalities and among the newly created nation-states.

THE SEEDS OF REVOLT

If failed or semisuccessful modernization and unfinished nation-building were fertile soil for authoritarian rule and national hatreds, the conditions were also conducive to revolt. People rebelled against oppressive, authoritarian, exploitative regimes, against petrified social conditions, landlessness, poverty, and the sociopolitical exclusion of the bulk of the population from the body politic. Representatives of the peasant and worker masses and part of the political elite shared the Enlightenment belief in progress and the possibility of changing the course of history by rational action. However, they harbored rather different social ideals and concepts of progress. Politics in turn-of-the-century Central and Eastern Europe was thus characterized by various types of right- and left-wing populism and revolt.

This was also a consequence of the partial success of modernization, the rise of a small, educated intelligentsia, partly emerging from the ranks of the new burgher and white-collar strata, partly from the peasantry, workers, and various minority groups virtually excluded from the society. One could, however, find déclassé gentry-intellectuals and sometimes even aristocrats in their ranks. The mass leaders, right or left, nevertheless, mostly belonged to the modern urban intelligentsia and had an important impact on politics. A new peasant intelligentsia, mostly teachers, became instrumental in educating and mobilizing the peasants. They stood behind various self-help organizations and, sometimes, radical peasant movements. Self-educated peasants also played an important role in organizing, not only village reading rooms, but also strikes by harvesters and political demonstrations. The same was true of educated workers who became local leaders in urban working districts.

The Jewish minority, which suffered special segregation, also played an important role. When legal emancipation was followed by continued social exclusion, a part of the Jewish intelligentsia turned to political movements and parties that offered full and real emancipation—often to radical democratic movements, and even more often to socialism, which rejected nationalism and was, in principle, internationalist.

Unlike the early nineteenth-century noble-gentry intelligentsia, this was a new, modern layer, but it still displayed the Central and Eastern European legacy of prophetic public intellectuals with missionary zeal. Around the turn of the century, various types of mass leaders emerged. Charismatic politicians, the Czechs Tomáš Masarýk and Edvard Beneš, both modern intellectuals, the Hungarian Mihály Károlyi, an aristocrat turned democrat and later socialist, and Oszkár Jászi, an emancipated baptized Jewish intellectual, were uncompromising democrats who, after the war, formulated the futures of their countries. Peasant teachers such as the Romanian Ion Mihalache and the young Hungarian teacher Dezső Szabó became advocates of populism. Two Bulgarian schoolteachers, Damian Gruev and Gotse Delchev, founders of the Internal Macedonian Revolutionary Organization (IMRO), were leading nationalist leaders. The history professor Nicolae Iorga, the economics professor Alexandru Cuza, and the poet Octavian Goga, modern intellectuals partly educated in France and Germany, became the initiators, ideologues, and organizers of right-wing populist movements in Romania. Several leaders of the left-wing socialists in Poland and Hungary were Jewish intellectuals, including the legendary Rosa Luxemburg, Leon Jogiches-Tyszko, and Felix Kon, as well as Ernő Garami, Manó Buchinger, Jenő Varga, and Béla Kún. Déclassé gentry-turned-intellectuals also played a role. The Pole Ludwik Wariński, one of the founders of the first Polish workers' organization, and Constantin Stere, the father of Romanian populism, came from such families.

Whereas in the age of romantic nationalism, the gentry intelligentsia had been missionaries of nationalism, the new intelligentsia called for an end to authoritarianism and the promotion of democracy; real emancipation of the peasants by parceling out the large estates and granting them equal political rights; and the liberation of workers from bourgeois exploitation through international solidarity and socialist revolution. Wild, xenophobic right-wing populists offered other alternatives, substituting foreign capital and domestic Jewry for the class enemy, but were, however, just as romantic as their early nationalist counterparts and ready to meet their fates fulfilling their mission.

Political anti-Semitism emerged in the late nineteenth century as part of rising ethno-cultural, xenophobic nationalism. Its main argument focused on the role of Jews in the modern economy: their domination in banking and industry, their role and "overrepresentation" in trade, business, and intellectual occupations. The main argument was that a Jewish conspiracy was undermining the nation. Although political anti-Semitism replaced medieval religious anti-Semitism and looked on the Jews not as a religion but as an alien nation, it also used the arsenal of traditional religious anti-Semitism. One of the most interesting connections between the two was the explosion of a ritual murder mania, the medieval blood libel, during the 1880s and 1890s. In 1882, the dramatic Tiszaeszlár ritual murder accusation and trial in Hungary fostered a whole series of similar accusations. "The Jews need blood for their *challah* bread," a placard in Mladá Vožice in the Czech lands proclaimed. In 1891, a ritual murder was reported from Corfu, and next year from Xanten, in the Prussian Rhineland. The Kolín case in 1893 and the Hilsner case in 1899 in the Czech lands generated a "small industry of anti-Semitic, propagandistic literature." In all these cases, Jews were accused of murdering young Christian girls, often servants of Jewish families, around Jewish holy days to take their blood for the special holy day bread. These accusations could mobilize the mob and "added important psychological dimensions to the [anti-Semitic] rhetoric . . . Jews were not only stranglers of the nation but also sexual predators and murderers in a literal sense" (Kieval 2001, 183–87, 197). The revival of traditional religious anti-Semitism heralded the era of a new political anti-Semitism.

One of the first signs of political change and the opening of a new era was the rise of a self-conscious peasantry. It happened after long decades of political marginalization when the peasant majority of the population had neither political organizations nor representation. Peasant parties and movements were formed around the end of the century throughout Central and Eastern Europe. The demand for a second and full emancipation of the peasantry suddenly filled the air. The emancipation of the peasantry began in literature, in accord with the zeitgeist at the turn of the century. The Polish Nobel laureate Władisław Reymont's *The Peasants* created the first peasant literary heroes at the turn of the century. With its detailed description of peasant customs, rituals, family life, and work, it was also a perfect encyclopedia of peasant life. The book was translated into all European languages and played an important role in the literary emancipation of the peasantry. With Zsigmond Móricz's early twentieth-century novel *Sárarany,* Hungary's rebellious, oppressed landless peasants, living a life of Asiatic backwardness in their villages, entered Hungarian literature. The energetic hero, Dani Túri, seeks to help his fellow peasants get land. Although he exhibits genuine, mythic strength, he inevitably succumbs to the brutality of a barbaric world (Szabolcsi 1965, 166–67).

Endre Ady, the leading and most influential prophet-poet of early twentieth-century Hungary, called himself "grandson of György Dózsa," the sixteenth-century leader of the Hungarian peasant revolt. Ady warned about a bloody revolution:

> The summer is hot and the scythe cuts straight.
> Ah, you landlords . . . what will happen if Dózsa's vagabond people
> should spill over in angry, menacing might?
>
> (Makkai 1996, 403–4)

Early twentieth-century Central and Eastern European modern music also discovered the peasantry. The Czech-Moravian Leoš Janáček composed his first opera, *Janůfa,* in 1903, using Moravian peasant speech and folk song, and launched a musical war against traditional harmony with dissonance and broken melodies. Folk song also became the basis for the revolutionary new music of Béla Bartók, who, together with Zoltán Kodály, collected peasant songs. The publication of their *Hungarian Folk-Songs* in 1906 established their theory of peasant music. Bartók used the Asian pentatonic structure of genuine Hungarian folk music as the first, pentatonic theme of his opera *A kékszakállú herceg vára* (Bluebeard's Castle). Genuine peasant music, without variety of rhythm, without ornamentation or dynamic changes, became the music of revolt (Frigyesi 1988, 72, 253).

Literature and music exhibited a new intellectual responsibility for and a new way of thinking about the peasantry. This new trend clearly expressed the rising of the masses. The previously immobile and passive peasantry stepped onto the political stage with elemental strength. In Romania, Constantin Dobrescu-Argeş, a young teacher in Muntenia, initiated and organized public lectures, evening courses, established libraries, village cooperatives, and credit banks for peasants. His *ţărănism,* or political peasantism, opened a new chapter in Romanian history. In 1880, he also established a peasant committee, and the next year, a weekly journal, *Ţărănul* (Peasant). His activity led to the foundation of the first Partida Ţărănească (Peasant party) in 1895. Although this party was soon disbanded, the peasant movement gained ground. One of its main advocates was Spiru Haret's influential journal *Sămănătorul* (1901), which mobilized schoolteachers and promoted self-help activities in villages. Sămănătorism became an important movement in the country.

Poporanismul (*popor* means people) also emerged as a mass movement, advocated mostly by teachers and lower-middle-class people, and soon turned to right-wing populism. The adherents condemned Westernization and capitalist transformation, industrial development, and "nonproductive" trade in Romania and worked to preserve the country's peasant character. The influential populist leader Constantin Stere dreamed of a future Romania of smallholders. Born into a Bessarabian landowning family, Stere was deported to Siberia, then settled in Romania and became one of the leading advocates of the cause of the peasantry. In *Viaţa Româneasca,* Stere published excellent analyses of the situation of the peasant who "sells his labor at famine prices and pays an exorbitant rate for his land," and whose "condition is increasingly miserable." Stere saw improving the situation of the peasantry as the only way to preserve traditional Romanian values, which he claimed were undermined and endangered by the "plundering capital" of "parasite Jews." Populism was strongly mixed with anti-Semitism and xenophobia.

Populism was also strongly represented by peasant intellectuals, one of whose most important organizations was the Teachers' Association, which in 1913 elected the radical populist Ion Mihalache as its president. In 1906, Alexandru Vălescu and Vasile Kogălniceanu founded a new Peasant party. The masses had made their appearance in Romanian politics.

Peasant movements and riots also flooded Hungary during the 1890s. The landless pick-and-shovel men of the south Hungarian Orosháza organized a socialist association and celebrated May Day. The local authorities used the gendarmerie to disperse the demonstration, and over a hundred peasants were killed or wounded by gunfire. The next day, in nearby Békéscsaba, the army suppressed an actual uprising, and martial law was introduced. In June, Csanád County became the scene of a major riot, and again army units killed and wounded peasants. The wave of riots was finally quelled in September, after more than three months of skirmishes. A major trial imprisoned 112 peasants, 93 of them landless. "Peasant socialism" spread like wildfire in the Great Plain area. In 1893, a reading association was founded in Hódmezövásárhely, which organized a gathering in February 1894. The authorities reacted with force, and the charismatic peasant leader János Szántó Kovács was arrested. When the peasants attacked the city hall, the cavalry was used against them. In the trial that followed, twenty-seven peasant leaders were sentenced to thirty-seven years' imprisonment. The next year, a similar riot exploded in Szeged.

In the summer of 1897, a well-organized harvest strike of 15,000 peasants swept through fourteen counties in the Great Plain and trans-Danube area. Several atrocities, brutal gendarmerie actions, and bloodshed mobilized the peasants. This movement led to the formation of a landless-peasant-workers' party, the Független Szocialista Párt (Independent Socialist party) in 1897 by István Várkonyi, who was expelled from the Social Democratic party. Spontaneous movements sprang up to parcel out large estates in Nyírkalász, Mándok, and Gyüre. In the winter and spring of 1898, peasant uprisings erupted around the country. The government retaliated brutally. István Várkonyi was arrested and his newspaper was banned. By year's end, the country had been pacified (Hanák 1988, 135–37, 144–47, 190–96).

Peasant movements, populist organizations, peasant parties, and strikes were launched throughout the region. In partitioned Poland, the first peasant party, the Zwiazek Stronnictwo Chłopskiego (Union of Peasants party), appeared in Galicia in 1893. Two years later, the Polskie Stronnictwo Ludowe, a Polish populist party, began to liberate uneducated peasants from the patronage of the clergy. At their Rzeszów Conference in 1903, the populists demanded universal and equal balloting. Their social and economic demands were rather moderate, however, and their influence was limited. Most peasants were influenced by Dmowski's national slogans, and the more active landed peasants shared conservative principles.

In eastern Galicia, however, the rising political awareness of the peasantry was clearly exhibited by a widespread agricultural strike of Ukrainian and Polish farmhands in 1902 (Wandycz 1974, 279, 294–95).

Large estates did not exist in post-1878 Bulgaria, because the Ottoman estates had been parceled out among peasants in an egalitarian fashion. Partly because most of them were tiny and partly because farming methods remained medieval, Balkan poverty plots were, however, unable to support peasant families adequately. In 1899, after several bad harvests, the government introduced a new tax in kind. The 10 percent tax increase was the last straw: riots fanned out across the Bulgarian countryside. The Radoslavov government used the army, which killed several rebels. The turbulent end of the century led to the formation of the most important political organization of the peasantry, the Blgarski Zemedelski Naroden Sojuz, or Agrarian Union. In a few years, the highly energetic and talented Aleksandur Stamboliski became the leader of the party, which would be a decisive factor in postwar Bulgaria (Jelavich and Jelavich 1977, 194).

Throughout rural, peasant Central and Eastern Europe, the bulk of the peasantry, still uneducated and under the influence of landlords and the Church, remained passive or joined the nationalist camp. Significant peasant masses, first of all landless farmhands, but also well-to-do farmers, peasant intellectuals, and especially teachers, established the first political peasant parties and organized revolutionary populist movements, national demonstrations, and strikes, resulting in conflict with the gendarmerie and army.

The emerging politicized peasantry were, however, unable to influence prewar Central and Eastern European politics as yet. Nonetheless, their rise and activities heralded the future of the region. The mobilized peasantry became the mass base of revolutionary radicalism in various countries of the region, whose successful twentieth-century revolutions led either to left-wing dictatorships or bolstered right-wing populist movements. The deep disappointment and rebellion of the peasants fueled extremism on both the left and the right. It was World War I, however, that literally mobilized the peasants, armed them, taught them to fight in a disciplined way, and, above all, gave them the experience and euphoric feeling of strength in an organized struggle.

The peasantry dominated the societies of agricultural Central and Eastern Europe. A semisuccessful industrialization, however, created a few big industrial centers and rapidly growing cities. Turn-of-the-century Central and Eastern European realist literature discovered not only the peasantry but also the urban masses and their poverty. Writing under the pen name "B. Prus," Alexander Głowacki, a member of the great Polish realist trio, presented an authentic picture of Polish middle-class and professional life in his Dickensian descriptions of Warsaw. The Croats Ante Kovačić and Venceslav Novak and the Slovene Janko Kersnik also introduced social problems into South Slav literature. Village and small-town life are portrayed in Bora Stanković's 1911 Serbian realist novel *Nečista Krv* (Impure Blood).

The capital cities, with their industrial workers and modern middle-class population, with a new, modern intellectual layer and cosmopolitan fabric, were fertile soil for a fast-growing socialist movement. In Poland, even the socialist organizations were born out of the national struggle. Émigré "Reds," radical veterans of the 1863–64 insurrection, founded the International Workers' Association in London. Two generals of the uprising, Jarosław Dąbrowski and Walery Wróblewski, participated in the Paris Commune. The latter became a friend of Karl Marx and the Polish delegate to the General Council of the First International. Marxist theories spread in Poland. The first socialist circles and trade unions were established in Galicia, and the first organized strikes hit Poznań in 1872. As the imperial Chancellery's Third Section (the political police responsible for the security of the tsar) declared in the summer of 1873: "The Kingdom of Poland more than any other constitutes a favorable ground for the International." The members of the first socialist groupings were mostly students, but Ludwik Waryński established the first workers' organization in 1876. After a forced escape to Galicia, he returned to Warsaw and established the first socialist party, the Proletariat, in 1882. The internationalist character of the party immediately led to the foundation—by Bolesław Limanowski—of a rival, patriotic workers' organization, the Polish People. The dichotomy between the internationalist and patriotic wings of the Polish labor movement marked the nineteenth-century socialist movement in the country.

The first mass strikes of several thousand workers in Żyrardów, Lodz, and Warsaw in 1883 were suppressed by military force, which killed three and wounded fifteen people. Hundreds of arrests followed, and in January 1886, the first Polish socialists were hanged at the Warsaw citadel.

A major breakthrough and the foundation of the Social Democratic party occurred in 1892. Galician and Silesian Polish socialists founded the Polish Social Democratic party of Galicia and Silesia in Lwów, while four small socialist groups in Paris founded the Polish Socialist party (PPS) of Russian Poland. Its program applied the Erfurt program of the German socialists but also demanded independence and advocated the education of workers to elevate their class and national consciousness. Social justice and national independence became twins in the program of the PPS. The next year, an internationalist group, headed by Ignacy Daszyński and Rosa Luxemburg, harshly confronted the "social patriots," split off, and founded the Social Democratic party of the kingdom of Poland (SDKP). This party accepted the "organic incorporation" of Poland (with territorial autonomy) into the Russian state and argued for close collaboration with the Russian socialists for constitutional democracy and workers' rights, followed by proletarian revolution. The party had a limited base in Lithuania and Warsaw, while the PPS dominated the socialist movement in the Polish kingdom. The PPS's emerging charismatic leader, Jósef Piłsudski, rejected strikes, incorporated the tradition of insurrection and terrorist activities into the movement, and considered Russia the main enemy of the Polish people. The PPS, or at least a part of it, under Piłsudski's leadership, rapidly shifted toward a nationalist program. Confrontation became unavoidable during the revolutionary crisis of 1905–6.

Although the PPS refused to participate in a series of strikes and a May Day demonstration in 1904, a revolutionary wave emerged in Warsaw, Lodz, Radom, and other industrial centers, which culminated in a general strike in January 1905, accompanied by major demonstrations against autocracy and in favor of a democratic republic and workers' rights. A civil war was in the making. May Day demonstrations turned into a riot in 1905, unleashing the bloodiest confrontation between organized socialist workers, the authorities, and rightist groups, which organized pogroms. Dmowski's National Democratic party organized its National Workers' Association into squads, which frequently clashed with Piłsudski's socialists. More than a hundred people were killed. On June 22–23, barricades were built in Lodz, and a three-day street fight took several hundred victims. In November, a renewed fight led to the introduction of martial law.

The revolutionaries were exhausted, and the movement declined after 1906. Piłsudski's "permanent insurrectionist" faction was isolated within the PPS, which, at its eighth congress in Lwów in 1906 condemned this strategy and returned to the concept of social revolution in an autonomous Poland. Piłsudski's military organization was expelled from the party in November, and he gradually distanced himself from socialism. In 1908, he formed the Union of Active Resistance and began preparing his cadres for a coming armed national uprising (Dziewanowski 1959, 4–5, 11–49).

Strong labor movements grew up all over Central and Eastern Europe.

The Austrian socialist movement became the cradle of similar movements throughout the monarchy. The first workers' associations, self-help and educational groups, including the important Arbeiterbildungsverein, were established between 1848 and the 1860s. A mass demonstration of 20,000 in Vienna in 1869 clearly exhibited the strength of the rising movement. In 1874, the Congress of Neudörfl established the Sozialdemokratische Partei Österreich. As an answer to violent demonstrations and actions, a state of emergency was introduced in 1884, and more than 300 workers were expelled from Vienna. Antisocialist legislation (the anarchist law of 1886) and strong police pressure led to a split between moderates and radicals, but the party was reorganized and united by Viktor Adler and Karl Kautsky, the author of the party program at the Heinfeld Congress in December 1888–January 1889.

The Austrian Social Democratic party emerged as a real political force. From the outset, it had been a multiethnic Cis-Leithanian organization, and Czech socialists had participated in its foundation and work, but in 1878, seven distinctly autonomous national sections—German, Czech, Croat, Slovene, Italian, Polish, and Ukrainian—were created within it. Directed by a federal executive and a joint parliamentary faction, the Czech section of the party had 20,000 members in 1906. In 1913, this figure rose to 31,000, while the nearly half million strong Austrian trade unions included 70,000 Czech members. The separatist Czech Trade Union, additionally, counted more than 107,000 members (Macartney 1968, 684, 797). Major strikes were jointly organized throughout the industrial regions of Austria and Bohemia during the 1890s. Although the party's Brünn (Brno) program called for a solution to the nationality problem and demanded territorial autonomy for the various nationalities in 1899, its Czech branch gradually broke away and eventually became the Czech Social Democratic party in 1911.

The first Hungarian workers' organization, the Általános Munkásegylet (General Workers' Association) was modeled on Ferdinand Lassalle's German movement immediately after the Ausgleich, in February 1868. Marxist socialism, however, was a child of the Second International, founded in Paris on July 14, 1889, followed by a gathering of Austrian and Hungarian socialists in Pozsony (Bratislava) in September. This led to the foundation of the Magyarországi Szociáldemokrata Párt and the celebration of the first May Day in 1890. This party was so heavily under the tutelage of the Austrian party and so internationalist that its Declaration of Principles, a kind of party program, repeated the general slogans of the European socialist movement without even mentioning the most crucial social and political issues in Hungary, the agrarian and national questions.

In the early twentieth century, however, social democracy became a significant political factor in Hungary. In 1906, the number of unionized workers—only 10,000 in 1901—reached 130,000, and 200,000 workers participated in the nationwide strikes of 1907. The party daily, *Népszava,* had a circulation of 25,000. The party also published various local weeklies, and its theoretical periodical, *Szocializmus,* organized and educated rank-and-file socialists. Police terror against the socialist movement became an everyday phenomenon from the end of the nineteenth century on: between the summer of 1897 and 1899, more than 300 meetings were banned, one-third of the local organizations were abolished, 51 workers were killed, and 300 were sentenced to a total of 178 years imprisonment (Hanák 1988, 107–8, 206–7). Oppression strengthened the movement, however, and became a motivating factor after 1906. In May 1912, a general strike and demonstration called in support of the parliamentary struggle of the opposition clearly exhibited the strength of the Social Democratic party: a hundred thousand people demonstrating in Budapest were attacked by the police, who killed six (Erényi 1988, 674, 825–27). The poet Endre Ady wrote a poem dedicated to the socialist leader Ernő Garami entitled "We Are Running toward a Revolution!"

The international labor movement strongly influenced even the unindustrialized Balkan countries. The first workers' organizations appeared in Romania in the 1880s, and Constantine Dobrogeanu-Gherea spread Marxist theories. The Romanian Social Democratic party was founded in 1893 but dissolved in 1899. The socialist unions gained ground in 1907, however, and the party was reorganized under the leadership of the radical Christian Rakovski in 1910 (Niculae 1993).

The father of the Bulgarian socialist movement, Dimitur Blagoev, led in the founding of the Bulgarian Social Democratic party in 1891 and launched a struggle for comprehensive nationalization of private property, "from the biggest machine to the tailor's needle." Ianko Sakazov's "Broads," who advocated daily struggle for better working conditions and an alliance with the peasantry, opposed Blagoev's "Narrow" wing. From the 1890s on, strikes were organized, including a major railroad strike in 1907. Socialists became members of the parliament between 1899 and 1902, and, in 1913, thirty-seven socialist representatives were voted in. However, before the war, membership in the socialist-organized unions was less than 10,000, mostly teachers and white-collar workers.

The Serbian Social Democratic party was established in 1903, but attracted only a few hundred people. Just before the war, it still had fewer than three thousand members (Jelavich and Jelavich 1977, 204–5).

The socialist workers' movement put down strong roots in Central and

Eastern Europe. The workers' struggle for political rights and better working conditions established them as an important political force. Among
the socialist rank and file, small but important radical groupings emerged
with revolutionary programs and a readiness to fight the ruling regimes.
Like contemporary peasant movements and parties, they had only limited
influence at the time, but in a few countries of the region, these workers'
organizations were the seeds of revolt that, in the fertile soil of desperation at the end of the war, gave rise to revolution.

WORLD WAR I

EXPANSIONIST PLANS AND CONFLICTS in the "age of empire" (Hobs-bawm 1987) between 1870 and 1914 led to bloody confrontations between the main players. According to Cecil Rhodes's characterization of this epoch, "expansion was everything." J. A. Hobson spoke of the "conscious policy of imperialism" (Hobson [1905] 1938, 19). The two rival groups had been formed and prepared by the 1880s. The overture to an international war—the Bosnian crisis and the two Balkan wars—sent repercussions through the explosive Balkans, the dangerous "powder keg" of Europe. That area was actually the topic of discussion between Wilhelm II, emperor of Germany, and Archduke Franz Ferdinand, heir apparent of the aging emperor of Austria-Hungary, in the Bohemian Kanopíště after a long hunting party on June 4, 1914. They agreed to arrange provocative military exercises by the Austro-Hungarian army in Bosnia near the Serbian border. Franz Ferdinand arrived in Sarajevo in his general's uniform to participate in the maneuvers on June 28. The events that followed are well known: as Franz Ferdinand rode to a festive reception in an open car, a young Bosnian Serb nationalist, Gavrilo Princip, who belonged to a terrorist organization, known as the Black Hand, that sought to prevent a "trialist" reorganization of Austria-Hungary and espoused the dream of a Greater Serbia, assassinated the archduke and his wife.

The murder was an excellent excuse to begin the long-awaited showdown. On July 6, Wilhelm II, via Ambassador Szögyén-Marich, urged Austria-Hungary to act and, at the Potsdam meeting of the war council, ordered the German army on alert. The next day, a joint session of the Austrian and Hungarian cabinets decided to send an ultimatum that was clearly unacceptable to Serbia. The plan worked. On July 28, Emperor Franz Josef entered the study of his Bad Ischl hunting lodge. The future of Europe was hammered out in this small, 15- by 30-foot room, where he sat at his corner desk between two windows—surveyed by a bust of his dead wife, "Sisi," the empress Elisabeth, at the age of fifteen—and signed a declaration of war. Within three days, Wilhelm II had mobilized the German army.

The origins of the war were, however, much more complex, and seeking to explain them is far beyond the scope of this book. "A reader who commanded a knowledge of the main European languages could spend a lifetime on the books and articles which have been produced on the subject without getting near to the end; and the stream shows no sign of drying up," Philip Bell observed (Hayes 1992, 106).

The outbreak of the war, whatever the explanation, was a watershed. It was greeted with euphoria in Europe. Most people believed in the purifying effect of war and regarded it as a vehicle of renewal. Wilhelm II declared proudly that he no longer knew parties, but only Germans, and spoke of the "liberation and blessing" of the war, which broke down the barriers separating social classes. Most of the social democratic parties and the masses shared his view. "European culture is fighting against Russian barbarism," the Hungarian Social Democratic party proclaimed, exhorting its members to participate enthusiastically (*Népszava* 1914). The war seemed like a carnival, a great experience, and everybody believed it would end in a few months. The troops would return, Franz Josef said, "before the trees have shed their leaves."

The German military machine thought so too and planned a blitzkrieg, as it was later called. The essence of the Schlieffen Plan was a well-prepared, sudden attack against France, via Belgium, as fast as lightning, to knock France out first, and then turn against slow-moving Russia to win the war in two brief campaigns. This plan, however, failed in the fall of 1914. The German troops were held at the river Marne, about forty miles from Paris, as early as September, and an Anglo-French counterattack caused tremendous German losses. Instead of a rapid advance, trench warfare followed. The Germans were deadlocked in the west. Both sides dug endless trenches between the Swiss border and the English Channel. Along the French front line of about 270 miles, there were 6,250 miles of trenches— a front line, a second line of support trenches, and a third reserve trench. Both sides made several attempts to break through. All these attempts failed and made the western front a slaughterhouse, especially at Verdun, where 800,000 men died, and on the Somme River, where the British lost 400,000 and the Germans 200,000.

The eastern front was in permanent movement but without a decisive victory. A Russian offensive at the beginning of the war was successful, and Austria-Hungary nearly collapsed, but a German counteroffensive pushed the Russians back, conquering Poland. Austria-Hungary was more successful against Serbia and Romania but was deadlocked on the Italian front. The losses were shocking.

The interminable war offered some hope for Germany in 1917–18: the Russian revolution and armistice made possible a major regrouping of the German army and a decisive new offensive in the west. In February 1918, 3.7 million German soldiers, 44,000 big guns, and 3,670 airplanes attempted to break through the Allied front between Arras and Le Fère. The Entente, however, gathered 5 million soldiers, 4,500 airplanes, and 800 tanks and caused 1 million losses for the Germans. In July, an Allied counteroffensive ended the German endeavor. The last German offensive in early July on the Reims-Marne front also collapsed.

The temporary success of the Central Powers on the Italian front at Caporetto in 1917 was followed by the disaster at Piave in June 1918. Austria-Hungary lost 150,000 men and virtually collapsed; 2,100,000 of its soldiers and 55,000 officers were already in Russian POW camps. That summer, the number of deserters from the army reached 800,000.

The populations of the defeated countries lost hope and patience. Intellectuals and artists revolted against the war and the regimes that had initiated it. The Romanians Tristan Tzara and Marcel Janko left the country in protest and, with other artists, established the Dada movement in neutral Switzerland. Nihilist Dada, as Tzara interpreted it, was "a private guerrilla war" against the irrational reality of war-ridden Europe. Dadaist poetry, Tzara explained, reflected a world in which "words should not be believed . . . [because] they express the opposite . . . [of what they should mean, in a world where] lies circulate" (Tzara 1959, 295). The Hungarian Lajos Kassák, with László Moholy-Nagy, Victor Vasarely, and others, founded the avant-garde artists' circles *Tett* (Deed) and then *Ma* (Today) during the war. "The artist and writer," Kassák wrote, "will again be worker among workers and fighter among fighters." They protested not only "against the war, but against the society that tolerated such a war, and against an art that had its source in such a society" (Kassák 1972, 243). Desperate masses protested through strikes and often occupied the streets. In January 1918, half a million workers staged a strike in Berlin. In the same month, 700,000 workers struck in Vienna, and 100,000 people demonstrated in Budapest. The strikes spread to Bohemia and Galicia. In May, the Serb soldiers of the Sixth Infantry Regiment of the Austro-Hungarian army retreated from the front and began an armed uprising in the southern Hungarian city of Pécs. Hungarian miners joined in.

In the early fall of 1918, after the last failed offensives, it became evident that the Central Powers could not survive another winter, and their military and political leaders were forced to accept the impossibility of continuing the war. The decision was reached on September 27, 1918, in Vienna, and on September 29 in Berlin, and both the German and the Austro-Hungarian governments requested an armistice on October 4. On October 17, István Tisza, prime minister of Hungary at the beginning of the war, the embodiment of the old regime, told the parliament tersely: "The war is lost!" On the last day of that month, two military vehicles stopped in front of Tisza's house; four soldiers went in, and, after a brief, furious argument, shot and killed him. A German revolution dethroned the Hohenzollern dynasty and the Kaiser left the country.

The Great War was a unique historical event. It was the first war in which trucks, tanks, airplanes, and modern submarines were used, and in which the industrial capacity and technological preparedness of the countries influenced the outcome of battles. The human cost was incredible. Twenty-five percent of the 1891–95 French cohort was killed, altogether 1.4 million Frenchmen. Nearly 2 million Germans, 1.7 million Russians, 1.2 million Austrian-Hungarians, and nearly 0.8 million British died. During the five years of the war, 8 million people in all lost their lives, twice as many as in all previous conflicts between 1789 and 1914 (Graham 1998, 104). The victors were bankrupt, and the losers were on the brink of final collapse.

Noting that wars were usually not fought to the death or to total exhaustion, Eric Hobsbawm rightly asks: "Why was the First World War waged by the leading powers on both sides as a zero-sum game [i.e., as a war that could only be totally won or totally lost]?" The reason, he argues, was "that this war . . . was waged for unlimited ends . . . global political and maritime" power. "It was an absurd and self-defeating aim, which ruined both victors and vanquished" (Hobsbawm 1994, 29–30). Moreover, it destroyed the European community of nations and the structure of nineteenth-century European civilization. Hannah Arendt speaks of the "weird atmosphere of a Strindbergian family quarrel," of a "pervasive hatred of everybody and everything," and of an atmosphere of disintegration (Arendt 1966, 268). "Europe and large parts of Asia and Africa became one vast battlefield on which after years of struggle not armies but nations broke and ran," Winston Churchill noted after the war. "When all was over, Torture and Cannibalism were the only two expedients that the civilized, scientific, Christian States had been able to deny themselves: and they were of doubtful utility" (quoted by Johnson 1983, 13–14).

The war spectacularly closed the "long" nineteenth century, because it destroyed all the pillars of its world system. "Nineteenth-century civilization," Karl Polanyi writes, "rested on four institutions. The first was the balance-of-power system, which for a century prevented the occurrence of any long and devastating war between the Great Powers. The second was the international gold standard, which symbolized a unique organization of world economy. The third was the self-regulated market, which produced unheard-of material welfare. The fourth was the liberal state" (Polanyi [1944] 1964, 3). All these stable and interrelated institutions collapsed as a consequence of the war.

Along with the nineteenth-century European system, the entirety of the old Central and Eastern Europe exploded and submerged. As had rarely happened before in history, all the conflicts, internal and international, unsolved national-minority and social problems, exploded together and slashed the old empires and societies to pieces. The masses, previously unable to realize or even articulate their interests and demands, disenfranchised, deprived of the use of their mother tongue, and forced to cultivate their masters' land, became masters of their own destiny. The horror of the war offered important lessons and educated the masses. They learned about their strength acting together. They learned to organize and use weapons. Violence became the order of the day. In this chaotic situation, former members of minority elites, Tomáš Masarýk, Edvard Beneš, Iuliu Maniu, and Józef Piłsudski, peasant advocates such as Ion Mihalache and Alexander Stamboliski, workers' leaders such as Rosa Luxemburg and Béla Kún, quite a few of them outlaws, persecuted, arrested, or forced to emigrate a few years earlier, now took over. Those who were able to address the masses from one day to the next became masters of the situation. They were elevated by the rising masses, and they elevated the masses. The dream of an independent nation-state, unrealistic in the shadow of huge, invincible empires, was suddenly realized. From the North Sea to the Adriatic, a series of national revolutions reestablished independent nation-states in place of huge multiethnic empires. Poland was reunited and, together with the Baltic states, became independent. The vision of Greater Romania was realized, and new state formations, which had never existed before, such as Czechoslovakia and Yugoslavia, were easily forged together by active national elites and happily recognized by the victorious great powers. The dissolution of the empires left a rump Turkey, Austria, and Hungary in place of the Ottoman empire and Austria-Hungary. The dreams of land reform, of a just society and equal rights for all, unrealistic in the petrified old social-political structures, seemed to be within reach. Minorities, national and social alike, successfully revolted against oppressive majorities. National and social revolutions engulfed the entire region and sparked national and social euphoria. The crisis culminated in the Bolshevik revolution in Russia and the formation of workers' and peasant governments in Hungary and Bulgaria.

Although most of the social revolutions were suppressed, and various nineteenth-century institutions were reestablished, nineteenth-century Central and Eastern Europe, as contemporaries knew it, had come to an end. A new Central and Eastern Europe, transformed by successful national revolutions, emerged in the transitory power vacuum. "Recent political evolution has been favorable to the small peoples," Masarýk said confidently; "in a new Europe . . . the independence of even the smallest national individuality can be safeguarded" (Masarýk 1927, 371). All of the newly independent countries turned to protectionism and import substitution to achieve rapid industrialization. Quite a few introduced new constitutions to establish democracies. Like the war euphoria of a few years earlier, however, the national and revolutionary euphoria soon faded, along with national independence and economic and social modernization. In Central and Eastern Europe, the new era failed to open a new chapter of development and catching up with the West: instead, decades of crises followed (Berend 1998).

BIBLIOGRAPHY

Adanir, Fikret. 1989. "Tradition and Rural Change in Southeastern Europe during Ottoman Rule." In *The Origins of Backwardness in Eastern Europe,* ed. Daniel Chirot. Berkeley and Los Angeles: University of California Press.

Anderson, Benedict. 1983. *Imagined Communities: Reflections on the Origin and Spread of Nationalism.* London: Verso.

Andorka, Rudolf. 1978. *Determinants of Fertility in Advanced Societies.* London: Methuen.

———. 1994. "The Historical Demography of a Proper Hungarian Village: Atány in the Eighteenth and Nineteenth Centuries." *Journal of Family History* 19, no. 4.

Antologija srpske narodne epike Kosova i Metohije. 1974. Priština: Jedinstvo.

Appleby, Joyce, Lynn Hunt, and Margaret Jacob. *Telling the Truth about History.* New York: Norton, 1995.

Arany, János. 1914. *Toldi; Toldi's Eve; Ballads; Selected Lyrics.* Translated by William N. Loew. New York: Co-operative Press.

Arató, Endre. 1960. *A nemzetiségi kérdés története Magyarországon, 1790–1840.* Budapest: Akadémiai Kiadó.

———. 1971. *Kelet-Europa története a 19. század első felében.* Budapest: Akadémiai Kiadó.

Arendt, Hannah. 1966. *The Origins of Totalitarianism.* Cleveland: World Publishing Co.

Armengaud, André. 1973. "Population in Europe, 1700–1914." In *The Fontana Economic History of Europe,* vol. 3: *The Industrial Revolution,* ed. Carlo Cipolla. London: Collins/Fontana Books.

Armengaud, André, and Marcel R. Reinhard. 1961. *Histoire générale de la population mondiale.* Paris: Éditions Montchrestien.

Axenciuc, Victor. 1995. *Banca Natională României, 1880–1995.* Bucharest: Enciclopedică.

———. 1996. *Evoluția economica a României. Cercetări statistice-istorice (1859–1947).* Vol. 2. Bucharest: Academiei Române.

Az Életképek (1846–1848). 1970. Edited by Anna Tamás. Budapest: Akadémiai Kiadó.

Bahlcke, Joachim. 2000. "The Construction of the Past: Conception of History, the Formation of Tradition and Self-Representation in the Societies of Orders of East-Central Europe, 1500–1800." *German History* (London) 18, no. 2.

Bairoch, Paul. 1973. "European Foreign Trade in the Nineteenth Century: The Development of the Value and Volume of Exports." *Journal of European Economic History* 2, no. 2.

———. 1976a. "Europe's Gross National Product, 1800–1975." *Journal of European Economic History* 5, no. 2.

———. 1976b. *Commerce extérieur et développement économique de l'Europe au XIXe siècle*. Paris: Mouton.

Balázs, Éva H. 1967. *Berzeviczy Gergely a reformpolitikus*. Budapest: Akadémiai Kiadó.

The Balkan Range: A Bulgarian Reader. 1976. Edited by John Robert Colombo and Nikola Roussanoff. Toronto: Hounslow Press.

Banac, Ivo. 1984. *The National Question in Yugoslavia: Origins, History, Politics*. Ithaca, N.Y.: Cornell University Press.

Barac, Antun. 1955. *A History of Yugoslav Literature*. Belgrade: Committee for Foreign Cultural Relations.

Bárczi, Géza. 1975. *A magyar nyelv életrajza*. Budapest: Gondolat.

Bartók, Béla. [1934] 1986. "Népzenénk és a szomszédos népek népzenéje." In *Helyünk Európában: Nézetek és koncepciók a 20. századi Magyarországon*, ed. Iván T. Berend and Éva Ring. Budapest: Magvető.

Bauer, Leonhard, and Herbert Matis. 1988. *Geburt der Neuzeit. Vom Feudalsystem zur Marktgesellschaft*. Munich: Deutscher Taschenbuch Verlag.

Benda, Gyula. 2000. "A halálozás és halandóság Keszthelyen, 1747–1849." In *K.S.H. Népességtudományi Kutatóintézetének 2000. évi történeti demográfiai évkönyve*, ed. T. Faragó and P. Őri. Budapest: Központi Statisztikai Hivatal.

Benda, Kálmán. 1983. "A magyar Jakobínus mozgalom (1792–1795)." In *Magyarország Története, 1790–1848*, ed. Gyula Mérei. Budapest: Akadémiai Kiadó.

Bényi, Miklós. 1972. *Eötvös József olvasmányai*. Budapest: Akadémiai Kiadó.

Berend, Ivan T. 1986. "The Historical Evolution of Eastern Europe as a Region." In *Power, Purpose, and Collective Choice*, ed. Ellen Comisso and Laura D'Andrea Tyson. Ithaca, N.Y.: Cornell University Press.

———. 1996. *Central and Eastern Europe, 1944–1993: Detour from the Periphery to the Periphery*. Cambridge: Cambridge University Press.

———. 1998. *Decades of Crisis: Central and Eastern Europe before World War II*. Berkeley and Los Angeles: University of California Press.

Berend, Iván T., and György Ránki. 1955. *Magyarország gyáripara, 1900–1914*. Budapest: Szikra Kiadó.

———. 1974. *Hungary: A Century of Economic Development*. Newton Abbot, U.K.: David & Charles; New York: Barnes & Noble.

———. 1979. *Underdevelopment and Economic Growth: Studies in Hungarian Social and Economic History*. Budapest: Akadémiai Kiadó.

———. 1982. *The European Periphery and Industrialization*. Cambridge: Cambridge University Press.

———. 1987. *Európa gazdasága a 19. században, 1780–1914.* Budapest: Gondolat Kiadó.

Berend, Iván T., and Miklós Szuhay. 1978. *A tőkés gazdaság története Magyarországon, 1848–1944.* Budapest: Kossuth Könyvkiadó.

Berlin, Isaiah, Sir. 1978. *Russian Thinkers.* Edited by Henry Hardy and Aileen Kelly. New York: Viking Press.

———. 1999. *The Roots of Romanticism.* Edited by Henry Hardy. The A. W. Mellon Lectures in the Fine Arts, Bollingen series, 45. Princeton, N.J.: Princeton University Press.

Berzsenyi, Dániel. 1938. *Ismeretlen és kiadatlan levelei.* Budapest: Magyar Tudományos Akadémia Irodalomtörténeti Bizottsága.

Bezruč, Petr. 1909 [1929]. *Silesian Songs.* In *An Anthology of Czechoslovak Literature,* ed. and trans. Paul Selver. London: Kegan Paul, Trench, Trubner.

Bibó, István. 1986. *Válogatott tanulmányok,* vol. 1: *1935–1944;* vol. 2: *1945–1949.* Budapest: Magvető Kiadó.

Bihiku, Koço. 1980. *A History of Albanian Literature.* Tirana: The "8 Näntori" Publishing House.

Blejwas, Stanisłaus A. 1984. *Realism in Polish Politics: Warsaw Positivism and National Survival in Nineteenth-Century Poland.* New Haven, Conn.: Yale Concilium on International Studies.

Bocşan, Nicolae. 1998. "Ideea de naţiune şi principul naţionalităţilor la A.C. Popovici." In *Studii Istorice. Omagiu profesorului Camil Mureşanu.* Cluj-Napoca, Romania: Presa Universitară Clujeană.

Bodea, Cornelia. 1998. *1848 la Români.* Vol. 3. Bucharest: Enciclopedică.

Bogucka, Maria. 1993. "Social Structures and Customs in Early Modern Poland." *Acta Poloniae Historica* (Warsaw), no. 68.

Botev, Hristo. 1976. *Selected Works.* Edited by Stefana Tarinska. Sofia: Sofia Press.

Bowman, Shearer Davis. 1993. *Masters and Lords: Mid-Nineteenth-Century U.S. Planters and Prussian Junkers.* New York: Oxford University Press.

Bradley, John F. N. 1984. *Czech Nationalism in the Nineteenth Century.* Boulder, Colo.: East European Monographs.

Braudel, Fernand. 1979. *Civilisation matérielle, économie et capitalisme: XVe–XVIIIe siècle.* 3 vols. Paris: A. Colin, 1979. Translated by Siân Reynolds as *Civilization and Capitalism, 15th–18th Century* (1982–84; reprint, Berkeley and Los Angeles: University of California Press, 1992).

Brenner, Robert. 1985. "Agrarian Class-Structure and Economic Development in Pre-Industrial Europe" and "The Agrarian Roots of Capitalism." In *The Brenner Debate,* ed. T. H. Aston and C. H. E. Philpin. Cambridge: Cambridge University Press.

Brkić, Jovan. 1961. *Moral Concepts in Traditional Serbian Epic Poetry.* The Hague: Mouton.

Brock, Peter. 1969. "Polish Nationalism." In *Nationalism in Eastern Europe,* ed. Ivo Lederer and Peter Sugar. Seattle: University of Washington Press.

———. 1972. *Nationalism and Populism in Partitioned Poland.* London: Orbis Books.

———. 1977. *Polish Revolutionary Populism: A Study in Agrarian Socialist Thought from the 1830s to the 1850s.* Toronto: University of Toronto Press.

———. 1984. *The Slovak National Awakening: An Essay in the Intellectual History of East Central Europe.* Toronto: University of Toronto Press.

———. 1992. *Folk Cultures and Little Peoples: Aspects of National Awakening in East Central Europe.* Boulder, Colo.: East European Monographs.

Brubaker, Rogers. 1992. *Citizenship and Nationhood in France and Germany.* Cambridge, Mass.: Harvard University Press.

Brusatti, Alois. 1973. "Die wirtschaftliche Entwicklung." In *Die Habsburgmonarchie, 1848–1918,* ed. Adam Wandruszka and Peter Urbanitsch. Vol. 1. Vienna: Verlag der österreichischen Akademie der Wissenschaften.

Cameron, Rondo. 1961. *France and the Economic Development of Europe, 1800–1914.* Princeton, N.J.: Princeton University Press.

Căpreanu, Ion. 1994. *Partide și idei politice în România (1880–1947).* Bucharest: Didactică și Pedagogică.

Cărăbis, Vasile. 1996. *Tudor Vladimirescu.* Târgu-Jiu: Spicon.

Chamerska, Halina. 1996. "Women of Petty Nobility in the Polish Kingdom during the Nineteenth Century." *Acta Poloniae Historica* (Warsaw), no. 74.

Cipolla, Carlo, ed. 1973. *The Emergence of Industrial Societies.* Vol. 4 of *The Fontana Economic History of Europe.* Part Two. London: Collins/Fontana Books.

———. 1994. *Before the Industrial Revolution: European Society and Economy, 1000–1700.* New York: Norton.

Cobden, Richard. 1994. *The European Diaries of Richard Cobden, 1846–1849.* Edited by Miles Taylor. Aldershot, U.K.: Scolar Press.

Cojocariu, Mihai. 1995. *Partida nationala si constituirea statului român, 1856–1859.* Iași, Romania: Editura Universității "Al. I. Cuza."

Coleman, Arthus Prudden. 1934. *The Polish Insurrection of 1863 in the Light of New York Editorial Opinion.* Williamsport, Penn.: Bayard Press.

Connelly, John. 1999. Review of *Decades of Crisis: Central and Eastern Europe before World War II,* by Ivan T. Berend (Berkeley and Los Angeles: University of California Press, 1998). *Journal of Economic History* 59, no. 4 (December): 1096–98.

Constantinescu, Nicolae N. 1960. *Contribuții la istoria capitalului strain in Rominia.* București: Institutul de Cercetări Economice.

Crisp, Olga. 1967. "Russia, 1860–1914." In *Banking in the Early Stages of Industrialization. A Study in Comparative Economic History,* ed. Rondo Cameron, Olga Crisp, Hugh T. Patrick, and Richard Tilly. New York: Oxford University Press.

Cynarski, Stanisław. 1974. "Sarmatyzm—ideologia i styl zycia." In *Polska 17 wieku.* Warsaw: Wiedza Powszechna.

Czap, Peter. 1983. "A Large Family: The Peasants' Greatest Wealth: Serf Households in Mishino, Russia, 1814–1858." In *Family Forms in Historic Europe,* ed. Richard Wall. Cambridge: Cambridge University Press.

Czigány, Lóránt. 1984. *The Oxford History of Hungarian Literature from the Earliest Times to the Present.* Oxford: Oxford University Press.

Dányi, Dezső. 1994. "Villein Housholds of the Palóc Population, 1836–1843." *Journal of Family History* 19, no. 4.

———. 2000. "A 19. század végi hazai belső vándorlás néhány jellemzője." In *K.S.H. Népességtudományi Kutatóintézetének 2000. évi történeti demográfiai évkönyve*, ed. T. Faragó and P. Őri. Budapest: Központi Statisztikai Hivatal.

Darnton, Robert. 1997. "Free Spirit." Review of *The Sense of Reality: Studies in Ideas and Their History*, by Sir Isaiah Berlin, edited by Henry Hardy (New York: Farrar, Straus & Giroux, 1997). *New York Review of Books* 44, no. 11 (June 26): 11.

David, Thomas, and Elizabeth Spilman. 1999. "From Proto-Economic Nationalism to Economic Nationalism: Eastern Europe, 1780–1940" (MS).

Davies, Norman. 1986. *Heart of Europe: A Short History of Poland*. Oxford: Oxford University Press.

———. 1996. *Europe: A History*. Oxford: Oxford University Press.

Deák, István. 1992. *Beyond Nationalism: A Social and Political History of the Habsburg Officer Corps, 1848–1918*. New York: Oxford University Press.

Dean, Philis, and W. A. Cole. 1967. *British Economic Growth, 1688–1959*. Cambridge: Cambridge University Press.

De Bellaigue, Christopher. 2001. "Turkey's Hidden Past." *New York Review of Books* 48, no. 4 (March 8).

Dobbs, Betty Jo Teeter, and Margaret C. Jacob. 1995. *Newton and the Culture of Newtonianism*. Atlantic Highlands, N.J.: Humanities Press.

Dogaru, Vladimir. 1982. *Eminescu, musician al poeziei, Enescu, poet al muzicii*. Bucharest: Editura Ion Creangă.

Dolmányos, István. 1988. "A koalíció kormányzásának első szakasza." In *Magyarország története, 1890–1918*, ed. Péter Hanák. Budapest: Akadémiai Kiadó.

Donskov, Andrew, and Richard Sokoloski, eds. 1992. *Slavic Drama: The Question of Innovation*. Ottawa: University of Ottawa.

Dordevic, Mihailo, comp. 1984. *Anthology of Serbian Poetry: The Golden Age*. New York: Philosophical Library.

Dziewanowski, M. K. 1959. *The Communist Party of Poland*. Cambridge, Mass.: Harvard University Press.

Eckhart, Ferenc. 1922. *A bécsi udvar gazdasági politikája Magyarországon Mária Terézia korában*. Budapest: Budavári Tudományos Társaság.

Eidelberg, Philip Gabriel. 1974. *The Great Rumanian Peasant Revolt of 1907: Origins of a Modern Jacquerie*. Leiden: E. J. Brill.

Einstein, Alfred. 1947. *Music in the Romantic Era*. New York: Norton.

Elsie, Robert. 1995. *History of Albanian Literature*. Vol. 1. Boulder, Colo.: Social Science Monographs.

Eötvös, József. 1902a. *A XIX. század uralkodó eszméinek befolyása az álladalomra*. Budapest: Révai Testvérek.

———. 1902b. *Tanulmányok*. Budapest: Révai Testvérek.

Erényi, Tibor. 1988. "A szocialista munkásmozgalom" and "Az ellenzéki küzdelem fellendülése." In *Magyarország története, 1890–1918*, ed. Péter Hanák. Budapest: Akadémiai Kiadó.

Ernle, Lord. 1925. "The Land and Its People." In *Agriculture and Economic Growth in England, 1650–1815*, ed. Eric L. Jones. London: Methuen.

Ewen, Frederic. 1984. *Heroic Imagination: The Creative Genius of Europe from Waterloo (1815) to the Revolution of 1848*. Secaucus, N.J.: Citadel Press.

Fabre, Jean, 1963. *Lumières et romantisme: Énergie et nostalgie de Rousseau á Mickiewicz*. Paris: C. Klincksieck .

Feis, Herbert. 1965. *Europe: The World's Banker, 1870–1914: An Account of Foreign Investment and the Connection of World Finance with Diplomacy before World War I*. New York: Norton.

Fellner, Frigyes. 1916. "Das Volkseinkommen Österreichs und Ungarns." *Statistische Monatschrift* (Vienna).

Fényes, Elek. 1847. *Magyarország ismertetése statisztikai, földirati és történelmi szempontból*. Pest: Beimel.

Fischer-Galati, Stephen. 1969. *The Socialist Republic of Rumania*. Baltimore: John Hopkins Press.

Flinn, Michael. 1966. *The Origins of the Industrial Revolution*. London: Longmans.

Florea, Vasile. 1984. *Romanian Art: Modern and Contemporary Ages*. Bucharest: Meridiane Publishing House.

Freifeld, Alice. 1999. "The De-Germanization of the Budapest Stage." *Yearbook of European Studies*, no. 13.

———. 2000. *Nationalism and the Crowd in Liberal Hungary, 1848–1914*. Washington, D.C.: Woodrow Wilson Center Press.

Freudenberger, Herman. 1977. *The Industrialization of a Central European City: Brno and the Fine Woollen Industry in the Eighteenth Century*. Edington, U.K.: Pasold Research Fund.

Fric, Milan. [1907] 1991. "On the Woman Question." In *Incipient Feminists: Women Writers in the Slovak National Revival*, ed. Norma Rudinsky. Columbus, Ohio: Slavica Publishers.

Frigyesi, Judit. 1998. *Béla Bartók and Turn-of-the-Century Budapest*. Berkeley and Los Angeles: University of California Press.

Furst, Lilian R. 1980. *European Romanticism: Self-Definition. An Anthology*. London: Methuen.

Galbraith, John Kenneth. 1964. *Economic Development*. Rev. ed. Boston: Houghton Mifflin.

Gavrilova, Raina. 1999. *Bulgarian Urban Culture in the Eighteenth and Nineteenth Centuries*. Cranbury, N.J.: Susquehanna University Press.

Geréb, László. 1961. *A munkásügy irodalmunkban*. Budapest: Akadémiai Kiadó.

Gergely, András. 1983. "A magyar reformellenzék kialakulása és megszilárdulása (1830–1840)." In *Magyarország Története, 1790–1848*, ed. Gyula Mérei. Budapest: Akadémiai Kiadó.

Gerschenkron, Alexander, 1962. *Economic Backwardness in Historical Perspective*. Cambridge, Mass.: Harvard University Press, Belknap Press.

Glass, D. V., and D. E. C. Eversley. 1965. *Population in History: Essays in Historical Demography*. Chicago: Aldine.

Good, David F. 1984. *The Economic Rise of the Habsburg Empire, 1750–1914*. Berkeley and Los Angeles: University of California Press.

———. 1997. Review of *Central and Eastern Europe, 1944–1993: Detour from the Pe-*

riphery to the Periphery, by Ivan T. Berend (Cambridge: Cambridge University Press, 1996). H-net Book Review, March.

Graham, Darby. 1998. *The Origins of the First World War.* Harlow, U.K.: Longman.

Gross, Mirjana. 1960. *Vladavina Hrvatsko-Srpske Koalicije, 1906–1907.* Belgrade: Institute Društvenih Nauka.

Gross, Nachum T. 1971. "Economic Growth and the Consumption of Coal in Austria and Hungary." *Journal of Economic History* 31, no. 4 (December).

———. 1973. "The Industrial Revolution in the Habsburg Monarchy, 1750–1914." In *The Emergence of Industrial Societies,* vol. 4 of *The Fontana Economic History of Europe,* ed. Carlo Cipolla, pt. 1. London: Collins/Fontana Books.

Gunst, Péter. 1996. *Agrarian Development and Social Change in Eastern Europe, Fourteenth–Nineteenth Centuries.* Aldershot, U.K.; Brookfield, Vt.: Variorum.

Gutowski, Wojciech. 1991. *Pasje wyobrazni: Szkice o literaturze romantyzmu i Mlodej Polski.* Torun: Towarzystwo Naukowe w Toruniu.

Gyurgyák, János. 2001. *A zsidókérdés Magyarországon. Politikai eszmetörténet.* Budapest: Osiris Kiadó.

Hajnal, John. 1965. "European Marriage Patterns in Perspective." In *Population in History,* ed. D. V. Glass and D. E. C. Eversly. London: Edward Arnold.

———. 1983. "Two Kinds of Pre-Industrial Household Formation System." In *Family Forms in Historic Europe,* ed. Richard Wall. Cambridge: Cambridge University Press.

Halpern, Joel M., and Barbara Kerewsky Halpern, eds. 1972. *A Serbian Village in Historical Perspective.* New York: Holt, Rinehart & Winston.

Hanák, Péter. 1988. "Magyarország társadalma a századforduló idején," "Társadalmi és politikai küzdelmek az 1890–es évek első felében," and "A dualizmus válságának kezdetei a 19.század végén." In *Magyarország története, 1890–1918,* ed. Péter Hanák. Budapest: Akadémiai Kiadó.

———. 1992. "Jews and the Modernization of Commerce in Hungary, 1760–1848." In *Jews in the Hungarian Economy, 1760–1945,* ed. Michael K. Silber. Jerusalem: Magnes Press.

Härtel, Hans-Joachim, and Roland Schönfeld. 1998. *Bulgarien.* Regensburg: Verlag Friedrich Pustet.

Hatton, Timothy J., and Jeffrey G. Williamson. 1998. "International Migration 1850–1939: An Economic Survey." In *Historical Foundations of Globalization,* ed. James Foreman-Peck. Cheltenham, U.K.: Elgar Reference Collection.

Hayek, Friedrich A. 1976. *The Constitution of Liberty.* London: Routledge.

Hayes, Paul, ed. 1992. *Themes in Modern European History, 1890–1945.* London: Routledge.

Heilig, Balázs. 2000. "Paraszti háztartások és háztartásciklusok Szőlősardón a 19.század második felében." In *K.S.H. Népességtudományi Kutatóintézetének 2000. évi történeti demográfiai évkönyve,* ed. T. Faragó and P. Őri. Budapest: Központi Statisztikai Hivatal.

Heimann, Eduard. 1964. *History of Economic Doctrines.* New York: Oxford University Press.

Heller, Ágnes. 1992. "Europe: An Epilogue?" In *The Idea of Europe: Problems of*

National and Transnational Identity, ed. Brian Nelson, David Roberts, and Walter Veit. New York: Berg.

Herder, Johann Gottfried. [1784–91] 1968. *Reflections on the Philosophy of the History of Mankind.* Edited by Frank E. Manuel. Chicago: University of Chicago Press.

Hertz, Friedrich. 1917. *Die Produktionsgrundlagen der österreichischen Industrie vor und nach dem Kriege.* Vienna: Verlag für Fachliteratur.

Himka, John-Paul. 1988. *Galician Villagers and the Ukrainian National Movement in the Nineteenth Century.* New York: St. Martin's Press.

Hitchins, Keith. 1994. *Rumania, 1866–1947.* Oxford: Clarendon Press.

———. 1996. *The Romanians, 1774–1866.* Oxford: Clarendon Press.

Hobbes, Thomas. [1651] 1956. *Leviathan.* Chicago: Gateway.

Hobsbawm, Eric. 1962. *The Age of Revolution: Europe 1789–1848.* London: Weidenfeld & Nicholson.

———. 1987. *The Age of Empire, 1870–1914.* New York: Pantheon Books.

———. 1994. *Age of Extremes: The Short Twentieth Century, 1914–1991.* London: Michael Joseph.

Hobson, John A. [1905] 1938. *Imperialism: A Study.* London: Allen & Unwin.

Holmgren, Beth. 1998. *Rewriting Capitalism: Literature and the Market in Late Tsarist Russia and the Kingdom of Poland.* Pittsburgh: University of Pittsburgh Press.

Holton, Milne, and Vasa D. Mihailovich, eds. 1988. *Serbian Poetry from the Beginnings to the Present.* New Haven, Conn.: Yale Russian and East European Publications.

Hóman, Bálint, and Szekfű Gyula. 1935–36. *Magyar történet.* 2d ed. 5 vols. Budapest: Királyi Magyar Egyetemi Nyomda.

Homola-Skapska, Irena. 1992. "Girls' Education in the Kingdom of Poland (1815–1915)." In *Women in Polish Society,* ed. Rudolf Jaworski and Bianka Pietrow-Ennker. Boulder, Colo.: East European Monographs.

Horská, Pavla. 1994. "Historical Models of the Central European Family: Czech and Slovak Examples." *Journal of Family History* 19, no. 2.

Hossu, Andrei Iustin. 1995. *Istoria monarhiei române (10 mai 1866–30 decembrie 1947).* Bucharest: Romcart.

Hroch, Miroslaw. 1985. *Social Preconditions of National Revival in Europe: A Comparative Analysis of the Social Composition of Patriotic Groups among the Smaller European Nations.* Cambridge: Cambridge University Press.

Iacob, Gheorghe. 1996. *Economia României (1859–1939).* Iaşi, Romania: Fundaţiei Axis.

Iacob, Gheorghe, and Luminiţa Iacob. 1995. *Modernizare: Europenism.* 2 vols. Iaşi, Romania: Editura Universitatii "Al. I. Cuza."

Ihnatowicz, Ireneusz. 1988. *Spoleczenstwo polskie, 1864–1914.* Dzieje narodu i panstwa polskiego, III–51. Kraków: Krajowa Agencja Wydawnicza.

Ilincioiu, Ion, ed. 1991. *The Great Romanian Peasant Revolt of 1907.* Bucharest: Editura Academiei Române.

Inalcik, Halil. [1973] 1994. *The Ottoman Empire: The Classical Age, 1300–1600.* Translated by Norman Itzkowitz and Colin Imber. London: Phoenix.

Ioanid, Radu. 1992. "Iorga, Nicolae and Fascism." *Journal of Contemporary History* 27, no. 3 (July).

Iordache, Anastasie. 1987. *Apararea autonomiei Principatelor române 1821–1859.* Bucharest: Academiei Republicii Socialiste Romania.

Iorga, Nicolae. 1933. *Histoire de l'enseignement en pays Roumains.* Bucharest: Édition de la Caisse des Écoles.

Iparfelügyelői jelentések. 1910. Budapest: Statisztikai Hivatal.

Izdebski, Hubert. 1995. "Government and Self-Government in Partitioned Poland." In *Finland and Poland in the Russian Empire: A Comparative Study,* ed. Michael Branch, Janet Hartley, and Antoni Mączak. London: School of Slavonic and East European Studies, University of London.

Janos, Andrew C. 1982. *The Politics of Backwardness in Hungary, 1825–1945.* Princeton, N.J.: Princeton University Press.

Jedlicki, Jerzy. 1964. *Nieudana próba kapitalstycznej industrializacji.* Warsaw: Ksiazka i Wiedza.

———. 1999. *A Suburb of Europe: Nineteenth-Century Polish Approaches to Western Civilization.* Budapest: Central European University Press.

Jelavich, Charles, and Barbara Jelavich. 1977. *The Establishment of the Balkan National States, 1804–1920.* Seattle: University of Washington Press.

Jenks, Leland Hamilton. 1927. *The Migration of British Capital to 1875.* New York: Knopf.

Jezierski, Andrzej. 1967. *Handel zagraniczny Królestwa Polskiego 1815–1914.* Warsaw: Państwowe Wydawn.

Johnson, Paul. 1983. *Modern Times: The World from the Twenties to the Eighties.* New York: Harper & Row.

Jókai, Mór. [1870] 1968. *The Dark Diamonds [Fekete gyémántok].* Translated by Frances Gerard. Budapest: Corvina Press.

Jones, Eric Lionel. 1981. *The European Miracle: Environments, Economies, and Geopolitics in the History of Europe and Asia.* Cambridge: Cambridge University Press.

Jones, Eric Lionel, ed. 1967. *Agriculture and Economic Growth in England, 1650–1815.* London: Methuen.

Kadić, Ante. 1983. *The Tradition of Freedom in Croatian Literature.* Bloomington, Ind.: Croatian Alliance.

Kadlec, Jaroslav. 1987. *Přehled českých církevních dějin.* Prague: ZVON.

Kahk, Juhan. 1989. "The Baltic Region in the Nineteenth Century." In *Economy, Society, Historiography. Dedicated to Zsigmond Pál Pach on his 70th Birthday,* ed. Ferenc Glatz. Budapest: MTA Történettudományi Intézet.

Kann, Robert A. 1974. *A History of the Habsburg Empire, 1526–1918.* Berkeley and Los Angeles: University of California Press.

Kann, Robert, and Zdenek David. 1984. *The Peoples of the Eastern Habsburg Lands, 1526–1918.* Seattle: University of Washington Press.

Kapper, Siegfried. 1851. *Die Serbische Bewegung in Südungarn: Ein Beitrag zur Geschichte der ungarischen Revolution.* Berlin: F. Dunker.

Karanovich, Milenko. 1995. *The Development of Education in Serbia and Emergence of Its Intelligentsia (1838–1858).* Boulder, Colo.: East European Monographs.

Kassák, Lajos. 1972. *Az izmusok története.* Budapest: Magvető Kiadó.

Katus, László. 1979. "A népesedés és a társadalmi szerkezet változásai." In *Ma-gyarország Története, 1848–1890*, ed. Endre Kovács. Budapest: Akadémiai Kiadó.
———. 1992. "The Occupational Structure of Hungarian Jewry in the Eighteenth and Twentieth Centuries." In *Jews in the Hungarian Economy, 1760–1945*, ed. Michael K. Silber. Jerusalem: Magnes Press.

Kawyn, Stefan. 1953. *Polska publicystyka postępowa w kraju, 1831–1846*. Wrocław: Zakład Narodowy im. Ossolińskich.

Kemény, Gábor G., ed. 1956. *Iratok a nemzetiségi kérdés történetéhez Magyarországon a dualizmus korában*. 2 vols. Budapest: Akadémiai Kiadó.

Kenwood, A. George, and Alan L. Lougheed. 1971. *The Growth of the International Economy, 1820–1960*. London: Allen & Unwin.

Keyder, Caglar. 1991. "Creation and Destruction of Forms of Manufacturing: The Ottoman Example." In *Between Development and Underdevelopment, 1800–1870*, ed. Jean Batou. Geneva: Droz.

Kieval, Hillel J. 1988. *The Making of Czech Jewry: National Conflict and Jewish Society in Bohemia, 1870–1918*. New York: Oxford University Press.
———. 2000. *Languages of Community: The Jewish Experience in the Czech Lands*. Berkeley and Los Angeles: University of California Press.

Kindleberger, Charles P. 1962. *Foreign Trade and National Economy*. New Haven, Conn.: Yale University Press.

Kitromilides, Paschalis M. 1994. *Enlightment, Nationalism, Orthodoxy: Studies in the Culture and Political Thought of South-Eastern Europe*. Aldershot, U.K.: Variorum.

Kizwalter, Tomasz. 1990. "Polish Landed Gentry of the Mid Nineteenth Century and Modernization." *Acta Poloniae Historica* (Warsaw), no. 62.

Klíma, Arnošt. 1991. *Economy, Industry, and Society in Bohemia in the Seventeenth–Nineteenth Centuries*. Prague: Charles University.

Koch, Adolf. 1887. *Prince Alexander of Battenberg*. London: Whitaker.

Kochanowicz, Jacek. 1995. "The Economy of the Polish Kingdom: A Question of Dependence." In *Finland and Poland in the Russian Empire: A Comparative Study*, ed. Michael Branch, Janet Hartley, and Antoni Mączak. SSEES Occasional Papers, no. 29. London: School of Slavonic and East European Studies, University of London.

Kohn, Hans. 1944. *The Idea of Nationalism: A Study in Its Origins and Background*. New York: Macmillan.

Kolodziejczyk, Ryszard. 1986. "Die Warschauer Bourgeoisie in 19. Jahrhundert." In *Bürgertum und bürgerliche Entwicklung in Mittel- und Osteuropa*, ed. Vera Bácskai. Budapest: Közép és Kelet-Európai Kutatási Központ.

Komlos, John. 1983. *The Habsburg Monarchy as a Customs Union: Economic Development in Austria-Hungary in the Nineteenth Century*. Princeton, N.J.: Princeton University Press.

Korzon, Tadeusz. 1897–98. *Wewnętrzne dzieje Polski za Stanisława Augusta (1764–1794)*. Kraków: L. Zwoliński.

Kosáry, Domokos. 1942. *Kossuth és a Védegylet: A magyar nacionalizmus történetéhez*. Budapest: Atheneum.

——. 1980. *Művelődés a XVIII. századi Magyarországon*. Budapest: Akadémiai Kiadó.

Kosim, Jan. 1986. "Die Warschauer Kriegslieferanten zwischen 1780–1830." In *Bürgertum und bürgerliche Entwicklung in Mittel- und Osteuropa*, ed. Vera Bácskai. Budapest: Közep és Kelet-Európai Kutatási Központ.

Kostrowicka, Irena, Zbignev Landau, and Jerzy Tomaszewski. 1966. *Historia gospodarcza Polski XIX i XX wieku*. Warsaw: Książka i Wiedza.

Kowalczykowa, Alina, comp. 1991. *Idee programowe romantyków polskich: Antologia*. Warsaw: Zaklad Narodowy im. Ossolinskich—Wydawn.

Kowecki, Jerzy. 1971. "U początków nowoczesnogo narodu." In *Polska w epoce Oświecenia*, ed. Bogusław Leśnodorski. Warsaw: Wiedza Powszechna.

Kozik, Jan. 1986. *The Ukrainian National Movement in Galicia, 1815–1849*. Translated from the Polish by Andrew Gorski and Lawrence D. Orton. Edmonton: Canadian Institute of Ukrainian Studies, University of Alberta.

Krajcsi, Rezsö. 1907. *Az 1907. évi III. törvénycikk*. Budapest.

Krejcí, Karel. 1958. *Klassicismus a sentimentalismus v literaturách vychodnich a zapadnich Slovanu*. Prague: CSAV.

Krejcí, Oskar. 1995. *History of Elections in Bohemia and Moravia*. Boulder, Colo.: East European Monographs.

Krzyzanowski, Julian. 1931. *Polish Romantic Literature*. New York: Dutton.

Kula, Witold. 1947. *Historia gospodarcza Polski w dobie popowstaniowej, 1864–1918*. Warsaw: Książka i Wiezda.

——. 1983. *Historia, zacofanie, rozwój*. Warsaw: Czytelnik.

Kuznetz, Simon. 1966. *Modern Economic Growth: Rate, Structure and Spread*. New Haven, Conn.: Yale University Press.

——. 1967. "Quantitative Aspects of the Economic Growth of Nations: X-Levels and Structure of Foreign Trade: Long-Term Trends." *Economic Development and Cultural Change* 15, no. 2, pt. 2.

Lampe, John R., and Marvin R. Jackson. 1982. *Balkan Economic History, 1550–1950: From Imperial Borderlands to Developing Nations*. Bloomington: Indiana University Press.

Landes, David. 1969. *The Unbound Prometheus: Technological Change and Industrial Development in Western Europe from 1750 to the Present*. Cambridge: Cambridge University Press.

Landry, Adolphe. 1934. *La Révolution démographique: Études et essais sur les problèmes de la population*. Paris: Librairie du Recueil Sirey.

Laslett, Peter. 1960. "Introduction." In John Locke, *Two Treatises of Government*. Cambridge: Cambridge University Press.

Laue, Theodore H. von. 1969. *Sergei Witte and the Industrialization of Russia*. New York: Atheneum.

Lederer, Ivo. 1969. "Nationalism and the Yugoslavs." In *Nationalism in Eastern Europe*, ed. Ivo Lederer and Peter Sugar. Seattle: University of Washington Press.

Le Play, Frédéric. 1877–79. *Les Ouvriers européens*. 6 vols. Tours: A. Mame et fils.

Lippay, Zoltán. 1919. *A magyar birtokos osztály és a közélet*. Budapest: Franklin.

List, Friedrich. 1841. *Das nationale System der politischen Ökonomie*. Stuttgart: J. G. Cotta'scher Verlag.

Liszt, Ferenc. 1989. *Válogatott levelei (1824–1861)*. Budapest: Zeneműkiadó.

Locke, John. [1690] 1947. *Two Treatises on Government*. Edited by Thomas I. Cook. New York: Hafner.

Logio, George Clenton. 1932. *Rumania: Its History, Politics and Economics*. Manchester: Sherratt & Hughes.

Lord, Albert B. 1963. "Nationalism and the Muses in Balkan Slavic Literature in the Modern Period." In *The Balkans in Transition*, ed. Charles Jelavich and Barbara Jelavich. Berkeley and Los Angeles: University of California Press.

Lucas, Franc L. 1948. *The Decline and Fall of the Romantic Ideal*. Cambridge: Cambridge University Press.

Lukács, Ágnes B. 1977. "Eger demográfiai viszonyai az 1820–as években." Paper presented at conference on historical statistics, Budapest.

Lukács, György. 1977. *A történelmi regény*. Budapest: Magvető.

Lukacs, John. 1988. *Budapest 1900: A Historical Portrait of a City and Its Culture*. New York: Grove Weidenfeld.

Macartney, C. A. 1968. *The Habsburg Empire, 1790–1918*. London: Weidenfeld & Nicholson.

Mackenzie, Georgina M. M., and A. P. Irby. [1867] 1877. *Travels in the Slavonic Provinces of Turkey-in-Europe*. Vols. 1–3. 3d rev. ed. London: Bell & Daldy; Daldy, Isbister.

Mączak, Antoni. 1995. *Money, Prices and Power in Poland, Sixteenth–Seventeenth Centuries*. Aldershot, U.K.: Variorum.

Maddison, Angus. 1995. *Monitoring the World Economy, 1820–1992*. Paris: Development Centre of the Organisation for Economic Co-operation and Development.

Magdalena, Aldo de. 1974. "Rural Europe 1500–1750." In *The Sixteenth and Seventeenth Centuries*, vol. 2 of *The Fontana Economic History of Europe*, ed. Carlo Cipolla. London: Collins/Fontana Books.

Magin, Ján Baltazar. 1728. *Murices nobilissimae et norissimae diaetae Posoniensis scriptori sparsi sive Apologia*. Púchov, Slovakia.

Magyar Pénzügy. 1905. October 5.

Magyar Statisztikai Évkönyv. 1913. Budapest: Statisztikai Hivatal.

Magyar Statisztikai Évkönyv. 1915. Uj évfolyam XXI. Budapest: Statisztikai Hivatal.

Magyar Törvénytár, 1740–1835. Évi törvénycikkek. 1901. Budapest: Franklin Társulat.

Makkai, Adám, ed. 1996. *In Quest of the "Miracle Stag": The Poetry of Hungary*. Chicago: Atlantis-Centaur.

Makkai, László. 1976. "Feudalizmus és az eredeti jellegzetességek Európában." *Történelmi Szemle*, no. 1–2.

Manolova, Maria Georgieva. 1989. *Parlamentarizmut v Bulgariia, 1879–1894*. Sofia: Bulgarskata Akademia Naukite.

Marczali, Henrik. 1888. *Magyarország története II. József korában*. Budapest: Magyar Tudományos Akadémia Történelmi Bizottsága.

Marr, Wilhelm. [1873] 1879. *Der Sieg des Judenthums über das Germanenthum: Vom nicht confessionellen Standpunkt aus betrachtet*. Bern: R. Costenoble.

Marx, Karl. [1867] 1932. *Capital: A Critique of Political Economy.* Vol. 1. Chicago: Charles H. Kerr.

Marx, Karl, and Friedrich Engels. [1848] 1988. *The Communist Manifesto.* New York: Norton.

Masarýk, Tomáš. 1927. *The Making of a State: Memoires and Observations, 1914–1918.* London: Allen & Unwin.

Masoff, Ioan. 1964. *Eminescu și teatrul.* Bucharest: Editura Pentru Literatură.

Materiały do dziejów sejmu Czteroletniego. 1955–69. Edited by Janusz Woliński, Jerzy Michalski, and Emanuel Rostworowski. Wrocław: Ossolińskich.

Matlekovits, Sándor, ed. 1898. *Magyarország közgazdasági és közművelődési állapota ezer éves fennállásakor és az 1896. évi ezredévi kiállítás eredménye.* Vol. 9. Budapest: Pesti Könyvnyomda.

Matuška, Alexander. 1948. *Štúrovci.* Bratislava: Pravda.

Mayer, Arno J. 1981. *The Persistence of the Old Regime: Europe to the Great War.* New York: Pantheon Books.

McCagg, William. 1992. "Jewish Wealth in Vienna, 1670–1918." In *Jews in the Hungarian Economy, 1760–1945,* ed. Michael K. Silber. Jerusalem: Magnes Press.

McNeill, William, H. 1963. *The Rise of the West: A History of the Human Community.* Chicago: University of Chicago Press.

Meinecke, Friedrich. 1908. *Weltbürgertum und Nationalstaat: Studien zur Genesis des deutschen Nationalstaates.* Munich: R. Oldenbourg.

Melegh, Attila. 2000. "Házassagtörés Halason a 17–18. században." In *K.S.H. Népességtudományi Kutatóintézetének 2000.évi történeti demográfiai évkönyve,* ed. T. Faragó and P. Őri. Budapest: Központi Statisztikai Hivatal.

Melville, Ralph. 1998. *Adel und Revolution in Böhmen. Strukturwandel von Herrschaft und Gesellschaft in Österreich um Mitte des 19. Jahrhunderts.* Mainz: Philipp von Zabern.

Mendels, Franklin F. 1972. "Proto-industrialization: The First Phase of the Process of Industrialization." *Journal of Economic History* 32, no. 1 (March).

———. 1982. "Proto-industrialization: Theory and Reality." In *International Economic History Congress (8th),* "A" Themes. Budapest: Magyar Tudományos Akadémia.

Mérei, Gyula. 1951. *Magyar iparfejlődés, 1790–1848.* Budapest: MTT.

———, ed. 1983. *Magyarország története, 1790–1849.* Budapest: Akadémiai Kiadó.

Meriage, Lawrence P. 1987. *Russia and the First Serbian Insurrection, 1804–1813.* New York: Garland Publishing.

Michelson, Paul E. 1987. *Conflict and Crisis: Romanian Political Development, 1861–1871.* New York: Garland Publishing.

Mickiewicz, Adam. [1832] 1986. "Books of the Polish Nation and Pilgrimage." Quoted in Norman Davies, *Heart of Europe: A Short History of Poland.* Oxford: Oxford University Press.

Mikszáth, Kálmán. 1897. *Az apró gentry és a nép; harmincz kis elbeszélés.* Budapest: Révai Testvérek.

———. [1908] 1912. *A Noszty fiú esete Tóth Marival.* Budapest: Franklin Társulat.

Mill, John Stuart. 1848. *Principles of Political Economy with Some of Their Applications to Social Philosophy.* 2 vols. Boston: C. C. Little & J. Brown.

Miłosz, Cesław. 1983. *The History of Polish Literature.* Berkeley and Los Angeles: University of California Press.

Milward, Alan S., and S. B. Soul. 1977. *The Development of the Economies of Continental Europe, 1850–1914.* London: Allen & Unwin.

Mitchell, B. R. 1975. *European Historical Statistics, 1750–1970.* New York: Columbia University Press.

Mitrany, David. 1930. *The Land and the Peasant in Rumania.* London: H. Milford, Oxford University Press; New Haven, Conn.: Yale University Press.

Mitterauer, Michael, and Reinhard Sieder. 1982. *The European Family: Patriarchy to Partnership from the Middle Ages to the Present.* Oxford: Blackwell.

Mladenovic, Ivica. 1995. "Modern Serbian Architecture." In *The History of Serbian Culture,* ed. Pavle Ivic, trans. Randall A. Major. Edgware, Middlesex, U.K.: Porthill Publishers.

Molenda, Jan. 1991. "The Formation of National Consensus of the Polish Peasants and the Part They Played in the Regaining of Independence by Poland." *Acta Poloniae Historica* (Warsaw), no. 63–64.

Mols, Roger S. J. 1974. "Population of Europe, 1500–1700." In *The Sixteenth and Seventeenth Centuries,* vol. 2 of *The Fontana Economic History of Europe,* ed. Carlo Cipolla. London: Collins/Fontana Books.

Montesquieu, Charles-Louis, baron de. [1748] 1946. "The Spirit of Laws." In *Introduction to Contemporary Civilization in the West. A Source Book.* New York: Columbia University Press.

Monumenta Bulgarica: A Bilingual Anthology of Bulgarian Texts from the Ninth to the Nineteenth Centuries. 1996. Edited by Thomas Butler. Michigan Slavic Materials, no. 41. Ann Arbor: Michigan Slavic Publications.

Monumenta Serbocroatica: A Bilingual Anthology of Serbian and Croatian Texts from the Twelfth to the Nineteenth Century. 1980. Edited by Thomas Butler. Joint Committee on Eastern Europe, no. 6. Ann Arbor: Michigan Slavic Publications.

Moore, Barrington, Jr. 1966. *Social Origins of Dictatorship and Democracy: Lord and Peasant in the Making of the Modern World.* Boston: Beacon Press.

Mori, Giorgio. 1975. "The Genesis of Italian Industrialization." *Journal of European Economic History* 4, no. 7.

Mortier, Roland. 1969. *Clartés et ombres du siècle des lumières: Études sur le 18e siècle littéraire.* Geneva: Droz.

Mościcki, Henryk, ed. 1924. *Z filareckiego świata zhbiór wspomnień z lat, 1816–1824.* Warsaw: Instytut Wydawniczy "Bibljoteka Polska."

Moser, Charles A. 1972. *History of Bulgarian Literature, 865–1944.* The Hague: Mouton.

Mosse, George L. 1961. *The Culture of Western Europe: The Nineteenth and Twentieth Centuries.* Chicago: Rand McNally.

———. 1966. *The Crisis of German Ideology: Intellectual Origins of the Third Reich.* London: Weidenfeld & Nicolson.

Musson, Albert Eduard, and Eric Robinson. 1969. *Science and Technology in the Industrial Revolution.* Manchester: Manchester University Press.

Narusziewicz, Adam. 1780–86. *Historya narodu polskiego od poczatku Chrzescianstwa.* 6 vols. Warsaw: w Drukarni J. K. Mci.

Neagoe, Stelian. 1995. *Istoria guvernelor României.* Bucharest: Editura Machiavelli.

Nemoianu, Virgil. 1984. *The Taming of Romanticism: European Literature and the Age of Biedermeier.* Cambridge, Mass.: Harvard University Press.

Népszava [daily newspaper published in Budapest by the Social Democratic party]. 1914. August 3.

Neruda, Jan. 1983. "May, 1890." In *Czech Prose: An Anthology,* ed. William E. Harkins. Michigan Slavic Translations, no. 6. Ann Arbor: Michigan Slavic Publications, Dept. of Slavic Languages and Literatures, University of Michigan.

Nicolae, Vasile. 1993. *O istorie a social-democratiei române.* Vol. 1. Bucharest: Editura Noua Alternativaea.

Nisbet, Robert. 1980. *History of the Idea of Progress.* New York: Basic Books.

Novák, Arne. 1976. *Czech Literature.* Translated by Peter Kussi. Joint Committee on Eastern Europe Publication series, no. 4. Ann Arbor: Michigan Slavic Publications, University of Michigan.

Novaković, Stojan. 1995. *Kosovo: Srpske narodne pesme o boju na Kosovu.* Belgrade: Vukova Zadužbina.

Oprescu, George. 1984. *Pictura românească in secolul al XIX-lea.* Bucharest: Meridiane.

Österreichisches Institut für Wirtschaftsforschung. 1965. *Österreichs Volkseinkommen 1913 bis 1963.* Monatsberichte des österreichischen Institutes für Wirtschaftsforschung 14. Vienna: Österreichisches Institut für Wirtschaftsforchung.

Pach, Zsigmond Pál. 1963. *Nyugat-európai és magyarorszagi agrárfejlődés a XV–XVII. században.* Budapest: Kossuth Kiadó.

———. 1994. *Hungary and the European Economy in Early Modern Times.* Aldershot, U.K.: Variorum.

Palacký, František. 1998. "History of the Czech Nation in Bohemia and Moravia." Quoted in Derek Sayer, *The Coasts of Bohemia: A Czech History.* Princeton, N.J.: Princeton University Press.

Palairet, Michael. 1997. *The Balkan Economies, c. 1800–1914: Evolution without Development.* Cambridge: Cambridge University Press.

Pap, Gy. 1865. *A palóc népköltemények.* Sárospatak, Hungary: N.p.

Papanek, Juraj. 1780. *De regno, regibusque Slavorum atque cum prisci civilis, et ecclesiastici, tum hujius aevi statu genti Slavae anno Christi MDCCLXXX Quinque.* Ecclesi Typis J. J. Eng.

Pascu, Vasile. 1996. *Istoria modernă a românilor, 1821–1918.* Bucharest: Clio Nova.

Payzant, Geoffrey. 1991. *Eduard Hanslick and Ritter Berlioz in Prague: A Documentary Narrative.* Calgary: University of Calgary Press.

Pearson, Thomas S. 1989. *Russian Officialdom in Crisis: Autocracy and Local Self-Government, 1861–1900.* New York: Cambridge University Press.

Peckham, Morse, ed. 1965. *Romanticism: The Culture of the Nineteenth Century.* New York: George Braziller.

———. 1970. *The Triumph of Romaticism.* Columbia: University of South Carolina Press.

————. 1995. *Romanticism and Ideology*. Hanover, N.H.: Wesleyan University Press.

Peeters, Edward, and Alexandre Zlatanoff. 1909. *L'Éducation en Bulgarie, d'après les documents officiels du Ministère de l'instruction publique de Bulgarie*. Bruges: A. Moens-Patfoort.

Péter, László. 1997–98. "The Autocratic Principle of the Law and Civil Rights in Nineteenth-Century Hungary." In *Central European University, History Department Yearbook*. Budapest: Central European University Press.

Petőfi, Sándor. [1948] 1976. *Sixty Poems*. Translated into English verse by Eugénie Bayard Pierce and Emil Delmár. Millwood, N.Y.: Kraus Reprint Co.

————. 1985. *Költeményei*. Budapest: Helikon Kiadó.

Petrosjan, J. 1977. "Die Ideen 'der Europäisierung' in dem sozialpolitischen Leben des osmanischen Reiches in der Neuzeit (Ende des 18., Anfang des 20. Jahrhunderts)." In *La Révolution industrielle dans le sud-est européen XIX s*. Sofia: Institut d'Études balcaniques.

Petrovich, Michael B. 1980. "Religion and Ethnicity in Eastern Europe." In *Ethnic Diversity and Conflict in Eastern Europe,* ed. Peter F. Sugar. Santa Barbara, Calif.: ABC–Clio.

Phillips, Ursula. 1999. "The Upbringing and Education of Women as Represented in Novels by Nineteenth-Century Polish Women Writers." *Slavonic and East European Review* 77, no. 2 (April).

Piasecka, Maria. 1992. *Mistrzowie snu. Mickiewicz, Słowacki, Krasiński*. Wrocław: Zakład Narodowy im. Ossolińskich.

Pietrow-Ennker, Bianka. 1992. "Women in Polish Society. A Historical Introduction." In *Women in Polish Society,* ed. Rudolf Jaworski and B. Pietrow-Ennker. Boulder, Colo.: East European Monographs.

Pintea, Alexandru, and Gheorghe Ruscanu. 1995. *Băncile în economia românească (1774–1995)*. Bucharest: Economică.

Podjavorinská, Ludmila. [1909] 1976. "The Woman." In *An Anthology of Slovak Literature,* comp. Andrew Cincura. Riverside, Calif.: University Hardcovers.

Polanyi, Karl. [1944] 1964. *The Great Transformation: The Political and Economic Origins of Our Times*. Boston: Beacon Press.

Pollard, Sydney. 1974. *European Economic Integration, 1815–1970*. New York: Harcourt Brace Jovanovich.

Popovici, Aurel C. 1906. *Die Vereinigten Staaten von Gross-Österreich: Politische Studien zur Lösung der nationalen Fragen und staatsrechtlichen Krisen in Österreich-Ungarn*. Leipzig: B. Elischer Nachfolger.

Porter, Brian. 2000. *When Nationalism Began to Hate: Imagining Modern Politics in Nineteenth-Century Poland*. New York: Oxford University Press.

Pribram, K. 1907. *Geschichte der österreichischen Gewerbepolitik von 1740–1860*. Leipzig: Duncker & Humblot.

Prus, Bolesław. 1890. *Lalka: Powiesc*. Warsaw: Nakl. Gebethnera i Wolfa.

Půrš, Jaroslav. 1960. "The Industrial Revolution in the Czech-lands." *Historica* 2, no. 2 (Prague).

Pynsent, Robert B. 1994. *Questions of Identity: Czech and Slovak Ideas of Nationality and Personality*. Budapest: Central European University Press.

Radics, Katalin. 1997. "German Influences in East-European Linguistic Movements." In *Germany and Southeastern Europe—Aspects of Relations in the Twentieth Century,* ed. Roland Schönfeld. Munich: Südosteuropa-Gesellschaft.

Ranke, Leopold von. [1824] 1909. *History of the Latin and Teutonic Nations (1494 to 1514).* London: George Bell.

Ratajczak, Dobrochna, ed. 1992. *Dramat i teatr pozytywistyczny.* Wrocław: Wiedza o Kulturze.

Reiss, Hans Siegbert, ed. 1995. *The Political Thought of the German Romantics, 1793–1815.* Oxford: Blackwell.

Reymont, Władysław. 1925. *The Peasants: A Tale of Our Own Times: Autumn, Winter, Spring, Summer.* Translated by Michael H. Dziewicki. New York: Knopf.

Riasanovsky, Nicholas V. [1952] 1965. *Russia and the West in the Teaching of the Slavophiles: A Study of Romantic Ideology.* Gloucester, Mass.: Peter Smith.

Ring, Éva. 2001. *Lengyelországot az anarchia tartja fenn? A nemesi köztársaság válságának anatómiája.* Budapest: ELTE Eötvös Kiadó.

Roguski, Piotr. 1996. *Aufsätze zur Polnischen und Deutschen Romantik.* Munich: Otto Sagner.

Ronnas, Per. 1984. *Urbanization in Romania.* Stockholm: Stockholm School of Economics.

Rosen, Avram. 1995. *Participarea evreilor la dezvoltarea industriala a Bucureştiului: Din a doua jumatate a secolului al XIX-lea pâna în anul 1938.* Bucharest: Hasefer.

Rosetti, Radu D. 1907. *Pentru ce s'au răsculat ţăranii.* Bucharest: Ateliere grafice Socec & Co.

Rostow, W. W. 1963. *The Economics of Take-Off into Sustained Growth: Proceedings of a Conference Held by the International Economic Association.* New York: Macmillan.

Rousseau, Jean-Jacques. [1755] 1983. *Discourse on the Origin of Inequality.* Indianapolis: Hackett.

———. [1762] 1946. "The Social Contract." In *Introduction to Contemporary Civilization in the West. A Source Book.* New York: Columbia University Press.

Rudinsky, Norma. 1991. *Incipient Feminists: Women Writers in the Slovak National Revival.* Columbus: Slavica Publishers.

Rutkowski, Jan. 1928. "La Genèse du régime de la corvée dans l'Europe centrale depuis la fin du Moyen Âge." In *La Pologne au VIe Congrès international des Sciences historiques* (Oslo, 1928). Warsaw: Société polonaise d'histoire.

Sasarman, Gheorghe, ed. 1983. *Gîdirea estetică in arhitectura românească.* Bucharest: Meridiane.

Sayer, Derek. 1998. *The Coasts of Bohemia: A Czech History.* Princeton, N.J.: Princeton University Press.

Scharf, Christian. 1996. *Ausgleichspolitik und Pressekampf in der Ära Hohenwart: Die Fundamentalartikel von 1871 und der deutsch-tschechische Konflikt in Böhmen.* Munich: Oldenbourg.

Schifirnet, Constantin. 1996. *Civilizaţie moderna şi naţiune. Mihail Kogălniceanu, Titu Maiorescu, Mihai Eminescu.* Bucharest: Editura Didactică şi Pedagogică.

Schorske, Carl. 1980. *Fin-de-Siècle Vienna: Politics and Culture.* New York: Knopf.

Schumpeter, Joseph. 1955. *Imperialism and Social Classes*. New York: Meridian Books.

Schwarz, Arnold. 1913. *Die Lage der österreichischen Baumwollspinnerei*. Vienna: Manzsche.

Scurtu, Ioan. 1988. *Contribuţii privind viaţa politică din România*. Bucharest: Editura Ştiinţifică şi Enciclopedică.

Seccombe, Wally. 1992. *A Millennium of Family Change*. London: Verso.

Senelick, Laurence, ed. 1991. *National Theatre in Northern and Eastern Europe, 1746–1900*. Cambridge: Cambridge University Press.

Serban, F. 1983–94. "Modernisation de la langue roumaine." In *Language Reform: History and Future*, ed. István Fodor and Claude Hagège, vol. 3. Hamburg: Buske.

Serban, Michael. 1914. *Rumäniens Agrarverhältnisse*. Berlin: P. Parey.

Seton-Watson, Robert W. [1934] 1963. *A History of the Roumanians from Roman Times to the Completion of Unity*. New York: Archon Books.

Silber, Michael K. 1992. "A Jewish Minority in a Backward Economy: An Introduction." In Silber, ed., *Jews in the Hungarian Economy 1760–1945*. Jerusalem: Magnes Press.

Singer, Hans Wolfgang. 1950. "The Distribution of Gains between Investing and Borrowing Countries." *American Economic Review*, no. 50.

Slicher van Bath, B. H. 1963. *The Agrarian History of Western Europe, A.D. 500–1850*. Translated by Olive Ordish. New York: St. Martin's Press.

Śliwa, Michał. 1997. *Obcy czy swoi: z dziejów poglądów na kwestię żydowską w Polsce w XIX i XX wieku*. Kraków: Wydawn.

Słomkowska, Alina. 1974. *Dziennikarze warszawscy: Szkice z XIX wieku*. Warsaw: Państwowe Wydawnictwo Naukowe.

Smith, Adam. [1759] 1813. *The Theory of Moral Sentiments*. Edinburgh: W. Creech.

———. [1776] 1976. *An Inquiry into the Nature and Causes of the Wealth of Nations*. 2 vols. Chicago: University of Chicago Press.

Soltésová, Elena Maróthy. [1898] 1991. "The Need for Women's Education." In *Incipient Feminists: Women Writers in the Slovak National Revival*, ed. Norma Rudinsky. Columbus: Slavica Publishers.

Sombart, Werner. 1911. *Die Juden und das Wirtschaftsleben*. Leipzig: Duncker & Humblot.

Sőtér, István. 1973. *The Dilemma of Literary Science*. Budapest: Akadémiai Kiadó.

Souckova, Milada. 1958. *The Czech Romantics*. The Hague: Mouton.

Spector, Scott. 2000. *Prague Territories: National Conflict and Cultural Innovation in Franz Kafka's Fin de Siècle*. Berkeley and Los Angeles: University of California Press.

Spira, György. 1987. "Polgári forradalom 1848–1849." In *Magyarország Története, 1848–1890*, ed. Endre Kovács. Budapest: Akadémiai Kiadó.

Spiró, György. 1986. *A közép-kelet-európai dráma. A Felvilágosodástól Wyspianski szintéziséig*. Budapest: Magvető.

Stahl, Henri H. 1980. *Traditional Romanian Village Communities: The Transition from the Communal to the Capitalist Mode of Production in the Danube Region*.

Translated by Daniel Chirot and Holley Coulter Chirot. Cambridge: Cambridge University Press.

Stan, Apostol. 1995. *Putere politică şi democraţie in România, 1859–1918*. Bucharest: Editura Albatros.

Starr, S. Frederick. 1972. *Decentralization and Self-Government in Russia, 1830–1870*. Princeton, N.J.: Princeton University Press.

Stavrianos, Leften S. [1958] 1963. *The Balkans since 1453*. New York: Rinehart. New ed., New York: New York University Press, 2000.

Stoianov, Ivan. 1989. *Liberalnata partiia v kniahestvo Bulgariia, 1879–1886*. Sofia: Nauka.

Stoianovich, Traian. 1963. "The Social Foundation of Balkan Politics, 1750–1941." In *The Balkans in Transition*, ed. Charles Jelavich and Barbara Jelavich. Berkeley and Los Angeles: University of California Press.

Subotić, Milan. 1992. *Sricanje slobode: studije o počecima liberalne političke misli u Srbiji XIX veka*. Niš: Gradina.

Suchoff, Benjamin. 1995. *Bartók: Concerto for Orchestra*. London: Schirmer Books.

Sugar, Peter. 1999. *East European Nationalism, Politics and Religion*. Aldershot, U.K.; Brookfield, Vt.: Ashgate/Variorum.

Szabolcsi, Miklós, ed. 1965. *A magyar irodalom története 1905-től 1919-ig*. Vol. 5. Budapest: Akadémiai Kiadó.

Szász, Zoltán. 1987. "A konzervatív liberalizmus kora. A dualista-rendszer konszolidált időszaka." In *Magyarország története, 1848–1990*, ed. Endre Kovács. Budapest: Akadémiai Kiadó.

Széchenyi, István. 1830. *Hitel*. Pest: Petrózai Trattner.

———. 1925. *A kelet népe*. Budapest: Magyar Történelmi Társulat.

Széchenyi, István, and Miklós Wesselényi. 1985. *Feleselő naplók. Egy barátság kezdetei*. Budapest: Helikon.

Szekfű, Gyula. 1920. *Három nemzedék. Egy hanyatló kor története*. Budapest: Egyetemi Nyomda.

———. 1922. *A magyar bortermelő lelki alkata. Gazdaságtörténeti tanulmány*. Budapest: Minerva Társaság.

———. 1935. Vol. 3 of Hóman Bálint and Szekfű Gyula, *Magyar történet*. 2d ed. Budapest: Királyi Magyar Egyetemi Nyomda.

Szelenyi, Balazs. 1998. "German Burghers in Sixteenth- and Nineteenth-Century Hungary." Ph.D. diss., University of California, Los Angeles.

Sziklay, László. 1962. "A kelet-európai összehasonlító irodalomtörténetírás néhány elvi kérdéséről (XIX.század)." *Helikon: Világirodalmi Figyelö* (Budapest), no. 4.

Szlajfer, Henryk. 1991. "Enforced Industrialization: The Contrasting Examples of the Kingdom of Poland and Latin America in the First Half of the Nineteenth Century." In *Between Development and Underdevelopment, 1800–1870*, ed. Jean Batou. Geneva: Droz.

Szűcs, Jenő. 1955. *Városok és kézművesek a XVI. századi Magyarországon*. Budapest: Tudományos Ismeretterjesztő Társaság.

———. 1983. *Vázlat Európa három történeti régiójáról*. Budapest: Magvető.

Szwarc, A. 1993. "Educational Aspirations of Women in the Kingdom of Poland at the End of the Nineteenth Century." *Acta Poloniae Historica* (Warsaw), no. 68.

Tabellen zur Währungsstatistik. 1902. Part 2. Vienna: Hof- und Staatsdruckerei.

Talmon, Jacob L. 1960. *Political Messianism: The Romantic Phase.* London: Secker & Warburg.

———. 1979. *Romanticism and Revolt: Europe, 1815–1849.* New York: Norton.

Tazbir, Janusz. 1983. *Poland as the Rampart of Christian Europe: Myth and Historical Reality.* Warsaw: Interpress Publisher.

Thorlby, Anthony. 1966. *The Romantic Movement.* London: Longmans.

Tocqueville, Alexis de. [1856] 1978. *The Old Regime and the French Revolution.* Gloucester, Mass.: Peter Smith.

Todorova, Maria. 1977. "The Europeanization of the Ruling Elite of the Ottoman Empire during the Period of Reforms." In *La Révolution industrielle dans le sud-est européen en XIXe.* Sofia: Institut d'Études balcaniques.

———. 1997. *Imagining the Balkans.* New York: Oxford University Press.

Tomasevich, Jozo. 1955. *Peasants, Politics and Economic Change in Yugoslavia.* Stanford: Stanford University Press.

Topencharov, Vladimir. 1982. *Hristo Botev.* Paris: Unesco.

Topolski, Jerzy. 1982. *Zarys dziejów Polski.* Warsaw: Wydawnictwo Interpress.

———. 1994. *The Manorial Economy in Early-Modern East-Central Europe.* Aldershot, U.K.: Variorum.

Topolski, Jerzy, Witold Molik, and Krzysztof Makowski, eds. 1991. *Ideologie, poglady, mity w dziejach Polski i Europy XIX wieku.* Poznań: Uniwersytet im. A.Mickiewicza.

Tremel, Ferdinand. 1969. *Wirtschafts- und Sozialgeschichte Österreichs. Von den Anfängen bis 1955.* Vienna: Deuticke.

Trzecinkowski, Lech. 1995. "Toward a Modern Society: Economic and Cultural Activity as a Political Programme, 1800–1914." In *Finland and Poland in the Russian Empire: A Comparative Study,* ed. Michael Branch, Janet Hartley, and Antoni Mączak. London: School of Slavonic and East European Studies, University of London.

Turczynski, Emanuel. 1976. *Konfession und Nation:Zur Frühgeschichte der serbischen und rumänischen Nationsbildung.* Düsseldorf: Pädagogischer Verlag Schwann.

Tzara, Tristan. [1916] 1959. "Manifesto Dada." In Mario de Micheli, ed., *Le avanguardie artistiche del Novecento.* Collana di storia e cultura 17. Milan: Schwarz.

Üzemi és munkás statisztika. 1901, 1910. Budapest: Statisztikai Hivatal.

Varga, Jenő. 1912. *A magyar kartellek.* Budapest: Világosság Nyomda.

Várkonyi, Ágnes R. 1985. "Gazdaság és társadalom a 17.század második felében, 1648–1686." In *Magyarország Története, 1526–1686,* ed. Zsigmond Pál Pach. Budapest: Akadémiai Kiadó.

Vasary, I. 1989. "The Sin of Transdanubia: The One-Child System in Rural Hungary." *Continuity and Change,* no. 4.

Voltaire [François-Marie Arouet]. 1946. "Philosophical Dictionary," and "Essay on Toleration." In *Introduction to Contemporary Civilization in the West. A Source Book,* vol. 1. New York: Columbia University Press.

Vucinich, Wayne S. 1963. "Some Aspects of the Ottoman Legacy." In *The Balkans in Transition,* ed. Charles Jelavich and Barbara Jelavich. Berkeley and Los Angeles: University of California Press.

Walicki, Andrzej. 1991. *Russia, Poland, and Universal Regeneration: Studies on Russian and Polish Thought of the Romantic Epoch.* Notre Dame, Ind.: University of Notre Dame Press.

———. [1982] 1994. *Philosophy and Romantic Nationalism: The Case of Poland.* Notre Dame, Ind.: University of Notre Dame Press.

Walkingame, Francis. 1784. *The Tutor's Assistant: Being a Compendium of Arithmetic, and a Complete Question Book . . . by Francis Walkingame, writing-master and accomptant.* 20th ed. London: Printed for the author, and sold by J. Scatcherd, and I. Whitaker, successor to E. Johnson, Ave-Mary-Lane.

Wallerstein, Immanuel. 1974. *The Modern World-System: Capitalist Agriculture and the Origins of the European World-Economy in the Sixteenth Century.* New York: Academic Press.

Wandycz, Piotr S. 1974. *The Lands of Partitioned Poland, 1795–1918.* Seattle: University of Washington Press.

Wapinski, Roman. 1994. *Polska i male ojccyzny Polaków.* Wrocław: Zaklad Narodowy im. Ossolinskich.

Weber, Eugen. 1960. *Paths to the Present: Aspects of European Thought from Romanticism to Existentialism.* New York: Dodd, Mead.

———. 1972. *Europe since 1715: A Modern History.* New York: Norton.

Weber, Max. [1904–5] 2001. *The Protestant Ethic and the Spirit of Capitalism.* Translated by Talcott Parsons. New York: Routledge.

Wehler, Hans-Ulrich. 1973. *Das Deutsche Kaiserreich, 1871–1918.* Göttingen: Vandenhoeck & Ruprecht.

Welter, Beate. 1989. *Die Judenpolitik der rumänischen Regierung, 1866–1888.* Frankfurt: P. Lang.

Wesselényi, Miklós. [1833] 1986. *Balitéletekről.* Budapest: Közgazdasági és Jogi Könyvkiadó.

Wilcox, Walter F., and Imre Ferenczi. 1929–31. *International Migrations.* 2 vols. New York: National Bureau of Economic Research.

Witos, Wincenty. 1964. *Moje wspomnienia.* Vol. 1. Paryz: Instytut Literacki.

Wittlich, Petr. 1992. *Prague: Fin de siècle.* Translated by Maev de la Guardia. Paris: Flammarion.

Woytinsky, Wladimir S. 1925–28. *Die Welt in Zahlen.* 7 vols. Berlin: R. Mosse.

Wróbel, Piotr. 1991. *Zarys dziejów zydów na ziemiach polskich w latach, 1880–1918.* Warsaw: Wydawnictwa Uniwersytetu Warszawskiego.

Wýbicki, Józef. [1791] 1984. *Mysli polityczne o wolnosci cywilnej.* Wrocław: Zaklad Narodowy im. Ossolinskich.

Zarnowska, Anna. 1996. "Education of Working-Class Women in the Polish Kingdom." *Acta Poloniae Historica* (Warsaw), no. 74.

Zeletin, Ştefan. 1991. *Burghezia română: Origina şi rolul ei istoric.* Bucharest: Humanitas.

Zimányi, Vera. 1985. "Gazdasági és társadalmi fejlődés Mohácstól a 16.század végéig." In *Magyarország Története, 1526–1686,* ed. Zsigmond Pál Pach, vol. 3, pt. 1. Budapest: Akadémiai Kiadó.

INDEX

TEXT: 10/13 Galliard

DISPLAY: Galliard

COMPOSITOR: Integrated Composition Systems

PRINTER AND BINDER: Edwards Brothers, Inc.